P9-CNA-633

TREASURY OF
FAVORITE
BRAND NAME
RECIPES

10 Cookbooks in 1

Copyright © 1997 Publications International, Ltd.
All rights reserved. This publication may not be reproduced or quoted in whole or in part by any means whatsoever without written permission from:

Louis Weber, CEO
Publications International, Ltd.
7373 North Cicero Avenue
Lincolnwood, Illinois 60646.

Permission is never granted for commercial purposes.

All recipes and photographs that contain specific brand names are copyrighted by those companies and/or associations, unless otherwise specified. All photographs *except* those on pages 243, 249, 253, 255, 257, 261, 275, 277, 283, 292, 297, 299, 303, 307, 308, 314, 317, 333, 341, 349, 356, 361, 363, 364, 369, 373, 381, 505, 508, 511, 513, 516, 518, 521, 523, 524, 525, 528, 530, 536, 538, 539, 543, 546, 549, 550, 553 and 556 copyright © Publications International, Ltd.

DOLE® is a registered trademark of Dole Food Company, Inc.

Some of the products listed in this publication may be in limited distribution.

Front cover photography by Sanders Studios, Inc., Chicago

Pictured on the front cover *(center, then clockwise from top left):* Rosemary Chicken with Asparagus Lemon Rice *(page 92)*, Sicilian-Style Pasta Salad *(page 196)*, Chocolate and Raspberry Cream Torte *(page 460)*, Festive Chicken Dip *(page 246)*, Oriental Shrimp & Steak Kabobs *(page 38)*, Coffee Chip Drops *(page 404)*, Chocolate Cherry Oatmeal Fancies *(page 418)*, Orange-Glazed Date Nut Bars *(page 408)*, Almond Mocha Cookie Bars *(page 445)* and Tri-Colored Tuna Stuffed Mushrooms *(page 122)*.

Pictured on the back cover *(top to bottom):* Luscious Chocolate Cheesecake *(page 458)*, Albacore Stir-Fry *(page 164)* and Steak with Peppers *(page 58)*.

ISBN: 0-7853-2178-0

Library of Congress Catalog Card Number: 96-71291

Manufactured in U.S.A.

8 7 6 5 4 3 2 1

Nutritional Analysis: Nutritional information is given for some of the recipes in this publication. Each analysis is based on the food items in the ingredient list, except ingredients labeled as "optional" or "for garnish." When more than one ingredient choice is listed, the first ingredient is used for analysis. If a range for the amount of an ingredient is given, the nutritional analysis is based on the lowest amount. Foods offered as "serve with" suggestions are not included in the analysis unless otherwise stated.

Microwave Cooking: Microwave ovens vary in wattage. The microwave cooking times given in this publication are approximate. Use the cooking times as guidelines and check for doneness before adding more time. Consult manufacturer's instructions for suitable microwavable cooking dishes.

TREASURY OF
FAVORITE
BRAND NAME
RECIPES

10 Cookbooks in 1

PUBLICATIONS INTERNATIONAL, LTD.

Contents

Introduction

Today's busy lifestyle means few of us can spend hours in the kitchen creating complicated dishes. But you can still prepare spectacular meals for your family and friends by using reliable kitchen-tested recipes with easy-to-follow directions. **Treasury of Favorite Brand Name Recipes: 10 Cookbooks in 1** provides exactly what you need. There's no need to search through a stack of cookbooks to find menu ideas. Here in one easy-to-use and easy-to-store book are 10 fantastic cookbooks featuring some of our most popular titles. You'll find exciting appetizers, satisfying soups and salads, incomparable entrées, delicious desserts and unforgettable holiday recipes. Whether you're cooking for two or cooking for a crowd, you'll find a selection of recipes to fit your needs.

If you're looking for a way to turn everyday meals into great-tasting dishes, turn to *Lipton® Recipe Secrets®*. This reliable collection is bursting with appetizers, savory side dishes, grilling ideas and easy top-of-the-stove entrées featuring today's best-known kitchen helper—Lipton® Recipe Secrets® Soup Mixes. Also included are imaginative menu and entertaining suggestions to round out any meal.

For comforting and creative fare, look no further than *Chicken & Rice*. You'll be amazed by the versatility of this classic combination. Even busy families on a budget can make delightful dinners using such recipes as Tasty Skillet Chicken for Two, Lemon Chicken Rice and Spicy Marinated Chicken Kebabs over Rice. Tuna, another tremendously popular family staple, is delicious and convenient, plus a terrific choice for healthy eating. *StarKist® Tuna for Today* features many entrées that can be prepared in less that 30 minutes—a real bonus for families on the go. The book would not be complete without suggestions for those who like tuna in the traditional ways—sandwiches, soups and salads.

Italian cooking has become one of the most popular cuisines in America—and for good reason. Many traditional recipes are easy to make and simply fabulous. *Contadina® Italian Cooking* provides an appetizing array of dishes inspired by their Culinary Arts Center in Tuscany, Italy. Delight in authentic classics, such as Hearty Manicotti and Skillet Chicken Cacciatore, or try fresh new ideas such as Baked Steak Flamenco and Lasagne Roll-Ups. Mexican cooking now equals the popularity of Italian cuisine. Try using our *Sizzling Mexican Recipes* collection to get your next fiesta off to a great start. Serve up zesty salads, chilis and salsas or perhaps some spicy tacos, fajitas or enchiladas. For a creative twist, sample Red Chili Tortilla Torte or Layered Mexicali Casserole. Whether you're preparing an entire Mexican meal or just adding a flash of Mexican magic to one course, you'll find your favorite brand name recipes here.

Great Tasting Stir-Fries & More will show you that the versatile stir-frying technique extends far beyond the Orient and works wonderfully with a wide variety of ingredients. Included are irresistible recipes for salads and starters, beef, pork, chicken, seafood and vegetables. And, with the wide range of convenience foods available these days, such as precut meats and vegetables, you truly can make mouthwatering meals in minutes.

When warm weather comes your way, nothing is more alluring than the aroma of an outdoor barbecue. *BBQ & Outdoor Grilling* brings you a variety of tantalizing recipes developed especially for the grill. These backyard inspirations include burgers, ribs and kabobs, meats, poultry and seafood, and side-dish delights from breads to desserts. No matter what the occasion, you'll want to fire up the grill and get ready for some great outdoor cooking and eating.

What's a meal without dessert? In *Crisco® Cooking for a Year of Celebrations*, you'll discover five easy-to-make doughs that can be transformed into an amazing array of captivating cookies. Who can resist family favorites like chocolate chip or chewy oatmeal—and what about old-fashioned sugar, fudgy brownie and heavenly peanut butter cookies? Starting with these classic doughs, you'll discover how to make soft and moist cookies that will turn any get-together into a spectacular celebration.

Love dessert but worried about overindulging? *Hershey's Light & Luscious Desserts* is the perfect solution. The recipes use naturally low-fat cocoa instead of baking chocolate for rich chocolate flavor. Treat yourself to fabulous cakes and cheesecakes, creamy mousses, crunchy cookies—all with no more than 180 calories and 5 grams of fat per serving.

The easy-to-follow calendar format of *Simple Desserts Made Special with Cool Whip®* will help you choose desserts throughout the year. For quick and easy reference, the recipes are divided into "'Tis the Season," "Spring Sensations," "Summertime Celebrations" and "Autumn Delights." A bonus chapter entitled "Year-Round Fun for Kids" is sure to delight everyone.

As you page through **Treasury of Favorite Brand Name Recipes: 10 Cookbooks in 1,** you will find many suggestions for quick snacks, party-pleasing appetizers, family dinners, special occasion menus and incomparable cakes, cookies, pies and more. Don't let a shortage of time or creative ideas keep you from sharing special meals with family and friends. All the ideas and information you need are right here; all you need to do is step into the kitchen and begin!

Lipton.
RECIPE SOUP MIX

RECIPE SECRETS.

Contents

Three Bean Salsa, page 28

Anytime Appetizers

Can't Get Enough Chicken Wings

12 chicken wings (about 2 pounds)
½ cup butter or margarine, melted
1 envelope Lipton Recipe Secrets Savory Herb with Garlic Soup Mix
1 teaspoon cayenne pepper sauce* (optional)

Cut tips off chicken wings (save tips for soup). Cut chicken wings in half at joint. Deep fry, bake or broil until golden brown and crunchy.

In medium bowl, blend butter, savory herb with garlic soup mix and cayenne pepper sauce. Add hot cooked chicken wings; toss until coated. Serve, if desired, over greens with cut-up celery.   Makes 24 appetizers

*Use more or less according to taste desired.

Entertaining Suggestions: Serve with Mini Mexican Meatballs (page 17) and Roasted Red Pepper Dip (page 24).

Mediterranean Feta Dip

  1 envelope Lipton Recipe Secrets Vegetable Soup Mix
  1 container (16 ounces) sour cream
  4 ounces feta or blue cheese, crumbled
  ½ cup seeded diced cucumber
  2 tablespoons chopped red onion
  ½ teaspoon dried oregano leaves, crushed (optional)

In medium bowl, thoroughly blend all ingredients; cover and chill.

Makes about 2½ cups dip

Dipper Suggestions: Serve with assorted fresh vegetables, pita bread triangles and pitted ripe olives.

Buffalo Wings

24 chicken wings (about 4 pounds)
  1 envelope Lipton Recipe Secrets Golden Onion or Onion Soup Mix
  ½ cup butter or margarine, melted
  2 tablespoons white vinegar
  2 tablespoons water
  2 cloves garlic
1½ to 2 teaspoons ground red pepper
  1 teaspoon ground cumin (optional)
  1 cup Wish-Bone Chunky Blue Cheese Dressing

Cut tips off chicken wings (save tips for a soup). Cut chicken wings in half at joint. In food processor or blender, process golden onion soup mix, butter, vinegar, water, garlic, pepper and cumin until blended; set aside.

Broil chicken 12 minutes or until brown, turning after 6 minutes. Brush with ½ of the soup mixture, then broil 2 minutes or until crisp. Turn, then brush with remaining soup mixture and broil an additional minute. Serve with Wish-Bone Chunky Blue Cheese Dressing and celery sticks, if desired.

Makes 48 appetizers

Entertaining Suggestions: Serve with Caponata Spread (page 18) and Zesty Bruschetta (page 18).

12   Lipton® Recipe Secrets®

Spinach Rice Balls

1½ cups cooked rice
  1 package (10 ounces) frozen chopped spinach, cooked and well drained
  ½ cup shredded mozzarella cheese (about 1½ ounces)
  ⅓ cup plain dry bread crumbs
  2 eggs, slightly beaten
  ¼ cup grated Parmesan cheese
  ¼ cup milk
  1 teaspoon Dijon-style, country Dijon-style or brown prepared mustard
  1 envelope Lipton Recipe Secrets Golden Onion Soup Mix

Preheat oven to 375°F.

In medium bowl, combine all ingredients; shape into 1-inch balls. On well-greased baking sheet, arrange rice balls and bake 20 minutes or until golden. Serve warm and, if desired, with assorted mustards.

Makes about 2 dozen rice balls

Entertaining Suggestions: Serve with Golden Chicken Nuggets (page 20), Mini Mexican Meatballs (page 17) and Easy Italian Turnovers (recipe below) for an international appetizer buffet.

Easy Italian Turnovers

  1 envelope Lipton Recipe Secrets Savory Herb with Garlic Soup Mix
  1 pound ground beef
  1 onion, chopped
  ½ cup water
  ½ cup fresh bread crumbs
  2 tablespoons grated Parmesan cheese
  1 package (15 ounces) refrigerated pie crust for 2 crusts
      (9 inches *each*)

Preheat oven to 350°F.

In medium bowl, combine all ingredients except pie crust; set aside.

Open pie crusts; cut each into quarters to make 8 triangles. Place ¼ cup beef mixture on bottom half of each triangle. Fold over top half and seal edges using fork. Arrange on baking sheet and bake 25 minutes or until pastry is golden brown.

Makes 8 turnovers

♦ Also terrific with Lipton Recipe Secrets Onion-Mushroom Soup Mix.

Menu Suggestion: Serve with your favorite Lipton Soup and steamed fresh vegetables.

Polenta Triangles

3 cups cold water
1 cup yellow cornmeal
1 envelope Lipton Recipe Secrets Golden Onion or Onion Soup Mix
1 can (4 ounces) mild chopped green chilies, drained
½ cup thawed frozen *or* drained canned whole kernel corn
⅓ cup finely chopped roasted red peppers
½ cup shredded sharp Cheddar cheese (about 2 ounces)

In 3-quart saucepan, bring water to a boil over high heat. With wire whisk, stir in cornmeal, then golden onion soup mix. Reduce heat to low and simmer uncovered, stirring constantly, 25 minutes or until thickened. Stir in chilies, corn and roasted red peppers. Spread into lightly greased 9-inch square baking pan; sprinkle with cheese. Let stand 20 minutes or until firm; cut into triangles. Serve at room temperature or heat in oven at 350°F for 5 minutes or until warm.

Makes about 24 triangles

Menu Suggestion: Serve as an hors d'oeuvre or first course.

Taco Dip

1 envelope Lipton Recipe Secrets Onion Soup Mix
1 container (16 ounces) sour cream
1 package (8 ounces) cream cheese, softened
¼ pound ground beef, cooked, drained and crumbled
¾ cup shredded Monterey Jack or Cheddar cheese
    (about 3 ounces), divided
Shredded lettuce
Chopped tomato
Tortilla chips

Preheat oven to 350°F.

In shallow 1-quart casserole, combine onion soup mix, sour cream, cream cheese, ground beef and ½ cup shredded Monterey Jack cheese. Sprinkle remaining ¼ cup cheese over top. Bake uncovered 30 minutes or until heated through. Top with lettuce and tomato and serve with tortilla chips.

Makes about 3½ cups dip

♦ Also terrific with Lipton Recipe Secrets Onion-Mushroom Soup Mix.

Entertaining Suggestions: Serve with Zesty Bruschetta (page 18) and Party Peanut Crisp (page 25).

Top to bottom: Mediterranean Feta Dip (page 12), Polenta Triangles

Onion-Potato Pancakes

1 pound all-purpose potatoes, peeled
2 large eggs, beaten
1 envelope Lipton Recipe Secrets Onion or Savory Herb with
   Garlic Soup Mix
2 tablespoons olive or vegetable oil, divided

In food processor with grating attachment or with hand grater, coarsely grate potatoes; drain on several layers of paper towels until almost dry. In medium bowl, combine potatoes, eggs and onion soup mix.

In 12-inch nonstick skillet, heat 1 tablespoon oil over medium-high heat and drop ½ of the potato mixture by rounded tablespoons into skillet. Cook 1 minute on each side or until golden brown, pressing down lightly with spatula when turning; drain on paper towels. Repeat with remaining 1 tablespoon oil and remaining potato mixture.

Makes about 24 potato pancakes

Variation: Stir in 1 can (4 ounces) chopped green chilies, drained, *or* 1 can (7 ounces) corn, drained, with potatoes.

Serving Suggestion: Serve with applesauce and sour cream or plain yogurt.

Warm Broccoli 'n Cheddar Dip

1 envelope Lipton Recipe Secrets Vegetable Soup Mix
1 container (16 ounces) sour cream
1 package (10 ounces) frozen chopped broccoli or spinach, thawed and
   squeezed dry
1 cup shredded Cheddar cheese (about 4 ounces), divided

Preheat oven to 350°F.

In 1-quart casserole, combine vegetable soup mix, sour cream, broccoli and ¾ cup cheese. Top with remaining ¼ cup cheese. Bake uncovered 30 minutes or until heated through.

Makes about 3 cups dip

Dipper Suggestions: Serve with fresh vegetables, bread sticks or crackers.

Mini Mexican Meatballs

1 envelope Lipton Recipe Secrets Onion or Beefy Onion Soup Mix
1½ pounds ground beef
1 egg
1 tablespoon cornmeal (optional)
1 can (4 ounces) chopped green chilies, undrained, divided
1 can (14½ ounces) whole peeled tomatoes, undrained and chopped
1 teaspoon ground cumin (optional)

In medium bowl, combine onion soup mix, ground beef, egg, cornmeal and 1 tablespoon chilies; shape into 1-inch meatballs. In 12-inch skillet, brown meatballs over medium-high heat; drain. Add tomatoes, remaining chilies and cumin. Bring to a boil over high heat; cook 1 minute. Reduce heat to low and simmer covered 8 minutes or until meatballs are done. Serve, if desired, with tortilla chips.   Makes about 4 dozen meatballs

Entertaining Suggestions: Serve with Golden Chicken Nuggets (page 20) and White Pizza Dip (page 22).

The Famous Lipton California Dip

1 envelope Lipton Recipe Secrets Onion Soup Mix
1 container (16 ounces) sour cream

In small bowl, blend onion soup mix with sour cream; cover and chill at least 2 hours. Serve with your favorite dippers.   Makes about 2 cups dip

Note: For a creamier dip, add more sour cream.

Variations:
SENSATIONAL SPINACH DIP: Add 1 package (10 ounces) frozen chopped spinach, thawed and squeezed dry.

CALIFORNIA SEAFOOD DIP: Add 1 cup finely chopped cooked clams, crabmeat or shrimp, ¼ cup chili sauce and 1 tablespoon horseradish.

CALIFORNIA BACON DIP: Add ⅓ cup crumbled cooked bacon or bacon bits.

CALIFORNIA BLUE CHEESE DIP: Add ¼ pound crumbled blue cheese and ¼ cup finely chopped walnuts.

Dipper Suggestions: Serve with assorted cut-up fresh vegetables, crackers, bread sticks or toasted pita bread wedges.

Zesty Bruschetta

1 envelope Lipton Recipe Secrets Savory Herb with Garlic Soup Mix
3 tablespoons olive or vegetable oil
1 loaf French or Italian bread (about 18 inches long), sliced lengthwise
2 tablespoons shredded or grated Parmesan cheese

Preheat oven to 350°F.

Blend savory herb with garlic soup mix and oil. Brush onto bread, then sprinkle with cheese. Bake 3 minutes or until golden. Slice, then serve.

Makes 1 loaf, about 18 pieces

Entertaining Suggestions: Serve with Onion-Potato Pancakes (page 16) and Warm Broccoli 'n Cheddar Dip (page 16).

Caponata Spread

1½ tablespoons olive or vegetable oil
1 medium eggplant, diced (about 4 cups)
1 medium onion, chopped
1½ cups water, divided
1 envelope Lipton Recipe Secrets Savory Herb with Garlic Soup Mix
2 tablespoons chopped fresh parsley (optional)
Salt and pepper to taste
Pita chips or thinly sliced Italian or French bread

In 10-inch nonstick skillet, heat oil over medium heat and cook eggplant with onion 3 minutes. Add ½ cup water. Reduce heat to low and simmer covered 3 minutes. Stir in savory herb with garlic soup mix blended with remaining 1 cup water. Bring to a boil over high heat. Reduce heat to low and simmer uncovered, stirring occasionally, 20 minutes. Stir in parsley, salt and pepper. Serve with sliced bread.

Makes about 4 cups spread

♦ Also terrific with Lipton Recipe Secrets Onion-Mushroom Soup Mix.

Entertaining Suggestions: Serve with Easy Italian Turnovers (page 13) and Party Peanut Crisp (page 25).

Left to right: Zesty Bruschetta, Caponata Spread

Golden Chicken Nuggets

1 envelope Lipton Recipe Secrets Onion-Mushroom Soup Mix
¾ cup plain dry bread crumbs
1½ pounds boneless, skinless chicken breasts, cut into 1-inch pieces
3 tablespoons butter or margarine, melted

Preheat oven to 400°F.

Combine onion-mushroom soup mix with bread crumbs. Dip chicken in bread crumb mixture, coating well. In lightly greased 13×9-inch baking or roasting pan, arrange chicken in single layer. Drizzle with butter. Bake 10 minutes or until chicken is done, turning once.

Makes about 2 dozen nuggets

Note: Recipe can be doubled.

♦ Also terrific with Lipton Recipe Secrets Onion, Golden Onion or Savory Herb with Garlic Soup Mix.

Variation:
CAJUN-STYLE CHICKEN NUGGETS: Add 1½ teaspoons chili powder, 1 teaspoon ground cumin and ¼ teaspoon red pepper to bread crumb mixture.

Menu Suggestion: Serve with a mixed green salad and French fries.

Lipton Recipe Secrets Dip Recipes

1 envelope Lipton Recipe Secrets Beefy Onion, Golden Onion, Onion, Onion-Mushroom, Vegetable, Savory Herb with Garlic or Golden Herb with Lemon Soup Mix
1 container (16 ounces) sour cream

In small bowl, blend soup mix with sour cream. Cover and chill.

Makes about 2 cups dip

Note: For creamier dip, add more sour cream.

Serving Suggestions: For a terrific taste, stir in crumbled cooked bacon or bacon bits, shredded carrots or chopped radishes. Serve with potato chips, crackers or assorted fresh vegetables, such as celery or carrot sticks, green bell pepper strips or cherry tomatoes.

Baked Vegetable & Seafood Won Tons

  1 envelope Lipton Recipe Secrets Vegetable Soup Mix
  1 container (15 ounces) ricotta cheese
  ½ pound imitation crabmeat, chopped *or* 1½ cups chopped cooked shrimp
  ¼ teaspoon garlic powder
  ⅛ teaspoon ground black pepper
 40 refrigerated or thawed frozen won ton wrappers
    Water
  1 tablespoon olive or vegetable oil

Preheat oven to 350°F.

In medium bowl, combine vegetable soup mix, cheese, crabmeat, garlic powder and pepper. Place 1 tablespoon ricotta mixture on center of each won ton. Brush edges with water; fold each corner into center and press to seal. Arrange seam-side-down on lightly greased baking sheet; brush won tons with oil. Bake uncovered 25 minutes or until crisp and golden brown, turning once.

Makes 40 won tons

Note: Cover unbaked won tons with a damp cloth until ready to bake; brush with oil.

Entertaining Suggestions: Serve with Polenta Triangles (page 14) and Caponata Spread (page 18).

Extra Special Spinach Dip

  1 envelope Lipton Recipe Secrets Vegetable Soup Mix
  1 container (16 ounces) sour cream
  ½ cup regular or light mayonnaise
  ½ teaspoon lemon juice
  1 package (10 ounces) frozen chopped spinach, thawed and squeezed dry
  1 can (8 ounces) water chestnuts, drained and chopped

In medium bowl, blend vegetable soup mix, sour cream, mayonnaise and lemon juice. Stir in spinach and water chestnuts; chill at least 2 hours. Serve with your favorite dippers. Makes about 3 cups dip

♦ Also terrific with Lipton Recipe Secrets Savory Herb with Garlic or Fiesta Herb with Red Pepper Soup Mix.

Variations: Stir in 2 tablespoons chopped green onions, radishes or crumbled blue cheese; or omit water chestnuts and add 1 cup chopped apple.

White Pizza Dip

1 envelope Lipton Recipe Secrets Savory Herb with Garlic Soup Mix
1 container (8 ounces) sour cream
1 cup (8 ounces) ricotta cheese
1 cup shredded mozzarella cheese (about 4 ounces), divided
¼ cup (1 ounce) chopped pepperoni (optional)
1 loaf Italian or French bread, sliced and toasted

Preheat oven to 350°F.

In shallow 1-quart casserole, combine savory herb with garlic soup mix, sour cream, ricotta cheese, ¾ cup shredded mozzarella and pepperoni. Sprinkle with remaining ¼ cup cheese.

Bake uncovered 30 minutes or until heated through. Serve with bread.

Makes about 2 cups dip

Entertaining Suggestions: Serve with Golden Chicken Nuggets (page 20) and Onion-Potato Pancakes (page 16).

Snappy Party Snacks

8 cups oven-toasted rice, corn and/or wheat cereal
1 cup unsalted dry roasted mixed nuts
1 envelope Lipton Recipe Secrets Onion or Savory Herb with Garlic Soup Mix
½ cup butter or margarine, melted

Preheat oven to 300°F.

In large bowl, combine cereal, nuts and onion soup mix. Add butter and toss thoroughly. Turn onto baking sheet and bake 10 minutes.

Makes about 9 cups party snacks

Variation: For extra fun party snacks, after baking add any combination of the following to equal 2 cups: bite-size chewy real fruit snacks, semi-sweet chocolate chips, raisins, shredded coconut, small pretzels and mini-marshmallows.

Menu Suggestion: Serve with Fresco Marinated Chicken (page 42) and cole slaw or potato salad.

White Pizza Dip

Roasted Red Pepper Dip

1 envelope Lipton Recipe Secrets Onion Soup Mix
1 package (8 ounces) cream cheese, softened
1 jar (7 ounces) roasted red peppers packed in oil, undrained
½ teaspoon dried basil leaves, crushed (optional)
¼ teaspoon dried oregano leaves, crushed (optional)

In food processor or blender, combine all ingredients until smooth. Cover and chill at least 2 hours.   Makes about 2 cups dip

♦ Also terrific with Lipton Recipe Secrets Onion-Mushroom or Savory Herb with Garlic Soup Mix.

Dipper Suggestions: Use mozzarella sticks, bread sticks, sliced pepperoni, cooked tortellini, pitted ripe olives or cherry tomatoes.

Four Cheese Spread

1 package (8 ounces) cream cheese, softened
1 cup shredded Swiss cheese (about 4 ounces)
1 cup shredded Fontina or Monterey Jack cheese (about 3 ounces)
½ cup sour cream
¼ cup grated Parmesan cheese
¼ cup finely chopped fresh basil leaves *or* 1½ teaspoons dried basil leaves, crushed
1 tablespoon finely chopped parsley
1 tablespoon lemon juice
1 envelope Lipton Recipe Secrets Vegetable Soup Mix

Line 4-cup mold or bowl with waxed paper or dampened cheese cloth; set aside.

With food processor or electric mixer, combine all ingredients until smooth. Pack into prepared mold; cover and chill. To serve, unmold onto serving platter and remove waxed paper. Garnish, if desired, with additional chopped parsley and basil.   Makes about 3½ cups spread

Serving Suggestions: Serve with assorted crackers, bagel chips or cucumber slices.

Party Peanut Crisp

1 envelope Lipton Recipe Secrets Onion Soup Mix
¾ cup all-purpose flour
¾ cup butter or margarine, softened
½ cup firmly packed brown sugar
1 egg
1 teaspoon ground cumin (optional)
1 cup spoon-size shredded wheat cereal
1 cup natural whole almonds
1 cup unsalted peanuts

Preheat oven to 350°F.

Line jelly-roll pan with aluminum foil; spray with nonstick cooking spray and set aside. In large bowl with electric mixer, combine onion soup mix, flour, butter, brown sugar, egg and cumin until well blended. Stir in remaining ingredients; spread into prepared pan. Bake 25 minutes or until golden brown. Cool completely on wire rack. To serve, break into pieces. Store in airtight container up to 2 weeks.

Makes 1½ pounds (40 pieces) peanut crisp

Entertaining Suggestions: Serve as an appetizer with Mediterranean Feta Dip (page 12) and Polenta Triangles (page 14).

♦ Vegetable Crudités ♦

Offer fresh vegetables in a basket or clean clay flower pot lined with the outer leaves of fresh lettuce or cabbage. To hold a dip, carefully hollow out a cabbage head or a large bell pepper. The dip and cut vegetables may be prepared a day ahead and stored, tightly wrapped, in the refrigerator.

Savory Side Dishes

Oven-Roasted Vegetables

  1 envelope Lipton Recipe Secrets Savory Herb with Garlic Soup Mix
1½ pounds assorted fresh vegetables*
  2 tablespoons olive or vegetable oil**

Preheat oven to 450°F.

In large plastic bag or bowl, add all ingredients. Close bag and shake, or toss in bowl, until vegetables are evenly coated. In 13×9-inch baking or roasting pan arrange vegetables; discard bag. Bake, uncovered, stirring once, 20 minutes or until vegetables are tender.   Makes about 4 (½-cup) servings

*Use any combination of the following, sliced: zucchini, yellow squash, red, green or yellow bell peppers, carrots, celery and mushrooms.

**Substitution: Spray pan lightly with nonstick cooking spray and replace oil with 2 tablespoons water.

♦ Also terrific with Lipton Recipe Secrets Golden Herb with Lemon, Onion or Golden Onion Soup Mix.

Menu Suggestion: Serve with roasted chicken and a tossed green salad.

Oven-Roasted Vegetables

Lipton California Mashed Potatoes

2 pounds all-purpose potatoes, peeled, if desired, and cut into chunks
  Water
2 tablespoons chopped fresh parsley (optional)
1 envelope Lipton Recipe Secrets Onion Soup Mix
¾ cup milk, heated to boiling
½ cup sour cream

In 3-quart saucepan, cover potatoes with water. Bring to a boil over high heat. Reduce heat to low and simmer uncovered 20 minutes or until potatoes are very tender; drain. Return potatoes to saucepan. Mash potatoes. Stir in parsley and onion soup mix blended with hot milk and sour cream.

Makes about 8 servings

♦ Also terrific with Lipton Recipe Secrets Golden Onion, Golden Herb with Lemon or Savory Herb with Garlic Soup Mix.

Menu Suggestion: Serve with pork chops, beef or chicken and your favorite vegetable.

Three Bean Salsa

1 envelope Lipton Recipe Secrets Savory Herb with Garlic Soup Mix
½ cup water
1 large tomato, chopped
1 cup drained canned cannellini or red kidney beans
1 cup drained canned black or pinto beans
1 cup drained canned chick-peas or garbanzo beans
2 teaspoons white or white wine vinegar (optional)

In 12-inch skillet, blend savory herb with garlic soup mix with water. Bring to a boil over high heat; stir in tomato. Reduce heat to low and simmer 3 minutes. Stir in beans and simmer 3 minutes or until heated through. Stir in vinegar. Garnish, if desired, with chopped fresh parsley or cilantro.

Makes about 4 cups bean salsa

Menu Suggestion: Serve as a side dish or topping with grilled poultry, beef, lamb or pork.

Three Bean Salsa

Mashed Potatoes Florentine

2 pounds all-purpose potatoes, peeled, if desired, and cut into chunks
  Water
7 cups trimmed, washed and drained fresh spinach or kale leaves (about
  ½ pound)*
1 envelope Lipton Recipe Secrets Savory Herb with Garlic Soup Mix
½ cup milk
¼ cup butter or margarine

In 3-quart saucepan, cover potatoes with water. Bring to a boil over high
heat. Reduce heat to low and simmer uncovered 20 minutes or until potatoes
are very tender. Stir in spinach and cook an additional 2 minutes or until spinach is
wilted; drain. Return potatoes and spinach to saucepan; mash potatoes
with spinach.

Meanwhile, in small saucepan, heat savory herb with garlic soup mix, milk and
butter over low heat, stirring occasionally, until butter is melted. Stir into potato
mixture.   Makes about 8 servings

*Substitution: Use 1 package (10 ounces) frozen chopped spinach, thawed and
drained.

◆ Also terrific with Lipton Recipe Secrets Golden Onion or Golden Herb with
  Lemon Soup Mix.

Menu Suggestion: Serve with Cornish hens, roasted chicken or steak.

Green Bean Tart

1 refrigerated pie crust or pastry for single-crust pie
1 egg yolk (optional)
2 tablespoons water (optional)
1 envelope Lipton Recipe Secrets Vegetable Soup Mix
¼ cup milk
¼ cup grated Swiss or white Cheddar cheese (about 2 ounces)
1 egg
8 ounces fresh green beans, cooked and drained

Preheat oven to 375°F. On lightly floured cookie sheet, unfold pie crust. Fold
crust edges over 1 inch to form rim. Brush with egg yolk beaten with water.
Bake 9 minutes; set aside. In medium bowl, blend vegetable soup mix, milk,
cheese and egg. Arrange green beans on prepared crust; evenly pour soup
mixture over beans. Bake uncovered 15 minutes or until crust is golden and
mixture is set.   Makes 1 tart

Menu Suggestion: Serve as an hors d'oeuvre, first course or side dish.

Orzo Casserole

  2 tablespoons butter or margarine
  1 clove garlic, finely chopped
1½ cups uncooked orzo pasta
  1 envelope Lipton Recipe Secrets Onion or Onion-Mushroom Soup Mix
3¼ cups water
  6 ounces shiitake or white mushrooms, sliced
  ¼ cup chopped fresh parsley

In 3-quart heavy saucepan, melt butter over medium heat and cook garlic with orzo, stirring constantly, 2½ minutes or until golden. Stir in onion soup mix blended with water. Bring to a boil over high heat. Reduce heat to low and simmer covered 10 minutes. Add mushrooms; do not stir. Simmer covered 10 minutes. Stir in parsley. Turn into serving bowl. *Liquid will not be totally absorbed.* Let stand 10 minutes or until liquid is absorbed.

Makes about 10 (½-cup) servings

Variation:
SAVORY ORZO CASSEROLE: Increase water to 4 cups and use Lipton Recipe Secrets Savory Herb with Garlic Soup Mix.

Menu Suggestion: Serve with your favorite ham, pork, lamb or beef recipe.

Golden Herb Stuffing

2 tablespoons butter or margarine
1 medium carrot, diced
1 rib celery, diced
1 small onion, finely chopped
1 envelope Lipton Recipe Secrets Savory Herb with Garlic or
    Golden Herb with Lemon Soup Mix
2 cups fresh bread crumbs
¼ cup milk or water
½ cup chopped walnuts or pecans (optional)

In 10-inch skillet, melt butter over medium heat and cook carrot, celery and onion, stirring occasionally, 4 minutes.

In medium bowl, combine vegetables with remaining ingredients; toss well. Makes enough stuffing for 1 roasting chicken, 2 Cornish hens, 8 pork chops or 8 fish fillets. Or, turn into 1-quart baking dish and bake covered at 375°F for 25 minutes. Remove cover and bake an additional 5 minutes or until top is lightly browned.

Makes 4 (½-cup) servings

Menu Suggestion: Serve as above with whole berry cranberry sauce and baked apples.

Oven Entrées

Golden Glazed Flank Steak

1 envelope Lipton Recipe Secrets Onion Soup Mix
1 jar (12 ounces) apricot or peach preserves
½ cup water
1 beef flank steak (about 2 pounds), cut into thin strips
2 medium green, red and/or yellow bell peppers, sliced
Hot cooked rice

In small bowl, combine onion soup mix, preserves and water; set aside. On foil-lined grill or in bottom of broiler pan, with rack removed, arrange steak and peppers; top with soup mixture. Grill or broil, turning once, until steak is done. Serve over hot rice.   Makes about 8 servings

Menu Suggestion: Serve with Lipton Iced Tea and fresh fruit topped with shredded coconut for dessert.

Golden Glazed Flank Steak

Country Roasted Chicken Dinner

1 envelope Lipton Recipe Secrets Savory Herb with Garlic Soup Mix
2 tablespoons honey
1 tablespoon water
1 tablespoon butter or margarine, melted
1 roasting chicken (5 to 6 pounds)
3 pounds all-purpose and/or sweet potatoes, cut into chunks

Preheat oven to 350°F.

In small bowl, blend savory herb with garlic soup mix, honey, water and butter.

In 18×12-inch roasting pan, arrange chicken, breast side up; brush with soup mixture. Cover loosely with aluminum foil. Roast 30 minutes; drain. Arrange potatoes around chicken and continue roasting covered, stirring potatoes occasionally, 1 hour or until meat thermometer reaches 175°F and potatoes are tender. *If chicken reaches 175°F before potatoes are tender, remove chicken to serving platter and keep warm. Continue roasting potatoes until tender.*

Makes about 8 servings

Note: Insert meat thermometer into thickest part of thigh between breast and thigh; make sure tip does not touch bone.

♦ Also terrific with Lipton Recipe Secrets Golden Herb with Lemon or Golden Onion Soup Mix.

Menu Suggestion: Serve with a mixed green salad, warm biscuits and Lipton Iced Tea.

♦ Quick Crumb Toppings ♦

For a zippy crumb topping for vegetable, chicken or tuna casseroles, combine Lipton Recipe Secrets Onion Soup Mix with fresh bread crumbs, melted butter or margarine and shredded cheese; broil until golden.

♦

Country Roasted Chicken Dinner

Southwestern Meat Loaf

   1 **envelope Lipton Recipe Secrets Onion Soup Mix**
   2 **pounds ground beef**
   2 **cups crushed cornflakes or bran flakes cereal (about 3 ounces)**
1½ **cups frozen *or* drained canned whole kernel corn**
   1 **small green bell pepper, chopped**
   2 **eggs**
¾ **cup water**
⅓ **cup ketchup**

Preheat oven to 350°F.

In large bowl, combine all ingredients. In 13×9-inch baking or roasting pan, shape into loaf. Bake 1 hour or until done. Let stand 10 minutes before serving.

Makes about 8 servings

♦ Also terrific with Lipton Recipe Secrets Onion-Mushroom or Beefy Onion Soup Mix.

Menu Suggestion: Serve with salsa, corn bread and Lipton Iced Tea.

Spanish-Style Chicken & Rice

   2 **tablespoons olive or vegetable oil**
   1 **clove garlic, finely chopped**
   1 **cup uncooked regular rice**
   1 **envelope Lipton Recipe Secrets Onion Soup Mix**
2½ **cups hot water**
   1 **cup frozen peas, partially thawed**
½ **cup chopped red or green bell pepper**
   8 **green olives, sliced**
   1 **chicken (2½ to 3 pounds), cut into serving pieces**

Preheat oven to 400°F.

In 13×9-inch baking or roasting pan, combine oil with garlic; heat in oven 5 minutes. Stir in uncooked rice until coated with oil. Add onion soup mix blended with hot water; stir in peas, pepper and olives. Press chicken pieces into rice mixture. Bake 35 minutes or until chicken is done and rice is tender. Cover and let stand 10 minutes before serving.

Makes about 4 servings

Menu Suggestion: Serve with cooked green beans and fresh fruit for dessert.

Southwestern Meat Loaf

From the Grill

Oriental Shrimp & Steak Kabobs

1 envelope Lipton Recipe Secrets Savory Herb with Garlic or Onion Soup Mix
¼ cup soy sauce
¼ cup lemon juice
¼ cup olive or vegetable oil
¼ cup honey
½ pound uncooked medium shrimp, peeled and deveined
½ pound boneless sirloin steak, cut into 1-inch cubes
16 cherry tomatoes
2 cups mushroom caps
1 medium green bell pepper, cut into chunks

In 13×9-inch glass baking dish, blend savory herb with garlic soup mix, soy sauce, lemon juice, oil and honey; set aside. On skewers, alternately thread shrimp, steak, tomatoes, mushrooms and green pepper. Add prepared skewers to baking dish; turn to coat. Cover and marinate in refrigerator, turning skewers occasionally, at least 2 hours. Remove prepared skewers, reserving marinade. Grill or broil, turning and basting frequently with reserved marinade, until shrimp turn pink and steak is done. Do not brush with marinade during last 5 minutes of cooking.

Makes about 8 servings

Menu Suggestion: Serve with corn-on-the-cob, a mixed green salad and grilled garlic bread.

Oriental Shrimp & Steak Kabobs

Grilled Pasta Salad

    4 medium zucchini and/or yellow squash, sliced
    1 medium Spanish onion, halved and cut into large chunks
    1 envelope Lipton Recipe Secrets Savory Herb with
        Garlic Soup Mix
    ¼ cup olive or vegetable oil
    8 ounces penne, rotini or ziti pasta, cooked and drained
    ¾ cup diced roasted red peppers
    ¼ cup red wine vinegar, apple cider vinegar or white vinegar

On broiler pan or heavy-duty aluminum foil, arrange zucchini and onion. Brush with savory herb with garlic soup mix blended with oil. Broil or grill 5 minutes or until golden brown and crisp-tender.

In large bowl, toss cooked pasta, vegetables, roasted peppers and vinegar. Serve warm or at room temperature.

                        Makes about 4 main-dish or 8 side-dish servings

♦ Also terrific with Lipton Recipe Secrets Golden Onion Soup Mix.

Menu Suggestion: Serve with hot crusty bread and a spinach salad.

Grilled Greek-Style Chicken

    1 container (8 ounces) plain yogurt
    ¼ cup chopped fresh mint or parsley leaves
    1 envelope Lipton Recipe Secrets Savory Herb with Garlic Soup Mix
    1 pound boneless, skinless chicken breast halves

In small shallow glass baking dish, blend yogurt, mint and savory herb with garlic soup mix. Add chicken and turn to coat. Cover and marinate in refrigerator, turning chicken occasionally, at least 2 hours. Remove chicken, reserving marinade. Grill or broil chicken, turning once and basting with reserved marinade, until chicken is done.   Makes about 4 servings

Menu Suggestion: Serve with Oven-Roasted Vegetables (page 26) and rice pilaf.

Grilled Pasta Salad

Fresco Marinated Chicken

1 envelope Lipton Recipe Secrets Savory Herb with Garlic Soup Mix
½ cup water
2 tablespoons olive or vegetable oil
1 teaspoon lemon juice or vinegar
1 pound boneless, skinless chicken breast halves

In large nonaluminum baking dish, blend savory herb with garlic soup mix, water, oil and lemon juice; add chicken and turn to coat. Cover and marinate in refrigerator at least 1 hour or overnight.

On broiler pan or grill lined with heavy-duty aluminum foil lightly sprayed with nonstick cooking spray, arrange chicken. Pour ½ of the marinade over chicken. Grill or broil, turning once and pouring remaining marinade over chicken, until done.   *Makes about 4 servings*

♦ Also terrific with Lipton Recipe Secrets Golden Onion or Golden Herb with Lemon Soup Mix.

Menu Suggestion: Serve with a tomato salad and cooked rice tossed with mushrooms and sliced green onions.

Grilled Reuben Burgers

1 envelope Lipton Recipe Secrets Onion-Mushroom Soup Mix
1½ pounds ground beef
½ cup water
½ cup shredded Swiss cheese (about 2 ounces)
1 tablespoon crisp-cooked crumbled bacon or bacon bits
½ teaspoon caraway seeds (optional)

In large bowl, combine all ingredients; shape into 6 patties. Grill or broil until done. Top, if desired, with heated sauerkraut and additional bacon.
                                     Makes 6 servings

♦ Also terrific with Lipton Recipe Secrets Onion or Beefy Onion Soup Mix.

Menu Suggestion: Serve with coleslaw, pickles and Lipton Iced Tea.

Fresco Marinated Chicken

Top-of-Stove Entrées

No-Peek Skillet Chicken

  1 chicken (2½ to 3 pounds), cut into serving pieces (with or without skin)
  2 tablespoons olive or vegetable oil
  1 can (14½ ounces) whole peeled tomatoes, undrained and chopped
  ½ cup sliced fresh or drained canned mushrooms
  1 clove garlic, minced
  1 envelope Lipton Recipe Secrets Onion Soup Mix
    Hot cooked noodles

Rinse chicken; pat dry. In 12-inch skillet, heat oil over medium-high heat and brown chicken; drain. Stir in tomatoes, mushrooms and garlic combined with onion soup mix. Bring to a boil over high heat. Reduce heat to low and simmer covered 45 minutes or until chicken is done. Serve over hot noodles and sprinkle, if desired, with chopped fresh parsley.   Makes about 6 servings

♦ Also terrific with Lipton Recipe Secrets Savory Herb with Garlic, Golden Herb with Lemon or Beefy Onion Soup Mix.

Menu Suggestion: Serve with a mixed green salad and Lipton Iced Tea.

No-Peek Skillet Chicken

Savory Chicken with Mushrooms & Spinach

2 tablespoons olive or vegetable oil, divided
1 pound boneless, skinless chicken breast halves, pounded thin
8 ounces fresh spinach leaves, rinsed and drained*
1½ cups sliced fresh or drained canned mushrooms
1 envelope Lipton Recipe Secrets Savory Herb with Garlic Soup Mix
1 cup water

In 12-inch skillet, heat 1 tablespoon oil over medium-high heat and cook chicken until done; remove and keep warm.

In same skillet, heat remaining 1 tablespoon oil over medium heat and cook spinach and mushrooms, stirring frequently, 3 minutes. Stir in savory herb with garlic soup mix blended with water. Bring to a boil over high heat; continue boiling, stirring occasionally, 1 minute or until sauce is thickened. To serve, arrange chicken over vegetable mixture.

Makes about 4 servings

*Substitution: Use 1 package (10 ounces) frozen leaf spinach, thawed and squeezed dry.

♦ Also terrific with Lipton Recipe Secrets Golden Herb with Lemon or Golden Onion Soup Mix.

Menu Suggestion: Serve with Lipton California Mashed Potatoes (page 28) and warm dinner rolls.

♦ Simple Tricks with Lipton Recipe Secrets Soup Mixes ♦

Substitute 1 envelope Lipton Recipe Secrets Golden Onion Soup Mix blended with 1½ to 2 cups water for 1½ to 2 cups chicken broth in your recipes. You'll get more flavor...plus a bonus of tender onion pieces.

Substitute 1 envelope Lipton Recipe Secrets Onion, Onion-Mushroom or Beefy Onion Soup Mix blended with 2 cups water for every 2 cups beef broth needed in a recipe.

Combine Lipton Recipe Secrets Onion Soup Mix with sour cream and use as a topping for nachos, tacos or baked potatoes.

Savory Chicken with Mushrooms & Spinach

Country French Chicken Breasts

1 tablespoon butter or margarine
1 pound boneless, skinless chicken breast halves
1 envelope Lipton Recipe Secrets Savory Herb with Garlic or
　　Golden Onion Soup Mix
1 cup water
1 tablespoon lemon juice
4 lemon slices (optional)
　Hot cooked rice

In 12-inch skillet, melt butter over medium-high heat and brown chicken.
Stir in savory herb with garlic soup mix blended with water and lemon
juice; arrange lemon slices on chicken. Reduce heat to low and simmer
covered 10 minutes or until sauce is slightly thickened and chicken is done.
To serve, arrange chicken over hot rice and spoon sauce over chicken.

Makes about 4 servings

Menu Suggestion: Serve with your favorite Lipton Soup.

Pork Chops Piquante

2 teaspoons olive or vegetable oil, divided
4 pork chops, ¾ inch thick
1 medium onion, thinly sliced
1½ teaspoons ketchup
½ cup dry white wine
1 envelope Lipton Recipe Secrets Savory Herb with Garlic Soup Mix
1¼ cups water
2 tablespoons finely sliced sweet gherkin pickles

In 12-inch skillet, heat 1 teaspoon oil over medium-high heat and brown chops;
remove and set aside. In same skillet, heat remaining 1 teaspoon oil over medium
heat and brown onion. Add ketchup and cook over medium heat, stirring
frequently, 1 minute. Add wine and boil over high heat 1 minute. Stir in savory
herb with garlic soup mix blended with water. Bring to a boil over high heat;
reduce heat to low. Return pork chops to skillet and simmer covered 10 minutes.
Add pickles and continue simmering 5 minutes or until pork is done.

Makes about 4 servings

Menu Suggestion: Serve with baked potatoes and applesauce.

Country French Chicken Breasts

Frittata with Artichokes

1 envelope Lipton Recipe Secrets Savory Herb with Garlic Soup Mix
8 eggs
¾ cup milk
1 teaspoon butter or margarine
1 cup diced and drained canned artichoke hearts (about 4 ounces)

In medium bowl, blend savory herb with garlic soup mix, eggs and milk; set aside. In omelet pan or 8-inch skillet, melt butter over low heat and cook egg mixture, lifting set edges with spatula and tilting pan to allow uncooked mixture to flow to bottom. When bottom is set, top with artichokes. Reduce heat to low and simmer covered 3 minutes or until eggs are set.

Makes about 4 servings

♦ Also terrific with Lipton Recipe Secrets Golden Herb with Lemon or Golden Onion Soup Mix.

Menu Suggestion: Serve with Lipton Noodle Soup and a mixed green salad.

Chicken Breasts with Savory Mustard Herb Sauce

2 tablespoons olive or vegetable oil, divided
1 pound boneless, skinless chicken breast halves
1 medium zucchini, sliced
1½ cups sliced fresh or drained canned mushrooms
1 envelope Lipton Recipe Secrets Savory Herb with Garlic or
    Golden Onion Soup Mix
¾ cup water
2 teaspoons Dijon-style, country Dijon-style or brown prepared mustard

In 12-inch skillet, heat 1 tablespoon oil over medium-high heat and cook chicken 5 minutes or until almost done, turning once; remove and keep warm. In same skillet, heat remaining 1 tablespoon oil over medium heat and cook zucchini and mushrooms, stirring frequently, 3 minutes. Return chicken to skillet; stir in savory herb with garlic soup mix blended with water and mustard. Bring to a boil over high heat. Reduce heat to low and simmer covered 5 minutes or until chicken is done. To serve, arrange chicken on serving platter and top with sauce mixture.

Makes about 4 servings

Menu Suggestion: Serve with cooked noodles and a fresh fruit salad.

Frittata with Artichokes

"Messy Hanks"

1 envelope Lipton Recipe Secrets Onion Soup Mix
¾ cup chili sauce
¼ cup grape jelly
2 tablespoons water
1 pound ground beef
1 medium green bell pepper, finely chopped
6 hoagie or hamburger rolls or English muffins

In small bowl, combine onion soup mix, chili sauce, grape jelly and water. In 10-inch skillet, brown ground beef with green pepper over medium-high heat; drain. Stir in soup mixture. Bring to a boil over high heat. Reduce heat to low and simmer uncovered, stirring occasionally, 5 minutes or until slightly thickened. Serve on rolls.

Makes about 6 servings

♦ Also terrific with Lipton Recipe Secrets Beefy Onion, Onion-Mushroom or Savory Herb with Garlic Soup Mix.

Menu Suggestion: Serve with a lettuce and tomato salad, tortilla chips and ice cream with a choice of toppings.

Chicken & Artichoke Sauté

2 tablespoons olive or vegetable oil, divided
1 chicken (2½ to 3 pounds), quartered
1 medium onion, chopped
1 envelope Lipton Recipe Secrets Savory Herb with
    Garlic Soup Mix
1½ cups water
1 can (15 ounces) artichoke hearts, drained

In 12-inch skillet, heat 1½ tablespoons oil over medium-high heat and brown chicken. Remove chicken and drain. In same skillet, add remaining ½ tablespoon oil and cook onion 2 minutes. Stir in savory herb with garlic soup mix blended with water; bring to a boil over high heat. Return chicken to skillet; add artichokes. Reduce heat to low and simmer covered 20 minutes or until chicken is done.

Makes about 4 servings

♦ Also terrific with Lipton Recipe Secrets Golden Herb with Lemon Soup Mix.

Menu Suggestion: Serve over hot cooked rice, couscous or noodles.

"Messy Hanks"

Country Chicken Stew with Dumplings

1 tablespoon olive or vegetable oil
1 chicken (3 to 3½ pounds), cut into serving pieces (with or without skin)
4 large carrots, cut into 2-inch pieces
3 ribs celery, cut into 1-inch pieces
1 large onion, cut into 1-inch wedges
1 envelope Lipton Recipe Secrets Savory Herb with Garlic Soup Mix
1½ cups water
½ cup apple juice
   Parsley Dumplings, optional (recipe follows)

In heavy saucepot or 6-quart Dutch oven, heat oil over medium-high heat and brown ½ of the chicken; remove and set aside. Repeat with remaining chicken. Return chicken to Dutch oven. Stir in carrots, celery, onion and savory herb with garlic soup mix blended with water and apple juice. Bring to a boil over high heat. Reduce heat to low and simmer covered 25 minutes or until chicken is done and vegetables are tender.

Meanwhile, prepare Parsley Dumplings. Drop 12 rounded tablespoonfuls of batter into simmering broth around chicken. Continue simmering covered 10 minutes or until toothpick inserted in center of dumpling comes out clean. Season stew, if desired, with salt and ground black pepper.

                                        Makes about 6 servings

PARSLEY DUMPLINGS: In medium bowl, combine 1⅓ cups all-purpose flour, 2 teaspoons baking powder, 1 tablespoon chopped fresh parsley and ½ teaspoon salt; set aside. In measuring cup, blend ⅔ cup milk, 2 tablespoons melted butter or margarine and 1 egg. Stir milk mixture into flour mixture just until blended.

Variation: Add 1 pound quartered red potatoes to stew with carrots; eliminate dumplings.

♦ Also terrific with Lipton Recipe Secrets Golden Onion or Golden Herb with Lemon Soup Mix.

Menu Suggestion: Serve this as a meal-in-one!

Country Chicken Stew with Dumplings

Crunchy Cutlets with Corn Salsa

1 egg, beaten
1 tablespoon plus 1 cup water, divided
1 pound boneless, skinless chicken breast halves, pounded to ¼-inch thickness
½ cup yellow cornmeal
½ teaspoon salt
2 tablespoons plus 1½ teaspoons olive or vegetable oil, divided
2 green onions, sliced (about ¾ cup)
1 large red bell pepper, diced (about 1 cup)
1 package (10 ounces) frozen whole kernel corn, partially thawed
1 envelope Lipton Recipe Secrets Golden Onion or Golden Herb with Lemon Soup Mix
1 to 2 tablespoons chopped fresh cilantro (optional)

In small bowl, beat egg with 1 tablespoon water. Dip chicken in egg, then cornmeal combined with salt. In 12-inch skillet, heat 1 tablespoon oil over medium-high heat and cook ½ of the chicken 4 minutes or until done, turning once. Remove chicken to platter; keep warm. Repeat with remaining chicken and 1 tablespoon oil.

Wipe out skillet. Heat remaining 1½ teaspoons oil in skillet over medium heat and cook green onions and red pepper 1 minute, stirring constantly. Add corn and golden onion soup mix blended with remaining 1 cup water. Bring to a boil over high heat. Reduce heat to low and simmer 7 minutes or until vegetables are tender and liquid is thickened. Stir in cilantro. To serve, spoon corn salsa over chicken.

Makes about 4 servings

Menu Suggestion: Serve with a tomato salad and pineapple slices for dessert.

Fish Fillets with Ragoût Sauce

1½ teaspoons butter or margarine
3 large red, green and/or yellow bell peppers, cut into very thin strips (about 3 cups)
3 tablespoons dry white wine or water
1 envelope Lipton Recipe Secrets Savory Herb with Garlic or Golden Onion Soup Mix
1½ cups water
1 tablespoon lemon juice
1 pound fish fillets

In 12-inch skillet, melt butter over medium heat and cook peppers, stirring occasionally, 5 minutes or until softened. Remove ½ of the peppers; reserve. Add wine to skillet and bring to a boil over high heat, stirring frequently. Stir in savory herb with garlic soup mix blended with water and lemon juice. Bring to a boil over high heat. Reduce heat to low and continue simmering 10 minutes or until sauce is slightly thickened.

Meanwhile, top fish with equal portions of reserved peppers; roll up and secure with wooden toothpicks. Arrange fish in skillet and simmer covered 8 minutes or until fish flakes. Remove toothpicks before serving.

Makes about 4 servings

Menu Suggestion: Serve with rice pilaf and hot crusty bread.

Hearty Bistro Chicken

   2 tablespoons olive or vegetable oil
   1 chicken (2½ to 3 pounds), cut into serving pieces (with or without skin)
   2 ears fresh or frozen corn, cut into 1½-inch pieces
   1 package (8 ounces) frozen snap peas *or* 1 package (10 ounces) frozen green
      beans
   1 cup frozen sliced or baby carrots
   1 envelope Lipton Recipe Secrets Onion Soup Mix
   2 cups water
  ¼ cup sherry (optional)
   2 tablespoons Dijon-style, country Dijon-style or brown prepared mustard
   2 tablespoons all-purpose flour
   1 container (8 ounces) sour cream

In 12-inch skillet, heat oil over medium-high heat and brown chicken; drain. Add corn, peas and carrots; then add onion soup mix blended with water, sherry and mustard. Bring to a boil over high heat. Reduce heat to low and simmer covered 20 minutes or until chicken is done.

Remove chicken and vegetables to serving platter and keep warm; reserve liquid. Boil reserved liquid over high heat 10 minutes. Remove from heat and stir in flour blended with sour cream; return to heat. Bring just to the boiling point over medium-high heat. Reduce heat to low and simmer, stirring constantly, until sauce is thickened, about 3 minutes. To serve, pour sauce over chicken and vegetables.

Makes about 4 servings

♦ Also terrific with Lipton Recipe Secrets Golden Herb with Lemon, Golden Onion or Savory Herb with Garlic Soup Mix.

Menu Suggestion: Serve with a mixed green salad and fresh fruit for dessert.

Steaks with Peppers

2 tablespoons olive or vegetable oil
1½ pounds boneless beef chuck steaks, ½ inch thick (about 4 to 5)
2 medium red, green and/or yellow bell peppers, cut into thin strips
1 clove garlic, finely chopped (optional)
1 medium tomato, coarsely chopped
1 envelope Lipton Recipe Secrets Onion or Onion-Mushroom Soup Mix
1 cup water

In 12-inch skillet, heat oil over medium-high heat and brown steaks. Remove steaks. Add peppers and garlic to skillet; cook over medium heat 5 minutes or until peppers are crisp-tender. Stir in tomato, then onion soup mix blended with water; bring to a boil over high heat. Reduce heat to low. Return steaks to skillet and simmer uncovered, stirring sauce occasionally, 25 minutes or until steaks and vegetables are tender.

Makes about 4 servings

Menu Suggestion: Serve with steak fries or baked potatoes.

Savory Chicken Breasts Provençal

1 tablespoon olive or vegetable oil
2 whole chicken breasts (about 1 pound each), split
¼ cup dry white wine or water
1 large tomato, chopped
1 envelope Lipton Recipe Secrets Savory Herb with Garlic Soup Mix
¾ cup water
2 tablespoons sliced pitted ripe olives
1 tablespoon chopped fresh parsley (optional)

In 12-inch skillet, heat oil over medium-high heat and brown chicken 10 minutes, turning once; drain. Remove chicken and keep warm. Add wine to skillet and boil over high heat 2 minutes, stirring brown bits from bottom of skillet. Stir in tomato and savory herb with garlic soup mix blended with water. Bring to a boil over high heat. Reduce heat to low and return chicken to skillet. Simmer covered 20 minutes or until chicken is done. Top with olives and parsley.

Makes about 4 servings

♦ Also terrific with Lipton Recipe Secrets Golden Onion or Golden Herb with Lemon Soup Mix.

Menu Suggestion: Serve with hot buttered rice or noodles.

Steaks with Peppers

Chicken & Rice

New Ideas for Old Favorites

Contents

Classic Arroz con Pollo, page 74

Chicken Basics

◆

It's no wonder that chicken is America's favorite meat. High in protein and vitamins, low in fat and calories, chicken's popularity has grown as rapidly as America's appetite for healthy eating. Its versatility has long been recognized by chefs and novice cooks alike—and even busy families on a budget find it convenient and affordable. Adaptable to many seasonings and compatible with a great variety of fruits, vegetables—and of course—rice, you could eat chicken every day and never experience the same flavors.

Broiler chickens, young birds about 6½ weeks old and weighing between 2½ and 5 pounds, represent more than 95 percent of all chicken sold in supermarkets today. The National Broiler Council offers recipes in this publication that reflect the reasons for chicken's universal appeal—taste, versatility, economic value, convenience and good nutrition. The Council recommends that cooks master the following basic buying, handling, storage, preparation tips and techniques to ensure the wholesomeness of each recipe.

BUYING GUIDE

Knowing how much chicken to buy and being able to identify the many different forms that are available is important for any cook. A general rule of thumb is to buy ½ to ¾ pound per person of bone-in chicken and ¼ to ½ pound per person of boneless meat. A 3½-pound whole chicken will generously feed a family of four.

As America's demand for chicken has grown, so has the variety of forms in which chicken is available in the supermarket. Popular cuts of chicken are packaged together for convenience. Boneless, skinless chicken breasts are tender cuts that are great for gourmet dishes as well as quick family suppers. Breast and leg quarters are good cuts for grilling and are often sold in jumbo packs. Drumsticks, favorites with children, and wings, popular with crowds of any age, can be found in convenient party packs either fresh or frozen.

Be sure to inspect the chicken before purchasing. Check to make sure that the skin is bright, ranging in color from creamy white to deep yellow, and free of bruises and discolorations. It should never look gray or pasty. Odors could signal spoilage. The chicken should be plump and well shaped, both signs of meatiness.

All chicken found in supermarkets must pass government inspection, and each package should be stamped with a government inspection seal indicating wholesomeness. Some packages will have an additional Grade A stamp, which insures top quality chicken. Look for the package's "sell by" date, which tells you the last day the chicken should be bought. Avoid buying any packages that are broken or loosely wrapped.

HANDLING AND STORAGE

Fresh, raw chicken can be stored in its original wrap for up to two days in the refrigerator. Freeze chicken immediately if you do not plan to use it within two days. You can freeze in the original packaging for up to two months; if you plan to freeze it longer, double-wrap or rewrap with freezer paper, foil or plastic wrap. Freeze well wrapped chicken parts for up to nine months. When freezing whole chickens, remove and rinse giblets (if any); pat dry with paper towels. Trim away any excess fat. Tightly wrap, label, date and freeze both chicken and giblets in separate heavy-duty plastic, paper or foil wraps.

Always thaw chicken in the refrigerator or microwave. A general guideline is to allow 24 hours thawing time for a 5-pound whole chicken in the refrigerator; allow about 5 hours per pound for thawing chicken pieces. *Never* thaw chicken at room temperature; this promotes bacterial growth.

Wash all preparation surfaces and utensils thoroughly with hot, soapy water after contact with raw meat and before using utensils for other food preparation. If bacteria are transferred, they could contaminate other foods. With careful handling and proper cooking, this is easily prevented.

PREPARING CHICKEN

Simmering a whole broiler is an easy way to provide meat for recipes calling for cooked chicken. Place a 3½-pound chicken in a large saucepan with enough water to cover. Add 1 teaspoon salt, ½ teaspoon black pepper and, if desired, chopped vegetables such as an onion, a carrot or a celery rib. Cover; simmer for 45 minutes or until a fork can be inserted with ease and the juices run clear, not pink. This makes about 3 cups of chicken meat and 2½ cups of stock.

Whole breasts can also be **poached**. Place the chicken breasts in a saucepan. Cover with water; add 1 teaspoon salt, ½ teaspoon black pepper and chopped vegetables, if desired. Simmer for 20 minutes before checking for doneness. Two whole breasts, or 1½ pounds, will yield about 3 cups of cooked meat.

Microwaving is another way to prepare cooked chicken. Arrange 2 breast halves in a single layer in shallow microwave dish; cover with wax paper. Cook on HIGH for 8 minutes, rotating dish after 4 minutes. Since microwave ovens vary in wattage, check for doneness and return the chicken to the microwave for additional cooking if pink in the center.

CHECKING FOR DONENESS

Whatever method you use for cooking chicken, it should always be cooked thoroughly. The most accurate test is a meat thermometer. Whole chickens should be cooked to an internal temperature of 180°F. Cook bone-in parts to 170°F and boneless parts to 160°F. Ground chicken should be cooked to 165°F. Keep cooked chicken either hot (140° to 165°F) or cold (refrigerated at 40°F or less). Never leave chicken at room temperature for more than two hours. When a thermometer isn't available, test bone-in chicken by inserting a fork into the chicken. If the meat is tender and all juices run clear, the chicken is done. For boneless chicken, check that meat is no longer pink in the center.

The Good News Is ... Rice

What a welcome phrase these days, especially when it brings easy-to-use information about health and fitness.

At the USA Rice Council the news keeps getting better. We have been urged to evaluate the favorite foods in our diets in order to avoid health problems. In the process, we have learned that rice not only maintains its position of esteem, but is also earning new praise. Here's a favorite we don't have to give up—a nutrition-savvy food that fits perfectly into our health-conscious lifestyles.

This versatile world-popular grain almost does it all. It is low in fat and calories and is cholesterol free. All the recipes in this collection provide nutritional analyses, and there is even a chapter on low-fat recipes in which each serving provides 30 percent or less of the calories from fat.

Overall, these recipes demonstrate how rice remarkably combines with chicken in all kinds of dishes—from appetizers to salads to marvelous entrées. There's even a chapter on desserts that further highlights the versatility of rice. In addition, rice comes in several shapes and forms. You'll never be bored!

THE THREE TYPES OF RICE

Long Grain: Long and slender, these grains are 3 to 4 times as long as they are wide. Cooked grains remain separate, light and fluffy. The perfect choice for salad, side-dish or main-dish recipes.

Medium Grain: Plump but not round, these grains when cooked are more moist and tender than long grain. Ideal for risottos, molds and desserts.

Short Grain: Almost round, the grains tend to cling together when cooked—just right for puddings.

FORMS OF RICE

Brown: Rice from which only the hull has been removed. When cooked, it has a slightly chewy texture and nutlike flavor. An excellent source of rice bran.

Parboiled: Unmilled rice is soaked, steamed and dried before milling. Nutrients stay within the grain. A favorite of cooks who like fluffy-but-separate results.

Precooked: Rice is cooked and dehydrated after milling. It takes less time to prepare than other forms.

Regular-Milled White Rice: Rice after it has been completely milled, removing the bran layers. Vitamins and minerals are added for enrichment. This rice is labeled either milled rice, milled white rice, polished rice or polished white rice.

Aromatic Rice: Rices which provide authentic flavor in many ethnic cuisines. A variety of aromatic rices are grown in America. All the aromatic rices have the aroma and flavor of roasted nuts or popcorn. In some aromatic varieties, the grains cook up separate and fluffy. Other aromatic varieties are classified as soft cooking rices, where the grains tend to cling together when cooked. Aromatic rices are available in both white and brown rice forms.

HOW TO PREPARE RICE

1 cup uncooked rice	Liquid*	Cooking Time
Regular-milled long grain	1¾ to 2 cups	15 minutes
Regular-milled medium or short rice	1½ to 1¾ cups	15 minutes
Brown	2 to 2½ cups	45 to 50 minutes
Parboiled	2 to 2½ cups	20 to 25 minutes
Precooked	Follow package directions	Follow package directions
Flavored or seasoned mixes	Follow package directions	Follow package directions

Combine 1 cup rice, liquid (see chart above), 1 teaspoon salt (optional) and 1 tablespoon butter or margarine (optional) in 2- to 3-quart saucepan. Bring to a boil; stir once or twice. Reduce heat; cover and simmer. Cook according to time specified on chart. If rice is not quite tender or liquid is not absorbed, replace lid and cook 2 to 4 minutes more. Fluff with fork.

Cooked rice may be stored in the refrigerator for up to one week or in the freezer up to six months.

*Liquids other than water that can be used include: chicken broth, bouillon, consommé, tomato or vegetable juice (1 part water, 1 part juice), fruit juice, such as orange or apple (1 part water, 1 part juice).

MICROWAVE OVEN INSTRUCTIONS

Combine 1 cup rice, liquid (see chart above), 1 teaspoon salt (optional) and 1 tablespoon butter or margarine (optional) in 2- to 3-quart deep microproof baking dish. Cover and cook on HIGH 5 minutes or until boiling. Reduce setting to MEDIUM (50% power) and cook 15 minutes (20 minutes for parboiled rice and 30 minutes for brown rice). Fluff with fork.

For Starters

◆

*Begin your meals with these appetizing
appetizers and savory soups!*

BUFFALO CHICKEN WINGS

24 chicken wings
1 teaspoon salt
¼ teaspoon ground black
   pepper
4 cups vegetable oil for frying
¼ cup butter or margarine

¼ cup hot pepper sauce
1 teaspoon white wine vinegar
   Celery sticks
1 bottle (8 ounces) blue cheese
   dressing

Cut tips off wings at first joint; discard tips. Cut remaining wings into two
parts at the joint; sprinkle with salt and pepper. Heat oil in deep fryer or
heavy saucepan to 375°F. Add half the wings; fry about 10 minutes or until
golden brown and crisp, stirring occasionally. Remove with slotted spoon;
drain on paper towels. Repeat with remaining wings. Melt butter in small
saucepan over medium heat; stir in pepper sauce and vinegar. Cook until
thoroughly heated. Place wings on large platter. Pour sauce over wings.
Serve warm with celery and dressing for dipping.

Makes 24 appetizers

Each appetizer provides 173 calories, 9 grams protein, 15 grams fat,
4 grams saturated fat, 1 gram carbohydrate, 0 grams dietary fiber,
34 milligrams cholesterol and 174 milligrams sodium.

Buffalo Chicken Wings

PARTY CHICKEN TARTS

2 tablespoons butter or
 margarine
1 cup chopped fresh
 mushrooms
¼ cup finely chopped celery
¼ cup finely chopped onion
2 tablespoons all-purpose flour
1½ cups chopped cooked chicken
6 tablespoons sour cream

½ teaspoon garlic salt
1 package (10 ounces) flaky
 refrigerator biscuits
 (10 to 12 count)
Vegetable cooking spray
1 tablespoon butter or
 margarine, melted
Grated Parmesan cheese

Melt 2 tablespoons butter in large skillet until hot. Add mushrooms, celery and onion; cook and stir 4 to 5 minutes. Sprinkle with flour; stir in chicken and sour cream. Cook until thoroughly heated. Stir in garlic salt; set aside. Cut each biscuit into quarters; press each piece into miniature muffin tins coated with cooking spray to form tart shell. Brush each piece with melted butter. Bake at 400°F 6 minutes. Remove from oven; *reduce oven temperature to 350°F.* Fill each tart with 1 teaspoon chicken mixture; sprinkle with cheese. Bake 14 to 15 minutes more. Serve immediately.

Makes 40 to 48 appetizers

Note: For ease in serving at party time, prepare filling ahead and cook tarts 5 minutes. Fill and bake just before serving for best flavor.

Each appetizer provides 49 calories, 2 grams protein, 3 grams fat, 1 gram saturated fat, 4 grams carbohydrate, 0 grams dietary fiber, 8 milligrams cholesterol and 131 milligrams sodium.

ORIENTAL CHICKEN BALLS

1 tablespoon butter or
 margarine
1 tablespoon all-purpose flour
½ cup warm milk
3 tablespoons finely chopped
 onion
1 cup chopped cooked chicken
1 teaspoon lemon juice

1 tablespoon chopped fresh
 parsley
½ teaspoon salt
⅛ teaspoon ground black
 pepper
⅓ cup cornstarch
 Vegetable oil for frying
 Sweet and sour sauce

continued on page 70

Party Chicken Tarts

Oriental Chicken Balls, continued

Melt butter in small skillet over medium heat until hot; stir in flour and cook until smooth and lightly browned. Slowly stir in milk until sauce is thick and smooth. Bring to a boil, stirring constantly. Stir in onion; cook about 5 minutes over low heat. Stir in chicken, lemon juice, parsley, salt and pepper; transfer to small bowl. Refrigerate until cold. Shape into 1-inch balls; keep refrigerated until ready to cook. Place cornstarch on wax paper. Roll chicken balls in cornstarch. Heat 1 inch oil in large skillet to 375°F. Add chicken balls; cook only until light brown. Serve hot with sweet and sour sauce for dipping.

Makes 10 servings (about 30 to 34 appetizers)

Each serving (3 appetizers) provides 201 calories, 4 grams protein, 16 grams fat, 3 grams saturated fat, 10 grams carbohydrate, 0 grams dietary fiber, 16 milligrams cholesterol and 166 milligrams sodium.

TORTILLA RICE SOUP

Vegetable cooking spray
1/3 cup sliced green onions
4 cups chicken broth
2 cups cooked rice
1 can (10 1/2 ounces) diced tomatoes with green chiles, undrained
1 cup cooked chicken breast cubes

1 can (4 ounces) chopped green chiles, undrained
1 tablespoon lime juice
Salt to taste
Tortilla chips
1/2 cup chopped tomato
1/2 avocado, cut into small cubes
4 lime slices for garnish
Fresh cilantro for garnish

Heat Dutch oven or large saucepan coated with cooking spray over medium-high heat until hot. Add onions; cook and stir until tender. Add broth, rice, tomatoes and juice, chicken and chiles. Reduce heat to low; cover and simmer 20 minutes. Stir in lime juice and salt. Just before serving, pour into soup bowls; top with tortilla chips, tomato and avocado. Garnish with lime slices and cilantro.   *Makes 4 servings*

Each serving provides 305 calories, 16 grams protein, 10 grams fat, 0 grams saturated fat, 36 grams carbohydrate, 1 gram dietary fiber, 27 milligrams cholesterol and 1601 milligrams sodium.

Tortilla Rice Soup

Straight from the Skillet

◆

*Discover these one-dish meals for complete
busy-day menus.*

ORANGE CHICKEN STIR-FRY

½ cup orange juice
2 tablespoons sesame oil, divided
2 tablespoons soy sauce
1 tablespoon dry sherry
2 teaspoons grated fresh ginger
1 teaspoon grated orange peel
1 clove garlic, minced
1½ pounds boneless, skinless
   chicken breast, cut into
   strips

3 cups mixed fresh vegetables,
   such as green bell pepper,
   red bell pepper, snow peas,
   carrots, green onions,
   mushrooms and/or onions
1 tablespoon cornstarch
½ cup unsalted cashew bits or
   halves
3 cups hot cooked rice

Combine orange juice, 1 tablespoon oil, soy sauce, sherry, ginger, orange
peel and garlic in large glass bowl. Add chicken; marinate in refrigerator
1 hour. Drain chicken, reserving marinade. Heat remaining 1 tablespoon oil
in large skillet or wok over medium-high heat. Add chicken; stir-fry 3
minutes or until chicken is light brown. Add vegetables; stir-fry 3 to
5 minutes or until vegetables are crisp-tender. Combine cornstarch and
marinade; add to skillet and stir until sauce boils and thickens. Stir in
cashews; cook 1 minute more. Serve over hot rice.

Makes 6 servings

Each serving provides 590 calories, 48 grams protein, 20 grams fat, 4 grams
saturated fat, 53 grams carbohydrate, 4 grams dietary fiber, 109 milligrams
cholesterol and 822 milligrams sodium.

Orange Chicken Stir-Fry

CLASSIC ARROZ CON POLLO

2 tablespoons olive oil
1 cut up chicken
2 cups uncooked rice*
1 cup chopped onion
1 medium-size red bell pepper, chopped
1 medium-size green bell pepper, chopped
1 clove garlic, minced
1½ teaspoons salt, divided
1½ teaspoons dried basil
4 cups chicken broth
1 tablespoon lime juice
⅛ teaspoon ground saffron *or* ½ teaspoon ground turmeric
1 bay leaf
2 cups chopped tomatoes
½ teaspoon ground black pepper
1 cup fresh or frozen green peas
Fresh basil for garnish

Heat oil in large Dutch oven over medium-high heat until hot. Add chicken; cook 10 minutes or until brown, turning occasionally. Remove chicken; keep warm. Add rice, onion, red pepper, green pepper, garlic, ¾ teaspoon salt and basil to pan; cook and stir 5 minutes or until vegetables are tender and rice is browned. Add broth, lime juice, saffron and bay leaf. Bring to a boil; stir in tomatoes. Arrange chicken on top and sprinkle with remaining ¾ teaspoon salt and black pepper. Cover; reduce heat to low. Cook 20 minutes more. Stir in peas; cover and cook 10 minutes more or until fork can be inserted into chicken with ease and juices run clear, not pink. Remove bay leaf. Garnish with basil. Serve immediately. *Makes 8 servings*

*Recipe based on regular-milled long grain white rice. If using other types of rice, refer to rice cooking chart (page 65).

Each serving provides 408 calories, 24 grams protein, 13 grams fat, 3 grams saturated fat, 48 grams carbohydrate, 2 grams dietary fiber, 54 milligrams cholesterol and 1016 milligrams sodium.

Classic Arroz con Pollo

CHICKEN MANGO STIR-FRY

1 cup chicken broth, divided
¼ cup orange juice
1 tablespoon low-sodium soy sauce
1 tablespoon cornstarch
1 teaspoon sugar
1 tablespoon vegetable oil
1½ pounds boneless, skinless chicken breast, cut into ¼-inch strips

1 jalapeño pepper, seeded and minced
1 medium-size red bell pepper, cut into 1-inch squares
1½ cups diced fresh mangos* (about 2 medium)
6 green onions, sliced
2 cloves garlic, minced
⅛ teaspoon ground cinnamon
3 cups hot cooked rice

Combine ¾ cup broth, orange juice, soy sauce, cornstarch and sugar in small bowl; set aside. Heat oil in large skillet or wok over high heat until hot. Add chicken; stir-fry about 2 minutes or until chicken is no longer pink in center. Remove from skillet; keep warm. Add jalapeño, red pepper and remaining ¼ cup broth to skillet. Stir-fry 2 minutes. Add mangos, onions, garlic and cinnamon. Return chicken to skillet; stir well. Stir in broth mixture. Cook over high heat about 2 minutes or until thick and bubbly. Serve over hot rice.   *Makes 4 servings*

*Bottled mangos, diced, may be substituted.

Each serving provides 481 calories, 45 grams protein, 10 grams fat, 2 grams saturated fat, 52 grams carbohydrate, 2 grams dietary fiber, 109 milligrams cholesterol and 767 milligrams sodium.

SIMPLE MARINATED CHICKEN BREASTS

2 teaspoons Dijon mustard
1 clove garlic, minced
½ teaspoon salt
½ teaspoon ground black pepper
⅛ teaspoon dried savory
⅛ teaspoon dried tarragon

2 tablespoons olive oil, divided
¼ cup dry white wine
4 boneless, skinless chicken breast halves (about 1½ pounds)
½ cup warm water
Fresh thyme for garnish

Combine mustard, garlic, salt, pepper, savory, tarragon, 1 tablespoon oil and wine in small bowl. Place chicken in shallow dish; pour marinade mixture over chicken, turning to coat. Cover; marinate in refrigerator overnight. Heat remaining 1 tablespoon oil in large skillet over medium heat until hot. Add chicken, reserving marinade; cook 15 minutes or until brown and no longer pink in center, turning occasionally. Remove to warm platter. Place marinade and warm water in skillet. Bring to a boil; cook and stir about 3 minutes. Pour over chicken. Garnish with thyme. Serve immediately.

Makes 4 servings

Each serving provides 152 calories, 27 grams protein, 4 grams fat, 1 gram saturated fat, 0 grams carbohydrate, 0 grams dietary fiber, 73 milligrams cholesterol and 64 milligrams sodium.

PIZZA-FLAVORED CHICKEN TACOS

1 pound ground chicken
1 small onion, chopped
1 small green bell pepper, chopped
1 cup chopped fresh mushrooms
1 clove garlic, minced
1 tablespoon all-purpose flour
1/2 teaspoon salt
1/2 teaspoon dried basil
1/2 teaspoon dried oregano
1/4 teaspoon ground black pepper
1 can (8 ounces) tomato sauce
1/2 cup water
12 taco shells, warmed
Shredded mozzarella cheese, grated Parmesan cheese, chopped tomatoes, chopped onion, shredded lettuce and sliced black olives for toppings

Cook and stir chicken in large nonstick skillet over medium-high heat 5 minutes or until no longer pink. Add onion, green pepper, mushrooms and garlic; cook 5 minutes or until vegetables are tender. Sprinkle with flour, salt, basil, oregano and black pepper. Stir in tomato sauce and water; bring to a boil. Reduce heat to low; simmer, uncovered, 15 minutes. To serve, spoon chicken mixture into taco shells; sprinkle with mozzarella and Parmesan cheeses, then add tomato, onion, lettuce and olives.

Makes 6 servings (2 tacos each)

Each serving provides 305 calories, 23 grams protein, 13 grams fat, 4 grams saturated fat, 25 grams carbohydrate, 4 grams dietary fiber, 58 milligrams cholesterol and 725 milligrams sodium.

LOUISIANA JAMBALAYA

1½ pounds chicken tenders
½ teaspoon salt
½ teaspoon ground black
   pepper
1 tablespoon vegetable oil
¾ pound smoked turkey
   sausage, cut into ¼-inch
   slices
2 medium onions, chopped
1 large green bell pepper,
   chopped

1 cup chopped celery
1 clove garlic, minced
2 cups uncooked rice*
¼ to ½ teaspoon ground red
   pepper
2½ cups chicken broth
1 cup sliced green onions
1 medium tomato, chopped
   Celery leaves for garnish

Season chicken with salt and black pepper. Heat oil in large saucepan or Dutch oven over high heat until hot. Add chicken, stirring until brown on all sides. Add sausage; cook 2 to 3 minutes. Remove chicken and sausage from saucepan; set aside. Add chopped onions, green pepper, celery and garlic to same saucepan; cook and stir over medium-high heat until crisp-tender. Stir in rice, red pepper, broth and reserved chicken and sausage; bring to a boil. Reduce heat to low; cover and simmer 30 minutes. Stir in green onions and tomato. Garnish with celery leaves. Serve immediately.

Makes 8 servings

*Recipe based on regular-milled long grain white rice. If using other types of rice, refer to rice cooking chart (page 65).

To microwave: Season chicken with salt and black pepper. Place oil in deep 3-quart microproof baking dish. Add chicken; cover with wax paper and cook on HIGH 3 minutes, stirring after 2 minutes. Add sausage; cover with wax paper and cook on HIGH 1 minute. Remove chicken and sausage with slotted spoon; set aside. Add chopped onions, green pepper, celery and garlic to same dish. Cover and cook on HIGH 4 minutes, stirring after 2 minutes. Stir in rice, red pepper, broth and reserved chicken and sausage; cover and cook on HIGH 8 minutes or until boiling. Reduce setting to MEDIUM (50% power); cover and cook 30 minutes, stirring after 15 minutes. Stir in green onions and tomato. Let stand 5 minutes before serving. Garnish with celery leaves. Serve immediately.

Each serving provides 403 calories, 32 grams protein, 10 grams fat, 1 gram saturated fat, 46 grams carbohydrate, 2 grams dietary fiber, 79 milligrams cholesterol and 739 milligrams sodium.

Louisiana Jambalaya

TASTY SKILLET CHICKEN FOR TWO

1 tablespoon butter or
  margarine
2 chicken breast halves
½ cup chopped onion
1 large tomato, chopped
1 tablespoon Worcestershire
  sauce

½ teaspoon dry mustard
½ teaspoon salt
¼ teaspoon ground black
  pepper
Hot cooked rice (optional)

Melt butter in medium skillet over medium-high heat until hot. Add chicken; cook 5 minutes or until brown, turning occasionally. Add onion; cook 2 minutes or until onion is tender. Add tomato, Worcestershire, mustard, salt and pepper; bring to a boil. Reduce heat to low; cover and simmer 20 minutes or until fork can be inserted into chicken with ease and juices run clear, not pink. Serve with hot rice. *Makes 2 servings*

Each serving provides 295 calories, 31 grams protein, 14 grams fat, 6 grams saturated fat, 11 grams carbohydrate, 3 grams dietary fiber, 98 milligrams cholesterol and 800 milligrams sodium.

LEMON CHICKEN RICE

1 tablespoon olive oil
1 pound boneless, skinless
  chicken breast, cut into
  strips
1 clove garlic, crushed
1 cup uncooked rice*

1 can (14½ ounces) chicken
  broth
1 tablespoon grated lemon
  peel
½ teaspoon ground black
  pepper

Heat oil in large skillet over medium-high heat until hot. Add chicken and garlic; cook and stir until browned. Stir in rice and broth. Cover and cook 15 minutes or until liquid is absorbed. Stir in lemon peel and pepper. Serve immediately. *Makes 4 servings*

*Recipe based on regular-milled long grain white rice. If using other types of rice, refer to rice cooking chart (page 65).

Each serving provides 369 calories, 31 grams protein, 8 grams fat, 0 grams saturated fat, 40 grams carbohydrate, 0 grams dietary fiber, 72 milligrams cholesterol and 496 milligrams sodium.

Tasty Skillet Chicken for Two

What's for Dinner?

◆

*Rely on these family favorites that are
also great for entertaining.*

CHICKEN FAJITAS

1/4 cup orange juice
2 tablespoons lime juice
2 tablespoons lemon juice
1 clove garlic, minced
4 boneless, skinless chicken
    breast halves (about
    1 1/2 pounds)
1 teaspoon chili powder
1/2 teaspoon salt
1 tablespoon vegetable oil
1 medium-size red bell pepper,
    cut into strips

1 medium-size green bell
    pepper, cut into strips
1 medium-size yellow bell
    pepper, cut into strips
1 medium onion, sliced
10 flour tortillas, warmed
1 cup sour cream
1 cup salsa
1 can (2 1/4 ounces) sliced
    black olives, drained

Combine orange juice, lime juice, lemon juice and garlic in large bowl.
Season chicken with chili powder and salt. Place chicken in juice mixture,
turning to coat. Cover; marinate in refrigerator 30 minutes. Remove
chicken. Place marinade in small saucepan. Bring to a boil over medium-
high heat; keep warm. Place chicken on broiler rack or grill about 6 inches
from heat. Broil or grill, turning and basting with marinade, 10 minutes or
until no longer pink in center. Heat oil in large skillet over medium-high
heat until hot. Add peppers and onion; cook and stir about 5 minutes or
until onion is tender. Slice chicken into strips; add to pepper-onion
mixture. Divide chicken-pepper mixture evenly in centers of tortillas. Roll
up tortillas; top each with dollop of sour cream, salsa and olives. Serve
immediately. *Makes 5 servings (2 fajitas each)*

Each serving provides 518 calories, 31 grams protein, 22 grams fat, 8 grams
saturated fat, 51 grams carbohydrate, 4 grams dietary fiber, 79 milligrams
cholesterol and 526 milligrams sodium.

Chicken Fajitas

STUFFED CHICKEN BREASTS WITH HERBED BUTTER SAUCE

8 boneless, skinless chicken breast halves (about 3 pounds)
½ teaspoon salt
¼ teaspoon ground black pepper
½ cup butter or margarine, softened
2 tablespoons chopped fresh parsley
½ teaspoon ground oregano
½ teaspoon dried rosemary, crushed
½ teaspoon dried basil

4 ounces Swiss cheese, cut into 8 strips
¼ cup all-purpose flour
1 egg, beaten
⅔ cup dry bread crumbs
½ cup dry white wine
1 teaspoon vegetable oil
½ cup red bell pepper strips
½ cup green bell pepper strips
4 cups cooked rice
1 tablespoon cornstarch
1 tablespoon cold water
Fresh oregano and rosemary sprigs for garnish

Place chicken between plastic wrap; pound with meat mallet or rolling pin to ¼-inch thickness. Sprinkle chicken with salt and black pepper. Combine butter, parsley, oregano, rosemary and basil in small bowl. Place 1½ teaspoons herb butter on centers of breast halves, reserving remaining herb butter. Place one cheese strip in center of each breast half. Roll up chicken with cheese inside; tuck in ends. Roll in flour, then dip in egg. Coat with bread crumbs. Place in ungreased 13×9-inch baking dish; bake at 375°F 15 minutes. Stir wine into remaining herb butter in small saucepan; heat over low heat until butter melts. Pour over chicken; bake 20 minutes more. Heat oil in large skillet over medium heat until hot. Add red and green bell peppers; cook and stir until crisp-tender. Add rice; toss lightly. Heat thoroughly. Serve chicken over rice. Pour pan drippings into small saucepan. Dissolve cornstarch in water. Add to drippings; heat until mixture boils and thickens, stirring constantly. Serve with chicken and rice. Garnish with oregano and rosemary. *Makes 8 servings*

Each serving provides 477 calories, 35 grams protein, 20 grams fat, 11 grams saturated fat, 34 grams carbohydrate, 1 gram dietary fiber, 140 milligrams cholesterol and 434 milligrams sodium.

Stuffed Chicken Breast with Herbed Butter Sauce

YA GOTTA EMPANADA

1 package (4.4 to 6.8 ounces) Spanish rice mix, prepared according to package directions
1 cup shredded cooked chicken
1 cup (4 ounces) shredded Cheddar cheese
½ cup sliced green onions
¼ cup chopped black olives
1 package (15 ounces) refrigerated pie crust

Combine rice, chicken, cheese, onions and olives in large bowl. Spoon half of rice mixture on half of each pie crust. Fold crust over filling. Seal and crimp edges. Place on baking sheet. Bake at 400°F 20 to 22 minutes or until golden brown. Cut each empanada in half. Serve immediately.

Makes 4 servings (½ empanada each)

Each serving provides 683 calories, 27 grams protein, 35 grams fat, 6 grams saturated fat, 67 grams carbohydrate, 2 grams dietary fiber, 58 milligrams cholesterol and 668 milligrams sodium.

GLAZED CHICKEN

⅔ cup ketchup
⅓ cup white wine vinegar
2 tablespoons brown coarse-grain mustard
¾ teaspoon salt
¼ teaspoon ground black pepper
8 chicken breast halves (about 3 pounds)
Vegetable cooking spray
¼ cup butter or margarine, melted
2 tablespoons honey

Combine ketchup, vinegar, mustard, salt and pepper in shallow large glass dish. Add chicken, turning to coat. Cover; marinate in refrigerator overnight. Remove chicken to shallow glass baking dish coated with cooking spray, reserving marinade. Bake at 325°F 45 minutes. Combine marinade, butter and honey in small saucepan; bring to a boil over medium-high heat, stirring until smooth. Brush chicken with sauce; bake 15 minutes more or until fork can be inserted into chicken with ease and juices run clear, not pink. Serve immediately. *Makes 8 servings*

Each serving provides 217 calories, 30 grams protein, 9 grams fat, 3 grams saturated fat, 3 grams carbohydrate, 0 grams dietary fiber, 86 milligrams cholesterol and 299 milligrams sodium.

Ya Gotta Empanada

SPICY MARINATED CHICKEN KEBABS OVER RICE

½ cup white wine
¼ cup lime juice
¼ cup vegetable oil
2 cloves garlic, minced
1 jalapeño pepper, seeded and finely chopped
2 tablespoons chopped fresh cilantro
½ teaspoon salt
½ teaspoon ground black pepper

1½ pounds boneless, skinless chicken breast, cut into 1-inch cubes
1 medium-size red onion, cut into 1-inch pieces
2 medium-size red or green bell peppers, cut into 1-inch pieces
2 medium-size yellow squash, cut into 1-inch pieces
12 wooden or metal skewers*
Vegetable cooking spray
3 cups hot cooked rice

Combine wine, lime juice, oil, garlic, jalapeño, cilantro, salt and black pepper in gallon size plastic resealable food bag. Add chicken, onion, red peppers and squash. Seal; toss to coat vegetables. Marinate in refrigerator 30 to 45 minutes. Remove chicken and vegetables. Place marinade in small saucepan. Bring to a boil over medium-high heat; keep warm. Alternate chicken and vegetables on skewers. Place on broiler rack coated with cooking spray; brush with marinade. Broil 4 to 6 inches from heat 8 to 10 minutes, turning and basting occasionally with marinade. (Do not baste during last 5 minutes of cooking.) Serve over hot rice.   *Makes 6 servings*

*Soak wooden skewers in water before using to prevent burning. Spray metal skewers with vegetable cooking spray before using.

Each serving provides 280 calories, 30 grams protein, 5 grams fat, 1 gram saturated fat, 28 grams carbohydrate, 2 grams dietary fiber, 73 milligrams cholesterol and 262 milligrams sodium.

Spicy Marinated Chicken Kebabs over Rice

BAKED CHICKEN BOMBAY

2 teaspoons paprika
½ teaspoon ground cumin
½ teaspoon ground coriander
¼ teaspoon ground ginger
⅛ teaspoon ground red pepper
8 boneless, skinless chicken thighs (about 1¼ pounds)
2 tablespoons plus 1 teaspoon lemon juice, divided
2 tablespoons reduced-calorie margarine, melted

1 cup plain dry bread crumbs
Vegetable cooking spray
8 ounces plain nonfat yogurt, at room temperature
½ cup fresh cilantro leaves
¼ cup fresh mint leaves
¼ teaspoon salt
Lemon slices for garnish
Hot cooked rice (optional)

Combine paprika, cumin, coriander, ginger and red pepper in small bowl. Place chicken between plastic wrap; pound with meat mallet or rolling pin to ½-inch thickness. Sprinkle paprika mixture on both sides of chicken. Combine 2 tablespoons lemon juice and margarine in shallow bowl. Dip chicken in margarine mixture. Roll in bread crumbs to coat. Place on baking sheet coated with cooking spray. Bake at 425°F 17 to 20 minutes or until no longer pink in center. Combine yogurt, cilantro, mint, salt and remaining 1 teaspoon lemon juice in blender or food processor; process until smooth. To serve, pour sauce over chicken. Garnish with lemon slices. Serve with hot rice. *Makes 4 servings*

Each serving provides 374 calories, 33 grams protein, 16 grams fat, 4 grams saturated fat, 25 grams carbohydrate, 1 gram dietary fiber, 99 milligrams cholesterol and 535 milligrams sodium.

Baked Chicken Bombay and Brown Rice and Shiitake Pilaf (page 106)

High Flavor– Low Fat

◆

*Try these delectable recipes—
you won't miss the fat.*

ROSEMARY CHICKEN WITH ASPARAGUS LEMON RICE

¼ cup dry white wine
3 cloves garlic, minced
1 tablespoon finely chopped fresh rosemary
1 tablespoon vegetable oil
1 tablespoon low-sodium soy sauce
1 teaspoon sugar
½ teaspoon ground black pepper
6 boneless, skinless chicken breast halves (about 2¼ pounds)

Vegetable cooking spray
3 cups cooked rice (cooked in low-sodium chicken broth)
10 spears asparagus, blanched and cut into 1-inch pieces (¼ pound)
1 teaspoon grated lemon peel
1 teaspoon lemon pepper
½ teaspoon salt
Lemon slices for garnish
Fresh rosemary sprigs for garnish

Combine wine, garlic, rosemary, oil, soy sauce, sugar and pepper in large shallow glass dish. Add chicken, turning to coat; cover and marinate in refrigerator at least 1 hour. Heat large skillet coated with cooking spray over medium-high heat until hot. Add chicken and marinade; cook 7 minutes on each side or until brown and no longer pink in center. Combine rice, asparagus, lemon peel, lemon pepper and salt in large bowl. To serve, spoon rice on individual serving plates. Cut chicken into strips; fan over rice. Garnish with lemon and rosemary.   *Makes 6 servings*

Each serving provides 294 calories (20% of calories from fat), 30 grams protein, 6 grams fat, 1 gram saturated fat, 25 grams carbohydrate, 1 gram dietary fiber, 73 milligrams cholesterol and 437 milligrams sodium.

*Rosemary Chicken with
Asparagus Lemon Rice*

CHICKEN PHYLLO WRAPS

Vegetable cooking spray
1 pound ground chicken
1 cup chopped fresh
    mushrooms
1 medium onion, chopped
3 cups cooked rice (cooked
    without salt and fat)
1 cup nonfat low-salt ricotta
    cheese
1 package (10 ounces) chopped
    spinach, thawed and well
    drained
1 can (2¼ ounces) sliced
    black olives, drained
¼ cup pine nuts, toasted*
2 cloves garlic, minced
1 teaspoon ground oregano
1 teaspoon lemon pepper
12 phyllo dough sheets

Coat large skillet with cooking spray; heat over medium-high heat until hot. Add chicken, mushrooms and onion; cook and stir 2 to 4 minutes or until chicken is no longer pink and vegetables are tender. Reduce heat to medium. Add rice, ricotta cheese, spinach, olives, nuts, garlic, oregano and lemon pepper; cook and stir 3 to 4 minutes until well blended and thoroughly heated. Working with 1 phyllo sheet at a time, spray 1 sheet with cooking spray; fold sheet in half lengthwise. Place ¾ to 1 cup rice mixture on one end of phyllo strip. Fold left bottom corner over mixture, forming a triangle. Continue folding back and forth into triangle at end of strip. Repeat with remaining phyllo sheets and rice mixture. Place triangles, seam sides down, on baking sheets coated with cooking spray. Coat tops of each triangle with cooking spray. Bake at 400°F 15 to 20 minutes or until golden brown. Serve immediately.　　*Makes 12 servings*

*To toast nuts, place on baking sheet. Bake at 350°F 5 to 7 minutes or until lightly browned.

Each serving provides 219 calories (26% of calories from fat), 12 grams protein, 6 grams fat, 2 grams saturated fat, 25 grams carbohydrate, 1 gram dietary fiber, 27 milligrams cholesterol and 224 milligrams sodium.

Chicken Phyllo Wrap

LIGHT 'N' LEAN CHICKEN BREASTS

Vegetable cooking spray
4 chicken breast halves,
  skinned (about 1½ pounds)
½ teaspoon ground black
  pepper, divided
2 cloves garlic, halved
1 cup low-sodium chicken
  broth

½ cup dry white wine
2 teaspoons cornstarch
⅔ cup skim milk
1 teaspoon finely chopped
  fresh chives
2 cups hot cooked rice
  (cooked without salt
  and fat)

Coat skillet with cooking spray; heat over medium heat until hot. Add chicken; sprinkle with ¼ teaspoon pepper. Cook 20 minutes or until brown, turning occasionally. Reduce heat to low; add garlic. Cook 10 minutes more or until fork can be inserted into chicken with ease and juices run clear, not pink. Remove chicken; keep warm. Add broth and wine to garlic. Bring to a boil over high heat; boil 5 minutes. Reduce heat to low. Stir cornstarch into milk and slowly add mixture to skillet. Sprinkle with remaining ¼ teaspoon pepper; cook and stir 2 minutes or until thickened. Return chicken to skillet. Spoon sauce over chicken; sprinkle with chives. Simmer 5 minutes or until thoroughly heated. Serve with hot rice.

Makes 4 servings

Each serving provides 299 calories (13% of calories from fat), 31 grams protein, 4 grams fat, 1 gram saturated fat, 27 grams carbohydrate, 0 grams dietary fiber, 74 milligrams cholesterol and 121 milligrams sodium.

WARM CHICKEN SALAD WITH RED ONIONS AND RICE

6 boneless, skinless chicken
  breast halves (about
  2¼ pounds)
1 tablespoon dried oregano
½ teaspoon ground black
  pepper
½ teaspoon salt
1 tablespoon olive oil
1 medium-size red bell pepper,
  cut into julienned strips
1 small red onion, sliced

⅓ cup low-sodium chicken
  broth
2 tablespoons balsamic
  vinegar
2 tablespoons drained capers
  (optional)
1 tablespoon white wine
2 teaspoons sugar
3 cups cooked rice (cooked
  without salt and fat)
6 large romaine lettuce leaves

continued on page 98

Light 'n' Lean Chicken Breasts

Warm Chicken Salad with Red Onions and Rice, continued

Sprinkle chicken with oregano, black pepper and salt. Heat oil in large skillet over medium-high heat until hot; add chicken. Cook about 7 minutes on each side or until brown and no longer pink in center. Remove chicken; keep warm. Add red pepper and onion to skillet; cook and stir 2 to 3 minutes or until crisp-tender. Stir in broth, vinegar, capers, wine and sugar; cook 3 to 4 minutes or until thickened slightly. Combine rice with broth mixture in large bowl; toss. Place 1 lettuce leaf on each plate; arrange rice mixture over lettuce. Slice chicken; fan over rice.   *Makes 6 servings*

Each serving provides 288 calories (19% of calories from fat), 30 grams protein, 6 grams fat, 1 gram saturated fat, 27 grams carbohydrate, 1 gram dietary fiber, 73 milligrams cholesterol and 270 milligrams sodium.

RICE STUFFED BAKED APPLES

1 cup uncooked rice*	½ cup chopped dried apricots
1 cup water	½ cup chopped pecans
¾ cup apple juice	¼ cup maple syrup
6 large baking apples	3 tablespoons brown sugar
¾ cup raisins	1 tablespoon lemon juice
½ cup fresh or frozen	1½ teaspoons ground allspice
cranberries, chopped	1 teaspoon vanilla extract

Combine rice, water and apple juice in 2- to 3-quart saucepan. Bring to a boil over high heat; stir once or twice. Reduce heat to low; cover and simmer 15 minutes or until rice is tender and liquid is absorbed. Set aside. Core apples leaving 1½-inch walls and bottoms intact; set aside. Peel top halves, if desired. Combine rice, raisins, cranberries, apricots, pecans, syrup, brown sugar, lemon juice, allspice and vanilla in large bowl. Stuff apples with rice mixture and place in shallow glass baking dish. Place remaining rice mixture around apples. Cover with foil; bake at 350°F 50 to 60 minutes or until apples are fork-tender. Serve immediately.

Makes 6 servings

*Recipe based on regular-milled long grain white rice. For medium grain rice, use ¾ cup water and cook 15 minutes. For parboiled rice, use 1¼ cups water and cook 20 to 25 minutes. For brown rice, use 1¼ cups water and cook 45 to 50 minutes.

Each serving provides 450 calories (15% of calories from fat), 5 grams protein, 8 grams fat, 1 gram saturated fat, 96 grams carbohydrate, 8 grams dietary fiber, 0 milligrams cholesterol and 9 milligrams sodium.

Rice Stuffed Baked Apple

Tasty Toss-Ups & Great Go-Withs

◆

*Create these main-dish salads for lighter fare
and round out meals with these
splendid side dishes.*

BORDER BLACK BEAN CHICKEN SALAD

1/4 cup olive oil, divided
1 1/2 pounds boneless, skinless
  chicken breast, cut into
  2-inch strips
1 clove garlic, minced
1/2 jalapeño pepper, seeded and
  finely chopped
1 1/4 teaspoons salt, divided
4 cups torn romaine lettuce
1 can (15 to 16 ounces) black
  beans, drained and rinsed

1 cup peeled and seeded
  cucumber cubes
1 cup red bell pepper strips
1 cup chopped tomato
1/2 cup chopped red onion
1/3 cup tomato vegetable juice
2 tablespoons fresh lime juice
1/2 teaspoon ground cumin
1/2 cup chopped pecans,
  toasted*
Fresh parsley for garnish

Heat 2 tablespoons oil in large skillet over medium heat until hot. Add chicken; stir-fry 2 minutes or until no longer pink in center. Add garlic, jalapeño and 3/4 teaspoon salt; stir-fry 30 seconds. Combine chicken mixture, lettuce, beans, cucumber, red pepper, tomato and onion in large salad bowl. Combine tomato juice, lime juice, remaining 2 tablespoons oil, cumin and remaining 1/2 teaspoon salt in small jar with lid; shake well. Add to skillet; heat over medium heat until slightly warm. Pour warm dressing over chicken mixture; toss to coat. Sprinkle with pecans. Garnish with parsley. Serve immediately. *Makes 4 servings*

*To toast nuts, see directions on page 94.

Each serving provides 572 calories, 50 grams protein, 29 grams fat, 4 grams saturated fat, 30 grams carbohydrate, 4 grams dietary fiber, 109 milligrams cholesterol and 913 milligrams sodium.

Border Black Bean Chicken Salad

ATHENIAN RICE WITH FETA CHEESE

1 tablespoon olive oil
1 cup chopped red onion
1 red bell pepper, chopped
1 clove garlic, minced
3 cups cooked rice
½ cup sun-dried tomatoes, softened* and cut into julienned strips
1 can (4½ ounces) sliced black olives

1 tablespoon chopped fresh parsley
1½ teaspoons dried oregano
½ cup crumbled feta cheese
1 tablespoon lemon juice
¼ teaspoon ground black pepper
Fresh oregano for garnish

Heat oil in large skillet over medium-high heat until hot. Add onion, red pepper and garlic; cook and stir until onion is tender. Stir in rice, tomatoes, olives, parsley and oregano; heat thoroughly. Remove from heat; add cheese, lemon juice and black pepper. Stir until well blended. Garnish with oregano. Serve immediately. *Makes 6 servings*

*To soften sun-dried tomatoes, place in ⅓ cup boiling water; stir to coat. Let stand 10 minutes; drain water.

Each serving provides 204 calories, 5 grams protein, 7 grams fat, 2 grams saturated fat, 31 grams carbohydrate, 2 grams dietary fiber, 8 milligrams cholesterol and 612 milligrams sodium.

SUMMER PILAF

1 tablespoon butter
½ cup thinly sliced green onions
⅓ cup pine nuts or slivered almonds
1 clove garlic, minced

3 cups cooked rice (cooked in chicken broth)
¼ teaspoon salt
¼ teaspoon ground black pepper
¼ teaspoon dried thyme

Melt butter in large skillet over medium-high heat until hot. Add onions, nuts and garlic; cook and stir 3 to 5 minutes or until nuts are lightly browned. Add rice, salt, pepper and thyme; cook and stir 3 to 5 minutes or until well blended. Serve immediately. *Makes 6 servings*

Each serving provides 181 calories, 5 grams protein, 8 grams fat, 2 grams saturated fat, 25 grams carbohydrate, 0 grams dietary fiber, 5 milligrams cholesterol and 414 milligrams sodium.

Athenian Rice with Feta Cheese

LAYERED CHICKEN SALAD

1 chicken, cooked, skinned,
  boned and chopped
  (about 3 cups)
2 cups alfalfa sprouts
1 can (8 ounces) sliced water
  chestnuts, drained

1 small red onion, thinly sliced
  and broken into rings
½ cup oil-free Italian dressing
½ teaspoon ground black
  pepper

Layer half each of chicken, sprouts, water chestnuts and onion in medium glass bowl. Sprinkle with half each of dressing and pepper. Repeat layers. Cover and refrigerate at least 2 hours. Serve cold.   *Makes 4 servings*

Variation: Layer salad as directed on four individual serving plates, dividing ingredients evenly.

Each serving provides 241 calories, 29 grams protein, 7 grams fat, 2 grams saturated fat, 14 grams carbohydrate, 1 gram dietary fiber, 85 milligrams cholesterol and 411 milligrams sodium.

BLACK BEAN PILAF

1 tablespoon olive oil
1 medium onion, sliced
1 can (15 to 16 ounces) black
  beans, drained and rinsed
½ cup drained and chopped
  sun-dried tomatoes in oil

¼ teaspoon salt
¼ teaspoon ground black
  pepper
3 cups cooked brown rice
  (cooked in chicken broth)

Heat oil in large skillet over medium-high heat until hot. Add onion, beans, tomatoes, salt and pepper; cook 3 to 5 minutes or until flavors are well blended. Stir in rice; heat thoroughly. Serve immediately.

Makes 6 servings

Each serving provides 239 calories, 9 grams protein, 6 grams fat, 1 gram saturated fat, 39 grams carbohydrate, 2 grams dietary fiber, 0 milligrams cholesterol and 464 milligrams sodium.

Layered Chicken Salad

BROWN RICE AND SHIITAKE PILAF

1 tablespoon olive oil
1 cup (about 2 ounces) sliced
    fresh shiitake mushrooms
1 cup asparagus spears, cut
    into 1-inch pieces
1 clove garlic, minced
3 cups cooked brown rice
1/4 cup pine nuts, toasted*

1/4 cup sliced green onions
1 tablespoon grated lemon
    peel
1/2 teaspoon salt
1/2 teaspoon ground black
    pepper
Baked chicken (optional)

Heat oil in large skillet over medium-high heat until hot. Add mushrooms, asparagus and garlic; cook and stir 1 to 2 minutes or until tender. Add rice, nuts, onions, lemon peel, salt and pepper. Stir until well blended; heat thoroughly. Serve with chicken.   *Makes 6 servings*

*To toast nuts, place on baking sheet. Bake at 350°F 5 to 7 minutes or until lightly browned.

Each serving provides 173 calories, 5 grams protein, 7 grams fat, 0 grams saturated fat, 26 grams carbohydrate, 3 grams dietary fiber, 0 milligrams cholesterol and 397 milligrams sodium.

HERBED WALNUT RICE

1 tablespoon butter or
    margarine
1/2 cup chopped onion
1/2 cup shredded carrot
1/2 cup chopped walnuts
1/4 teaspoon dried marjoram
1/4 teaspoon dried thyme

1/8 teaspoon dried rosemary,
    crushed
3 cups cooked rice (cooked in
    chicken broth)
2 tablespoons chopped fresh
    parsley

Melt butter in large skillet over medium-high heat until hot. Add onion, carrot, walnuts, marjoram, thyme and rosemary; cook and stir until vegetables are crisp-tender. Stir in rice and parsley; heat thoroughly. Serve immediately.   *Makes 6 servings*

Each serving provides 205 calories, 6 grams protein, 9 grams fat, 2 grams saturated fat, 26 grams carbohydrate, 1 gram dietary fiber, 5 milligrams cholesterol and 319 milligrams sodium.

CRUNCHY CURRIED CHICKEN SALAD

1 chicken, cooked, skinned,
   boned and cut into small
   cubes
3 cups cooked rice
2 cans (11 ounces *each*)
   mandarin oranges, drained
½ medium-size red onion,
   sliced

1 rib celery, thinly sliced
¾ cup plain nonfat yogurt
¼ cup honey
2 tablespoons lemon juice
1 teaspoon curry powder
¼ teaspoon salt
⅓ cup chopped dry roasted
   peanuts

Combine chicken, rice, oranges, onion and celery in large bowl; cover and refrigerate until chilled. Combine yogurt, honey, lemon juice, curry and salt in small bowl; stir until well combined. Cover and refrigerate until chilled. To serve, pour dressing over salad; toss gently. Sprinkle with peanuts.

Makes 6 servings

Each serving provides 376 calories, 25 grams protein, 9 grams fat, 2 grams saturated fat, 50 grams carbohydrate, 1 gram dietary fiber, 57 milligrams cholesterol and 383 milligrams sodium.

RICE MEDALLIONS

3 cups cooked brown rice
2 carrots, shredded
1 red bell pepper, shredded
1 leek, cut into julienned strips
   or 4 green onions, sliced
1 medium zucchini, shredded

4 eggs, slightly beaten
1 clove garlic, minced
½ teaspoon salt
¼ teaspoon ground white
   pepper
Vegetable oil for frying

Combine rice, carrots, red pepper, leek, zucchini, eggs, garlic, salt and white pepper in large bowl; mix thoroughly. Heat ¼ inch oil in large skillet until hot. Spoon ¼ cup rice mixture into skillet; flatten with spatula to make patty. Fry 3 to 5 minutes on each side or until golden brown. Repeat with remaining rice mixture. Serve immediately.

Makes 6 servings (3 patties each)

Each serving provides 320 calories, 8 grams protein, 19 grams fat, 4 grams saturated fat, 30 grams carbohydrate, 3 grams dietary fiber, 147 milligrams cholesterol and 453 milligrams sodium.

FLORIDA RICE AND AVOCADO SALAD

3 cups cooked rice, cooled
2 cups chopped cooked
 chicken
2 avocados, peeled and cut into
 ½-inch cubes
1 cup diagonally sliced celery
½ green bell pepper, cut into
 julienned strips
¼ cup minced onion
3 tablespoons lemon juice

2 tablespoons vegetable oil
1½ teaspoons salt
1 teaspoon sugar
¼ teaspoon ground white
 pepper
1 clove garlic, minced
 Hot pepper sauce to taste
 Salad greens (optional)
 Tomato wedges or roses
 for garnish

Combine rice, chicken, avocados, celery, green pepper and onion in large bowl. Place lemon juice, oil, salt, sugar, white pepper, garlic and pepper sauce in small jar with lid; shake well. Pour over rice mixture. Toss lightly. Cover and refrigerate 1 to 2 hours. Adjust seasonings, if necessary. Serve on salad greens. Garnish with tomato wedges. *Makes 6 servings*

Each serving provides 344 calories, 16 grams protein, 18 grams fat, 1 gram saturated fat, 31 grams carbohydrate, 2 grams dietary fiber, 38 milligrams cholesterol and 845 milligrams sodium.

CHINESE CHICKEN SALAD

3 cups cooked rice, cooled
1½ cups cooked chicken breast
 cubes (about 1 whole
 breast)
1 cup sliced celery
1 can (8 ounces) sliced water
 chestnuts, drained
½ cup sliced fresh mushrooms
¼ cup sliced green onions

¼ cup chopped red bell pepper
¼ cup sliced black olives
2 tablespoons vegetable oil
2 tablespoons lemon juice
1 tablespoon soy sauce
½ teaspoon ground ginger
¼ to ½ teaspoon ground white
 pepper
 Lettuce leaves

Combine rice, chicken, celery, water chestnuts, mushrooms, onions, red pepper and olives in large bowl. Place oil, lemon juice, soy sauce, ginger and white pepper in small jar with lid; shake well. Pour over rice mixture. Toss lightly. Serve on lettuce leaves. *Makes 4 servings*

Each serving provides 350 calories, 20 grams protein, 10 grams fat, 0 grams saturated fat, 45 grams carbohydrate, 2 grams dietary fiber, 41 milligrams cholesterol and 644 milligrams sodium.

Florida Rice and Avocado Salad

Tempting Treasures

◆

**Indulge in these scrumptious desserts—
perfect for the grand finale!**

RICE PUDDING TARTS

1 cup cooked rice
1 cup low-fat milk
1/3 cup sugar
1/4 cup raisins
1/8 teaspoon salt
2 eggs, beaten
3/4 cup heavy cream

1/2 teaspoon vanilla extract
1/4 teaspoon almond extract
6 frozen tartlet pastry shells,
   partially baked and cooled
1/8 teaspoon ground nutmeg
   for garnish
Fresh berries for garnish
Fresh mint for garnish

Combine rice, milk, sugar, raisins and salt in medium saucepan. Cook over medium-low heat 30 to 35 minutes or until thick and creamy, stirring frequently. Remove from heat; add one-fourth rice mixture to eggs. Return egg mixture to saucepan; stir in cream and extracts. Spoon equally into pastry shells; sprinkle with nutmeg. Place tarts on baking sheet. Bake at 350°F 20 to 30 minutes or until pudding is set. Cool on wire rack 1 hour. Use knife to loosen pastries from aluminum containers; unmold. Garnish with berries and mint. Serve at room temperature. Refrigerate remaining tarts.   *Makes 6 servings*

Each tart provides 353 calories, 7 grams protein, 20 grams fat, 1 gram saturated fat, 37 grams carbohydrate, 1 gram dietary fiber, 118 milligrams cholesterol and 277 milligrams sodium.

Rice Pudding Tart

WEST COAST BRANDIED RICE

1 cup firmly packed brown
   sugar
1/2 cup butter or margarine
2 apples, cored and chopped
1 cup golden raisins

1/2 cup brandy
5 cups cooked brown rice*
1 cup chopped walnuts
1 1/2 teaspoons ground cinnamon
1 pint vanilla ice cream

Combine brown sugar and butter in large skillet. Cook over medium heat until sugar is dissolved. Stir in apples, raisins and brandy. Cook until apples are crisp-tender, stirring constantly. Fold in rice, walnuts and cinnamon. Serve topped with vanilla ice cream. *Makes 8 servings*

*Medium or long grain white rice may be substituted.

Each serving provides 612 calories, 7 grams protein, 26 grams fat, 0 grams saturated fat, 85 grams carbohydrate, 5 grams dietary fiber, 46 milligrams cholesterol and 399 milligrams sodium.

CHOCOLATE RICE PUDDING

2 1/2 cups low-fat milk
2 cups cooked rice
1/2 cup sugar

1/4 cup semisweet chocolate
   chips
1 teaspoon vanilla extract

Combine milk, rice, sugar and chocolate in 2- to 3-quart saucepan. Cook over medium heat about 20 minutes or until pudding is thick and creamy, stirring often. Remove from heat; stir in vanilla. Spoon into serving dishes. Let stand 10 minutes. Serve warm or cold. *Makes 6 servings*

Each serving provides 220 calories, 5 grams protein, 4 grams fat, 3 grams saturated fat, 41 grams carbohydrate, 0 grams dietary fiber, 8 milligrams cholesterol and 177 milligrams sodium.

West Coast Brandied Rice

RICE PUDDING WITH RASPBERRY SAUCE AND CRÈME ANGLAISE

1⅓ cups cooked rice
1⅓ cups warm low-fat milk
¼ cup sugar
⅛ teaspoon salt
2 eggs, beaten
1 teaspoon vanilla extract
Raspberry Sauce (recipe follows)

Crème Anglaise (recipe follows)
Fresh raspberries for garnish
Fresh mint for garnish

Combine rice, milk, sugar and salt in medium bowl; whisk in eggs and vanilla. Pour rice mixture into 8 greased ovenproof molds or custard cups. Place molds in baking pan. Pour hot water in pan to 1-inch depth. Bake at 350°F 30 to 35 minutes or until knife inserted into centers comes out clean. Cool completely. To serve, pour equal amounts of Raspberry Sauce and Crème Anglaise on individual serving plates. Unmold pudding over sauces. Garnish with raspberries and mint. *Makes 8 servings*

RASPBERRY SAUCE

1 package (10 ounces) frozen sweetened raspberries, thawed

2 teaspoons cornstarch

Combine raspberries and cornstarch in small saucepan over medium heat. Cook 5 to 7 minutes or until thickened, stirring constantly. Strain mixture; cool completely.

CRÈME ANGLAISE

1 cup low-fat milk
2 tablespoons sugar

2 teaspoons cornstarch
1 egg yolk, beaten

Combine milk, sugar and cornstarch in small saucepan over medium heat. Cook 5 to 7 minutes or until almost thickened, stirring constantly. Whisk 2 tablespoons of hot mixture into egg yolk; stir back into hot mixture. Heat 1 to 3 minutes, stirring constantly. Cool completely.

Each serving provides 176 calories, 5 grams protein, 3 grams fat, 1 gram saturated fat, 31 grams carbohydrate, 3 grams dietary fiber, 88 milligrams cholesterol and 149 milligrams sodium.

Rice Pudding with Raspberry Sauce and Crème Anglaise

RICE PUDDING PEAR TART

1 sheet prepared refrigerated
   pie crust
2 cups dry red wine
1 teaspoon ground cinnamon
2 large pears, peeled, halved
   and cored
2 cups cooked rice
2 cups half and half

½ cup plus 1 tablespoon sugar,
   divided
2 tablespoons butter or
   margarine
¼ teaspoon salt
2 eggs, beaten
1 teaspoon vanilla extract

Prepare pie crust according to package directions. Place in 10-inch tart pan. Bake at 450°F 8 to 10 minutes or until lightly browned; set aside. *Reduce oven temperature to 350°F.* Place wine and cinnamon in 10-inch skillet. Bring to a boil over high heat; add pears. Reduce heat to low; cover and poach 10 minutes. Turn pears; poach 5 to 10 minutes more or until tender. Remove from wine; set aside pears and discard wine mixture. Combine rice, half and half, ½ cup sugar, butter and salt in 3-quart saucepan. Cook over medium heat 12 to 15 minutes or until slightly thickened, stirring occasionally. Gradually stir one-fourth of rice mixture into eggs; return egg mixture to saucepan, stirring constantly. Cook 1 to 2 minutes more. Remove from heat; stir in vanilla. Pour rice mixture into baked crust. Place pears, cut sides down, on cutting board. Cut thin lengthwise slits into each pear, one-third down from stem end. Fan pears over rice mixture. Bake 30 minutes or until rice mixture is set. Remove from oven; sprinkle with remaining 1 tablespoon sugar. Broil tart about 4 to 5 inches from heat source 1 to 2 minutes or until top is browned. Cool before serving.   *Makes 8 servings (one 10-inch tart)*

Each serving provides 445 calories, 7 grams protein, 20 grams fat, 0 grams saturated fat, 50 grams carbohydrate, 2 grams dietary fiber, 86 milligrams cholesterol and 398 milligrams sodium.

Rice Pudding Pear Tart

Contents

Albacore Stir-Fry, page 164

TUNA *for* TODAY

People love the taste and convenience of StarKist® tuna. But besides having great flavor, tuna is a terrific food for healthy eating. Did you know that tuna is a good source of niacin and vitamin B_{12}, which are important for heart health, and the protein in tuna is easier to digest than other meat protein. Also, a two-ounce serving of StarKist Chunk Light water-packed tuna has *less cholesterol** and *less saturated fat*** than chicken or beef. These are a few of the reasons that make tuna a smart choice and a wonderful substitute for meat and poultry dishes.

When selecting tuna, choose StarKist, America's best-loved and most trusted brand.*** Our tuna products are consistently great tasting because of our strict quality controls that continually monitor the entire packing process—from the sea to the can. Our dolphin-safe policy was the first in the industry and one we are firmly committed to, along with millions of our consumers.

Charlie the Tuna
StarKist's spokefish and all-time purveyor of good taste

StarKist tuna offers meal magic to prevent menu boredom. The secret to its magic is not only its fantastic versatility, but also the ease with which delicious entrées are ready to enjoy. Many of these recipes are prepared in 30 minutes or less—a real plus for today's busy cooks. For instance, a can of tuna combined with a variety of fresh vegetables and canned tomatoes makes the sensational Tuna and Caponata Sauce. This sauce is ready to serve over your choice of pasta in an easy 25 minutes.

Those of you who like your tuna in the traditional ways—sandwiches, soups and salads—are in for a treat. There are old favorites, such as Tuna Supper Sandwiches, and innovative creations, such as Spicy Tuna Empanadas and Nutty Albacore Salad Pitas. These are just a sampling of the tasty tuna dishes you'll find here.

The recipes that follow suggest using Solid White (albacore) tuna or offer a choice between Solid White and Chunk Light tuna. To help guide your decision, here is some information about these different types of tuna. Solid White tuna comes from albacore tuna. It is packed as a solid fillet and is firm, white and mild. These characteristics make it a great substitute for chicken. It is often referred to as the gold standard of tuna.

Chunk Light tuna is packed in a chunk style instead of a solid fillet. It is light in color and comes from either yellowfin (ahi) or skipjack tuna. Chunk Light tuna is most commonly used in sandwiches, spreads and family-style baked dishes.

You'll enjoy the compliments from your family and friends when you serve these mouth-watering StarKist dishes. Bon Appetit!

For Chunk Light Tuna in Spring Water

*30% less cholesterol than chicken (30mg versus 43mg) and 33% less than beef (30mg versus 45mg) based on two-ounce serving

**72% less saturated fat than chicken (0.18g versus 0.65g) and 94% less than beef (0.18g versus 3.2g) based on two-ounce serving

***1992 Tuna Usage and Attitude Study

Appetizers &
SNACKS

Tri-Colored Tuna Stuffed Mushrooms

This assortment of stuffed mushrooms is not just great looking; the smoked Gouda cheese complements the tuna flavor.

30 medium mushrooms, cleaned and stems removed
2 tablespoons melted butter or margarine
1 cup finely chopped onion
1 tablespoon vegetable oil
1 can (6 ounces) StarKist Solid White or Chunk Light Tuna, drained and flaked
½ cup shredded smoked Gouda cheese, divided
1 red bell pepper, seeded and puréed*
1 package (10 ounces) frozen spinach soufflé
¼ cup mayonnaise, divided
¼ cup grated Parmesan cheese, divided
½ teaspoon curry powder

Lightly coat mushroom caps with melted butter; divide into 3 groups of 10. Sauté onions in hot oil until tender. *In each of 3 small bowls, place ⅓ tuna and ⅓ sautéed onions.* In first small bowl, add ¼ cup Gouda cheese and red bell pepper purée.

In second small bowl, add ¼ cup spinach soufflé,** 2 tablespoons mayonnaise, 2 tablespoons Parmesan cheese and curry powder. In third small bowl, add remaining ¼ cup Gouda cheese, remaining 2 tablespoons mayonnaise and remaining 2 tablespoons Parmesan cheese. Fill 10 mushrooms with filling from each bowl. Arrange on baking sheet; bake in 350°F oven 10 to 12 minutes. Serve hot.

Makes 30 servings

*To purée bell pepper: Place seeded and coarsely chopped red pepper into blender or food processor with metal blade. Blend or process until puréed.

**Keep remainder frozen until ready to use.

Prep Time: 40 minutes

Tri-Colored Tuna Stuffed Mushrooms

Tuna and Olive Spread

This quick and easy spread will be a family favorite in no time.

1 can (6 ounces) StarKist Solid White or Chunk Light Tuna, drained
1 hard-cooked egg *or* 2 hard-cooked egg whites
½ cup soft cream cheese
¼ cup prepared green onion dip
1 can (4¼ ounces) chopped ripe olives
Salt and pepper to taste
Snipped chives and paprika, for garnish
Crackers, assorted breads or raw vegetables

In food processor bowl with metal blade, place tuna, egg, cream cheese and onion dip; process until smooth. Transfer to bowl; stir in olives, salt and pepper. Chill several hours or overnight before serving. Serve or mold into special shape, if desired. Garnish with chives and paprika. Serve with crackers.

Makes about 12 servings

Prep Time: 5 minutes

Creamy Tuna Dip with Dill

Whip up this dip using lighter ingredients for great taste with less guilt.

1 can (6 ounces) StarKist Solid White or Chunk Light Tuna, drained and chunked
1 package (8 ounces) light cream cheese
½ cup light mayonnaise
½ cup light sour cream
2 green onions, including tops, cut into 1-inch pieces
1 tablespoon dried dill weed
2 teaspoons lemon juice
½ teaspoon garlic salt
¼ teaspoon white pepper
Fresh raw vegetables for dipping

In food processor bowl with metal blade, place tuna, cream cheese, mayonnaise, sour cream, onions, dill, lemon juice, garlic salt and white pepper. Pulse on and off until blended. Pour into small bowl; chill several hours or overnight before serving with vegetables.

Makes 8 to 10 servings

Note: Mixture will be soft. For firmer dip, use regular cream cheese, mayonnaise and sour cream in place of the light varieties.

Prep Time: 5 minutes

Tuna and Olive Spread

Hot Artichoke and Tuna Spread

This hot appetizer spread is excellent on plain or toasted French bread and assorted crackers. It's a great addition to any cocktail party.

> 1 can (6 ounces) StarKist Solid White or Chunk Light Tuna, drained
> 1 jar (12 ounces) marinated artichoke hearts, drained
> 1 to 2 cloves garlic
> 1 cup shredded mozzarella cheese
> ½ cup grated Parmesan cheese
> ¼ cup chopped canned green chiles
> 1 tablespoon minced green onion
> 2 to 3 tablespoons mayonnaise
> Hot pepper sauce to taste
> French bread or assorted crackers

In food processor bowl with metal blade, place all ingredients except bread. Process until well blended but not puréed. Transfer mixture to ovenproof serving dish. Bake, uncovered, in 350°F oven about 30 minutes or until mixture is golden. Serve hot with French bread.

Makes 12 servings

Note: This mixture may be baked in small hollowed bread shell. Wrap in foil; bake as above. Open top of foil last 5 minutes of baking.

Tip: Mixture keeps well, tightly covered, in refrigerator for up to 5 days.

Prep Time: 35 minutes

Tuna Potato Boats

This hearty appetizer can double as a light meal.

> 4 russet potatoes, baked and halved lengthwise
> 1 can (12 ounces) StarKist Solid White or Chunk Light Tuna, drained and flaked
> ¾ cup shredded Cheddar cheese
> ¼ cup finely chopped green onions
> ¼ cup cooked and crumbled bacon
> ¼ cup sour cream

Scoop out potatoes, leaving ¼-inch shells; place potato pulp in bowl. Add tuna, cheese, onions, bacon and sour cream; mix just enough to blend together but still remain chunky. Spoon into potato shells. Bake in 375°F oven 15 minutes or until potatoes are hot and cheese is melted. *Makes 8 servings*

Tip: Use microwave to cook potatoes and heat finished stuffed potatoes.

Prep Time: 30 minutes

Hot Artichoke and Tuna Spread

Tuna in Crispy Won Ton Cups

This is great for kids to make.

18 won ton skins, *each*
    3¼ inches square
    Butter or olive oil cooking
    spray
1 can (6 ounces) StarKist Solid
    White or Chunk Light Tuna,
    drained and flaked
⅓ cup cold cooked orzo (rice-
    shaped pasta) or cooked rice
¼ cup Southwestern ranch-style
    vegetable dip with jalapeños
    or other sour cream dip
¼ cup drained pimiento-stuffed
    green olives, chopped
3 tablespoons sweet pickle
    relish, drained
    Paprika, for garnish
    Parsley sprigs, for garnish

Cut won tons into circles with 3-inch round cookie cutter. Spray miniature muffin pans with cooking spray. Place one circle in each muffin cup; press to sides to mold won ton to cup. Spray each won ton with cooking spray. Bake in 350°F oven 6 to 8 minutes or until golden brown; set aside.

In small bowl, gently mix tuna, orzo, dip, olives and relish. Refrigerate filling until ready to serve. Remove won ton cups from muffin pan. Use rounded teaspoon to fill each cup; garnish with paprika and parsley.

Makes 18 servings

Tip: Cups may be made a day ahead; store in airtight container. Reheat in 350°F oven 1 to 2 minutes to recrisp.

Prep Time: 20 minutes

Tuna Tapenade

Tapenade is a flavorful spread made in the South of France. Serve with brightly colored fresh vegetables, or use to stuff tomatoes or hard-cooked eggs.

1 can (12 ounces) StarKist Solid
    White or Chunk Light Tuna,
    drained and chunked
1 can (6 ounces) pitted ripe
    olives, drained
4 to 6 anchovy fillets, drained
¼ cup drained capers
2 tablespoons lemon juice
1 tablespoon Dijon-style
    mustard
1 teaspoon dried basil
⅛ teaspoon ground black pepper
2 cloves garlic
⅓ cup extra-virgin olive oil
    Raw vegetables, crisp wheat
    crackers or pita bread

In food processor bowl with metal blade, place tuna, olives, anchovies, capers, lemon juice, mustard, basil, pepper and garlic. Add oil very slowly through feed tube while processing. Chill several hours before serving with vegetables.

Makes 12 servings

Prep Time: 7 minutes

Tuna in Crispy Won Ton Cups

Soups &

SANDWICHES

Albacore Corn Chowder

This chowder is a thick, rich soup with chunks of tuna and vegetables.

 2 tablespoons butter or
    margarine
 ½ cup sliced celery
 ½ cup chopped onion
 ¾ cup chopped carrot
 2 to 3 tablespoons flour
 1 teaspoon dried thyme or
    Italian seasoning
 1 can (17 ounces) cream-style
    corn
 2 cups milk
 1 can (12 ounces) StarKist Solid
    White Tuna, drained and
    flaked
 1 cup water
 1 teaspoon chicken flavor
    instant bouillon

In medium saucepan, melt butter over medium heat; sauté celery, onion and carrot about 3 minutes. Add flour and thyme; blend well. Cook 3 more minutes. Add corn, milk, tuna, water and bouillon, stirring to blend. Cover and simmer *(do not boil)* 5 minutes to heat through, stirring occasionally.

Makes 4 servings

Prep Time: 20 minutes

Peanut-ty Tuna Sandwiches

This recipe combines interesting flavors and textures.

 3 tablespoons mayonnaise
 2 tablespoons crunchy-style
    peanut butter
 ¼ teaspoon curry powder
 ¼ teaspoon lemon peel
 1 can (6 ounces) StarKist Solid
    White or Chunk Light Tuna,
    drained and flaked
 1 tablespoon finely minced
    green onion
 8 slices whole wheat bread
 4 lettuce leaves (optional)
 4 tomato slices (optional)

In small bowl, combine mayonnaise, peanut butter, curry powder and lemon peel; blend well. In medium bowl, combine tuna and onion; stir in mayonnaise mixture. Spread onto 4 slices of bread. Add lettuce leaves and tomato slices, if desired; top with remaining 4 bread slices.

Makes 4 servings

Prep Time: 8 minutes

Albacore Corn Chowder

StarKist Vegetable Gazpacho

Broiled or grilled vegetables lend a hearty, roasted flavor to this adaptation of a classic soup.

  1 large onion, quartered
  1 medium zucchini, halved
     lengthwise
  1 yellow or crookneck squash,
     halved lengthwise
  1 red bell pepper
  1 yellow bell pepper
  3/4 cup bottled olive oil vinaigrette
     dressing
  1 can (6 ounces) StarKist Solid
     White Tuna, drained and
     chunked
  3 pounds firm ripe tomatoes,
     chopped
  2 cucumbers, peeled, seeded and
     chopped
  2 to 3 cloves fresh garlic,
     minced or pressed
  1/2 cup fresh sourdough
     breadcrumbs
  1 1/2 to 2 cups tomato juice

Preheat broiler. Brush onion quarters, zucchini and squash halves and whole peppers with dressing; reserve remaining dressing. Broil 6 to 8 minutes, turning occasionally until vegetables are roasted and pepper skins blister and turn black. Remove from broiler. Place peppers in paper bag; close bag and let stand 15 minutes before peeling. Cool remaining vegetables. Peel skin from peppers; seed and remove membrane. Cut all roasted vegetables in large pieces; place in food processor bowl with metal blade. Process until coarsely chopped. Transfer to large bowl; add tuna, tomatoes, cucumbers, garlic, breadcrumbs, 1 1/2 cups tomato juice and remaining dressing. Blend thoroughly. Add remaining 1/2 cup tomato juice to thin, if necessary.

Makes 6 to 8 servings

Prep Time: 30 minutes

Tuna Supper Sandwiches

Kids love making and eating these super supper buns.

  2 cups shredded Cheddar cheese
  1/3 cup chopped green onions,
     including tops
  1/3 cup chopped red bell pepper
  1 can (2 1/4 ounces) sliced ripe
     olives, drained
  2 tablespoons minced fresh
     parsley
  1 teaspoon curry powder
     Seasoned salt to taste
  1 can (12 ounces) StarKist Solid
     White or Chunk Light Tuna,
     drained and chunked
  1/2 cup light mayonnaise
  6 soft French rolls (7 inches
     each), halved lengthwise

In medium bowl, place cheese, onions, red pepper, olives, parsley, curry powder and salt; mix lightly. Add tuna and mayonnaise; toss lightly with fork. Cover baking sheet with foil; place rolls on foil. Spread about 1/3 cup mixture on each half. Bake in 450°F oven 10 to 12 minutes or until tops are bubbling and beginning to brown. Cool slightly before serving.

Makes 12 servings

Prep Time: 18 minutes

StarKist Vegetable Gazpacho

Spicy Tuna Empanadas

Kids will enjoy making and eating these empanadas.

- **1 can (6 ounces) StarKist Solid White or Chunk Light Tuna, drained and flaked**
- **1 can (4 ounces) diced green chiles, drained**
- **1 can (2¼ ounces) sliced ripe olives, drained**
- **½ cup shredded sharp Cheddar cheese**
- **1 chopped hard-cooked egg Salt and pepper to taste**
- **¼ teaspoon hot pepper sauce**
- **¼ cup medium thick and chunky salsa**
- **2 packages (15 ounces *each*) refrigerated pie crusts Additional salsa**

In medium bowl, place tuna, chiles, olives, cheese, egg, salt, pepper and hot pepper sauce; toss lightly with fork. Add ¼ cup salsa and toss again; set aside. Following directions on package, unfold crusts (roll out slightly with rolling pin if you prefer thinner crust); cut 4 circles, 4 inches *each*, out of each crust. Place 8 circles on foil-covered baking sheets; wet edge of each circle with water. Top each circle with ¼ cup lightly packed tuna mixture. Top with remaining circles, stretching pastry slightly to fit; press edges together and crimp with fork. Cut slits in top crust to vent. Bake in 425°F oven 15 to 18 minutes or until golden brown. Cool slightly. Serve with additional salsa.   *Makes 8 empanadas*

Prep Time: 25 minutes

Tuna and Watercress Tea Sandwiches

Tea sandwiches were never this easy; the food processor makes quick work of blending the ingredients. Now, just boil the water for tea.

- **1 can (6 ounces) StarKist Solid White Tuna, drained and chunked**
- **½ cup butter or margarine, softened**
- **½ cup watercress leaves, firmly packed**
- **2 tablespoons lemon juice**
- **¼ teaspoon salt**
- **⅛ teaspoon white pepper**
- **24 slices thin white or wheat sandwich bread, crusts removed Additional watercress, for garnish**

In food processor bowl with metal blade, place tuna, butter, ½ cup watercress, lemon juice, salt and white pepper. Pulse on and off until watercress is finely chopped and mixture is blended. Spread tuna mixture on half the bread slices; top with remaining slices. Cut into squares or triangles. Serve or refrigerate up to 2 hours. Garnish with additional watercress.
Makes 12 servings

Note: Day-old bread is best for making tea sandwiches; it is easier to slice. Use a serrated knife.

Prep Time: 15 minutes

Spicy Tuna Empanadas

Mini Tuna Tarts

This is an easy recipe for kids to make and it's also great for a picnic.

1 can (6 ounces) StarKist Solid White or Chunk Light Tuna, drained and flaked
2 tablespoons mayonnaise
2 tablespoons sweet pickle relish
1 green onion, including tops, minced
¾ cup shredded Monterey Jack cheese
Salt and pepper to taste
1 package (10 count) refrigerated flaky biscuits

In small bowl, combine tuna, mayonnaise, pickle relish, onion and cheese; mix well. Add salt and pepper. Separate each biscuit into 2 halves. Press each half in bottom of lightly greased muffin pan to form a cup. Spoon scant tablespoon tuna mixture into each muffin cup. Bake in 400°F oven 8 to 10 minutes or until edges of biscuits are just golden. Serve hot or cold.

Makes 20 servings

Prep Time: 15 minutes

Chunky Albacore Chowder

A savory, piping hot chowder that will satisfy the hunger of everyone in your family.

1 can (10¾ ounces) low fat cream of broccoli soup
1 can (10¾ ounces) low fat cream of mushroom soup
1¼ cups low fat milk, divided
1 teaspoon ground cumin
4 to 6 drops hot pepper sauce
⅓ cup red bell pepper, chopped in ¼-inch pieces
⅓ cup chopped green onions, including tops
½ cup light sour cream
1 can (6 ounces) StarKist Solid White Tuna, drained and chunked
⅓ cup fresh cilantro or parsley leaves, lightly packed, finely minced
½ teaspoon salt
¼ teaspoon white pepper

In 2-quart saucepan, mix together soups, milk, cumin and hot pepper sauce. Heat over medium heat about 5 minutes, stirring occasionally. Add red pepper and onions; whisk in sour cream. Stir in tuna; heat gently *(do not boil)*. Stir cilantro, salt and white pepper into soup.

Makes 4 servings

Prep Time: 15 minutes

Mini Tuna Tarts

Nutty Albacore Salad Pitas

What a great combination of tastes and textures!

1 can (6 ounces) StarKist Solid White Tuna, drained and flaked
½ cup mayonnaise
⅓ cup chopped celery
¼ cup raisins or seedless grape halves
¼ cup chopped walnuts, pecans or almonds
½ teaspoon dried dill weed
Salt and pepper to taste
2 pita breads, halved
Curly leaf lettuce leaves

In medium bowl, combine tuna, mayonnaise, celery, raisins, nuts and dill; mix well. Add salt and pepper. Line each pita bread pocket with lettuce leaf; fill with ¼ tuna mixture.

Makes 4 servings

Prep Time: 10 minutes

New York Deli-Style Tuna

For an authentic taste, use real New York style bagels that have a shiny crust and firm texture.

1 can (6 ounces) StarKist Solid White Tuna, drained and flaked
1 hard-cooked egg, minced
3 tablespoons minced celery
1 tablespoon chopped ripe olives
3 to 4 tablespoons mayonnaise
2 teaspoons mustard (optional)
1 tablespoon drained capers (optional)
3 New York style bagels, split
3 ounces cream cheese, softened
Baby kosher dill pickles, thinly sliced lengthwise
Thinly sliced red onion rings

In medium bowl, combine tuna, egg, celery, olives and mayonnaise. Stir in mustard and capers, if desired; blend well. Chill.

To serve, toast bagels; spread each half with ½ ounce cream cheese. Top *each* with 3 pickle slices, about 3 tablespoons tuna mixture and red onion rings; serve open face.

Makes 6 servings

Prep Time: 10 minutes

Nutty Albacore Salad Pita

Fabulous

◆◆◆

SALADS

Thai-Style Tuna and Fruit Salad with Sweet-Sour-Spicy Dressing

This dressing skimps on fat, but has a rich taste.

   8 lettuce leaves (use different
       varieties for color)
   2 tablespoons chopped fresh
       cilantro
   2 tablespoons chopped fresh
       mint leaves
   1 can (6 ounces) StarKist Solid
       White Tuna, drained and
       chunked
   ⅓ cup sliced cucumber
   ⅓ cup drained mandarin oranges
   ⅓ cup red seedless grape halves
   ¼ cup thinly sliced red onion
       Sweet-Sour-Spicy Dressing
       (recipe follows)
   ⅓ cup chopped cashews or
       peanuts

On platter, arrange half of lettuce. Break up remaining lettuce into bite-sized pieces and place over lettuce on platter. Sprinkle cilantro and mint over lettuce. Arrange tuna, cucumber, oranges, grapes and onion on top. Refrigerate, covered, while preparing Sweet-Sour-Spicy Dressing. Pour dressing over salad; sprinkle with cashews.

Makes 4 servings

Variation: Chop or tear all lettuce into bite-sized pieces; combine with remaining ingredients. Toss with dressing.

Sweet-Sour-Spicy Dressing
       Lime
   3 cloves garlic
   2 serrano chiles, halved, seeded
       and cut in pieces
   ¼ cup lime juice
   1½ tablespoons nam pla (fish
       sauce) or soy sauce
   1 tablespoon sugar

Peel ½ of lime with vegetable peeler. In blender or small food processor, place lime peel, garlic, chiles, lime juice, nam pla and sugar. Process until mixture is blended and lime peel, garlic and chiles are finely chopped.

Prep Time: 20 minutes

Thai-Style Tuna and Fruit Salad
with Sweet-Sour-Spicy Dressing

Albacore Salad Puttanesca with Garlic Vinaigrette

This dish may become a staple in your meal planning.

- 2 cups cooked, chilled angel hair pasta
- 2 cups chopped, peeled plum tomatoes
- 1 can (4¼ ounces) chopped* ripe olives, drained
- 1 cup Garlic Vinaigrette Dressing (recipe follows)
- 1 can (6 ounces) StarKist Solid White Tuna, drained and flaked
- ¼ cup chopped fresh basil leaves

In large bowl, combine chilled pasta, tomatoes, olives and 1 cup Garlic Vinaigrette Dressing. Add tuna and basil leaves; toss. Serve immediately.
Makes 2 servings

*If you prefer, the olives may be sliced rather than chopped.

Garlic Vinaigrette Dressing

- ⅓ cup red wine vinegar
- 2 tablespoons lemon juice
- 1 to 2 cloves garlic, minced or pressed
- 1 teaspoon freshly ground black pepper
  Salt to taste
- 1 cup olive oil

In small bowl, whisk together vinegar, lemon juice, garlic, pepper and salt. Slowly add oil, whisking continuously, until well blended.

Prep Time: 10 minutes

StarKist Salad Niçoise

Enjoy this classic tuna salad.

- ¾ pound new red potatoes, cooked in their jackets, chilled and diced
- 1½ pounds fresh green beans, trimmed and blanched
- 8 sliced plum tomatoes *or* 1 pint cherry tomatoes, halved
- ¾ cup niçoise olives or halved ripe olives
- ½ cup thinly sliced red onion rings
- 3 tablespoons finely chopped Italian parsley
- ¾ teaspoon medium-grind black pepper
  Salt to taste
- 4 hard-cooked eggs, cut in quarters
- 1 can (12 ounces) StarKist Solid White Tuna, drained and chunked
- 1 cup bottled vinaigrette dressing, divided

On large platter, arrange all ingredients except dressing. Cover with plastic wrap; chill. Just before serving, drizzle about ½ cup dressing over all ingredients; serve remaining dressing on side.
Makes 4 to 6 servings

Note: Look for niçoise olives in gourmet section of supermarket or in Italian deli.

Prep Time: 30 minutes

Albacore Salad Puttanesca with Garlic Vinaigrette

Fruity Brown Rice Salad with Raspberry Vinaigrette

This is an easy recipe to halve or double.

 2 cups cooked brown rice
 2 cups small broccoli flowerets, blanched and chilled
 2 cups fresh or canned pineapple chunks
 1 can (11 ounces) mandarin oranges, drained
 ½ cup slivered red bell pepper
 ½ cup chopped red onion
     Raspberry Vinaigrette Dressing (recipe follows)
 1 can (12 ounces) StarKist Solid White Tuna, drained and chunked
 6 to 8 Bibb lettuce cups

In large bowl, mix together rice, broccoli, pineapple, oranges, red pepper and onion. Add Raspberry Vinaigrette Dressing; toss. Refrigerate several hours before serving. Just before serving, add tuna; toss gently. Serve in lettuce cups.   *Makes 6 to 8 servings*

Raspberry Vinaigrette Dressing
 ¼ cup raspberry vinegar or apple cider vinegar
 2 tablespoons orange or lemon juice
 1 tablespoon brown sugar
 1 teaspoon seasoned salt
 ½ teaspoon crushed red pepper
 1 medium clove garlic, finely minced or pressed
 ½ cup olive oil

In small bowl, whisk together vinegar, orange juice, brown sugar, seasoned salt, crushed red pepper and garlic. Slowly add oil, whisking continuously until well blended.

Prep Time: 15 minutes

Oriental Albacore Salad

Try an Oriental-flavored bottled dressing to complement this salad.

 1 can (12 ounces) StarKist Solid White Tuna, drained and chunked
 1 cup bean sprouts
 ½ cup sliced celery
 ⅓ cup sliced green onions, including tops
 1 can (11 ounces) mandarin oranges, drained
 ½ to ¾ cup bottled Oriental salad dressing
 4 to 5 cups salad greens, romaine, iceberg, purple cabbage, savoy cabbage and bok choy
 ½ cup crisp chow mein noodles or chopped cashews

In large bowl, combine tuna, bean sprouts, celery, onions, oranges and dressing; toss gently. Add salad greens; toss again. Top each serving with chow mein noodles.
          Makes 6 servings

Prep Time: 15 minutes

Fruity Brown Rice Salad with Raspberry Vinaigrette

Tuna Pasta Primavera Salad

This salad is chock-full of garden vegetables. Don't hesitate to use any fresh vegetables you have.

     2 cups cooked and chilled small shell pasta
1 ½ cups halved cherry tomatoes
     ½ cup thinly sliced carrots
     ½ cup sliced celery
     ½ cup chopped seeded peeled cucumber
     ½ cup thinly sliced radishes
     ½ cup thawed frozen peas
     ¼ cup slivered red bell pepper
     2 tablespoons minced green onion, including tops
     1 can (12 ounces) StarKist Solid White or Chunk Light Tuna, drained and chunked
     1 cup salad dressing of choice
       Bibb or red leaf lettuce
       Fresh herbs, for garnish

In large bowl, combine all ingredients except lettuce and herbs. Chill several hours. If using oil and vinegar dressing, stir salad mixture occasionally to evenly marinate ingredients. Place lettuce leaves on each plate; spoon on salad. Garnish with fresh herbs, if desired.

Makes 6 servings

Prep Time: 25 minutes

Sunshine Albacore and Orange Salad

Here we combine oranges and grapes for a refreshing salad.

     2 oranges, peeled
     1 can (6 ounces) StarKist Solid White Tuna, drained and chunked
     1 cup chopped Belgian endive
     1 cup seedless green grape halves
     ¼ cup thinly sliced purple cabbage
       Sunshine Dressing (recipe follows)
       Lettuce leaves
     2 tablespoons slivered almonds, toasted

Slice oranges crosswise into rounds; cut rounds into quarters. In medium bowl, combine oranges with tuna, endive, grapes and cabbage. Toss with Sunshine Dressing; serve on lettuce leaves. Sprinkle each serving with almonds.

Makes 2 servings

Sunshine Dressing

     ½ cup plain yogurt
     2 tablespoons mayonnaise
     2 to 3 tablespoons orange juice
     1 to 1 ½ teaspoons orange peel
     ⅛ teaspoon paprika
       Salt to taste

In small bowl, combine all ingredients; blend well.

Prep Time: 10 minutes

Tuna Pasta Primavera Salad

Sensational
SAUCES

Ricotta Green Chiles and Albacore Sauce

You will love the rich taste of this sauce made with low fat dairy products.

1 egg, lightly beaten
1 cup (8 ounces) reduced fat ricotta cheese
1 cup low fat milk
¼ cup grated Parmesan cheese
2 tablespoons diced green chiles
1 jar (2 ounces) sliced or diced pimiento, drained
½ teaspoon garlic salt
½ teaspoon ground black pepper
1 can (6 ounces) StarKist Solid White Tuna, drained and chunked
2 cups hot cooked rice

In 1½-quart saucepan, combine all ingredients except tuna and rice; blend well. Heat thoroughly over low heat. Add tuna and rice; heat 1 more minute. *Makes 4 servings*

Note: For a spicier sauce, substitute fresh roasted and chopped Anaheim chiles for the green chiles.

Prep Time: 15 minutes

Creamy Tuna Broccoli and Swiss Sauce

Enjoy this special and easy-to-prepare dish at home.

1 can (10¾ ounces) cream of broccoli soup
½ cup half & half
½ cup shredded Swiss cheese
2 cups chopped cooked broccoli*
1 jar (2 ounces) sliced pimiento, drained
1 can (6 ounces) StarKist Solid White or Chunk Light Tuna, drained and chunked
Hot cooked pasta or rice

In medium saucepan, combine soup, half & half and cheese; cook over low heat, stirring to blend well. Stir in broccoli, pimiento and tuna; continue cooking until sauce is thoroughly heated. Serve over pasta.
Makes 2 servings

*Or substitute 1 package (10 ounces) frozen broccoli cuts, cooked and drained.

Prep Time: 15 minutes

Creamy Tuna Broccoli and Swiss Sauce

Tuna and Caponata Sauce

This savory tuna and vegetable sauce is great tossed with hot pasta.

    Olive oil
  2 cups diced, peeled eggplant
  ½ cup chopped onion
  ½ cup chopped celery
  ½ cup coarsely grated carrot
  ¼ pound mushrooms, chopped
  1 can (14½ ounces) Italian
      pasta-style tomatoes*
  1 can (6 ounces) StarKist Solid
      White or Chunk Light Tuna,
      drained and flaked
    Salt and pepper to taste
    Hot cooked pasta

In 3-quart saucepan, heat several tablespoons olive oil over medium-high heat; sauté ⅓ of eggplant until browned. Remove from pan; set aside. Repeat until all eggplant is browned and reserved. Heat several tablespoons oil; sauté onion, celery, carrot and mushrooms until onion is tender. Return eggplant to saucepan; stir in tomatoes and tuna. Simmer about 15 minutes; add salt and pepper. Serve over pasta.

Makes 4 servings

*Or substitute 1 can (14½ ounces) cut-up tomatoes, ½ teaspoon minced or pressed garlic and 1 teaspoon Italian herb seasoning.

Note: This recipe is easily doubled.

Prep Time: 25 minutes

Creamy Tuna Spinach and Ricotta Sauce

Almost a meal in itself, but plan to serve this delicious sauce over toasted French rolls or steamed rice.

  2 tablespoons butter or
      margarine
  1 package (10 ounces) frozen
      chopped spinach, thawed
      and squeezed dry
  2 tablespoons diced green chiles
  ½ to 1 teaspoon minced or
      pressed fresh garlic
  2 eggs, lightly beaten
 1¼ cups half & half
  1 cup (8 ounces) ricotta cheese
  ¼ cup grated Parmesan cheese
  ¾ teaspoon seasoned salt
  ½ teaspoon ground black pepper
  ½ teaspoon dried thyme, crushed
  1 can (12 ounces) StarKist Solid
      White or Chunk Light Tuna,
      drained and chunked
  3 French rolls, halved and
      toasted or steamed rice

In heavy 1½-quart saucepan, melt butter over medium heat; sauté spinach, chiles and garlic. In bowl, combine eggs, half & half, ricotta, Parmesan cheese and seasonings. Add ricotta mixture to sautéed spinach; blend well. Cook over medium heat until sauce begins to thicken. Add tuna; continue cooking until tuna is thoroughly heated. Serve over French rolls.

Makes 6 servings

Prep Time: 20 minutes

Tuna and Caponata Sauce

StarKist Garden Albacore Sauce

This vegetable and Swiss cheese sauce is perfect over pasta or rice.

2 cups chicken broth
1 package (1.8 ounces) white
    sauce mix
1 cup shredded Swiss cheese
1 can (6 ounces) StarKist Solid
    White Tuna, drained and
    chunked
1 cup sliced mushrooms
1 cup sliced bell pepper, green,
    red and/or yellow
1 cup sliced green beans,
    blanched
½ teaspoon seasoned pepper
    blend
    Hot cooked pasta or rice

In 1½-quart saucepan, combine
chicken broth and white sauce mix;
blend with wire whisk. Cook over
medium-high heat, whisking
constantly, until sauce thickens.
Reduce heat to low; add Swiss
cheese, stirring until melted. Add
tuna, mushrooms, bell peppers,
green beans and pepper blend; heat
thoroughly. Serve over pasta.

Makes 4 servings

Prep Time: 20 minutes

Creamy Cilantro and Chile Sauce

This sauce is excellent over rice, pasta or toasted cornbread.

1 cup coarsely chopped onion
½ cup fresh cilantro leaves
1 can (7 ounces) whole green
    chiles, seeded
1 to 2 cloves garlic
1 tablespoon dried oregano
½ teaspoon ground cumin
¼ teaspoon salt
1 cup shredded Monterey Jack
    cheese
1 can (6 ounces) StarKist Solid
    White Tuna, drained
½ cup sour cream
    Toasted cornbread, hot cooked
    rice or pasta
1 tablespoon toasted sesame
    seeds, for garnish

In food processor bowl with metal
blade, combine onion, cilantro,
chiles and garlic; process until
smooth and thick. Transfer mixture
to 1-quart saucepan. Add oregano,
cumin and salt; heat over low heat,
stirring frequently. Just before
serving, stir in cheese, tuna and sour
cream, stirring just until heated and
cheese is melted *(do not boil)*.
Serve immediately over cornbread.
Garnish with sesame seeds.

Makes 4 servings

Note: For a more piquant flavor,
substitute fresh roasted Anaheim
chiles for the canned mild green
chiles.

Prep Time: 15 minutes

StarKist Garden Albacore Sauce

Prime-Time

TEMPTATIONS

Homestyle Tuna Pot Pie

Making a pot pie has never been easier.

> 1 package (15 ounces) refrigerated pie crusts
> 1 can (12 ounces) StarKist Solid White or Chunk Light Tuna, drained and chunked
> 1 package (10 ounces) frozen peas and carrots, thawed and drained
> ½ cup chopped onion
> 1 can (10¾ ounces) cream of potato or cream of mushroom soup
> ⅓ cup milk
> ½ teaspoon poultry seasoning or dried thyme, crushed
> Salt and pepper to taste

Line 9-inch pie pan with one crust; set aside. Reserve second crust. In medium bowl, combine remaining ingredients; mix well. Pour tuna mixture into pie shell; top with second crust. Crimp edges to seal. Cut slits in top crust to vent. Bake in 375°F oven 45 to 50 minutes or until golden brown.

Makes 6 servings

Prep Time: 55 to 60 minutes

Sesame Almond Rice Dinner

This Indian dish's sweet raisins and hot chili complement the tuna and rice.

> 1 tablespoon sesame oil
> 1 teaspoon minced or pressed fresh garlic
> ⅓ cup slivered almonds
> 1 cup long grain white rice
> ¾ cup golden raisins
> 1 to 1½ teaspoons chili powder
> 2 cups chicken broth
> 1 can (6 ounces) StarKist Solid White Tuna, drained and chunked

In 1½-quart saucepan with tight-fitting lid, heat oil over medium-high heat. Add garlic, almonds and rice; sauté until golden. Stir in raisins, chili powder and chicken broth. Bring to a boil; cover. Reduce heat; simmer about 20 minutes or until rice has absorbed all liquid. Stir in tuna; serve. *Makes 4 servings*

Tip: Serve with steamed broccoli spears and chutney.

Prep Time: 30 minutes

Homestyle Tuna Pot Pie

Spicy Tuna and Linguine with Garlic and Pine Nuts

A great meal-in-a-dish that impresses company and uses only one pan.

    2 tablespoons olive oil
    4 cloves garlic, minced
    2 cups sliced mushrooms
    ½ cup chopped onion
    ½ teaspoon crushed red pepper
    2½ cups chopped plum tomatoes
    1 can (14½ ounces) chicken
        broth *plus* water to equal
        2 cups
    ½ teaspoon salt
    ¼ teaspoon coarsely ground
        black pepper
    1 package (9 ounces) uncooked
        fresh linguine
    1 can (12 ounces) StarKist Solid
        White Tuna, drained and
        chunked
    ⅓ cup chopped fresh cilantro
    ⅓ cup toasted pine nuts or
        almonds

In 12-inch skillet, heat olive oil over medium-high heat; sauté garlic, mushrooms, onion and red pepper until golden brown. Add tomatoes, chicken broth mixture, salt and black pepper; bring to a boil.

Separate uncooked linguine into strands; place in skillet and spoon sauce over. Reduce heat to simmer; cook, covered, 4 more minutes or until cooked through. Toss gently; add tuna and cilantro and toss again. Sprinkle with pine nuts.

Makes 4 to 6 servings

Prep Time: 12 minutes

Creamy Scalloped Potatoes and Tuna

What a fabulous way to cook potatoes and tuna!

    2 cups milk
    2 cups whipping cream
    2 cloves garlic, minced
    2½ pounds (about 6 medium)
        white or russet potatoes
    ¾ teaspoon salt
    ½ teaspoon white pepper
    1 tablespoon butter or margarine
    1 can (12 ounces) StarKist Solid
        White or Chunk Light Tuna,
        drained and chunked
    1½ cups shredded mozzarella
        cheese

In 3-quart saucepan over medium heat, heat milk, cream and garlic while preparing potatoes. Peel potatoes; slice about ⅛ to ¼ inch thick. Add potatoes, salt and white pepper to milk mixture; heat to simmering.

Grease 11×7-inch casserole with butter; spoon potato-milk mixture into dish. Bake 25 minutes; remove from oven. Add tuna, stirring gently; top with cheese. Bake 35 more minutes or until potatoes are cooked through and top is golden brown. Let stand, covered, about 15 minutes to thicken.   *Makes 6 to 8 servings*

Prep Time: 70 minutes

Spicy Tuna and Linguine with Garlic and Pine Nuts

Easy Three Cheese Tuna Soufflé

This is a great do-ahead dish for the entire family.

 4 cups large croutons*
2½ cups milk
 4 large eggs
 1 can (10¾ ounces) cream of celery soup
 3 cups shredded cheese, use a combination of Cheddar, Monterey Jack and Swiss
 1 can (12 ounces) StarKist Solid White or Chunk Light Tuna, drained and flaked
 1 tablespoon butter or margarine
 ½ cup chopped celery
 ½ cup finely chopped onion
 ¼ pound mushrooms, sliced

In bottom of lightly greased 13×9-inch baking dish, arrange croutons. In medium bowl, beat together milk, eggs and soup; stir in cheeses and tuna. In small skillet, melt butter over medium heat. Add celery, onion and mushrooms; sauté until onion is soft.

Spoon sautéed vegetables over croutons; pour egg-tuna mixture over top. Cover; refrigerate overnight. Remove from refrigerator 1 hour before baking; bake in 325°F oven 45 to 50 minutes or until hot and bubbly.   *Makes 8 servings*

*Use garlic and herb or ranch-flavored croutons.

Prep Time: 60 minutes

Tuna Manicotti in Creamy Dill Sauce

This traditional dish is seasoned with a light, lemony dill sauce.

 2 tablespoons butter or margarine
 ¼ cup chopped onion
 ¼ cup chopped celery
 ¾ cup chopped mushrooms
 ¼ cup grated Parmesan cheese
 3 tablespoons mayonnaise
1½ cups Quick White Sauce, divided (page 168)
 3 tablespoons lemon juice
 1 tablespoon dried dill weed
 Salt and pepper to taste
 1 can (12 ounces) StarKist Solid White or Chunk Light Tuna, drained and flaked
 6 manicotti shells, cooked al dente, rinsed and drained
 ½ cup shredded mozzarella cheese

In small saucepan, melt butter over medium heat; sauté onion, celery and mushrooms until onion is soft; cool. In large bowl, combine Parmesan cheese, mayonnaise, ¾ cup white sauce, lemon juice, dill, salt and pepper; blend well. Stir in tuna and sautéed vegetables; blend well.

Carefully stuff manicotti shells; arrange in baking dish. Pour remaining ¾ cup white sauce over stuffed manicotti; sprinkle mozzarella cheese over sauce. Bake in 350°F oven 30 minutes or until heated through.
          Makes 4 to 6 servings

Prep Time: 45 minutes

Easy Three Cheese Tuna Soufflé

Tuna and Broccoli Bake

Enjoy this quick and easy-to-prepare light tuna and broccoli dish.

- 1 package (16 ounces) frozen broccoli cuts, thawed and well drained
- 2 slices bread, cut in ½-inch cubes
- 1 can (12 ounces) StarKist Solid White or Chunk Light Tuna, drained and chunked
- 3 eggs
- 2 cups cottage cheese
- 1 cup shredded Cheddar cheese
- ¼ teaspoon ground black pepper

Place broccoli on bottom of 2-quart baking dish. Top with bread cubes and tuna. In medium bowl, combine eggs, cottage cheese, Cheddar cheese and pepper. Spread evenly over tuna mixture. Bake in 400°F oven 30 minutes or until golden brown and puffed.

Makes 4 servings

Prep Time: 35 minutes

Herbed Rice and Creamy Corn

The sweet creamed corn and bell peppers harmonize with the savory herbs and rice.

- 1 cup long grain white rice
- 1 can (14½ ounces) chicken broth
- ½ teaspoon garlic powder
- ¼ teaspoon dried thyme, crushed
- ¼ teaspoon dried oregano, crushed
- 1 can (17 ounces) cream-style corn
- ½ cup chopped green bell pepper
- ½ cup chopped red bell pepper
- 1 can (12 ounces) StarKist Solid White or Chunk Light Tuna, drained and chunked

In 1½-quart saucepan with tight-fitting lid, combine rice, chicken broth, garlic powder, thyme and oregano. Bring to a boil; cover. Reduce heat; simmer about 15 minutes. Stir in corn and bell peppers; cover. Continue cooking 5 to 8 more minutes or until rice is tender. Stir in tuna.

Makes 4 servings

Prep Time: 25 minutes

Tuna and Broccoli Bake

Tuna Puffs with Tomato-Orange Salsa

These tuna puffs bake quickly in muffin pans.

   2 large eggs
   ¾ cup coarsely crushed cheese
      cracker crumbs
   ¼ cup evaporated milk
   2 tablespoons melted butter
   1 tablespoon lemon juice
   1 teaspoon ground cumin
   ¼ to ½ teaspoon liquid red
      pepper
   1 can (12 ounces) StarKist Solid
      White or Chunk Light Tuna,
      drained and chunked
   ⅓ cup minced green onions,
      including tops
   Salt and pepper to taste
   Quick Tomato-Orange Salsa or
      Fresh Tomato-Orange Salsa
      (recipes follow)

In medium bowl, beat eggs with whisk; blend in crumbs, milk, butter, lemon juice, cumin and liquid red pepper; blend. Add tuna, onions, salt and pepper.

Spray 6 (2½-inch) muffin cups with cooking spray. Divide tuna mixture among cups. Bake in 375°F oven 20 to 25 minutes or until toothpick inserted near center comes out clean. Prepare desired salsa recipe. Serve Tuna Puffs with Quick Tomato-Orange Salsa or Fresh Tomato-Orange Salsa.

Makes 6 servings

Tip: Crush crackers in plastic bag with rolling pin.

Quick Tomato-Orange Salsa

   ½ cup thick and chunky salsa
   1 tablespoon frozen orange juice
      concentrate

In small bowl, stir salsa and orange juice concentrate together. Serve with Tuna Puffs. Refrigerate leftovers.

Fresh Tomato-Orange Salsa

   ½ cup plum tomatoes chopped in
      ¼-inch pieces
   ½ cup oranges or mandarin
      oranges chopped in
      ½-inch pieces
   2 tablespoons red onion
      chopped in ¼-inch pieces
   2 tablespoons chopped fresh
      cilantro
   1 to 2 tablespoons minced
      serrano chiles

In small bowl, gently mix all ingredients together. Serve with Tuna Puffs. Refrigerate leftovers.

Prep Time: 45 minutes

*Tuna Puffs with
Tomato-Orange Salsa*

Main-Dish
MAGIC

Albacore Stir-Fry

Enjoy the flavors of the Orient with this easy-to-prepare stir-fry.

   3 tablespoons vegetable oil
   1/2 cup sliced onion
   1 clove garlic, minced or pressed
   1 bag (16 ounces) frozen
      Oriental vegetables, thawed
      and drained*
   1 can (12 ounces) StarKist Solid
      White Tuna, drained and
      chunked
   3 tablespoons soy sauce
   1 tablespoon lemon juice
   1 tablespoon water
   1 teaspoon sugar
   2 cups hot cooked rice

In wok or large skillet, heat oil over medium-high heat; sauté onion and garlic until onion is soft. Add vegetables; cook about 3 to 4 minutes or until vegetables are crisp-tender. Add tuna, soy sauce, lemon juice, water and sugar. Cook 1 more minute; serve over rice.

Makes 4 servings

*May use 4 cups fresh vegetables, such as carrots, peapods, broccoli, bell peppers, mushrooms, celery and bean sprouts.

Prep Time: 20 minutes

Tuna Cakes

This is a quick and easy version of a classic seafood dish.

   1 1/4 cups breadcrumbs, divided
   1 can (12 ounces) StarKist Solid
      White or Chunk Light Tuna,
      drained and flaked
   3/4 cup shredded Cheddar cheese
   1/4 cup mayonnaise
   1 egg, lightly beaten
   1/3 cup bottled ranch dressing
   1/2 cup finely chopped onion
   1/2 cup finely chopped red or
      green bell pepper (optional)
   2 tablespoons vegetable oil,
      divided

In large bowl, combine 1/2 cup breadcrumbs with remaining ingredients except oil. Shape mixture into 8 patties, coating with remaining breadcrumbs. In nonstick skillet, heat 1 tablespoon oil over medium heat; cook 4 tuna cakes about 3 minutes per side. Repeat cooking process with remaining 1 tablespoon oil and 4 tuna cakes.

Makes 4 servings

Prep Time: 25 minutes

Albacore Stir-Fry

Biscuit-Topped Tuna Bake

This recipe is a real family pleaser. For a fun look, snip each biscuit into fourths before placing on top of the casserole.

2 tablespoons vegetable oil
½ cup chopped onion
½ cup chopped celery
1 can (12 ounces) StarKist Solid White or Chunk Light Tuna, drained and chunked
1 can (10¾ ounces) cream of potato soup
1 package (10 ounces) frozen peas and carrots, thawed
¾ cup milk
¼ teaspoon ground black pepper
¼ teaspoon garlic powder
1 can (7½ ounces) refrigerator flaky biscuits

In large skillet, heat oil over medium-high heat; sauté onion and celery until onion is soft. Add remaining ingredients except biscuits; heat thoroughly. Transfer mixture to 1½-quart casserole. Arrange biscuits around top edge of dish; bake in 400°F oven 10 to 15 minutes or until biscuits are golden brown.   *Makes 4 to 6 servings*

Prep Time: 25 minutes

Albacore and Asparagus Pasta

This simple recipe's rich taste will really surprise you.

½ pound uncooked angel hair pasta
1 tablespoon olive oil
1 can (10¾ ounces) cream of asparagus soup
¾ cup half & half
1 can (6 ounces) StarKist Solid White Tuna, drained and chunked
½ pound asparagus, trimmed, cut into 1-inch pieces and blanched *or* 1 package (10 ounces) frozen asparagus, thawed and drained
½ teaspoon lemon juice
Freshly ground black pepper to taste
¼ cup grated Parmesan cheese
1 tablespoon minced fresh parsley

Cook pasta according to package directions; drain, toss with olive oil. Keep warm. Meanwhile, in medium saucepan, combine soup and half & half; blend well. Stir in tuna, blanched asparagus, lemon juice and black pepper. Heat thoroughly; serve over pasta. Sprinkle with cheese and parsley.   *Makes 2 servings*

Prep Time: 15 minutes

Biscuit-Topped Tuna Bake

Baked Potatoes with Tuna and Broccoli in Cheese Sauce

With a microwave, this is an almost instant dinner-winner.

- 2 medium baking potatoes (6 to 8 ounces *each*)
- 1 package (10 ounces) frozen broccoli in cheese sauce
- 1 can (6 ounces) StarKist Solid White Tuna, drained and chunked
- 1 teaspoon chili powder
- ¼ cup minced green onions, including tops
- 2 slices cooked, crumbled bacon

Microwave Directions: Wash and pierce potatoes; microwave on HIGH 8 minutes. Wrap in foil; let stand to finish cooking while preparing broccoli. Microwave vented pouch of broccoli on HIGH 5 minutes. In medium microwaveable bowl, combine tuna and chili powder. Gently stir in broccoli. Cover; heat on HIGH 1½ more minutes or until heated through. Cut potatoes in half lengthwise. Top with broccoli-tuna mixture; sprinkle with onions and bacon.   *Makes 2 servings*

Note: Recipe can easily be doubled for 4 — just cook a little longer in the microwave.

Prep Time: 20 minutes

Curried Tuna Shells

Curry used to be considered an exotic seasoning. Today, curry is used in all types of dishes to create a unique flavor. Young children will give this rave reviews.

- 1 to 2 tablespoons vegetable oil
- ½ cup chopped onion
- ½ cup chopped red bell pepper
- 1 medium zucchini, chopped
- 2 cups Quick White Sauce (recipe follows)
- 1½ teaspoons curry powder
- 1 can (6 ounces) StarKist Solid White or Chunk Light Tuna, drained and flaked
- 6 ounces large pasta shells, cooked according to package directions

In large skillet, heat oil over medium-high heat; sauté onion and bell pepper until onion is soft. Add zucchini; sauté 2 more minutes. In large saucepan, combine white sauce with curry powder; blend well. Stir in tuna, cooked pasta and sautéed vegetables. Heat thoroughly; serve.
Makes 4 servings

Quick White Sauce: In small saucepan, mix together 1 package (1.8 ounces) white sauce mix, 1½ cups milk or half & half and ¾ cup chicken broth. Bring to a boil over medium heat, stirring constantly. Reduce heat; cook 1 more minute, stirring constantly.

Prep Time: 20 minutes

Baked Potatoes with Tuna and Broccoli in Cheese Sauce

StarKist Garden Spaghetti

This light, lemony sauce complements the tuna and vegetables.

- ½ pound whole wheat spaghetti
- 2 tablespoons butter or margarine
- 1 small onion, sliced
- ¼ pound mushrooms, sliced
- 2 cups chicken or vegetable broth
- 2 tablespoons flour
- 2 tablespoons lemon juice
- 2 tablespoons drained chopped pimiento
- 1 teaspoon grated lemon peel
- 1 teaspoon dried thyme, crushed
- ¼ teaspoon garlic powder
  Salt and pepper to taste
- 1 can (12 ounces) StarKist Solid White or Chunk Light Tuna, drained and chunked
- 2 cups cooked sliced carrots
- 2 cups cooked broccoli flowerets
  Tomato wedges, for garnish

Cook spaghetti according to package directions; drain, rinse and keep warm over medium-high heat. In large skillet, melt butter over medium heat; sauté onion 2 to 3 minutes. Add mushrooms; continue cooking 1 to 2 minutes.

In medium bowl, combine broth, flour, lemon juice, pimiento, lemon peel, thyme, garlic powder, salt and pepper. Add to onion-mushroom mixture; cook about 5 minutes over medium-high heat or until slightly thickened. Stir in tuna, carrots and broccoli; heat. Gently toss with spaghetti. Serve with tomato, if desired.　　*Makes 6 servings*

Prep Time: 25 minutes

StarKist Swiss Potato Pie

Easy enough for kids to make and definitely family pleasing. This may be assembled in the morning and cooked that evening.

- 1 cup milk
- 4 large eggs, beaten
- 4 cups frozen shredded hash brown potatoes, thawed
- 2 cups shredded Swiss cheese
- ½ to 1 cup chopped green onions, including tops
- ½ cup sour cream
- ½ cup chopped green bell pepper (optional)
- ½ teaspoon garlic powder
- 1 can (6 ounces) StarKist Solid White Tuna, drained and flaked

In large bowl, combine all ingredients. Pour into lightly greased deep 10-inch pie plate. Bake in 350°F oven 1 hour and 20 minutes or until golden and crusty. Let stand a few minutes before slicing into serving portions.

Makes 6 servings

Prep Time: 90 minutes

StarKist Garden Spaghetti

Broiled Tomatoes Stuffed with Tuna

Look for Crimini (Italian brown) mushrooms for a special flavor.

- 6 ripe beefsteak tomatoes
- 1 to 2 tablespoons butter or margarine
- 1 teaspoon minced or pressed fresh garlic
- ½ medium onion, cut in half
- 5 ounces Crimini (Italian brown) mushrooms, cleaned and trimmed*
- 1 can (12 ounces) StarKist Solid White or Chunk Light Tuna, drained and flaked
- 3 cups French or sourdough coarse fresh breadcrumbs
- 1 cup shredded mozzarella cheese
- Olive oil

Halve each tomato; use fork to break up cut surface of each half, pressing down to make shallow well. Arrange in baking dish.

In medium skillet, heat butter over low heat; sauté garlic. In food processor bowl with metal blade, finely chop onion; transfer to skillet and sauté until onion is soft. Place mushrooms in food processor bowl; finely mince (*do not over process*).

Transfer mushrooms to skillet; sauté with onion and garlic. In large bowl, combine tuna, sautéed garlic, onion and mushrooms, breadcrumbs and cheese. Fill each tomato with generous ½ cup filling. Drizzle olive oil over filled tomato halves; bake in 450°F oven 10 to 12 minutes until heated through. Place under broiler just until tops are lightly browned and crisp.   *Makes 6 servings*

*Regular domestic white mushrooms may be used.

Tip: To make fresh breadcrumbs, process ½ pound French bread in food processor bowl fitted with metal blade. Freeze remaining breadcrumbs for a later use.

Prep Time: 25 minutes

Potato Tuna au Gratin

A quick and easy family favorite.

- 1 package (5 or 6 ounces) Cheddar cheese au gratin potatoes
- 1 can (12 ounces) StarKist Solid White or Chunk Light Tuna, drained and chunked
- ¼ cup chopped onion
- 1 package (16 ounces) frozen broccoli cuts, cooked and drained
- ¾ cup shredded Cheddar cheese
- ¼ cup breadcrumbs

Prepare potatoes according to package directions. While potatoes are standing, stir in tuna and onion. Arrange cooked broccoli in bottom of lightly greased 11×7-inch baking dish. Pour tuna-potato mixture over broccoli; top with cheese. Broil 3 to 4 minutes or until cheese is bubbly. Sprinkle breadcrumbs over top.

Makes 6 servings

Prep Time: 35 minutes

Broiled Tomatoes Stuffed with Tuna

Albacore Vegetable Pilaf

Sour cream and lemon bring a fresh and lively taste to this pilaf.

   1 cup long grain white rice
   1 can (14½ ounces) chicken broth
   ¼ cup water
   2 to 3 tablespoons lemon juice
   1 teaspoon dried dill weed
   ½ teaspoon salt
   ¼ teaspoon ground black pepper
   ¼ teaspoon garlic powder
   ½ cup chopped red bell pepper
   ½ cup chopped green bell pepper
   ½ cup chopped zucchini
   ½ cup corn
   1 cup sour cream
   1 can (12 ounces) StarKist Solid White Tuna, drained and chunked

In medium saucepan with tight-fitting lid, combine rice, chicken broth, water, lemon juice, dill, salt, black pepper and garlic powder. Bring to a boil; cover. Reduce heat; simmer 15 minutes. Stir in vegetables; cover and continue cooking 5 to 7 more minutes or until all liquid is absorbed. Stir in sour cream and tuna. Serve hot or cold. *Makes 6 servings*

Prep Time: 30 minutes

Tuna Cream Cheese Omelets

These omelets make cooking for 1 or 2 a snap.

   1 teaspoon butter or margarine
   4 to 6 large eggs
      Water
   2 ounces cream cheese with chives, cut into ½-inch cubes, divided
   2 tablespoons drained and chopped roasted red peppers, divided
   1 can (6 ounces) StarKist Solid White or Chunk Light Tuna, drained and chunked, divided
   1 tablespoon light sour cream, divided
      Salt and pepper to taste

In small nonstick skillet, melt butter over medium-high heat. Beat 2 or 3 large eggs with 1 teaspoon water per egg. Stir in half of cream cheese and half of peppers. Pour into hot skillet; cook, using back of spatula to push cooked portion of eggs toward center, letting liquid flow underneath.

When eggs are cooked on bottom and top is nearly dry, sprinkle half the tuna over half the omelet. Fold omelet in half; slide onto plate. Top with half of sour cream; sprinkle with salt and pepper. Repeat for second omelet. *Makes 2 omelets*

Prep Time: 8 minutes

Albacore Vegetable Pilaf

Tuna and Broccoli Fettucini

Enjoy this reduced fat version of creamy fettucini.

4 cups broccoli flowerets
½ pound fettucini noodles
1 cup (8 ounces) part skim ricotta cheese
½ cup low fat milk
⅓ cup grated Parmesan cheese
½ teaspoon garlic salt
½ teaspoon Italian herb seasoning
Salt and pepper to taste
1 can (12 ounces) StarKist Solid White or Chunk Light Tuna, drained and chunked

In large saucepan of boiling water, cook broccoli until crisp-tender. Remove with slotted spoon to serving bowl. In same saucepan, cook fettucini; drain, rinse and add to broccoli. In same saucepan, combine remaining ingredients except tuna; mix well. Heat thoroughly, stirring frequently, until sauce is smooth and thick. Add tuna. Pour over fettucini and broccoli; toss gently. *Makes 5 servings*

Prep Time: 25 minutes

Tuna Mac and Cheese

Here's the dish that every kid loves; it's ready in a flash.

1 package (7¼ ounces) macaroni and cheese dinner
1 can (12 ounces) StarKist Solid White or Chunk Light Tuna, drained and chunked
1 cup frozen peas
½ cup shredded Cheddar cheese
½ cup milk
1 teaspoon Italian herb seasoning
¼ teaspoon garlic powder (optional)
1 tablespoon grated Parmesan cheese

Prepare macaroni and cheese dinner according to package directions. Add remaining ingredients except Parmesan cheese. Pour into 1½-quart microwavable serving dish. Cover with vented plastic wrap; microwave on HIGH 2 minutes. Stir; continue heating on HIGH 2½ to 3½ more minutes or until cheese is melted and mixture is heated through. Sprinkle with Parmesan cheese. *Makes 5 to 6 servings*

Prep Time: 20 minutes

Tuna and Broccoli Fettucini

Contents

Penne with Creamy Tomato Sauce, page 214

WELCOME TO THE BIRTHPLACE OF FRESH IDEAS

Situated amidst the splendor of the hills of Tuscany, Italy, is Casa Buitoni, Contadina's renowned Culinary Arts Center. Here the expert chefs of Contadina, adhering to genuine traditions of Italian cuisine, create quick, easy and delicious recipes and proudly deliver them from our house to yours.

Contadina products uphold the highest standards of quality and taste — attributes that have earned Contadina a place of honor in American kitchens for generations. All of the Contadina recipes featured in this publication are examples of authentic Italian recipes that are both quick and simple — an approach to cooking preferred by today's busy cooks. Each is truly a rewarding experience, especially for those who share a love of Italian food.

When it comes to finding the freshest ideas in Italian cooking, come to Contadina.

The Freshest Ideas in Italian Cooking™

APPETIZERS & SNACKS

Authentic Italian dining starts with any one of these appetizers or pizzas featuring the traditional flavors of Italy—Calzone Italiano, Classic Pepperoni Pizza, Tortellini Kabobs and more. No matter what your choice, you won't be disappointed!

Three-Pepper Pizza

Makes 8 servings

1 cup (*half* of 14.5-ounce can) CONTADINA Chunky Pizza Sauce with Three Cheeses
1 (12-inch) pizza crust
1½ cups (6 ounces) shredded mozzarella cheese, *divided*
½ *each:* red, green and yellow bell peppers, sliced into thin rings
2 tablespoons shredded Parmesan cheese
1 tablespoon chopped fresh basil or 1 teaspoon dried basil leaves, crushed

Spread pizza sauce onto crust to within 1 inch of edge. Sprinkle with *1 cup* mozzarella cheese, bell peppers, *remaining* mozzarella cheese and Parmesan cheese. Bake according to pizza crust package directions or until crust is crisp and cheese is melted. Sprinkle with basil.

Muffin Pizza Italiano

Makes 2 servings

1 sandwich-size English muffin, split, toasted
2 tablespoons CONTADINA Pizza Squeeze
8 slices pepperoni
¼ cup sliced fresh mushrooms
¼ cup (1 ounce) shredded mozzarella cheese

Spread muffin halves with pizza squeeze. Top with pepperoni, mushrooms and cheese. Bake in preheated 400°F. oven for 8 to 10 minutes or until cheese is melted.

Three-Pepper Pizza

Pizzette with Basil

Makes about 30 pizzettes

⅔ cup (6-ounce can)
   CONTADINA Italian-Style
   Tomato Paste
2 tablespoons (1 ounce) softened
   cream cheese
2 tablespoons chopped fresh basil
   or 2 teaspoons dried basil
   leaves, crushed
1 loaf (1 pound) Italian bread,
   sliced ¼ inch thick, toasted
8 ounces mozzarella cheese,
   thinly sliced
   Whole basil leaves (optional)
   Freshly ground black pepper
   (optional)

In small bowl, combine tomato paste, cream cheese and chopped basil. Spread *2 teaspoons* tomato mixture onto each toasted bread slice; top with 1 slice (about ¼ ounce) mozzarella cheese. Broil 6 to 8 inches from heat for 1 to 2 minutes or until cheese begins to melt. Top with whole basil leaves and pepper, if desired.

Pizza-Stuffed Mushrooms

Makes 12 large or 24 medium appetizers

12 large or 24 medium fresh
   mushrooms
¼ cup chopped green bell pepper
¼ cup chopped pepperoni or
   cooked, crumbled Italian
   sausage
1 cup (*half* of 15-ounce can)
   CONTADINA Pizza Sauce
½ cup (2 ounces) shredded
   mozzarella cheese

Wash and dry mushrooms; remove stems. Chop ¼ cup stems. In small bowl, combine chopped stems, bell pepper, meat and pizza sauce. Spoon mixture into mushroom caps; top with cheese. Broil 6 to 8 inches from heat for 2 to 3 minutes or until cheese is melted and mushrooms are heated through.

Pizzette with Basil

Tortellini Kabobs

Makes 12 servings

**2 tablespoons olive or vegetable
oil**
1 large clove garlic, minced
**2 cups (15-ounce can)
CONTADINA Tomato Sauce**
2 tablespoons capers
**2 tablespoons chopped fresh basil
or 2 teaspoons dried basil
leaves, crushed**
1 teaspoon Italian herb seasoning
**¼ teaspoon crushed red pepper
flakes**
**6 cups of the following kabob
ingredients: cooked, drained
meat- or cheese-filled
tortellini, cocktail franks,
smoked sausage pieces,
cooked medium shrimp,
whole button mushrooms,
green bell pepper chunks,
cooked broccoli flowerets,
cauliflowerets and onion
pieces**

In medium skillet, heat oil. Add
garlic; sauté for 30 seconds. Stir in
tomato sauce, capers, basil, Italian
seasoning and red pepper flakes.
Bring to a boil. Reduce heat to low;
simmer, uncovered, for 5 to 10
minutes or until heated through,
stirring occasionally. Remove from
heat. In medium bowl, combine
kabob ingredients; cover with
tomato sauce mixture. Cover and
marinate in refrigerator for 15
minutes or longer, if desired.
Remove kabob ingredients from
marinade, reserving marinade. Place
kabob ingredients on skewers. Broil
5 inches from heat until heated
through, turning once during
cooking and brushing with reserved
marinade.

Mini Nacho Pizza

Makes 2 servings

**1 sandwich-size English muffin,
split, toasted**
½ cup refried beans, *divided*
**2 tablespoons CONTADINA
Pizza Squeeze, *divided***
**½ cup (2 ounces) shredded
cheddar cheese, *divided***
**2 tablespoons diced green chiles,
drained (optional)**

Spread each muffin half with ¼ *cup*
refried beans and *1 tablespoon* pizza
squeeze; sprinkle with ¼ *cup*
cheese. Bake in preheated 400°F.
oven for 10 minutes or until cheese
is melted. Sprinkle with chiles, if
desired.

Tortellini Kabobs

Sicilian Caponata

Makes 4½ cups

5 tablespoons olive or vegetable oil, *divided*
8 cups (1½ pounds) cubed unpeeled eggplant
2½ cups onion slices
1 cup chopped celery
1¾ cups (14.5-ounce can) CONTADINA Pasta Ready Chunky Tomatoes with Olive Oil, Garlic and Spices, undrained
⅓ cup chopped pitted ripe olives, drained
¼ cup balsamic or red wine vinegar
2 tablespoons capers
2 teaspoons granulated sugar
½ teaspoon salt
Dash of ground black pepper

In medium skillet, heat *3 tablespoons* oil. Add eggplant; sauté for 6 minutes. Remove eggplant from skillet. In same skillet, heat *remaining* oil. Add onion and celery; sauté for 5 minutes or until vegetables are tender. Stir in tomatoes and juice and eggplant; cover. Bring to a boil. Reduce heat to low; simmer for 15 minutes or until eggplant is tender. Stir in olives, vinegar, capers, sugar, salt and pepper; simmer, uncovered, for 5 minutes, stirring occasionally.

Barbecue Dipping Sauce

Makes about 2 cups

1¾ cups (15-ounce can) CONTADINA Pizza Sauce
¼ cup firmly packed brown sugar
2 tablespoons vinegar
1 tablespoon prepared mustard
½ teaspoon liquid smoke

In medium saucepan, combine pizza sauce, brown sugar, vinegar, mustard and liquid smoke. Bring to a boil. Reduce heat to low; simmer, uncovered, for 5 minutes, stirring occasionally. Serve with chicken nuggets, meatballs, shrimp or cocktail franks, if desired.

Sicilian Caponata

Classic Pepperoni Pizza

Makes 8 servings

1 cup (*half* of 14.5-ounce can)
  CONTADINA Chunky Pizza
  Sauce with Mushrooms
1 (12-inch) pizza crust
1½ cups (6 ounces) shredded
  mozzarella cheese, *divided*
1.5 ounces (about 25 slices) sliced
  pepperoni
1 tablespoon chopped fresh
  parsley

Spread pizza sauce onto crust to within 1 inch of edge. Sprinkle with *1 cup* cheese, pepperoni and *remaining* cheese. Bake according to pizza crust package directions or until crust is crisp and cheese is melted. Sprinkle with parsley.

Three-Way Salsa

Makes about 5 cups

3½ cups (*two* 14.5-ounce cans)
  CONTADINA Recipe Ready
  Diced Tomatoes, undrained
1 cup (8-ounce can)
  CONTADINA Tomato Sauce
1 large onion, finely chopped
  (about 1 cup)
½ cup (4-ounce can) diced green
  chiles, drained
⅓ cup chopped green bell pepper
1 large clove garlic, minced
2 tablespoons chopped fresh
  cilantro
½ teaspoon cumin
½ teaspoon salt
¼ teaspoon ground black pepper

In medium bowl, combine tomatoes and juice, tomato sauce, onion, chiles, bell pepper, garlic, cilantro, cumin, salt and black pepper; cover. Chill thoroughly. Serve with tortilla chips, cut-up fresh vegetables or bread sticks, if desired.

Note: For medium-hot salsa, add ½ to 1 teaspoon minced jalapeño peppers. For very hot salsa, add 2 to 3 teaspoons minced jalapeño peppers and 10 drops hot pepper sauce.

Classic Pepperoni Pizza

Calzone Italiano

Makes 4 servings

Pizza dough for one 14-inch pizza
1¾ cups (15-ounce can) CONTADINA Pizza Sauce, *divided*
3 ounces sliced pepperoni *or* ½ pound crumbled Italian sausage, cooked, drained
2 tablespoons chopped green bell pepper
1 cup (4 ounces) shredded mozzarella cheese
1 cup (8 ounces) ricotta cheese

Divide dough into 4 equal portions. Place on lightly floured, large, rimless cookie sheet. Press or roll out dough to 7-inch circles. Spread *2 tablespoons* pizza sauce onto half of each circle to within ½ inch of edge; top with ¼ each: pepperoni, bell pepper and mozzarella cheese. Spoon ¼ cup ricotta cheese onto remaining half of each circle; fold dough over. Press edges together tightly to seal. Cut slits into top of dough to allow steam to escape. Bake in preheated 350°F. oven for 20 to 25 minutes or until crusts are golden brown. Meanwhile, heat *remaining* pizza sauce; serve over calzones.

Note: If desired, 1 large calzone may be made instead of 4 individual calzones. To prepare, shape dough into 1 (13-inch) circle. Spread ½ *cup* pizza sauce onto half of dough; proceed as above. Bake for 25 minutes.

Chunky Three-Cheese and Chicken Pizza

Makes 8 servings

1 cup (*half* of 14.5-ounce can) CONTADINA Chunky Original Pizza Sauce
1 (12-inch) pizza crust
4 ounces cooked chicken, chopped (about 1 cup)
1 cup (4 ounces) cubed mozzarella cheese
½ cup (2 ounces) cubed cheddar cheese
¼ cup (1 ounce) shredded Parmesan cheese
2 tablespoons chopped fresh basil or 2 teaspoons dried basil leaves, crushed (optional)

Spread pizza sauce onto crust to within 1 inch of edge. Top with chicken, mozzarella cheese, cheddar cheese and Parmesan cheese. Bake according to pizza crust package directions or until crust is crisp and cheese is melted. Sprinkle with basil, if desired.

Calzone Italiano

SOUPS & SALADS

In search of a quick-to-fix meal that is light, yet satisfying? Nothing hits the spot better than a thick, robust minestrone, a beautifully arranged antipasto salad or a fresh-from-the-sea cioppino. Page through this first-rate collection of savory soups and satisfying main-dish salads for creative recipe ideas.

Minestrone

Makes 8 cups

3 slices bacon, diced
½ cup chopped onion
1 large clove garlic, minced
2½ cups (*two* 10½-ounce cans) beef broth
1½ cups water
1¾ cups (15½-ounce can) Great Northern white beans, undrained
⅔ cup (6-ounce can) CONTADINA Tomato Paste
1 teaspoon Italian herb seasoning
¼ teaspoon ground black pepper
2 medium zucchini, sliced (about 2 cups)
1 package (10 ounces) frozen mixed vegetables
½ cup elbow macaroni, uncooked
½ cup (2 ounces) grated Parmesan cheese (optional)

In large saucepan, sauté bacon until crisp. Add onion and garlic; sauté until onion is tender. Add broth, water, beans and liquid, tomato paste, Italian seasoning and pepper. Reduce heat to low; simmer, uncovered, for 10 minutes. Add zucchini, mixed vegetables and macaroni. Return to a boil over high heat, stirring to break up vegetables. Reduce heat to low; simmer for 8 to 10 minutes or until vegetables and macaroni are tender. Sprinkle with Parmesan cheese just before serving, if desired.

Minestrone

Sicilian-Style Pasta Salad

Makes 10 servings

1 pound dry rotini pasta, cooked, drained, chilled

3½ cups (*two* 14.5-ounce cans) CONTADINA Pasta Ready Chunky Tomatoes with Crushed Red Pepper or Pasta Ready Chunky Tomatoes with Three Cheeses, undrained

1 cup sliced yellow bell pepper

1 cup halved zucchini slices

8 ounces cooked bay shrimp

½ cup (2.25-ounce can) sliced pitted ripe olives, drained

2 tablespoons balsamic vinegar

In large bowl, combine pasta, tomatoes and juice, bell pepper, zucchini, shrimp, olives and vinegar; toss well. Cover. Chill before serving.

Easy Antipasto Salad

Makes 6 servings

1¾ cups (14.5-ounce can) CONTADINA Stewed Tomatoes, drained

½ cup thinly sliced cucumber

½ cup thinly sliced onion

1 cup (*two* 6-ounce jars) marinated artichoke hearts, drained, cut in half

1 ounce thinly sliced salami (optional)

½ cup sliced pitted ripe olives, drained

½ cup thinly sliced green bell pepper

½ cup Italian dressing

In 1-quart casserole dish, layer tomatoes, cucumber, onion, artichoke hearts, salami, olives and bell pepper. Pour dressing over salad; cover. Chill before serving.

Southern Italian Clam Chowder

Makes 8 cups

2 slices bacon, diced

1 cup chopped onion

½ cup chopped peeled carrots

½ cup chopped celery

3½ cups (*two* 14.5-ounce cans) CONTADINA Recipe Ready Diced Tomatoes, undrained

1 cup (8-ounce can) CONTADINA Tomato Sauce

1 cup (8-ounce bottle) clam juice

½ teaspoon chopped fresh rosemary or ¼ teaspoon dried rosemary leaves, crushed

⅛ teaspoon ground black pepper

1½ cups (*two* 6½-ounce cans) chopped clams, undrained

In large saucepan, sauté bacon until crisp. Add onion, carrots and celery; sauté for 2 to 3 minutes or until vegetables are tender. Stir in tomatoes and juice, tomato sauce, clam juice, rosemary and pepper. Bring to a boil. Reduce heat to low; simmer, uncovered, for 15 minutes. Stir in clams and juice. Simmer for 5 minutes or until heated through.

Sicilian-Style Pasta Salad

Cioppino

Makes about 14 cups

2 tablespoons olive or vegetable oil
1½ cups chopped onion
1 cup chopped celery
½ cup chopped green bell pepper
1 large clove garlic, minced
3½ cups (28-ounce can) CONTADINA Whole Peeled Tomatoes, undrained
⅔ cup (6-ounce can) CONTADINA Tomato Paste
1 teaspoon Italian herb seasoning
1 teaspoon salt
½ teaspoon ground black pepper
2 cups water
1 cup dry red wine or chicken broth
3 pounds white fish, shrimp, scallops, cooked crab, cooked lobster, clams and/or oysters (in any proportion)

In large saucepan, heat oil. Add onion, celery, bell pepper and garlic; sauté until vegetables are tender. Add tomatoes and juice, tomato paste, Italian seasoning, salt, black pepper, water and wine. Break up tomatoes with spoon. Bring to a boil. Reduce heat to low; simmer, uncovered, for 15 minutes. To prepare fish and seafood: Scrub clams and oysters under running water. Place in ½ inch boiling water in separate large saucepan; cover. Bring to a boil. Reduce heat to low; simmer just until shells open, about 3 minutes. Set aside. Cut crab, lobster, fish and scallops into bite-sized pieces. Shell and devein shrimp.

Add fish to tomato mixture; simmer for 5 minutes. Add scallops and shrimp; simmer for 5 minutes. Add crab, lobster and reserved clams; simmer until heated through.

Milan Chickpea Soup

Makes about 10 cups

⅔ cup (6-ounce can) CONTADINA Tomato Paste
4 cups water or chicken broth
3½ cups (*two* 15½-ounce cans) chickpeas or garbanzo beans, undrained
½ pound mild Italian sausage, casings removed, sliced ½ inch thick
1 cup sliced fresh mushrooms
1 cup chopped onion
1½ teaspoons salt
¼ teaspoon ground black pepper
¼ teaspoon marjoram
2 teaspoons grated Parmesan cheese

In large saucepan, combine tomato paste and water; stir until well blended. Add chickpeas and liquid, sausage, mushrooms, onion, salt, pepper and marjoram; stir. Cover. Bring to a boil. Reduce heat to low; simmer for 30 minutes, stirring occasionally. Sprinkle with Parmesan cheese just before serving.

Cioppino

Cool Italian Tomato Soup

Makes 6 cups

1¾ cups (14.5-ounce can)
   CONTADINA Pasta Ready
   Chunky Tomatoes with
   Crushed Red Pepper,
   undrained
2 cups tomato juice
½ cup half-and-half
2 tablespoons lemon juice
1 large cucumber, peeled, diced
   (about 2 cups)
1 medium green bell pepper,
   diced (about ½ cup)
Chopped fresh basil (optional)
Croutons (optional)

In blender container, place tomatoes and juice, tomato juice, half-and-half and lemon juice; blend until smooth. Pour into large bowl or soup tureen; stir in cucumber and bell pepper. Sprinkle with basil and croutons just before serving, if desired.

Seafood Salad

Makes 6 servings

4 tablespoons olive or vegetable
   oil, *divided*
½ cup diced onion
2 cloves garlic, minced
8 ounces medium shrimp, peeled,
   deveined
8 ounces medium scallops
¼ teaspoon salt
¼ teaspoon ground black pepper
1 cup Italian bread cubes
1¾ cups (14.5-ounce can)
   CONTADINA Recipe Ready
   Diced Tomatoes, drained
2 cups torn salad greens
1 cup yellow bell pepper, cut into
   strips
2 tablespoons chopped fresh
   Italian parsley
1 tablespoon white wine vinegar

In medium skillet, heat *1 tablespoon* oil. Add onion and garlic; sauté for 1 minute. Add shrimp, scallops, salt and black pepper; sauté for 3 minutes. Remove from heat. In small skillet, heat *1 tablespoon* oil. Add bread cubes; sauté until golden brown. In large bowl, place seafood mixture, tomatoes, greens, bell pepper, parsley, *remaining* oil and vinegar; toss lightly. Top with bread cubes.

Cool Italian Tomato Soup

Spicy Shrimp Cocktail

Makes 6 servings

2 tablespoons olive or vegetable oil

¼ cup finely chopped onion

1 tablespoon chopped green bell pepper

1 clove garlic, minced

1 cup (8-ounce can) CONTADINA Tomato Sauce

1 tablespoon chopped pitted green olives, drained

¼ teaspoon crushed red pepper flakes

1 pound cooked shrimp, chilled

In small skillet, heat oil. Add onion, bell pepper and garlic; sauté until vegetables are tender. Stir in tomato sauce, olives and red pepper flakes. Bring to a boil. Reduce heat to low; simmer, uncovered, for 5 minutes. Cover. Chill thoroughly. Just before serving, combine sauce with shrimp in small bowl. Serve over mixed greens, if desired.

Tomato-Lentil Soup

Makes 9 cups

2 tablespoons olive or vegetable oil

2 cups chopped onion

1 cup sliced celery

1 carrot, peeled, sliced

6 cups water

1 cup dry lentils

⅔ cup (6-ounce can) CONTADINA Tomato Paste

½ cup dry red wine or chicken broth

¼ cup chopped fresh parsley or 1 tablespoon dried parsley flakes

3 small (½ ounce total) chicken bouillon cubes

1 teaspoon salt

½ teaspoon Worcestershire sauce

¼ teaspoon ground black pepper Shredded or grated Parmesan cheese (optional)

In large saucepan, heat oil over medium-high heat. Add onion, celery and carrot; sauté until vegetables are tender. Stir in water, lentils, tomato paste, wine, parsley, bouillon cubes, salt, Worcestershire sauce and pepper. Bring to a boil. Reduce heat to low; simmer, uncovered, for 45 to 50 minutes or until lentils are tender. Sprinkle with Parmesan cheese, if desired.

Spicy Shrimp Cocktail

Chickpea and Shrimp Soup

Makes 12 cups

1 tablespoon olive or vegetable oil
1 cup diced onion
2 cloves garlic, minced
2 quarts (*four* 10½-ounce cans) beef broth
1¾ cups (14.5-ounce can) CONTADINA Pasta Ready Chunky Tomatoes with Olive Oil, Garlic and Spices, undrained
1¾ cups (15½-ounce can) chickpeas or garbanzo beans, drained
⅔ cup (6-ounce can) CONTADINA Italian-Style Tomato Paste
8 ounces medium shrimp, cooked
½ teaspoon salt
¼ teaspoon ground black pepper
2 tablespoons chopped fresh Italian parsley or 2 teaspoons dried parsley flakes

In large saucepan, heat oil over medium-high heat. Add onion and garlic; sauté for 1 minute. Stir in broth, tomatoes and juice, chickpeas and tomato paste. Bring to a boil. Reduce heat to low; simmer, uncovered, for 10 minutes. Add shrimp, salt and pepper; simmer for 3 minutes or until heated through. Sprinkle with parsley just before serving.

Artichoke and Olive Salad

Makes 10 servings

1 pound dry rotini pasta, cooked, drained, chilled
3½ cups (*two* 14.5-ounce cans) CONTADINA Pasta Ready Chunky Tomatoes Primavera, undrained
½ cup (6-ounce jar) artichoke hearts, packed in water, drained, sliced
½ cup Italian dressing
½ cup (2.25-ounce can) sliced pitted ripe olives, drained
¼ cup chopped fresh parsley or 2 teaspoons dried parsley flakes, crushed
¼ cup sliced green onions
½ cup sliced almonds, toasted

In large bowl, combine pasta, tomatoes and juice, artichoke hearts, dressing, olives, parsley and green onions; toss well. Cover. Chill before serving. Sprinkle with almonds just before serving.

Chickpea and Shrimp Soup

PASTA SAUCES

Make any night pasta night! Top off your favorite hot cooked pasta with this enticing collection of select sauces. From garden fresh Portofino Primavera to savory Bolognese Sauce, you're sure to find that perfect sauce to suit your every need.

Giardiniera Sauce

Makes 8 servings

1 tablespoon olive or vegetable oil
2 cups sliced fresh mushrooms
1 cup chopped onion
½ cup sliced green bell pepper
2 cloves garlic, minced
1¾ cups (14.5-ounce can) CONTADINA Stewed Tomatoes, undrained
½ cup chicken broth
⅓ cup (*half* 6-ounce can) CONTADINA Tomato Paste
2 teaspoons Italian herb seasoning
½ teaspoon salt (optional)
1 pound dry pasta, cooked, drained, kept warm

In large skillet, heat oil. Add mushrooms, onion, bell pepper and garlic; sauté for 3 to 4 minutes or until vegetables are tender. Stir in tomatoes and juice, broth, tomato paste, Italian seasoning and salt. Bring to a boil. Reduce heat to low; simmer, uncovered, for 10 minutes, stirring occasionally. Serve over pasta.

Giardiniera Sauce

Roma Artichoke and Tomato Ragu

Makes 4 servings

1¾ cups (14.5-ounce can)
    CONTADINA Recipe Ready
    Diced Tomatoes, drained
½ cup (6-ounce jar) marinated
    artichoke hearts, sliced,
    undrained
¼ cup sliced pitted ripe olives,
    drained
2 tablespoons chopped fresh
    parsley or 2 teaspoons dried
    parsley flakes
2 tablespoons chopped fresh basil
    or 2 teaspoons dried basil
    leaves, crushed
1 clove garlic, minced
¼ teaspoon salt
⅛ teaspoon ground black pepper
8 ounces dry pasta, cooked,
    drained, kept warm
1 tablespoon chopped parsley
    (optional)

In medium bowl, combine tomatoes, artichoke hearts and juice, olives, parsley, basil, garlic, salt and pepper. Cover; chill for several hours to blend flavors. Heat before serving. Serve over pasta. Sprinkle with parsley, if desired.

Bolognese Sauce

Makes 8 servings

1 tablespoon olive or vegetable
    oil
1 cup chopped onion
½ cup diced celery
3 cloves garlic, minced
8 ounces lean ground beef
1¾ cups (15-ounce can)
    CONTADINA Tomato Puree
⅔ cup (6-ounce can)
    CONTADINA Italian-Style
    Tomato Paste
½ cup beef broth
⅓ cup dry red wine or water
2 teaspoons chopped fresh
    marjoram or 1 teaspoon
    dried marjoram leaves,
    crushed
1 teaspoon salt (optional)
1 pound dry pasta, cooked,
    drained, kept warm

In large skillet, heat oil. Add onion, celery and garlic; sauté for 3 to 4 minutes or until vegetables are tender. Add ground beef; cook for 5 to 7 minutes or until evenly browned, stirring occasionally. Add tomato puree, tomato paste, broth, wine, marjoram and salt. Bring to a boil. Reduce heat to low; simmer, uncovered, for 10 to 15 minutes or until heated through, stirring occasionally. Serve over pasta.

Roma Artichoke and Tomato Ragu

Portofino Primavera

Makes 8 servings

2 tablespoons olive or vegetable
   oil
1 small onion, chopped (about
   1 cup)
1 large clove garlic, minced
1¾ cups (14.5-ounce can)
   CONTADINA Recipe Ready
   Diced Tomatoes, undrained
⅔ cup (6-ounce can)
   CONTADINA Tomato Paste
1 cup chicken broth or water
1 cup quartered sliced zucchini
½ cup sliced pitted ripe olives,
   drained
2 tablespoons capers
½ teaspoon salt
1 pound dry pasta, cooked,
   drained, kept warm

In medium saucepan, heat oil. Add
onion and garlic; sauté for 1 minute.
Add tomatoes and juice, tomato
paste, broth, zucchini, olives, capers
and salt. Bring to a boil. Reduce heat
to low; simmer, uncovered, for 15 to
20 minutes or until heated through,
stirring occasionally. Serve over
pasta.

Olive Lovers' Pasta Sauce

Makes 6 servings

1 tablespoon olive or vegetable
   oil
2 cloves garlic, minced
1¾ cups (15-ounce can)
   CONTADINA Tomato Puree
1¾ cups (14.5-ounce can)
   CONTADINA Recipe Ready
   Diced Tomatoes, undrained
½ cup beef broth
1 cup pitted ripe olives, drained,
   quartered
1 cup pitted green olives,
   drained, quartered
¾ cup sliced green onions
¼ cup pine nuts, coarsely
   chopped
1 tablespoon dried basil leaves,
   crushed
½ teaspoon granulated sugar
¼ teaspoon ground black pepper
¾ pound dry pasta, cooked,
   drained, kept warm

In medium skillet, heat oil. Add
garlic; sauté for 30 seconds. Stir in
tomato puree, tomatoes and juice,
broth, olives, green onions, pine
nuts, basil, sugar and pepper. Bring
to a boil. Reduce heat to low;
simmer, uncovered, for 10 to 12
minutes or until heated through,
stirring occasionally. Serve over
pasta.

Portofino Primavera

MAIN DISHES

Mention Italian entrées and thoughts turn to thick, rich lasagne casseroles and dinner plates piled high with steaming pasta covered with delicious sauces. In addition to these recipe classics, this chapter is full of countless other main-dish favorites, such as Italian Garden Fusilli and Hearty Manicotti.

Hearty Manicotti

Makes 4 to 5 servings

- 1 package (10 ounces) frozen chopped spinach, thawed, squeezed dry
- 2 cups (15-ounce container) ricotta cheese
- 1 egg, lightly beaten
- ½ cup (2 ounces) grated Parmesan cheese
- ⅛ teaspoon ground black pepper
- 8 to 10 dry manicotti shells, cooked, drained
- 1⅓ cups (*two* 6-ounce cans) CONTADINA Italian-Style Tomato Paste
- 1⅓ cups water
- ½ cup (2 ounces) shredded mozzarella cheese

In medium bowl, combine spinach, ricotta cheese, egg, Parmesan cheese and pepper; mix well. Spoon into manicotti shells. Place in ungreased 12×7½-inch baking dish. In small bowl, combine tomato paste and water; pour over manicotti. Sprinkle with mozzarella cheese. Bake in preheated 350°F. oven for 30 to 40 minutes or until heated through.

Hearty Manicotti

Penne with Creamy Tomato Sauce

Makes 4 servings

1 tablespoon olive or vegetable oil
½ cup diced onion
2 tablespoons dry vermouth, white wine or chicken broth
1¾ cups (14.5-ounce can) CONTADINA Pasta Ready Chunky Tomatoes Primavera, undrained
½ cup heavy whipping cream
8 ounces dry penne or rigatoni, cooked, drained, kept warm
1 cup pitted ripe olives, drained, sliced
½ cup (2 ounces) grated Parmesan cheese
¼ cup sliced green onions

In large skillet, heat oil. Add diced onion; sauté for 2 to 3 minutes or until onion is tender. Add vermouth; cook for 1 minute. Stir in tomatoes and juice, cream, pasta, olives and Parmesan cheese; heat thoroughly, stirring occasionally. Sprinkle with green onions.

Eggplant Italiano Open-Faced Sandwiches

Makes 8 servings

1 medium eggplant (about 1½ pounds), peeled, cut into 8 slices
2 eggs, lightly beaten
1 cup CONTADINA Seasoned Bread Crumbs
½ cup olive or vegetable oil, *divided*
4 sandwich-size English muffins, split, toasted
1¾ cups (14.5-ounce can) CONTADINA Pasta Ready Chunky Tomatoes with Olives, drained
½ cup (2 ounces) shredded mozzarella cheese

In shallow dish, dip eggplant slices into eggs; coat with bread crumbs. In large skillet, heat *2 tablespoons* oil over medium heat. Add eggplant slices, a few at a time, to skillet. Cook for 2 to 3 minutes on each side or until golden brown. Remove from oil with slotted spoon. Drain on paper towels. Repeat with *remaining* oil and eggplant. Place muffin halves on large, ungreased baking sheet; top with eggplant, tomatoes and cheese. Bake in preheated 350°F. oven for 5 to 7 minutes or until cheese is melted.

Penne with Creamy Tomato Sauce

Lasagne Roll-Ups

Makes 8 servings

1 pound mild Italian sausage, casings removed
½ cup chopped onion
1 clove garlic, minced
1⅓ cups (12-ounce can) CONTADINA Tomato Paste
1⅔ cups water
1 teaspoon dried oregano leaves, crushed
½ teaspoon dried basil leaves, crushed
1 egg
1 package (10 ounces) frozen chopped spinach, thawed, squeezed dry
2 cups (15-ounce container) ricotta cheese
1½ cups (6 ounces) shredded mozzarella cheese, *divided*
1 cup (4 ounces) grated Parmesan cheese
½ teaspoon salt
¼ teaspoon ground black pepper
8 dry lasagne noodles, cooked, drained, kept warm

In large skillet, crumble sausage. Add onion and garlic; cook until sausage is no longer pink. Drain. Stir in tomato paste, water, oregano and basil; cover. Bring to a boil. Reduce heat to low; simmer, uncovered, for 20 minutes. In medium bowl, beat egg lightly. Add spinach, ricotta cheese, *1 cup* mozzarella cheese, Parmesan cheese, salt and pepper. Spread about *½ cup* cheese mixture onto each noodle; roll up. Place,

seam side down, in 12×7½-inch baking dish. Pour sauce over rolls; top with *remaining* mozzarella cheese. Bake in preheated 350°F. oven for 30 to 40 minutes or until heated through.

Vegetables Italiano

Makes 4 servings

2 tablespoons olive or vegetable oil
1 cup sliced peeled carrots
¾ cup halved onion slices
2 cloves garlic, minced
1¾ cups (14.5-ounce can) CONTADINA Stewed Tomatoes, undrained
3 cups sliced zucchini
1 cup fresh mushrooms, halved
¼ teaspoon salt, or to taste
⅛ teaspoon ground black pepper
8 ounces dry spaghetti, cooked, drained, kept warm

In large skillet, heat oil. Add carrots, onion and garlic; sauté for 3 minutes. Stir in tomatoes and juice, zucchini, mushrooms, salt and pepper. Bring to a boil. Reduce heat to low; simmer, uncovered, for 5 to 6 minutes or until vegetables are crisp-tender. Serve over spaghetti.

Lasagne Roll-Up

Contadina Classic Lasagne

Makes 10 servings

- 1 tablespoon olive or vegetable oil
- 1 cup chopped onion
- ½ cup chopped green bell pepper
- 2 cloves garlic, minced
- 1½ pounds lean ground beef
- 3½ cups (*two* 14.5-ounce cans) CONTADINA Recipe Ready Diced Tomatoes, undrained
- 1 cup (8-ounce can) CONTADINA Tomato Sauce
- ⅔ cup (6-ounce can) CONTADINA Tomato Paste
- ½ cup dry red wine or beef broth
- 1½ teaspoons salt
- 1 teaspoon dried oregano leaves, crushed
- 1 teaspoon dried basil leaves, crushed
- ½ teaspoon ground black pepper
- 1 egg
- 1 cup (8 ounces) ricotta cheese
- 2 cups (8 ounces) shredded mozzarella cheese, *divided*
- 1 pound dry lasagne noodles, cooked, drained, kept warm

In large skillet, heat oil. Add onion, bell pepper and garlic; sauté for 3 minutes or until vegetables are tender. Add ground beef; cook for 5 to 6 minutes or until evenly browned. Add tomatoes and juice, tomato sauce, tomato paste, wine, salt, oregano, basil and black pepper; bring to a boil. Reduce heat to low; simmer, uncovered, for 20 minutes, stirring occasionally. In medium bowl, beat egg slightly. Stir in ricotta cheese and *1 cup* mozzarella cheese. In ungreased 13×9-inch baking dish, layer noodles, *half* of meat sauce, noodles, all of ricotta cheese mixture, noodles and *remaining* meat sauce. Sprinkle with *remaining* mozzarella cheese. Bake in preheated 350°F. oven for 25 to 30 minutes or until heated through. Let stand for 15 minutes before cutting to serve.

Contadina Classic Lasagne

Italian Garden Fusilli

Makes 6 to 8 servings

1¾ cups (14.5-ounce can) CONTADINA Recipe Ready Diced Tomatoes, undrained
1 cup (4 ounces) cut fresh green beans
¼ teaspoon dried rosemary leaves, crushed
½ teaspoon garlic salt
1 small zucchini, thinly sliced (about 1 cup)
1 small yellow squash, thinly sliced (about 1 cup)
1 cup (12-ounce jar) marinated artichoke hearts, undrained
1 cup frozen peas
½ teaspoon salt, or to taste
¼ teaspoon ground black pepper, or to taste
8 ounces dry fusilli, cooked, drained, kept warm
¼ cup (1 ounce) shredded Parmesan cheese

In large skillet, combine tomatoes and juice, green beans, rosemary and garlic salt. Bring to a boil. Reduce heat to low; cover. Simmer for 3 minutes. Add zucchini and yellow squash; cover. Simmer for 3 minutes or until vegetables are tender. Stir in artichoke hearts and juice, peas, salt and pepper; heat through. Add pasta; toss to coat well. Sprinkle with Parmesan cheese just before serving.

Pasta Primavera with Italian Sausage

Makes 4 servings

8 ounces mild Italian sausage, casings removed, sliced
1 small onion, diced (about ½ cup)
1 large clove garlic, minced
1 medium zucchini, sliced (about 1 cup)
1¾ cups (14.5-ounce can) CONTADINA Pasta Ready Chunky Tomatoes Primavera, undrained
½ cup sliced pitted ripe olives, drained
¼ cup dry red wine or beef broth
8 ounces dry pasta, cooked, drained, kept warm
Chopped fresh basil (optional)
Grated Parmesan cheese (optional)

In large skillet, cook sausage until no longer pink. Remove sausage from skillet, reserving drippings in skillet. Add onion and garlic to skillet; sauté for 1 minute. Add zucchini; sauté for 2 minutes. Reduce heat to medium. Add tomatoes and juice, olives, wine and sausage; simmer, uncovered, for 5 to 7 minutes or until heated through. Serve over pasta. Sprinkle with basil and Parmesan cheese, if desired.

Italian Garden Fusilli

FISH & POULTRY

Discover how to accent the delicate flavors of fresh fish and tender poultry with this captivating collection of great-tasting Italian-style recipes. Choose from Chicken Marengo, full of chunky fresh vegetables, spicy Clams Diablo or a variety of other mouthwatering delicacies.

Poached Seafood Italiano

Makes 4 servings

1 tablespoon olive or vegetable oil
1 large clove garlic, minced
¼ cup dry white wine or chicken broth
4 salmon steaks or fillets (6 ounces *each*)
1¾ cups (14.5-ounce can) CONTADINA Pasta Ready Chunky Tomatoes with Olives or Pasta Ready Chunky Tomatoes with Three Cheeses or Pasta Ready Chunky Tomatoes Primavera, undrained
2 tablespoons chopped fresh basil (optional)

In large skillet, heat oil. Add garlic; sauté for 30 seconds. Add wine. Bring to a boil. Add salmon; cover. Reduce heat to medium; simmer for 6 minutes. Add tomatoes and juice; simmer for 2 minutes or until salmon flakes easily when tested with fork. Sprinkle with basil just before serving, if desired.

Poached Seafood Italiano

Chicken Marengo

Makes 6 servings

2 tablespoons olive or vegetable
   oil
2½ to 3 pounds skinned frying
   chicken pieces or 1½ pounds
   (about 6) boneless, skinless
   chicken breast halves
½ cup chopped onion
½ cup chopped green bell pepper
½ cup sliced fresh mushrooms
1 clove garlic, minced
1¾ cups (14.5-ounce can)
   CONTADINA Recipe Ready
   Diced Tomatoes, undrained
⅔ cup (6-ounce can)
   CONTADINA Tomato Paste
½ cup dry red wine
½ cup chicken broth
1 teaspoon Italian herb seasoning
½ teaspoon salt
⅛ teaspoon ground black pepper

In large skillet, heat oil. Add chicken;
cook until browned on all sides.
Remove chicken from skillet,
reserving any drippings in skillet.
Add onion, bell pepper, mushrooms
and garlic to skillet; sauté for 5
minutes. Add tomatoes and juice,
tomato paste, wine, broth, Italian
seasoning, salt and black pepper.
Return chicken to skillet. Bring to a
boil. Reduce heat to low; cover.
Cook for 30 to 40 minutes or until
chicken is no longer pink in center.
Serve over hot cooked rice or pasta,
if desired.

Note: Red wine can be omitted.
Increase chicken broth to 1 cup.

Seafarers' Supper

Makes 4 to 6 servings

1 tablespoon olive or vegetable
   oil
1 cup chopped green bell pepper
½ cup chopped onion
2 cloves garlic, minced
1¾ cups (14.5-ounce can)
   CONTADINA Italian-Style
   Stewed Tomatoes, undrained
1 cup chicken broth
⅔ cup (6-ounce can)
   CONTADINA Italian-Style
   Tomato Paste
¼ teaspoon salt
¼ teaspoon ground black pepper
1 pound orange roughy, cut into
   1-inch pieces
12 ounces dry linguine, cooked,
   drained, kept warm
   Chopped fresh Italian parsley
   (optional)

In large skillet, heat oil. Add bell
pepper, onion and garlic; sauté for 3
minutes or until vegetables are crisp-
tender. Stir in tomatoes and juice,
broth, tomato paste, salt and black
pepper. Bring to a boil. Reduce heat
to low; simmer, uncovered, for 5
minutes. Add orange roughy; simmer
for 5 minutes or until fish flakes
easily when tested with fork. Spoon
over pasta. Sprinkle with parsley, if
desired.

Chicken Marengo

Turkey Roulade

Makes 10 servings

1½ **pounds (10 slices) uncooked, boneless turkey breast**
2 **cups (15-ounce container) ricotta cheese**
1½ **cups (6 ounces) shredded mozzarella cheese,** *divided*
1 **package (10 ounces) frozen chopped spinach, thawed, squeezed dry**
½ **teaspoon garlic salt**
1 **tablespoon olive or vegetable oil**
½ **cup chopped onion**
2 **cloves garlic, minced**
1¾ **cups (14.5-ounce can) CONTADINA Recipe Ready Diced Tomatoes, undrained**
⅔ **cup (6-ounce can) CONTADINA Tomato Paste**
1 **cup chicken broth**
1 **teaspoon Italian herb seasoning**
1 **teaspoon salt**
¼ **teaspoon ground black pepper**

Pound turkey slices between 2 pieces of plastic wrap to ⅛-inch thickness. In medium bowl, combine ricotta cheese, *1 cup* mozzarella cheese, spinach and garlic salt. Spread ⅓ *cup* cheese mixture onto each turkey slice; roll up. Secure with toothpicks. Place rolls in greased 13×9-inch baking dish. In large skillet, heat oil. Add onion and garlic; sauté for 2 minutes. Add tomatoes and juice, tomato paste, broth, Italian seasoning, salt and pepper. Bring to a boil. Reduce heat to low; simmer, uncovered, for 10 minutes. Spoon sauce over rolls; cover. Bake in preheated 425°F. oven for 20 to 25 minutes or until turkey is done. Sprinkle with *remaining* mozzarella cheese. Bake for 5 minutes or until cheese is melted.

Clams Diablo

Makes 6 servings

2 **tablespoons olive or vegetable oil**
½ **cup chopped onion**
1 **clove garlic, minced**
1¾ **cups (14.5-ounce can) CONTADINA Recipe Ready Diced Tomatoes, undrained**
¼ **cup dry red wine or chicken broth**
½ **teaspoon dried thyme leaves, crushed**
¼ **teaspoon salt**
¼ **teaspoon crushed red pepper flakes**
1½ **pounds scrubbed fresh clams**
2 **tablespoons chopped fresh parsley or 2 teaspoons dried parsley flakes**

In medium skillet, heat oil. Add onion and garlic; sauté for 1 minute. Stir in tomatoes and juice, wine, thyme, salt and red pepper flakes. Bring to a boil. Reduce heat to low; simmer, uncovered, for 10 minutes, stirring occasionally. Add clams; cover. Simmer for 5 minutes or until clams have opened. Discard any clams that do not open. Sprinkle with parsley just before serving.

Turkey Roulade

Seafood Marinara with Linguine

Makes 6 servings

2 tablespoons olive or vegetable oil, *divided*

1 cup chopped onion

3 large cloves garlic, minced

1¾ cups (14.5-ounce can) CONTADINA Recipe Ready Diced Tomatoes, undrained

1¾ cups (14.5-ounce can) chicken broth

1⅓ cups (12-ounce can) CONTADINA Tomato Paste

½ cup dry red wine or water

1 tablespoon chopped fresh basil or 2 teaspoons dried basil leaves, crushed

2 teaspoons chopped fresh oregano or ½ teaspoon dried oregano leaves, crushed

1 teaspoon salt

8 ounces fresh or frozen medium shrimp, peeled, deveined

8 ounces fresh or frozen bay scallops

1 pound dry linguine, cooked, drained, kept warm

In large skillet, heat *1 tablespoon* oil. Add onion and garlic; sauté for 2 minutes. Add tomatoes and juice, broth, tomato paste, wine, basil, oregano and salt. Bring to a boil. Reduce heat to low; simmer, uncovered, for 10 minutes. In small skillet, heat *remaining* oil. Add shrimp and scallops; sauté for 3 to 4 minutes or until shrimp turn pink. Add to sauce; simmer for 2 to 3 minutes or until heated through. Serve over pasta.

Chicken Italiano

Makes 6 to 8 servings

1½ to 2 pounds (6 to 8) boneless, skinless chicken breast halves

¼ cup all-purpose flour

3 tablespoons olive or vegetable oil, *divided*

2 cups sliced onion

⅔ cup (6-ounce can) CONTADINA Tomato Paste

1¾ cups (14.5-ounce can) chicken broth

3 medium carrots, peeled, sliced (about 1½ cups)

2 teaspoons garlic salt

1 teaspoon Italian herb seasoning

⅛ teaspoon crushed red pepper flakes (optional)

2 medium zucchini, sliced (about 1½ cups)

In shallow bowl, coat chicken with flour. In large skillet, heat *2 tablespoons* oil over medium-high heat. Add chicken; cook for 2 to 3 minutes on each side or until golden brown. Remove chicken from skillet. Add *remaining* oil to skillet; heat. Add onion; sauté until tender. Stir in tomato paste, broth, carrots, garlic salt, Italian seasoning and red pepper flakes. Return chicken to skillet; spoon sauce over chicken. Bring to a boil. Reduce heat to low; cover. Simmer for 25 minutes or until chicken is no longer pink in center. Add zucchini; simmer for 5 minutes. Serve over hot cooked pasta, if desired.

Seafood Marinara with Linguine

Swordfish Messina Style

Makes 8 servings

- 2 tablespoons olive or vegetable oil
- ½ cup chopped fresh parsley
- 2 tablespoons chopped fresh basil or 2 teaspoons dried basil leaves, crushed
- 2 cloves garlic, minced
- 1 cup (8-ounce can) CONTADINA Tomato Sauce
- ¾ cup sliced fresh mushrooms
- 1 tablespoon capers
- 1 tablespoon lemon juice
- ⅛ teaspoon ground black pepper
- 3 pounds swordfish or halibut steaks

In small saucepan, heat oil. Add parsley, basil and garlic; sauté for 1 minute. Reduce heat to low. Add tomato sauce, mushrooms and capers. Bring to a boil. Reduce heat to low; simmer, uncovered, for 5 minutes. Stir in lemon juice and pepper. Place swordfish in single layer in greased 13×9-inch baking dish; cover with sauce. Bake in preheated 400°F. oven for 20 minutes or until fish flakes easily when tested with fork.

Chicken in Cilantro Sauce

Makes 6 servings

- 1 tablespoon olive or vegetable oil
- 1 *each:* small green, red and yellow bell peppers, sliced into ¼-inch-thick rings
- 1½ pounds (about 6) boneless, skinless chicken breast halves
- 2 cups (15-ounce can) CONTADINA Tomato Sauce
- ½ cup chopped fresh cilantro
- ½ cup coarsely chopped onion
- 1 clove garlic, minced
- ⅛ teaspoon salt

In medium skillet, heat oil. Add bell peppers; sauté until crisp-tender. Remove peppers from skillet, reserving any liquid in skillet. Add chicken to skillet; cook until browned on both sides. Remove skillet from heat; cover to keep chicken warm. In blender container, place tomato sauce, cilantro, onion, garlic and salt; blend until smooth. Pour over chicken in skillet. Return skillet to heat. Bring to a boil. Reduce heat to low; simmer, uncovered, for 15 to 20 minutes or until chicken is no longer pink in center. Remove chicken to serving platter; top with peppers. Serve with sauce.

Swordfish Messina Style

Skillet Chicken Cacciatore

Makes 6 servings

2 tablespoons olive or vegetable oil
1 cup sliced red onion
1 medium green bell pepper, cut into strips (about 1 cup)
2 cloves garlic, minced
1 pound (about 4) boneless, skinless chicken breast halves
1¾ cups (14.5-ounce can) CONTADINA Pasta Ready Chunky Tomatoes with Mushrooms, undrained
¼ cup dry white wine or chicken broth
½ teaspoon salt
¼ teaspoon ground black pepper
1 tablespoon chopped fresh basil or 1 teaspoon dried basil leaves, crushed

In large skillet, heat oil over medium-high heat. Add onion, bell pepper and garlic; sauté for 1 minute. Add chicken; cook until browned on both sides. Add tomatoes and juice, wine, salt and black pepper. Bring to a boil. Reduce heat to low; simmer, uncovered, for 15 to 20 minutes or until chicken is no longer pink in center. Serve over hot cooked rice or pasta, if desired. Sprinkle with basil.

Tomato and Salmon Quiche

Makes 6 servings

1 tablespoon olive or vegetable oil
1½ cups chopped fresh mushrooms
½ cup chopped shallots
1¾ cups (14.5-ounce can) CONTADINA Recipe Ready Diced Tomatoes, drained
½ teaspoon salt
¼ teaspoon ground white pepper
1¾ cups (*two* 7½-ounce cans) LIBBY'S Pacific Keta or Pink Salmon, drained
3 tablespoons thinly sliced green onion
2 tablespoons grated Parmesan cheese
3 eggs
¾ cup heavy whipping cream
1 *unbaked* 9-inch pie shell

In medium skillet, heat oil. Add mushrooms and shallots; sauté for 2 minutes. Stir in tomatoes, salt and pepper. Cook for 2 minutes or until most of liquid is evaporated. Remove from heat. Remove skin and bones from salmon, if desired; discard. Stir salmon, green onion and Parmesan cheese into mushroom mixture. In medium bowl, beat eggs lightly; stir in cream. Bake pie shell in preheated 400°F. oven for 5 minutes. Spoon salmon filling into hot pie shell; pour egg mixture over filling. Bake at 350°F. for 25 minutes or until center is set. Let stand for 5 minutes before cutting to serve.

Skillet Chicken Cacciatore

MEATS

With a simple, delicious Italian sauce, you can transform beef, sausage or any other meat into an authentic Italian main dish. Try fresh-tasting Italian Sausage Supper or Baked Steak Flamenco tonight.

Italian-Style Meat Loaf

Makes 8 servings

1 egg
1½ pounds lean ground beef or turkey
8 ounces hot or mild Italian sausage, casings removed
1 cup CONTADINA Seasoned Bread Crumbs
1 cup (8-ounce can) CONTADINA Tomato Sauce, *divided*
1 cup finely chopped onion
½ cup finely chopped green bell pepper

In large bowl, beat egg lightly. Add ground beef, sausage, bread crumbs, *¾ cup* tomato sauce, onion and bell pepper; mix well. Press into ungreased 9×5-inch loaf pan. Bake, uncovered, in preheated 350°F. oven for 60 minutes. Spoon *remaining* tomato sauce over meat loaf. Bake for an additional 15 minutes or until no longer pink in center; drain. Let stand for 10 minutes before serving.

Italian-Style Meat Loaf

Sirloin Steak Monte Carlo

Makes 4 to 6 servings

2 tablespoons olive or vegetable oil

1¾ pounds sirloin steak

½ cup sliced onion

1 large clove garlic, minced

¼ cup pine nuts

1¾ cups (14.5-ounce can) CONTADINA Italian-Style Tomatoes, undrained

2 tablespoons capers

½ teaspoon dried oregano leaves, crushed

½ teaspoon dried basil leaves, crushed

¼ teaspoon crushed red pepper flakes

In medium skillet, heat oil over medium-high heat. Add steak; cook for 4 to 5 minutes on each side for medium-rare. Remove steak to platter, reserving any drippings in skillet; keep warm. Add onion, garlic and pine nuts to skillet; sauté for 5 minutes or until onion is tender and nuts are lightly toasted. Add tomatoes and juice, capers, oregano, basil and red pepper flakes; simmer, uncovered, for 5 minutes. Serve over steak.

Sloppy Joes

Makes 4 servings

8 ounces lean ground beef or turkey

½ cup finely chopped onion

½ cup CONTADINA Pizza Sauce

2 sandwich-size English muffins, split, toasted

½ cup (2 ounces) shredded cheddar cheese

In medium skillet, brown ground beef with onion; drain. Stir in pizza sauce; simmer, uncovered, for 5 to 8 minutes or until heated through, stirring occasionally. Spoon mixture evenly onto muffin halves; sprinkle with cheese. Broil 6 to 8 inches from heat for 1 to 2 minutes or until cheese is melted.

Sirloin Steak Monte Carlo

Italian Sausage Supper

Makes 6 servings

1 pound mild Italian sausage,
   casings removed
1 cup chopped onion
3 medium zucchini, sliced
   (about 1½ cups)
⅔ cup (6-ounce can)
   CONTADINA Tomato Paste
1 cup water
1 teaspoon dried basil leaves,
   crushed
½ teaspoon salt
3 cups cooked rice
1 cup (4 ounces) shredded
   mozzarella cheese
¼ cup (1 ounce) grated Romano
   cheese

In large skillet, brown sausage with onion, stirring to break up sausage; drain, reserving 1 tablespoon drippings. Spoon sausage mixture into greased 2-quart casserole dish. Add zucchini to skillet; sauté for 5 minutes or until crisp-tender. In medium bowl, combine tomato paste, water, basil and salt. Stir in rice. Spoon over sausage mixture. Arrange zucchini slices on top; sprinkle with mozzarella and Romano cheeses. Cover. Bake in preheated 350°F. oven for 20 minutes.

Baked Steak Flamenco

Makes 6 servings

¼ cup all-purpose flour
½ teaspoon seasoned salt
⅛ teaspoon ground black pepper
1½ pounds trimmed round steak,
   cut into strips
½ cup thinly sliced onion
1 cup thin green bell pepper rings
1 cup sliced fresh mushrooms
1¾ cups (14.5-ounce can)
   CONTADINA Italian-Style
   Tomatoes, undrained
¼ cup horseradish sauce
1 tablespoon Worcestershire
   sauce

In large bowl or plastic food storage bag, combine flour, seasoned salt and black pepper. Add steak; toss to coat evenly. Place in greased 13×9-inch baking dish. Arrange onion, bell pepper and mushrooms on top of steak. Drain tomatoes, reserving juice. Slice tomatoes lengthwise; arrange on top of vegetables. In small bowl, combine reserved juice, horseradish sauce and Worcestershire sauce; pour evenly over all ingredients in baking dish. Bake, uncovered, in preheated 350°F. oven for 45 minutes to 1 hour or until steak is desired doneness.

Italian Sausage Supper

Sizzling
MEXICAN
RECIPES

◆ 🌵 ◆

Contents

Tex-Mex Chicken Fajitas, page 284

Salsas & Snacks

◆ ⚊ ◆

Deluxe Fajita Nachos

2½ cups shredded, cooked
　chicken
1 package (1.27 ounces)
　LAWRY'S® Spices &
　Seasonings for Fajitas
⅓ cup water
8 ounces tortilla chips
1¼ cups (5 ounces) shredded
　Cheddar cheese

1 cup (4 ounces) shredded
　Monterey Jack cheese
1 large tomato, chopped
1 can (2¼ ounces) sliced
　ripe olives, drained
¼ cup sliced green onions
　Salsa

In medium skillet, combine chicken, Spices & Seasonings for
Fajitas and water; blend well. Bring to a boil; reduce heat and
simmer 3 minutes. In large shallow ovenproof platter, arrange
chips. Top with chicken and cheeses. Place under broiler to melt
cheese. Top with tomato, olives, green onions and desired amount
of salsa. 　　　　　　　　　　　　　　*Makes 4 appetizer servings*

PRESENTATION: *Serve with guacamole and sour cream.*

SUBSTITUTION: *1¼ pounds cooked ground beef can be used in
place of shredded chicken.*

HINT: *For a spicier version, add sliced jalapeños.*

Deluxe Fajita Nachos

Spicy Empanadas

1 can (8¾ ounces)
   garbanzo beans,
   drained
1 teaspoon vegetable oil
¼ cup minced fresh onion
2 tablespoons minced
   green bell pepper
¼ teaspoon LAWRY'S®
   Garlic Powder with
   Parsley
2 tablespoons currants
2 tablespoons chopped
   pitted ripe olives

1 package (1.25 ounces)
   LAWRY'S® Taco Spices
   & Seasonings
1 teaspoon lemon juice
¼ cup (1 ounce) shredded
   Monterey Jack cheese
All-purpose flour
1 sheet frozen puff pastry,
   thawed
1 egg yolk, beaten

Preheat oven to 400°F. In food processor or blender, place garbanzo beans. Pulse 30 seconds to chop finely; set aside. In large skillet, heat oil. Add onion, bell pepper and Garlic Powder with Parsley; sauté 3 to 4 minutes or until vegetables are crisp-tender. Add beans, currants, olives, Taco Spices & Seasonings and lemon juice; cook until mixture thickens, stirring occasionally. Remove from heat; stir in cheese.

On lightly floured surface, roll out pastry sheet to approximately 18×10-inch rectangle; cut out six to eight 4-inch circles. Spoon equal amounts of filling onto half of each circle; fold pastry over to form half circle. Press edges together with fork to seal. Place empanadas on greased baking sheet; brush with egg yolk. Bake 18 to 20 minutes or until golden brown. Garnish as desired.

Makes 6 to 8 empanadas

PRESENTATION: *Great with salsa, dairy sour cream and peeled avocado slices.*

HINT: *Double recipe for more appetizers.*

Spicy Empanadas

Festive Chicken Dip

1½ pounds boneless skinless chicken breasts, finely chopped (about 3 cups)
¼ cup lime juice, divided
2 garlic cloves, minced
1 teaspoon salt
½ teaspoon ground black pepper
1 can (16 ounces) refried beans
1½ cups sour cream, divided
1 package (1¼ ounces) dry taco seasoning mix, divided
1 tablespoon picante sauce

1 avocado, chopped
1 tablespoon olive oil
1 cup (4 ounces) shredded sharp Cheddar cheese
1 small onion, finely chopped
2 tomatoes, finely chopped
1 can (2¼ ounces) sliced black olives, drained and chopped
1 bag (10 ounces) tortilla chips
Fresh cilantro for garnish

Place chicken in small bowl. Sprinkle with 3 tablespoons lime juice, garlic, salt and pepper; mix well. Set aside.

Combine beans, ½ cup sour cream, 2½ tablespoons taco seasoning and picante sauce in medium bowl. Spread bean mixture in bottom of shallow 2-quart casserole dish.

Combine avocado and remaining 1 tablespoon lime juice in small bowl; sprinkle over bean mixture. Combine remaining 1 cup sour cream and 2½ tablespoons taco seasoning in small bowl; set aside.

Heat oil in large skillet over high heat until hot; add chicken in single layer. Do not stir. Cook about 2 minutes or until chicken is brown on bottom. Turn chicken and cook until other side is brown and no liquid remains. Break chicken into separate pieces with fork. Layer chicken, sour cream mixture, cheese, onion and tomatoes over avocado mixture. Top with olives. Refrigerate until completely chilled. Serve with chips. Garnish with cilantro.

Makes 8 cups dip

Favorite recipe from **National Broiler Council**

Festive Chicken Dip

Southwestern Seafood Dip

1 (15-ounce) can pinto
   beans, rinsed and
   drained
1 tablespoon plus
   1 teaspoon taco
   seasoning mix
2 tablespoons fat-free sour
   cream
1 ripe avocado
1 tablespoon lime juice
1 tablespoon fat-free
   mayonnaise
¼ teaspoon Worcestershire
   sauce

⅛ teaspoon chili powder
⅛ teaspoon garlic powder
1 (8-ounce) package surimi
   seafood
½ cup (2 ounces) shredded
   reduced-fat sharp
   Cheddar cheese
½ small tomato, seeded and
   chopped
¼ cup whole kernel corn
3 tablespoons sliced black
   olives
2 tablespoons chopped
   green onion tops

Mash beans with a fork until almost smooth; stir in taco
seasoning mix and sour cream. Spread in an 8-inch circle on a
serving platter; set aside.

Coarsely chop avocado in a bowl; add lime juice, mayonnaise,
Worcestershire sauce, chili powder and garlic powder. Mash with
a fork until mixed well, but not quite smooth. Spread over bean
mixture.

Shred surimi seafood with fingers. Arrange mounds of seafood,
cheese, tomato, corn, olives and onions over avocado layer. Cover
and refrigerate until ready to serve, up to 2 hours. Let stand at
room temperature about 15 minutes before serving. Serve with
tortilla chips. *Makes about 8 appetizer servings*

Favorite recipe from **Surimi Seafood Education Center**

Southwestern Seafood Dip

Spicy Taco Dip

1 pound BOB EVANS
   FARMS® Italian Roll
   Sausage
1 (13-ounce) can refried
   beans
1 (8-ounce) jar medium
   salsa
2 cups (8 ounces) shredded
   Cheddar cheese

2 cups (8 ounces) shredded
   Monterey Jack cheese
1 (4-ounce) jar sliced black
   olives, drained
1 cup sliced green onions
   with tops
2 cups sour cream
1 (1-pound) bag tortilla
   chips

Preheat oven to 350°F. Crumble sausage into medium skillet.
Cook over medium heat until browned, stirring occasionally.
Drain off any drippings. Spread beans in ungreased 2½-quart
shallow baking dish, then top with sausage. Pour salsa over
sausage; sprinkle with cheeses. Sprinkle olives and onions over
top. Bake 20 to 30 minutes or until heated through. Spread with
sour cream while hot and serve with chips. Refrigerate leftovers.

Makes 12 to 16 servings

Salsa Italiano

1 pound (2 large) fresh
   California tomatoes,
   seeded and diced
½ cup chopped red onion
1 can (2.25 ounces) sliced
   ripe olives, drained
1 jar (6 ounces) marinated
   artichoke hearts
2 tablespoons lemon juice

2 garlic cloves, finely
   chopped
3 tablespoons chopped
   fresh basil
¼ teaspoon crushed hot red
   pepper flakes
¼ teaspoon salt
⅛ teaspoon ground black
   pepper

In a medium bowl, combine tomatoes, onion and olives. Slice
artichoke hearts, reserving marinade. Stir artichokes into tomato
mixture; set aside. In a small bowl, whisk together lemon juice,
garlic, basil, pepper flakes, salt, black pepper and 2 tablespoons
artichoke marinade. Gently mix dressing with tomato mixture.
Serve with roast or barbecued chicken.   *Makes about 2 cups*

Favorite recipe from **California Tomato Board**

Spicy Taco Dip

Sassy Salads & Sides

◆ ⛊ ◆

South-of-the-Border Salad

2 cups smoked fish, fresh
   or frozen
½ medium head lettuce,
   torn into 2-inch pieces
1 large peeled avocado, cut
   into 1-inch pieces
1 medium tomato, chopped
1 cup diagonally sliced
   celery
1 cup (4 ounces) shredded
   mild Cheddar cheese

½ cup cooked, drained
   garbanzo beans
½ cup chopped green
   onions
½ cup grated carrot
½ cup buttermilk-style
   salad dressing
1 package (4 ounces)
   tortilla chips, lightly
   crushed

Thaw fish if frozen. Break fish into bite-sized pieces. Combine all ingredients except salad dressing and tortilla chips. Toss well. Add dressing and tortilla chips and serve immediately.

Makes 6 servings

Favorite recipe from **Florida Department of Agriculture and Consumer Services, Bureau of Seafood and Aquaculture**

South-of-the-Border Salad

El Dorado Rice Casserole

1 can (14½ ounces) whole
   peeled tomatoes, cut up
1½ cups chicken broth
1 medium onion, chopped
1 tablespoon vegetable oil
1 cup uncooked long-grain
   rice

1 teaspoon LAWRY'S®
   Garlic Salt
1 cup dairy sour cream
1 can (4 ounces) diced
   green chilies, drained
1½ cups (6 ounces) shredded
   Monterey Jack cheese

Drain tomatoes, reserving juice. Add reserved juice to broth to make 2½ cups liquid; set aside. In medium saucepan, sauté onion in oil until tender. Add tomato-broth mixture, tomatoes, rice and Garlic Salt. Bring to a boil. Reduce heat; cover and simmer 25 minutes or until liquid is absorbed. In small bowl, combine sour cream and chilies. In 1½-quart casserole, layer ½ of prepared rice, ½ of sour cream mixture and ½ of cheese. Repeat. Bake at 350°F 20 minutes or until bubbly. *Makes 6 servings*

PRESENTATION: *Top casserole with avocado and pimiento slices.*

Black Bean Turkey Pepper Salad

¾ pound fully cooked
   honey-roasted turkey
   breast, cut into ¼-inch
   cubes
1 small red bell pepper, cut
   into ¼-inch cubes
1 small yellow bell pepper,
   cut into ¼-inch cubes
1 can (15 ounces) black
   beans, rinsed and
   drained

1 cup thinly sliced green
   onions
¾ cup chopped fresh
   cilantro
2 tablespoons olive oil
1 tablespoon red wine
   vinegar
1 teaspoon ground cumin
¼ teaspoon cayenne pepper

1. In large bowl combine turkey, red and yellow peppers, black beans, onions and cilantro.

2. In small bowl whisk together oil, vinegar, cumin and cayenne pepper. Fold dressing into turkey mixture. Cover and refrigerate 1 hour. *Makes 6 servings*

Favorite recipe from **National Turkey Federation**

El Dorado Rice Casserole

Hot Taco Salad

¾ **pound lean ground beef (80% lean)**
½ **cup chopped onion**
1 **package (6.8 ounces) RICE-A-RONI® Beef Flavor**
½ **cup salsa**
1 **teaspoon chili powder**

4 **cups shredded lettuce**
1 **medium tomato, chopped**
½ **cup (2 ounces) shredded Monterey Jack or Cheddar cheese**
½ **cup crushed tortilla chips (optional)**

1. In large skillet, brown ground beef and onion; drain. Remove from skillet; set aside.

2. In same skillet, prepare Rice-A-Roni Mix as package directs.

3. Stir in meat mixture, salsa and chili powder; continue cooking over low heat 3 to 4 minutes or until heated through.

4. Arrange lettuce on serving platter. Top with rice mixture, tomato and cheese. Top with tortilla chips, if desired.

Makes 5 servings

Mexican Pork Salad

1 **pound boneless pork loin, cut into 3×½×¼-inch strips**
4 **cups shredded lettuce**
1 **medium orange, peeled, sliced and quartered**
1 **medium avocado, peeled, seeded and diced**

1 **small red onion, sliced and separated into rings**
1 **tablespoon vegetable oil**
1 **teaspoon chili powder**
¾ **teaspoon salt**
½ **teaspoon dried oregano leaves, crushed**
¼ **teaspoon ground cumin**

Place lettuce on serving platter. Arrange orange, avocado and red onion over lettuce. Heat oil in large skillet; add chili powder, salt, oregano and cumin. Add pork loin strips and stir-fry over medium-high heat 5 to 7 minutes or until pork is tender. Spoon hot pork strips over lettuce mixture. Serve immediately.

Makes 4 servings

Favorite recipe from **National Pork Producers Council**

Hot Taco Salad

Soups, Stews & Chilies

◆ 🌵 ◆

Santa Fe Taco Stew

1 tablespoon vegetable oil
½ cup diced onion
½ teaspoon LAWRY'S®
    Garlic Powder with
    Parsley
1 package (1 ounce)
    LAWRY'S® Taco Spices
    & Seasonings
1 can (28 ounces) diced
    tomatoes, undrained
1 can (15 ounces) pinto
    beans, drained
1 can (8¾ ounces) whole
    kernel corn, drained

1 can (4 ounces) diced
    green chilies, drained
1 cup beef broth
½ teaspoon cornstarch
1 pound pork butt or beef
    chuck, cooked and
    shredded
Dairy sour cream
    (garnish)
Tortilla chips (garnish)
Fresh cilantro (garnish)

In Dutch oven or large saucepan, heat oil. Add onion and Garlic Powder with Parsley; sauté 2 to 3 minutes until onion is translucent and tender. Add Taco Spices & Seasonings, tomatoes, beans, corn and chilies; blend well. In small bowl, gradually blend broth into cornstarch using wire whisk. Stir into stew. Stir in cooked meat. Bring to a boil, stirring frequently. Reduce heat to low; simmer, uncovered, 30 minutes, stirring occasionally. (Or, simmer longer for a thicker stew.) *Makes 8 servings*

PRESENTATION: *Garnish each serving with sour cream, tortilla chips and fresh cilantro, if desired.*

VARIATION: *Substitute 3 cups cooked, shredded chicken for pork or beef.*

Santa Fe Taco Stew

Tex-Mex Chicken & Rice Chili

1 package (6.8 ounces)
   RICE-A-RONI® Spanish
   Rice
2¾ cups water
2 cups chopped cooked
   chicken or turkey
1 can (15 or 16 ounces)
   kidney beans or pinto
   beans, rinsed and
   drained
1 can (14½ or 16 ounces)
   tomatoes or stewed
   tomatoes, undrained

1 medium green bell
   pepper, cut into ½-inch
   pieces
1½ teaspoons chili powder
1 teaspoon ground cumin
½ cup (2 ounces) shredded
   Cheddar or Monterey
   Jack cheese (optional)
Sour cream (optional)
Chopped cilantro
   (optional)

1. In 3-quart saucepan, combine rice-vermicelli mix, contents of seasoning packet, water, chicken, beans, tomatoes, green pepper, chili powder and cumin. Bring to a boil over high heat.

2. Reduce heat to low; simmer, uncovered, about 20 minutes or until rice is tender, stirring occasionally.

3. Top with cheese, sour cream and cilantro, if desired.

Makes 4 servings

Salsa Corn Soup with Chicken

3 quarts chicken broth
2 pounds boneless skinless
   chicken breasts,
   cooked and diced
2 (10-ounce) packages
   frozen corn kernels,
   thawed

4 (11-ounce) jars
   NEWMAN'S OWN® All
   Natural Salsa
4 large carrots, cooked and
   diced

Bring chicken broth to a boil in Dutch oven. Add chicken, corn, salsa and carrots. Bring to a boil. Reduce heat and simmer until carrots are tender.

Makes 8 servings

Tex-Mex Chicken & Rice Chili

30-Minute Chili Olé

1 cup chopped onion
2 cloves garlic, minced
1 tablespoon vegetable oil
2 pounds ground beef
1 (15-ounce) can tomato
  sauce
1 (14½-ounce) can stewed
  tomatoes
¾ cup A.1.® Steak Sauce
1 tablespoon chili powder

1 teaspoon ground cumin
1 (16-ounce) can black
  beans, rinsed and
  drained
1 (11-ounce) can corn,
  drained
Shredded cheese, sour
  cream and chopped
  tomato for garnish

In 6-quart heavy pot, over medium-high heat, sauté onion and garlic in oil until tender. Add beef; cook and stir until browned. Drain; stir in tomato sauce, stewed tomatoes, steak sauce, chili powder and cumin. Heat to a boil; reduce heat to low. Cover; simmer for 10 minutes, stirring occasionally. Stir in beans and corn; simmer, uncovered, for 10 minutes. Serve hot; garnish with cheese, sour cream and tomato.

Makes 8 servings

Baja Corn Chowder

¼ cup butter or margarine
3 cans (17 ounces each)
  whole kernel corn,
  drained, divided
1 medium red bell pepper,
  diced
2 cups chicken broth
1 quart half-and-half
1 can (7 ounces) diced
  green chilies, drained

1 package (1.27 ounces)
  LAWRY'S® Spices &
  Seasonings for Fajitas
2 cups (8 ounces) shredded
  Monterey Jack cheese
½ teaspoon LAWRY'S®
  Seasoned Pepper
Hot pepper sauce to taste

In Dutch oven or large saucepan, melt butter. Add one can of corn and bell pepper; sauté 5 minutes. Remove from heat. In food processor or blender, place remaining two cans of corn and chicken broth; process until smooth. Add to Dutch oven with half-and-half, chilies and Spices & Seasonings for Fajitas. Return to heat. Bring just to a boil, stirring constantly. Remove from heat; blend in cheese, Seasoned Pepper and hot pepper sauce.

Makes 4 to 6 servings

Albóndigas Soup

1 pound ground beef
¼ cup long-grain rice
1 egg
1 tablespoon chopped
  fresh cilantro
1 teaspoon LAWRY'S®
  Seasoned Salt
¼ cup ice water
2 cans (14½ ounces each)
  chicken broth

1 can (14½ ounces) whole
  peeled tomatoes,
  undrained and cut up
¼ cup chopped onion
1 rib celery, diced
1 large carrot, diced
1 medium potato, diced
¼ teaspoon LAWRY'S®
  Garlic Powder with
  Parsley

In medium bowl, combine ground beef, rice, egg, cilantro, Seasoned Salt and ice water; form into small meatballs. In large saucepan, combine broth with vegetables and Garlic Powder with Parsley. Bring to a boil; add meatballs. Reduce heat; cover and simmer 30 to 40 minutes, stirring occasionally.

Makes 6 to 8 servings

PRESENTATION: *Serve with lemon wedges and warm tortillas.*

HINT: *For a lower salt version, use homemade chicken broth or low sodium chicken broth.*

Avocado Orange Soup

2 large ripe avocados,
  pitted
1 cup fresh orange juice
1 cup plain yogurt

½ teaspoon TABASCO®
  pepper sauce
¼ teaspoon salt
  Orange slices

In food processor or blender, blend avocados and orange juice. Add yogurt, TABASCO sauce and salt. Blend until smooth. Refrigerate until ready to serve. Garnish with orange slices.

Makes 4 servings

Tacos, Enchiladas & More

Skillet Steak Fajitas

½ cup A.1.® Steak Sauce
½ cup mild, medium or hot
    thick and chunky salsa
1 (1-pound) beef flank or
    bottom round steak,
    thinly sliced
1 medium onion, thinly
    sliced

1 medium green bell
    pepper, cut into strips
1 tablespoon margarine
8 (6½-inch) flour tortillas,
    warmed

Blend steak sauce and salsa. Place steak in glass dish; coat with ¼ cup salsa mixture. Cover; chill 1 hour, stirring occasionally.

In large skillet, over medium-high heat, cook onion and pepper in margarine for 3 minutes or until tender. Remove with slotted spoon; set aside. In same skillet, cook and stir steak for 5 minutes or until done. Add remaining salsa mixture, onion and pepper; cook until heated through. Serve with tortillas and your favorite fajita toppings, if desired. *Makes 4 servings*

Skillet Steak Fajitas

Tuna Fiesta Soft Tacos

⅓ cup mayonnaise
½ teaspoon garlic salt
½ teaspoon lemon pepper
  seasoning
1 can (6 ounces)
  STARKIST® Solid
  White or Chunk Light
  Tuna, drained and
  flaked
¼ cup chopped celery
1 hard-cooked egg,
  chopped
2 tablespoons finely
  chopped green onion

2 tablespoons finely
  chopped green bell
  pepper
1 tablespoon drained
  chopped pimiento
6 flour tortillas (6 inches
  each), warmed
1 cup shredded iceberg
  lettuce
½ cup shredded Colby or
  Monterey Jack cheese
  Salsa (optional)

In large bowl, combine mayonnaise, garlic salt, lemon pepper seasoning, tuna, celery, egg, onion, bell pepper and pimiento; mix thoroughly. Place generous ¼ cup filling on one side of each tortilla; top with lettuce and cheese. Fold tortilla over; serve with salsa, if desired. *Makes 6 servings*

Breakfast Quesadillas

1 pound BOB EVANS
  FARMS® Original
  Recipe Roll Sausage
4 eggs
4 (10-inch) flour tortillas

2 cups (8 ounces) shredded
  Monterey Jack cheese
½ cup chopped green
  onions with tops
½ cup chopped tomato
  Sour cream and salsa

Crumble sausage into large skillet. Cook over medium heat until sausage is browned, stirring occasionally. Drain off any drippings. Remove sausage to paper towels; set aside. Add eggs to same skillet; scramble until eggs are set but not dry. Remove eggs; set aside. Place 1 tortilla in same skillet. Top with half of each eggs, cheese, sausage, onions and tomato. Heat until cheese melts; top with another tortilla. Remove from skillet; cut into six equal wedges. Repeat with remaining tortillas, eggs, cheese, sausage, onions and tomato to make second quesadilla. Serve hot with sour cream and salsa. Refrigerate leftovers. *Makes 4 servings*

Tuna Fiesta Soft Taco

Bean and Vegetable Burritos

1 tablespoon olive oil
1 medium onion, thinly sliced
1 jalapeño pepper, seeded, minced
1 tablespoon chili powder
3 cloves garlic, minced
2 teaspoons dried oregano leaves, crushed
1 teaspoon ground cumin
1 large sweet potato, baked, cooled, peeled, diced *or* 1 can (16 ounces) yams in syrup, drained, rinsed, diced

1 can black beans or pinto beans, drained, rinsed
1 cup frozen whole kernel corn, thawed, drained
1 green bell pepper, chopped
2 tablespoons lime juice
¾ cup (3 ounces) shredded reduced fat Monterey Jack cheese
4 (10-inch) flour tortillas
Low fat sour cream (optional)

Preheat oven to 350°F. Heat oil in large saucepan or Dutch oven over medium-high heat. Add onion and cook, stirring often, 10 minutes or until golden. Add jalapeño, chili powder, garlic, oregano and cumin; stir 1 minute. Add 1 tablespoon water and stir; remove from heat. Stir in sweet potato, beans, corn, green pepper and lime juice.

Spoon 2 tablespoons cheese in center of each tortilla. Top with 1 cup filling. Fold all 4 sides around filling to enclose. Place burritos seam side down on baking sheet. Cover with foil and bake 30 minutes or until heated through. Serve with sour cream, if desired.

Makes 4 servings

Bean and Vegetable Burrito

Rice & Bean Burritos

FILLING
- 1 tablespoon olive or vegetable oil
- ½ cup sliced green onions
- 1 jalapeño pepper, seeded and chopped
- 2 to 3 cloves garlic, minced
- ½ pound lean ground beef, turkey or chicken

- 2 cups water
- 1 can (14½ ounces) chopped tomatoes, undrained
- 1 package (8 ounces) FARMHOUSE® Mexican Beans & Rice
- Salt and pepper

BURRITO FIXINGS
- 6 large *or* 12 small flour tortillas, softened
- Shredded Cheddar cheese

- Sour cream
- Prepared salsa

For filling, in large skillet, heat oil until hot. Cook and stir onions, jalapeño and garlic in hot oil until garlic is tender but not brown. Add ground meat; cook until meat is no longer pink. Add water and undrained tomatoes; bring to a boil. Add beans & rice and contents of seasoning packet. Reduce heat; cover and simmer 25 minutes. Season to taste with salt and pepper.

To assemble burritos, place ⅔ cup meat mixture in center of large tortilla (⅓ cup for small tortillas). Top with shredded cheese, sour cream and salsa. Fold up burrito style and serve immediately.

Makes 6 servings

Red Chili Tortilla Torte

- 2 cans (16 ounces) pinto beans or black beans, rinsed and drained
- ¼ cup low-salt chicken broth
- 1 tablespoon vegetable oil
- 2 large onions, sliced
- 2 red bell peppers, cut into ¼-inch strips
- 2 zucchini, thinly sliced

- 2 cloves garlic, minced
- 1 cup whole kernel corn
- 1 teaspoon ground cumin
- ½ teaspoon salt
- ¼ teaspoon cayenne pepper
- 6 (8-inch) flour tortillas
- 2 cups NEWMAN'S OWN® All Natural Salsa
- 2 cups (8 ounces) shredded Monterey Jack cheese

In food processor, combine pinto beans and chicken broth. Process until smooth; set aside. Heat oil in large nonstick skillet over medium heat. Add onions, bell peppers, zucchini and garlic; sauté until softened, 10 to 12 minutes. Add corn, cumin, salt and cayenne pepper; cook about 2 minutes.

Heat oven to 375°F. Grease 8-inch round baking dish. Spread ½ cup of pinto bean mixture on one flour tortilla; place on bottom of baking dish. Spoon 1 cup of the onion mixture on top of the beans. Spoon ⅓ cup of Newman's Own® All Natural Salsa on top of onion mixture; top with ⅓ cup of cheese. Repeat with remaining ingredients, ending with cheese. Bake until heated through, about 45 minutes. Let stand 10 minutes; cut into wedges to serve.   *Makes 8 to 10 servings*

Spicy Burrito Burgers

6 tablespoons prepared mild salsa, divided	**1 pound ground beef**
1 can (4 ounces) diced green chilies, divided	**4 (6-inch) flour tortillas**
¼ cup sour cream	**1 cup shredded lettuce**
Dash hot pepper sauce	**½ cup (2 ounces) shredded Cheddar cheese with taco seasonings**

Combine 2 tablespoons salsa, 2 tablespoons chilies, sour cream and hot pepper sauce in small bowl; set aside.

Combine beef, remaining 4 tablespoons salsa and remaining chilies in large bowl; mix well. Shape into four 4-inch oval patties.

Grill burgers over medium coals 8 to 10 minutes for medium or until desired doneness is reached, turning halfway through grilling time.

Place 1 burger in center of 1 tortilla. Top with one-quarter of the lettuce, cheese and sour cream mixture. Bring edges of tortilla together over top of burger; secure with toothpick if necessary. Remove toothpick before serving.   *Makes 4 servings*

Mexican Frittata

3 tablespoons butter or
  margarine
2 cups (8 ounces) frozen
  ready-to-cook hash
  brown potatoes with
  peppers and onions
  (O'Brien style),
  thawed*
5 eggs

½ cup salsa
¼ teaspoon salt
2 cups (8 ounces)
  SARGENTO® 4 Cheese
  Mexican Recipe Blend,
  divided
Sour cream (optional)
Chopped fresh cilantro
  (optional)

Melt butter in 10-inch ovenproof skillet over high heat. Swirl butter up side of pan to prevent frittata from sticking. Add potatoes to skillet; cook 3 minutes, stirring occasionally. Reduce heat to medium.

Beat eggs in medium bowl. Stir in salsa and salt. Stir in 1 cup of 4 Cheese Mexican Recipe Blend. Add egg mixture to skillet; stir gently to combine. Cover; cook 6 minutes without stirring or until eggs are set around edges. (Center will be wet.) Sprinkle remaining 1 cup cheese evenly over frittata. Place under preheated broiler 4 to 5 inches from heat source. Broil 2 to 3 minutes or until cheese is melted and eggs are set in center. Cut into wedges; serve with sour cream and cilantro, if desired.

Makes 4 servings

*To thaw frozen potatoes, microwave at HIGH 2 to 3 minutes.

Layered Mexicali Casserole

1 pound ground beef
1 (16-ounce) can
  ROSARITA® Refried
  Beans
1 (15-ounce) can HUNT'S®
  Tomato Sauce Special
1 (1.25-ounce) package
  taco seasoning mix
6 (8-inch) flour tortillas
1 (14½-ounce) can HUNT'S®
  Choice-Cut Tomatoes,
  drained

¾ cup sliced green onions
1 (4-ounce) can
  ROSARITA® Diced
  Green Chiles
1 (2¼-ounce) can sliced
  ripe olives, drained
4 cups (16 ounces)
  shredded Cheddar
  cheese
Sour cream (optional)
Avocado slices (optional)

In large skillet, brown ground beef; drain. Stir in beans, tomato sauce and taco seasoning. Bring to a boil; reduce heat and simmer 15 minutes. In lightly greased 13×9×2-inch baking dish, place 2 tortillas side by side on bottom of dish. Spread ⅓ of the meat mixture over tortillas and sprinkle with ⅓ of each of the tomatoes, green onions, chiles, olives and cheese. Repeat layers twice, ending with cheese.

Bake at 350°F for 40 minutes. Let stand 10 minutes before serving. Garnish each serving with sour cream and an avocado slice, if desired.   *Makes 8 to 10 servings*

Fiesta Pork Roast

1 (6- to 7-pound) pork loin
   roast
1 tablespoon salt
2 teaspoons onion powder
2 teaspoons garlic powder
½ teaspoon pepper
1½ cups water
8 small whole onions,
   peeled

¾ cup currant jelly
½ teaspoon hot pepper
   sauce
8 small seedless oranges,
   peeled
¼ cup water
3 tablespoons all-purpose
   flour

Combine salt, onion powder, garlic powder and pepper. Sprinkle on pork roast; rub into roast. Place roast in shallow roasting pan; insert meat thermometer. Roast at 325°F for 1 hour. Add 1½ cups water to pan. Place onions around roast. Combine currant jelly and hot pepper sauce; brush on roast and onions. Continue to roast for 1 hour or until meat thermometer registers 155°F to 160°F. Remove roast; let stand 5 to 10 minutes before slicing. Meanwhile, add oranges to hot liquid in pan; heat thoroughly. Remove onions and oranges; keep warm. To make gravy, combine ¼ cup water and flour; mix until smooth. Bring pan liquid to a boil; gradually stir in flour mixture. Cook and stir until thickened. Serve with onions and oranges.   *Makes 16 servings*

Favorite recipe from **National Pork Producers Council**

Tacos Picadillos

¾ **pound ground pork**
1 **medium onion, chopped**
½ **teaspoon ground
     cinnamon**
½ **teaspoon ground cumin**
1 **can (14½ ounces)
     DEL MONTE® Mexican
     Recipe Stewed
     Tomatoes**

⅓ **cup DEL MONTE®
     Seedless Raisins**
⅓ **cup toasted chopped
     almonds**
6 **flour tortillas**

In large skillet, brown meat with onion and spices over medium-high heat. Season to taste with salt and pepper, if desired. Stir in tomatoes and raisins. Cover and cook 10 minutes. Remove cover; cook over medium-high heat 5 minutes or until thickened, stirring occasionally. Just before serving, stir in almonds. Fill tortillas with meat mixture; roll to enclose. Garnish with lettuce, cilantro and sour cream, if desired. Serve immediately.

Makes 6 servings

HELPFUL HINT: *If ground pork is not available, boneless pork may be purchased and ground in food processor. Cut pork into 1-inch cubes before processing.*

Fantastic Pork Fajitas

1 **pound pork strips**
2 **teaspoons vegetable oil**
½ **medium onion, peeled
     and sliced**

1 **green pepper, seeded and
     sliced**
4 **flour tortillas, warmed**

Heat large nonstick skillet over medium-high heat. Add oil; heat until hot. Add pork strips, onion and pepper slices to skillet and stir-fry quickly 4 to 5 minutes. Roll up portions of the meat mixture in flour tortillas and serve with purchased salsa, if desired.

Makes 4 servings

Favorite recipe from **National Pork Producers Council**

Tacos Picadillos

Picadillo Chicken

1 broiler-fryer chicken, cut up (about 3½ pounds)
1½ tablespoons all-purpose flour
½ teaspoon salt
2 tablespoons vegetable oil
1 large onion, coarsely chopped
2 cloves garlic, minced
1 can (14½ ounces) stewed tomatoes
1 can (8 ounces) tomato sauce
⅓ cup raisins

⅓ cup sliced pickled jalapeños, drained
1 teaspoon ground cumin
¼ teaspoon ground cinnamon
⅓ cup toasted slivered almonds
Hot cooked rice (optional)
1 cup (4 ounces) SARGENTO® Fancy Supreme® Shredded Cheese For Nachos & Tacos

Rinse chicken; pat dry. Dust with flour and salt. In large skillet, brown chicken skin side down in hot oil over medium heat, about 5 minutes; turn. Add onion and garlic; cook 5 minutes more. Add stewed tomatoes, tomato sauce, raisins, jalapeños, cumin and cinnamon; heat to a boil. Reduce heat; cover and simmer 15 minutes. Uncover and simmer 5 to 10 minutes more or until chicken is tender and sauce is thickened.* Stir in almonds; serve over rice. Sprinkle with Nachos & Tacos cheese.

Makes 6 servings

*At this point, chicken may be covered and refrigerated up to 2 days before serving. Reheat before adding almonds.

Picadillo Chicken

Ensenada Fish Tacos

10 ounces halibut or orange roughy fillets, cut into 1-inch cubes
1 tablespoon vegetable oil
1 tablespoon lime juice
1 package (1.27 ounces) LAWRY'S® Spices & Seasonings for Fajitas
6 corn or flour tortillas (about 8 inches)
2½ cups shredded lettuce
½ cup diced tomatoes
¾ cup (3 ounces) shredded Monterey Jack or Cheddar cheese
2 tablespoons thinly sliced green onion
Dairy sour cream (garnish)
Guacamole (garnish)
Salsa (garnish)
Chopped fresh cilantro (garnish)

In shallow glass baking dish, place fish. Pour oil and lime juice over fish. Sprinkle with Spices & Seasonings for Fajitas; toss lightly to coat. Cover. Refrigerate 2 hours to marinate, occasionally spooning marinade over fish. In same dish, bake fish in 450°F oven 10 minutes or until fish flakes easily with fork; drain. To serve, evenly divide fish; place in center of each tortilla. Top with lettuce, tomatoes, cheese and green onion. Garnish as desired. *Makes 6 servings*

Turkey Tacos

1 pound ground turkey
2 tablespoons minced dried onion
1 tablespoon chili powder
1 teaspoon paprika
½ teaspoon *each* cumin, dried oregano and salt
¼ teaspoon garlic powder
⅛ teaspoon black pepper
10 taco shells
1 to 2 tomatoes, chopped
2 to 3 cups shredded lettuce
⅔ cup shredded reduced-fat Cheddar cheese

In large nonstick skillet over medium-high heat, cook and stir turkey, onion and seasonings 5 to 6 minutes or until turkey is no longer pink. Spoon mixture evenly into taco shells and top with tomatoes, lettuce and cheese. *Makes 5 servings*

Favorite recipe from **National Turkey Federation**

Ensenada Fish Tacos

Breakfast Burritos with Baked Citrus Fruit

4 green onions, thinly
   sliced, divided
1¼ cups frozen egg
   substitute, thawed
2 tablespoons diced mild
   green chilies
½ cup (2 ounces) shredded
   reduced fat Monterey
   Jack or Cheddar
   cheese

¼ cup lightly packed fresh
   cilantro
4 (7-inch) flour tortillas
¼ cup salsa
¼ cup low fat sour cream
   Baked Citrus Fruit
   (recipe follows)

Spray large nonstick skillet with cooking spray. Heat over medium heat. Set aside ¼ cup green onions. Add remaining onions, egg substitute and chilies to skillet. Cook, stirring occasionally, about 4 minutes or until eggs are softly set. Stir in cheese and cilantro. Continue cooking, folding eggs over until eggs are cooked to desired doneness, about 1 minute.

Stack tortillas and wrap in paper towels. Microwave at HIGH about 1 minute or until hot. Place one-quarter of eggs in center of each tortilla. Fold sides over filling to enclose. Place burritos seam side down on plates. Top each with salsa, sour cream and reserved green onions. Serve with Baked Citrus Fruit.

Makes 4 servings

Baked Citrus Fruit

2 oranges, peeled and
   sliced
1 grapefruit, peeled and
   sliced

1½ tablespoons lightly
   packed brown sugar
½ teaspoon ground
   cinnamon

Preheat oven to 400°F. Divide fruit slices into 4 portions. Arrange each portion on baking sheet, overlapping slices. Combine brown sugar and cinnamon in small bowl. Sprinkle 1 teaspoon brown sugar mixture over each serving of fruit. Bake 5 minutes or until fruit is hot.

Makes 4 servings

Breakfast Burritos with Baked
Citrus Fruit

Mexicali Beef & Rice

1 package (6.8 ounces)
   RICE-A-RONI® Beef
   Flavor
1 cup frozen corn *or* 1 can
   (8 ounces) whole
   kernel corn, drained
½ cup chopped red or
   green bell pepper

1 pound lean ground beef
   (80% lean)
Salt and pepper
   (optional)
Salsa (optional)
Sour cream (optional)

1. Prepare Rice-A-Roni Mix as package directs, stirring in frozen corn and red pepper during last 10 minutes of cooking.

2. While Rice-A-Roni is simmering, shape beef into four ½-inch-thick patties.

3. In lightly greased second large skillet, cook beef patties over medium heat, about 4 minutes on each side or until desired doneness. Season with salt and pepper, if desired.

4. Serve rice topped with cooked beef patties, salsa and sour cream, if desired. *Makes 4 servings*

Pork Tenderloin Mole

1½ pounds pork tenderloin
   (about 2 whole)
1 teaspoon vegetable oil
½ cup chopped onion
1 clove garlic, minced
1 cup Mexican-style chili
   beans, undrained
¼ cup chili sauce

¼ cup raisins
2 tablespoons water
1 tablespoon peanut butter
1 teaspoon unsweetened
   cocoa
Dash *each* salt, ground
   cinnamon and ground
   cloves

Place tenderloin in shallow baking pan. Roast at 350°F for 30 minutes or until juicy and slightly pink in center.

Heat oil in medium saucepan. Cook onion and garlic over low heat for 5 minutes. Combine onion and garlic with remaining ingredients in food processor; mix until almost smooth. Heat mixture in saucepan thoroughly over low temperature, stirring frequently. Serve over tenderloin slices. *Makes 6 servings*

Favorite recipe from **National Pork Producers Council**

Mexicali Beef & Rice

Tex-Mex Chicken Fajitas

6 boneless skinless chicken breast halves (about 1½ pounds), cut into strips

½ cup LAWRY'S® Mesquite Marinade with Lime Juice*

3 tablespoons plus 1½ teaspoons vegetable oil, divided

1 small onion, sliced and separated into rings

1 medium-sized green bell pepper, cut into strips

¾ teaspoon LAWRY'S® Garlic Powder with Parsley

½ teaspoon hot pepper sauce

1 medium tomato, cut into wedges

2 tablespoons chopped fresh cilantro

Flour tortillas, warmed

1 medium lime, cut into wedges

Pierce chicken several times with fork; place in large resealable plastic bag or bowl. Pour Mesquite Marinade with Lime Juice over chicken; seal bag or cover bowl. Refrigerate at least 30 minutes. Heat 1 tablespoon plus 1½ teaspoons oil in large skillet. Add onion, bell pepper, Garlic Powder with Parsley and hot pepper sauce; sauté 5 to 7 minutes or until onion is crisp-tender. Remove vegetable mixture from skillet; set aside. Heat remaining 2 tablespoons oil in same skillet. Add chicken; sauté 8 to 10 minutes or until chicken is no longer pink in center, stirring frequently. Return vegetable mixture to skillet with tomato and cilantro; heat through.   *Makes 4 to 6 servings*

PRESENTATION: *Serve with flour tortillas and lime wedges. Top with dairy sour cream, guacamole, salsa and pitted ripe olives as desired.*

*One package (1.27 ounces) Lawry's® Spices & Seasonings for Fajitas, ¼ cup lime juice and ¼ cup vegetable oil can be substituted.

Tex-Mex Chicken Fajitas

GREAT TASTING
STIR-FRIES
AND MORE

Contents

STIR-FRY ESSENTIALS

Stir-fry cooking—the art of rapidly cooking small pieces of food over high heat, usually in hot oil— is most often associated with Asian cuisines. **Great Tasting Stir-Fries and More** will convince you that the versatile stir-frying technique extends far beyond the Orient and works wonderfully with a wide variety of ingredients. This exciting new publication offers over 50 delicious opportunities to experience a vast assortment of tempting stir-fried creations, from exotic-tasting classic Chinese dishes to bold new flavor combinations reminiscent of Italian, Tex-Mex or spa cooking. Stir-frying lends itself to quick and nutritious menus while maximizing the flavors and textures of your ingredients. Read on for guidelines guaranteed to make your stir-fries an unforgettable success every time.

Here's a hot tip to keep in mind: Before beginning any recipe, read it all the way through at least once so you know what to expect and are sure not to miss any steps!

Getting Ready
Stir-frying can be broken down into two separate steps: (1) preparation of ingredients; and, (2) cooking. Because stir-frying requires constant attention during a relatively short cooking time, all ingredients should be cleaned, cut up, measured and arranged for easy access before you begin cooking. If possible, use different cutting boards for meats and vegetables (or wash the cutting board between uses with warm, soapy water). Knives should also be thoroughly cleaned after cutting raw meat, poultry and seafood. These precautions limit the possibility of spreading harmful bacteria between ingredients. To guarantee that meats and vegetables cook evenly, cut them into equal-sized pieces according to the recipe directions. Also, it may be easier to thinly slice meat and poultry that has been partially frozen first.

Heavy-duty resealable plastic food storage bags are perfect for marinating ingredients. Any foods marinated longer than 20 minutes should be marinated in the refrigerator. To prevent lumping, make sure to stir any mixtures containing cornstarch immediately before using.

Cook It Up

A wok is usually used for stir-frying, although a large, heavy skillet can work just as well. Because a wok has high, sloping sides, there is ample hot surface area to ensure even cooking. Also, the vigorously stirred and tossed ingredients are easily contained by a high-sided pan. Many kinds of woks are available: round- or flat-bottomed woks made of thin or heavy rolled steel, aluminum, stainless steel or copper as well as electric woks with nonstick finishes and thermostatic controls. Whichever type of wok you use, be sure to follow the manufacturer's instructions for using and taking care of it. Woks range widely in size from 12 to 24 inches in diameter. A 14-inch wok is an ideal choice because it can accommodate the typical amounts of ingredients without taking up too much space on the stove.

Remember: You can successfully stir-fry a little food in a large wok (or skillet) but a lot of food in a little wok will bring disappointing results.

The kind of oil used for stir-frying is also very important. Use vegetable oils such as peanut, corn, canola, soybean or a combination of these oils because they withstand high heat without smoking. Sesame oil, olive oil and butter burn easily.

When the ingredients are ready to go and you're set to cook, heat the wok until it's very hot. Next, add the oil; it takes only about 30 seconds to heat thoroughly when added to a hot pan. Usually, the meat, poultry or seafood is stir-fried first and removed from the wok. Then the vegetables are added to the wok, followed by the sauce. Finally, the meat is added back to finish cooking or just heat through.

Note: Because the choices of ingredients, heat sources and cooking equipment can vary greatly from reader to reader, the cooking times given in the recipes of this publication should be considered guidelines.

Salads & Starters

CHINATOWN STUFFED MUSHROOMS

24 large fresh mushrooms (about 1 pound), cleaned and stems trimmed
½ pound ground turkey
1 clove garlic, minced
¼ cup fine dry bread crumbs
¼ cup thinly sliced green onions
3 tablespoons reduced-sodium soy sauce, divided
1 teaspoon minced fresh ginger
1 egg white, slightly beaten
⅛ teaspoon crushed red pepper flakes (optional)

Remove stems from mushrooms; finely chop enough stems to equal 1 cup. Cook turkey with chopped stems and garlic in medium skillet over medium-high heat until turkey is no longer pink, stirring to separate turkey. Spoon off any fat. Stir in bread crumbs, green onions, 2 tablespoons soy sauce, ginger, egg white and crushed red pepper; mix well.

Brush mushroom caps lightly on all sides with remaining 1 tablespoon soy sauce; spoon about 2 teaspoons stuffing into each mushroom cap.* Place stuffed mushrooms on rack of foil-lined broiler pan. Broil 4 to 5 inches from heat 5 to 6 minutes or until hot. *Makes 24 appetizers*

*Mushrooms may be made ahead to this point; cover and refrigerate up to 24 hours. Add 1 to 2 minutes to broiling time for chilled mushrooms.

Chinatown Stuffed Mushrooms

Holland House® Stir-Fry Sauce

HOLLAND HOUSE® STIR–FRY SAUCE

1 teaspoon vegetable oil
1 bunch scallions, thinly sliced
2 cloves garlic, minced
¼ teaspoon ground ginger
¾ cup HOLLAND HOUSE®
　Sherry Cooking Wine
1 tablespoon reduced-sodium
　or regular soy sauce

1 cup reduced-sodium chicken
　broth
2 tablespoons cornstarch
1 to 2 tablespoons toasted
　sesame seeds (optional)

In medium saucepan, heat oil and cook scallions, garlic and ginger until scallions are just tender, about 4 minutes. Stir in Holland House® Cooking Wine, soy sauce and broth blended with cornstarch. Bring to a boil and stir 1 minute.

Serve as a sauce for grilled or broiled vegetables, steamed vegetables or with your favorite stir-fry recipe. Sprinkle with toasted sesame seeds, if desired.

Makes about 2 cups

STIR–FRIED BEEF & EGGPLANT SALAD

½ pound boneless tender beef steak (sirloin, rib eye or top loin)
⅓ cup KIKKOMAN® Stir-Fry Sauce
1 teaspoon distilled white vinegar
¼ to ½ teaspoon crushed red pepper
1 clove garlic, pressed
Lettuce leaves (optional)

3 cups finely shredded iceberg lettuce
3 tablespoons vegetable oil, divided
1 medium eggplant, cut into julienne strips
1 medium carrot, cut into julienne strips
6 green onions, cut into 1½-inch lengths, separating whites from tops

Cut beef across grain into thin slices, then into strips. Combine stir-fry sauce, vinegar, red pepper and garlic. Coat beef with 1 tablespoon of the stir-fry sauce mixture; set aside remaining mixture. Line edge of large shallow bowl or large platter with lettuce leaves; arrange shredded lettuce in center. Heat 1 tablespoon oil in hot wok or large skillet over high heat. Add beef and stir-fry 1 minute; remove. Heat remaining 2 tablespoons oil in same pan; add eggplant and stir-fry 6 minutes. Add carrot and white parts of green onions; stir-fry 3 minutes. Add green onion tops; stir-fry 2 minutes longer. Add remaining stir-fry sauce mixture and beef. Cook and stir just until beef and vegetables are coated with sauce. Spoon mixture over shredded lettuce; toss well to combine before serving. Serve immediately. *Makes 2 to 3 servings*

STIR–FRIED SHRIMP APPETIZERS

¼ cup KIKKOMAN® Soy Sauce
¼ cup dry white wine
¼ cup chopped green onions
1 clove garlic, pressed
1 teaspoon ground ginger

1 pound medium-size raw shrimp, peeled and deveined
3 tablespoons vegetable oil

Combine soy sauce, wine, green onions, garlic and ginger; stir in shrimp and let stand 15 minutes. Heat oil in hot wok or large skillet over medium-high heat. Drain shrimp and add to pan. Discard marinade. Stir-fry 1 to 2 minutes, or until shrimp are pink. Serve immediately. *Makes 8 servings*

ORIENTAL SALSA

1 cup diced unpeeled
    cucumber
½ cup chopped red bell pepper
½ cup thinly sliced green onions
⅓ cup coarsely chopped
    cilantro
1 clove garlic, minced
2 tablespoons reduced-sodium
    soy sauce

1 tablespoon rice vinegar
½ teaspoon Oriental sesame oil
¼ teaspoon crushed red pepper
    flakes
Easy Wonton Chips (recipe
    follows) or assorted fresh
    vegetables for dipping

Combine cucumber, bell pepper, onions, cilantro, garlic, soy sauce, rice vinegar, oil and crushed red pepper in medium bowl until well blended. Cover and refrigerate until serving time. Serve with Easy Wonton Chips or assorted fresh vegetables for dipping. Or, use as an accompaniment to broiled fish, chicken or pork.

Makes 1½ cups salsa

EASY WONTON CHIPS

1 tablespoon soy sauce
2 teaspoons vegetable oil
½ teaspoon sugar

¼ teaspoon garlic salt
12 wonton wrappers
Nonstick cooking spray

Preheat oven to 375°F. Combine soy sauce, oil, sugar and garlic salt in small bowl; mix well. Cut each wonton wrapper diagonally in half. Place on 15×10-inch jelly-roll pan coated with nonstick cooking spray. Brush soy mixture lightly but evenly over both sides of wrappers. Bake 4 to 6 minutes or until crisp and lightly browned, turning after 3 minutes. Transfer to cooling rack; cool completely.

Makes 2 dozen chips

Oriental Salsa and Easy Wonton Chips

BEEF, PORK & LAMB

LEMONY BEEF, VEGETABLES & BARLEY

1 pound lean ground beef
8 ounces mushrooms, sliced
1 medium onion, chopped
1 clove garlic, crushed
1 can (14 ounces) ready-to-
serve beef broth

½ cup quick-cooking barley
½ teaspoon salt
¼ teaspoon pepper
1 package (10 ounces) frozen
peas and carrots, defrosted
1 teaspoon grated lemon peel

1. In large nonstick skillet, cook and stir ground beef, mushrooms, onion and garlic over medium heat 8 to 10 minutes or until beef is no longer pink, breaking beef up into ¾-inch crumbles. Pour off drippings.

2. Stir in broth, barley, salt and pepper. Bring to a boil; reduce heat to medium-low. Cover tightly; simmer 10 minutes.

3. Add peas and carrots; continue cooking 2 to 5 minutes or until barley is tender. Stir in lemon peel.   *Makes 4 servings*

Favorite recipe from **National Cattlemen's Beef Association**

Lemony Beef, Vegetables & Barley

HUNAN STIR–FRY WITH TOFU

1 block tofu
½ pound ground pork
1 tablespoon dry sherry
1 teaspoon minced fresh
   gingerroot
1 clove garlic, minced
½ cup regular-strength chicken
   broth
1 tablespoon cornstarch

3 tablespoons KIKKOMAN® Soy
   Sauce
1 tablespoon vinegar
½ teaspoon crushed red pepper
1 tablespoon vegetable oil
1 onion, cut into ¾-inch pieces
1 green bell pepper, cut into
   ¾-inch pieces
Hot cooked rice

Cut tofu into ½-inch cubes; drain well on several layers of paper towels. Meanwhile, combine pork, sherry, ginger and garlic in small bowl; let stand 10 minutes. Blend broth, cornstarch, soy sauce, vinegar and red pepper; set aside. Heat wok or large skillet over medium-high heat; add pork. Cook, stirring to separate pork, about 3 minutes, or until lightly browned; remove. Heat oil in same pan. Add onion and bell pepper; stir-fry 4 minutes. Add pork and soy sauce mixture. Cook and stir until mixture boils and thickens. Gently fold in tofu; heat through. Serve immediately over rice.

Makes 4 servings

BEEF, PEPPERS AND TOMATO STIR–FRY

1 package (6.8 ounces) RICE-A-
   RONI® Beef Flavor
1 pound well-trimmed top
   sirloin steak
¼ cup margarine or butter,
   divided
   Salt and pepper (optional)
½ red or green bell pepper, cut
   into strips

½ yellow bell pepper, cut into
   strips
1 medium onion, sliced
4 plum tomatoes, sliced into
   quarters
2 tablespoons dry red wine
   or 1 tablespoon
   Worcestershire sauce

1. Prepare Rice-A-Roni® Mix as package directs.

2. While Rice-A-Roni® is simmering, thinly slice meat across the grain.

3. In second large skillet, melt 2 tablespoons margarine over medium-high heat. Sauté meat 5 minutes or until no longer pink. Remove from skillet; sprinkle with salt and pepper, if desired. Set aside; keep warm.

4. In same skillet, sauté peppers and onion in remaining 2 tablespoons margarine 3 minutes or until crisp-tender. Stir in meat.

5. Meanwhile, add tomatoes and wine to rice during last 5 minutes of cooking. Serve rice topped with meat mixture.

Makes 4 servings

Hot and Spicy Onion Beef

HOT AND SPICY ONION BEEF

2 tablespoons soy sauce,
  divided
1 tablespoon cornstarch,
  divided
¾ pound flank steak, thinly
  sliced across the grain
2 tablespoons dry sherry
1 teaspoon Oriental sesame oil
1 teaspoon chili paste
  (optional)

2 tablespoons vegetable oil
1 large onion (12 to
  14 ounces), sliced
  vertically
1 teaspoon minced garlic
  Dried whole red chili peppers
  to taste
1 tablespoon water

Combine 1 tablespoon soy sauce and 1 teaspoon cornstarch in medium bowl. Add beef; stir to coat. Let stand 30 minutes. Combine remaining tablespoon soy sauce, the sherry, sesame oil and chili paste in small bowl; set aside. Heat wok or large skillet over high heat. Add vegetable oil, swirling to coat sides. Add onion, garlic and chili peppers; cook and stir until onion is tender. Add beef; stir-fry 2 minutes or until lightly browned. Add soy sauce mixture and mix well. Combine remaining 2 teaspoons cornstarch and the water; mix into onion mixture. Cook and stir until sauce boils and thickens. *Makes about 4 servings*

Favorite recipe from **National Onion Association**

MONGOLIAN LAMB

SESAME SAUCE

1 tablespoon sesame seeds
¼ cup soy sauce
1 tablespoon dry sherry
1 tablespoon red wine vinegar
1½ teaspoons sugar

1 clove garlic, minced
1 green onion with top, finely
 chopped
½ teaspoon Oriental sesame oil

LAMB

1 pound boneless lean lamb*
 (leg or shoulder)
2 small leeks, trimmed and
 thoroughly cleaned
4 green onions with tops
2 medium carrots, shredded
1 medium zucchini, shredded
1 green bell pepper, cut into
 matchstick pieces

1 red bell pepper, cut into
 matchstick pieces
½ small head napa cabbage,
 thinly sliced
1 cup bean sprouts
4 tablespoons vegetable oil,
 divided
4 slices peeled fresh ginger,
 divided
Chili oil (optional)

For Sesame Sauce, place sesame seeds in small skillet. Carefully shake or stir over medium heat until seeds begin to pop and turn golden brown, about 2 minutes; cool. Crush seeds with mortar and pestle or place between paper towels and crush with rolling pin. Scrape up sesame paste with knife and transfer to small serving bowl. Add remaining sauce ingredients; mix well.

Slice meat across grain into 2×¼-inch strips. Cut leeks into 2-inch slivers. Repeat with green onions. Arrange meat and all vegetables on large platter. Have Sesame Sauce, vegetable oil, ginger and chili oil near cooking area.

Heat wok or electric griddle to 350°F. Cook one serving at a time. For each serving, heat 1 tablespoon vegetable oil. Add one slice ginger; cook and stir 30 seconds. Discard ginger. Add ½ cup meat strips; stir-fry until lightly browned, about 1 minute. Add 2 cups assorted vegetables; stir-fry 1 minute. Drizzle with 2 tablespoons Sesame Sauce; stir-fry 30 seconds. Season with a few drops chili oil. Repeat with remaining ingredients.

Makes 4 servings

*Or, substitute beef flank steak or boneless lean pork for the lamb.

Mongolian Lamb

SAVORY PORK & APPLE STIR–FRY

1 package (7.2 ounces) RICE-A-RONI® Rice Pilaf
1⅓ cups apple juice or apple cider, divided
1 pound boneless pork loin, pork tenderloin or skinless, boneless chicken breast halves
1 teaspoon paprika
1 teaspoon dried thyme leaves

½ teaspoon ground sage or poultry seasoning
½ teaspoon salt (optional)
2 tablespoons margarine or butter
2 medium apples, cored, sliced
1 teaspoon cornstarch
⅓ cup coarsely chopped walnuts

1. Prepare Rice-A-Roni® Mix as package directs, substituting 1 cup water and 1 cup apple juice for water in directions.

2. While Rice-A-Roni® is simmering, cut pork into 1½×¼-inch strips. Combine seasonings; toss with meat.

3. In second large skillet, melt margarine over medium heat. Stir-fry meat 3 to 4 minutes or just until pork is no longer pink.

4. Add apples; stir-fry 2 to 3 minutes or until apples are almost tender. Add combined remaining ⅓ cup apple juice and cornstarch. Stir-fry 1 to 2 minutes or until thickened to form glaze.

5. Stir in nuts. Serve rice topped with pork mixture.   *Makes 4 servings*

Savory Pork & Apple Stir-Fry

Oriental Beef & Noodle Toss

ORIENTAL BEEF & NOODLE TOSS

1 pound lean ground beef
2 packages (3 ounces each)
   Oriental flavor instant
   ramen noodles
2 cups water

2 cups frozen Oriental
   vegetable mixture
1/8 teaspoon ground ginger
2 tablespoons thinly sliced
   green onion

1. In large nonstick skillet, brown ground beef over medium heat 8 to 10 minutes or until beef is no longer pink, breaking up beef into 3/4-inch crumbles. Remove with slotted spoon; pour off drippings. Season beef with one seasoning packet from noodles; set aside.

2. In same skillet, combine water, frozen vegetables, noodles (broken into several pieces), ginger and remaining seasoning packet. Bring to a boil; reduce heat. Cover; simmer 3 minutes or until noodles are tender, stirring occasionally.

3. Return beef to skillet; heat through. Stir in green onion before serving.

Makes 4 servings

Favorite recipe from **National Cattlemen's Beef Association**

STIR–FRY TOMATO BEEF

1 cup uncooked long-grain
    white rice
1 pound flank steak
1 tablespoon cornstarch
1 tablespoon soy sauce
2 cloves garlic, minced

1 teaspoon minced gingerroot
   or ¼ teaspoon ground
   ginger
1 tablespoon vegetable oil
1 can (14½ ounces)
   DEL MONTE® Original
   Recipe Stewed Tomatoes

1. Cook rice according to package directions.

2. Cut meat in half lengthwise, and then cut crosswise into thin slices.

3. In medium bowl, combine cornstarch, soy sauce, garlic and ginger. Add sliced meat; toss to coat.

4. Heat oil in large skillet over high heat. Add meat; cook, stirring constantly, until browned. Add tomatoes; cook until thickened, about 5 minutes, stirring frequently.

5. Serve over hot rice. Garnish with chopped cilantro or green onions, if desired.

Makes 4 to 6 servings

GINGER BEEF QUICK–FRY

1 can (8 ounces) DOLE® Chunk
   Pineapple in Juice
½ pound top sirloin steak
2 cloves garlic, pressed
½ teaspoon ground ginger
2 tablespoons vegetable oil
6 tablespoons pale dry sherry
3 tablespoons soy sauce

½ cup water
2 tablespoons cornstarch
1 bunch radishes, cut into
   halves
1 green bell pepper, seeded and
   chunked
1 cup sliced green onions
   Shredded lettuce

Drain pineapple, reserving juice. Cut steak into ½-inch-thick strips. Quickly cook and stir steak with garlic and ginger in hot oil. Combine reserved juice, sherry, soy sauce, water and cornstarch. Stir into beef mixture. Add pineapple, radishes, bell pepper and onions. Cook until sauce is clear and thickened. Serve over bed of shredded lettuce.

Makes 2 servings

Quick Trick: Beef is easier to slice when partially frozen. For best results use a serrated knife.

Stir-Fry Tomato Beef

GOLDEN PORK STIR–FRY

Sweet and Sour Cooking
   Sauce (recipe follows)
2 tablespoons vegetable oil,
   divided
1 clove garlic, crushed or finely
   chopped
½ pound lean, boneless pork,
   cut into thin strips
2 cups broccoli florets

1 sweet red or green bell
   pepper, seeded and sliced
   into thin strips
1 Golden Delicious apple,
   cored and cut into 16 slices
4 cups sliced napa cabbage
   Cooked rice or noodles
   (optional)

1. Prepare Sweet and Sour Cooking Sauce; set aside. In large skillet or wok, heat 1 tablespoon oil over medium-high heat. Add garlic and stir-fry until lightly browned. Remove and discard garlic. Add pork to seasoned oil in skillet and stir-fry until browned; remove pork to bowl and reserve.

2. Add remaining tablespoon oil to skillet. Add broccoli and pepper; stir-fry about 1 minute. Add apple, cabbage, and reserved pork; stir-fry 2 minutes longer. Add Sweet and Sour Cooking Sauce and cook, stirring, until sauce thickens and coats all ingredients. Serve over rice or noodles.

Makes 4 servings

SWEET AND SOUR COOKING SAUCE: In small bowl, combine 2 tablespoons chicken broth or water, 1 tablespoon reduced-sodium soy sauce, 1 teaspoon cornstarch, 1 teaspoon sugar, 1 teaspoon grated fresh gingerroot, 1 teaspoon rice wine or cider vinegar, and ⅛ teaspoon crushed red pepper; stir until well-blended.

Favorite recipe from **Washington Apple Commission**

TERIYAKI BEEF

¾ pound sirloin tip steak, cut
   into thin strips
½ cup teriyaki sauce
¼ cup water
1 tablespoon cornstarch

1 teaspoon sugar
1 bag (16 ounces) BIRDS EYE®
   frozen Farm Fresh Mixtures
   Broccoli, Carrots and
   Water Chestnuts

• Spray large skillet with nonstick cooking spray; cook beef strips over medium-high heat 7 to 8 minutes, stirring occasionally.

• Combine teriyaki sauce, water, cornstarch and sugar; mix well.

• Add teriyaki sauce mixture and vegetables to beef. Bring to boil; quickly reduce heat to medium.

• Cook 7 to 10 minutes or until broccoli is heated through, stirring occasionally.

Makes 4 to 6 servings

BEEF & BROCCOLI PEPPER STEAK

1 tablespoon margarine or
  butter
1 pound well-trimmed top
  round steak, cut into thin
  strips

1 package (6.8 ounces) RICE-A-
  RONI® Beef Flavor
2 cups broccoli flowerets
½ cup red or green bell pepper
  strips
1 small onion, thinly sliced

1. In large skillet, melt margarine over medium heat. Add meat; sauté just until browned.

2. Remove from skillet; set aside. Keep warm.

3. In same skillet, prepare Rice-A-Roni® Mix as package directs; simmer 10 minutes. Add meat and remaining ingredients; simmer an additional 10 minutes or until most of liquid is absorbed and vegetables are crisp-tender. *Makes 4 servings*

Beef & Broccoli Pepper Steak

Beef & Vegetable Fried Rice

BEEF & VEGETABLE FRIED RICE

1 pound lean ground beef
2 cloves garlic, crushed
1 teaspoon grated fresh
    gingerroot *or* ¼ teaspoon
    ground ginger
2 tablespoons water
1 red bell pepper, cut into
    ½-inch pieces

1 package (6 ounces) frozen
    pea pods
3 cups cold cooked rice
3 tablespoons soy sauce
2 teaspoons dark sesame oil
¼ cup thinly sliced green onions

1. In large nonstick skillet, brown ground beef, garlic and ginger over medium heat 8 to 10 minutes or until beef is no longer pink, breaking beef up into ¾-inch crumbles. Remove with slotted spoon; pour off drippings.

2. In same skillet, heat water over medium-high heat until hot. Add bell pepper and pea pods; cook 3 minutes or until bell pepper is crisp-tender, stirring occasionally. Add rice, soy sauce and sesame oil; mix well. Return beef to skillet; heat through, about 5 minutes. Stir in green onions before serving.

Makes 4 servings

Favorite recipe from **National Cattlemen's Beef Association**

SPICY–SWEET PINEAPPLE PORK

¾ cup LAWRY'S® Hawaiian
    Marinade with Tropical
    Fruit Juices
1 tablespoon minced fresh
    gingerroot
1 pound pork loin, cut into
    ½-inch strips or cubes
1 cup salsa
3 tablespoons brown sugar
2 tablespoons cornstarch

2 cans (8 ounces each)
    pineapple chunks, divided
2 tablespoons vegetable oil,
    divided
1 green bell pepper, cut into
    chunks
3 green onions, diagonally
    sliced into 1-inch pieces
½ cup whole cashews

In large resealable plastic bag, combine Hawaiian Marinade with Tropical Fruit Juices and the ginger. Add pork and marinate in refrigerator 1 hour. In small bowl, combine salsa, brown sugar, cornstarch and juice from one pineapple can; set aside. In large hot skillet or wok heat 1 tablespoon oil. Stir-fry bell pepper and onions until onions are transparent; remove and set aside. Add remaining 1 tablespoon oil and pork to skillet; stir-fry 5 minutes or until just browned. Return bell pepper and onions to skillet. Stir salsa mixture; add to skillet. Cook until thickened, stirring constantly. Drain remaining can of pineapple. Add pineapple chunks from both cans and cashews; simmer 5 minutes.

Makes 6 servings

BROCCOLI BEEF STIR–FRY

½ cup beef broth
4 tablespoons HOLLAND
    HOUSE® Sherry Cooking
    Wine, divided
1 tablespoon soy sauce
1 tablespoon cornstarch
1 teaspoon sugar
2 tablespoons vegetable oil,
    divided

2 cups fresh broccoli florets
1 cup fresh snow peas
1 red bell pepper, cut into strips
1 pound boneless top round or
    sirloin steak, slightly
    frozen, cut into thin strips
1 clove garlic, minced
    Hot cooked rice

To make sauce, in small bowl, combine broth, 2 tablespoons cooking wine, soy sauce, cornstarch and sugar; mix well. Set aside. In large skillet or wok, heat 1 tablespoon oil. Stir-fry broccoli, snow peas and bell pepper 1 minute. Add remaining 2 tablespoons cooking wine. Cover; cook 1 to 2 minutes. Remove from pan. Heat remaining 1 tablespoon oil; add meat and garlic. Stir-fry 5 minutes or until meat is browned. Add sauce to meat; cook 2 to 3 minutes or until thickened, stirring frequently. Add vegetables; cook until thoroughly heated. Serve over cooked rice.

Makes 4 servings

STIR–FRY OF WILD RICE, SNOW PEAS AND PORK

3 tablespoons vegetable oil
½ pound pork tenderloin, sliced ¼ inch thick
1 cup sliced celery
1 cup sliced green onions
1 cup sliced fresh mushrooms
1 can (8 ounces) sliced water chestnuts, drained
½ pound fresh or thawed frozen snow peas
1 tablespoon grated fresh gingerroot
2 cups cooked wild rice
3 tablespoons soy sauce
1 tablespoon dry sherry
½ teaspoon salt
1 tablespoon cornstarch
½ cup cashews, sunflower seeds or shredded or cut-out carrots for garnish

Heat oil in heavy skillet or wok; add pork and stir-fry over high heat for 2 minutes until meat is no longer pink. Add celery, green onions, mushrooms, water chestnuts, snow peas and ginger. Stir-fry for 5 minutes over high heat until vegetables are crisp-tender. Add wild rice, stirring until evenly blended. Combine soy sauce, sherry and salt; mix into cornstarch. Add to skillet, cooking and stirring about 1 minute until thickened and rice mixture is coated with glaze. Garnish, if desired.   *Makes 4 servings*

Favorite recipe from **Minnesota Cultivated Wild Rice Council**

GINGER BEEF & NOODLE STIR–FRY

1 pound flank steak, cut into thin strips
½ cup LAWRY'S® Thai Ginger Marinade with Lime Juice
1 tablespoon vegetable oil
2 cups broccoli florettes
1 red bell pepper, chopped
2 tablespoons soy sauce
1 teaspoon cornstarch
1 teaspoon LAWRY'S® Garlic Powder with Parsley
1 package (7 ounces) chuka soba noodles (Japanese-style noodles) prepared according to package directions

In large resealable plastic bag combine beef and Thai Ginger Marinade with Lime Juice; marinate in refrigerator 30 minutes. In large skillet, heat oil. Stir-fry broccoli and bell pepper over high heat 2 minutes; remove and set aside. In same skillet cook beef over high heat about 5 to 7 minutes. In small bowl combine soy sauce, cornstarch and Garlic Powder with Parsley; blend well. Add to beef; cook over medium heat until sauce is thickened. Stir in broccoli and bell pepper; heat through. Spoon over noodles.   *Makes 4 servings*

Hint: Vermicelli noodles may be substituted for chuka soba noodles.

Ma-Po Bean Curd

MA–PO BEAN CURD

1 tablespoon Szechuan
    peppercorns* (optional)
¾ cup chicken broth
1 tablespoon soy sauce
1 tablespoon dry sherry
2 tablespoons vegetable oil
4 ounces ground pork
1 tablespoon hot bean sauce**
2 cloves garlic, minced

2 teaspoons minced fresh
    ginger
12 to 14 ounces bean curd,
    drained and cut into
    ½-inch cubes
2 green onions, thinly sliced
3 tablespoons water
4½ teaspoons cornstarch
1 teaspoon Oriental sesame oil

Place peppercorns in small skillet; shake over medium-low heat, until fragrant, about 2 minutes. Let cool. Crush peppercorns with mortar and pestle or place between paper towels and crush with hammer; set aside.

Combine chicken broth, soy sauce and sherry in small bowl; set aside. Heat vegetable oil in wok or large skillet over high heat. Add pork and stir-fry until pork is no longer pink, about 2 minutes. Add hot bean sauce, garlic and ginger. Stir-fry until meat absorbs color from bean sauce, about 1 minute. Add chicken broth mixture and bean curd to wok. Simmer, uncovered, 5 minutes. Stir in onions. Blend water and cornstarch in small cup. Add to wok; cook and stir until sauce boils and thickens slightly. Stir in sesame oil. Pass crushed peppercorns to sprinkle over individual servings, if desired. *Makes 3 to 4 servings*

*Szechuan peppercorns are very potent. Wear rubber or plastic gloves when crushing them and do not touch eyes or lips when handling.

**Available in the Oriental section of large supermarkets or in specialty grocery stores.

POULTRY

CHICKEN AND VEGETABLES WITH MUSTARD SAUCE

1 tablespoon sugar
2 teaspoons cornstarch
1½ teaspoons dry mustard
2 tablespoons reduced-sodium soy sauce
2 tablespoons water
2 tablespoons rice vinegar
1 pound boneless skinless chicken breasts
4 teaspoons vegetable oil, divided

2 cloves garlic, minced
1 small red bell pepper, cut into short thin strips
½ cup thinly sliced celery
1 small onion, cut into thin wedges
3 cups hot cooked Chinese egg noodles (3 ounces uncooked)
Celery leaves for garnish

Combine sugar, cornstarch and mustard in small bowl. Blend soy sauce, water and vinegar into cornstarch mixture until smooth. Cut chicken into 1-inch pieces. Heat 2 teaspoons oil in wok or large nonstick skillet over medium heat. Add chicken and garlic; stir-fry 3 minutes or until chicken is no longer pink. Remove and reserve.

Add remaining 2 teaspoons oil to wok. Add bell pepper, celery and onion; stir-fry 3 minutes or until vegetables are crisp-tender. Stir soy sauce mixture; add to wok. Cook and stir 30 seconds or until sauce boils and thickens. Return chicken with any accumulated juices to wok; heat through. Serve over Chinese noodles. Garnish, if desired.

Makes 4 servings

Chicken and Vegetables with Mustard Sauce

Lemon Chicken Herb Stir-Fry

LEMON CHICKEN HERB STIR–FRY

4½ teaspoons peanut oil
2 green onions, cut into 1-inch pieces
1 large carrot, cut into ½-inch julienne
1 can (8 ounces) bamboo shoots
2 cups broccoli florets
1 pound boneless skinless chicken breast halves or boneless pork loin, sliced into strips

1 cup LAWRY'S® Herb & Garlic Marinade with Lemon Juice
1 tablespoon soy sauce
½ teaspoon arrowroot
1 can (11 ounces) mandarin orange segments, drained (optional)
1 tablespoon sesame seeds

In large wok or skillet, heat oil. Cook and stir onions and carrot 3 to 5 minutes until just tender. Stir in bamboo shoots, broccoli and chicken. Stir-fry 7 to 9 minutes until meat is just cooked. In small bowl, whisk together Herb & Garlic Marinade with Lemon Juice, soy sauce and arrowroot. Add to skillet; continue cooking, stirring constantly until sauce forms glaze on mixture. Stir in orange segments, if desired, and sprinkle with sesame seeds. *Makes 6 servings*

TRADITIONAL FRIED RICE WITH TURKEY AND PINE NUTS

1 bag SUCCESS® Brown Rice
1 tablespoon vegetable oil
1 medium green bell pepper,
    chopped
¼ pound fresh mushrooms,
    sliced
1 small onion, chopped
¼ pound chopped cooked
    turkey
¼ cup pine nuts, toasted
2 tablespoons reduced-sodium
    soy sauce (optional)

Prepare rice according to package directions. Rinse with cold water until rice is cool.

Heat oil in large skillet or wok over medium heat. Add bell pepper, mushrooms and onion; cook and stir until tender. Add rice, turkey, pine nuts and soy sauce; heat thoroughly, stirring occasionally.

Makes 6 servings

SHANTUNG CHICKEN

1 whole chicken breast,
    skinned and boned
2 tablespoons cornstarch,
    divided
3 tablespoons KIKKOMAN® Soy
    Sauce, divided
1 tablespoon dry sherry
1 clove garlic, minced
1 cup water
3 tablespoons vegetable oil,
    divided
½ pound fresh bean sprouts
¼ pound green onions and tops,
    cut into 1½-inch lengths,
    separating whites from tops
1 tablespoon slivered fresh
    gingerroot
1 tablespoon sesame seed,
    toasted
Hot cooked noodles

Cut chicken into narrow strips. Combine 1 tablespoon *each* cornstarch and soy sauce with sherry and garlic in small bowl; stir in chicken. Let stand 5 minutes. Meanwhile, blend water, remaining 1 tablespoon cornstarch and 2 tablespoons soy sauce; set aside. Heat 1 tablespoon oil in hot wok or large skillet over high heat. Add chicken and stir-fry 2 minutes; remove. Heat remaining 2 tablespoons oil in same pan; add bean sprouts, white parts of green onions and ginger; stir-fry 3 minutes. Stir in chicken, soy sauce mixture, green onion tops and sesame seed. Cook and stir until mixture boils and thickens. Serve immediately over noodles.

Makes 4 servings

SWEET 'N' SOUR CHICKEN STIR-FRY

3 tablespoons ketchup
1 tablespoon vinegar
1 tablespoon soy sauce
2 boneless skinless chicken breasts, cut into 1-inch cubes
1 tablespoon vegetable oil

½ package (16 ounces) frozen stir-fry vegetables or other frozen vegetable combination (such as broccoli, bell peppers, mushrooms and onions)
1 can (20 ounces) DOLE® Pineapple Chunks, drained

• **Combine** ketchup, vinegar and soy sauce in small bowl; set aside.

• **Cook** and stir chicken in large skillet or wok in hot oil over medium-high heat until chicken is browned.

• **Stir** in vegetables; cover. Reduce heat to low; cook 2 to 3 minutes or until vegetables are tender-crisp, stirring occasionally. Stir in pineapple and sauce; cook and stir until pineapple is heated through.

Makes 6 servings

Tip: Fresh vegetable combinations can be used in place of frozen vegetables. When using fresh vegetables, add 2 tablespoons of juice from canned pineapple and increase cooking time to 4 minutes or until vegetables are tender-crisp.

SIMPLE STIR-FRY CHICKEN

2 tablespoons vegetable oil
4 boneless skinless chicken breast halves, sliced into thin strips
1 green bell pepper, cut into 1-inch slivers
3 green onions, diagonally sliced into ½-inch pieces

1 package (10 ounces) frozen green peas
1 can (4 ounces) sliced mushrooms, drained
½ cup LAWRY'S® Stir-Fry Oriental Style Cooking Sauce

In wok or large skillet, heat oil. Stir-fry chicken strips in hot oil. When chicken is almost cooked, stir in bell pepper and onions; continue to stir-fry until vegetables are just tender yet colorful. Add peas, mushrooms and Stir-Fry Oriental Style Cooking Sauce; toss and cook until heated thoroughly. Serve over hot cooked rice.

Makes 4 servings

Sweet 'n' Sour Chicken Stir-Fry

SANTA FE STIR–FRY

1 envelope LIPTON® Recipe
  Secrets® Onion Soup Mix*
¼ cup olive or vegetable oil
¼ cup water
1 tablespoon lime juice
  (optional)
½ teaspoon garlic powder

1 pound boneless skinless
  chicken breasts, cut into
  thin strips
2 cups frozen assorted
  vegetables, partially
  thawed and drained
Hot cooked rice

In 12-inch skillet, blend Onion Soup Mix, oil, water, lime juice and garlic powder; let stand 5 minutes. Bring to a boil over high heat; stir in chicken and vegetables. Cook uncovered, stirring frequently, 5 minutes or until chicken is done. Serve over hot rice. Garnish, if desired, with chopped fresh parsley and lime slices. *Makes about 4 servings*

*Also terrific with Lipton® Recipe Secrets® Onion-Mushroom or Savory Herb with Garlic Soup Mix.

LEMON TURKEY STIR–FRY

1 bunch green onions
½ pound medium-size
  mushrooms
1 small lemon
1 tablespoon Worcestershire
  sauce
2 teaspoons cornstarch
1 teaspoon honey
1 envelope chicken-flavored
  bouillon

1 package (16 ounces) turkey
  cutlets*
2 tablespoons vegetable oil
½ teaspoon LAWRY'S® Seasoned
  Salt
1 small zucchini, thinly sliced
1 small red bell pepper, thinly
  sliced

Cut green onions into 2-inch pieces; quarter mushrooms. Grate peel from lemon; place in small bowl. Squeeze juice into bowl. Stir in Worcestershire, cornstarch, honey, bouillon and ⅔ cup water. Cut turkey into ½-inch-wide strips. Heat oil in medium skillet; cook turkey with Seasoned Salt until turkey just loses its pink color, stirring constantly. Remove from skillet; set aside. In same skillet, cook zucchini, bell pepper, green onions and mushrooms until tender-crisp. Stir in cornstarch mixture. Cook, stirring until thickened. Add turkey; heat through.

Makes 4 servings

*1 pound cut-up cooked turkey can replace cutlets. Omit cooking stage of turkey and stir in at end to heat through.

Plum Chicken

PLUM CHICKEN

6 ounces fresh uncooked Chinese egg noodles
¼ cup plum preserves or jam
3 tablespoons rice wine vinegar
3 tablespoons reduced-sodium soy sauce
1 tablespoon cornstarch
3 teaspoons vegetable oil, divided

1 small red onion, thinly sliced
2 cups fresh snow peas, diagonally sliced into ½-inch pieces
12 ounces boneless skinless chicken breasts, cut into thin strips
4 medium plums or apricots, pitted and sliced

Cook noodles according to package directions, omitting salt. Drain and keep warm. Stir together plum preserves, vinegar, soy sauce and cornstarch in small bowl; set aside. Heat 2 teaspoons oil in large nonstick skillet or wok. Add onion and cook 2 minutes or until slightly softened. Add snow peas and cook 3 minutes. Remove mixture to bowl.

Heat remaining 1 teaspoon oil in skillet. Add chicken and cook over medium-high heat 2 to 3 minutes or until no longer pink. Push chicken to one side of skillet. Stir plum sauce; add to skillet. Cook and stir until thick and bubbly. Add vegetables and plums; stir to coat evenly. Cook 3 minutes or until heated through. Toss with noodles and serve immediately.

Makes 4 servings

ASPARAGUS CHICKEN WITH BLACK BEAN SAUCE

1 tablespoon dry sherry
4 teaspoons soy sauce, divided
5 teaspoons cornstarch, divided
1 teaspoon Oriental sesame oil
3 boneless skinless chicken breast halves, cut into bite-size pieces
1 tablespoon fermented, salted black beans*
1 teaspoon minced fresh ginger
1 clove garlic, minced
½ cup chicken broth
1 tablespoon oyster sauce
3 tablespoons vegetable oil, divided
1 pound fresh asparagus spears, trimmed and diagonally cut into 1-inch pieces
1 medium yellow onion, cut into 8 wedges and separated
2 tablespoons water

For marinade, combine sherry, 2 teaspoons soy sauce, 2 teaspoons cornstarch and the sesame oil in large bowl; mix well. Add chicken and stir to coat well. Let stand 30 minutes.

Place black beans in sieve and rinse under cold running water. Coarsely chop beans. Combine beans, ginger and garlic; finely chop all three together. Combine chicken broth, remaining 2 teaspoons soy sauce, the oyster sauce and remaining 3 teaspoons cornstarch in small bowl; mix well and set aside.

Heat 2 tablespoons vegetable oil in wok or large skillet over high heat. Add chicken and stir-fry about 3 minutes or until chicken is no longer pink. Remove and set aside. Heat remaining 1 tablespoon vegetable oil in wok. Add asparagus and onion; stir-fry 30 seconds. Add water; cover and cook, stirring occasionally, until asparagus is crisp-tender, about 2 minutes. Return chicken to wok. Stir chicken broth mixture and add to wok with bean mixture; cook and stir until sauce boils and thickens.

Makes 3 to 4 servings

*May be found in Oriental section of large supermarkets or specialty grocery stores.

Asparagus Chicken with Black Bean Sauce

HOISIN CHICKEN

1 whole chicken (3 to
   4 pounds), cut up
½ cup plus 1 tablespoon
   cornstarch, divided
1 cup water
3 tablespoons dry sherry
3 tablespoons cider vinegar
3 tablespoons hoisin sauce
4 teaspoons soy sauce
2 teaspoons instant chicken
   bouillon granules
   Vegetable oil for frying
2 teaspoons minced fresh
   ginger

2 medium yellow onions,
   chopped
8 ounces fresh broccoli, cut
   into 1-inch pieces
1 red or green bell pepper,
   chopped
2 cans (4 ounces each) whole
   button mushrooms, drained
   Hot cooked vermicelli
   (optional)
   Additional red bell pepper,
   cut into strips, for garnish

Rinse chicken; set aside. Combine 1 tablespoon cornstarch, water, sherry, vinegar, hoisin sauce, soy sauce and bouillon granules in small bowl; mix well and set aside.

Place remaining ½ cup cornstarch in large bowl. Add chicken pieces; stir to coat well. Heat oil in large skillet or wok over high heat to 375°F. Add ⅓ of the chicken pieces, one piece at a time; cook until no longer pink in center, about 5 minutes. Drain chicken pieces on paper towels. Repeat with remaining chicken.

Remove all but 2 tablespoons oil from skillet. Add ginger; stir-fry 1 minute. Add onions; stir-fry 1 minute. Add broccoli, bell pepper and mushrooms; stir-fry 2 minutes. Stir cornstarch mixture; add to skillet. Cook and stir until sauce boils and turns translucent. Return chicken to skillet. Cook and stir until chicken is thoroughly heated, about 2 minutes. Serve over hot vermicelli and garnish with bell pepper strips, if desired.

Makes 6 servings

Hoisin Chicken

CHICKEN CHOW MEIN

1 pound boneless skinless
    chicken breasts
2 cloves garlic, minced
1 package (6 ounces) frozen
    snow peas, thawed
1 teaspoon vegetable oil,
    divided
2 tablespoons reduced-sodium
    soy sauce

2 tablespoons dry sherry
3 large green onions, cut
    diagonally into 1-inch
    pieces
4 ounces uncooked Chinese egg
    noodles or vermicelli,
    cooked, drained and rinsed
1 teaspoon Oriental sesame oil

Cut chicken into 1-inch pieces. Toss with garlic in small bowl. Cut snow peas into halves. Heat ½ teaspoon vegetable oil in wok or large nonstick skillet over medium heat. Add chicken mixture; stir-fry 3 minutes or until chicken is no longer pink. Transfer to medium bowl; toss with soy sauce and sherry.

Heat remaining ½ teaspoon vegetable oil in wok. Add snow peas; stir-fry 1 minute. Add onions; stir-fry 30 seconds. Add chicken mixture; stir-fry 1 minute. Add noodles to wok; stir-fry 2 minutes or until heated through. Stir in sesame oil. Garnish, if desired. *Makes 4 servings*

Chicken Chow Mein

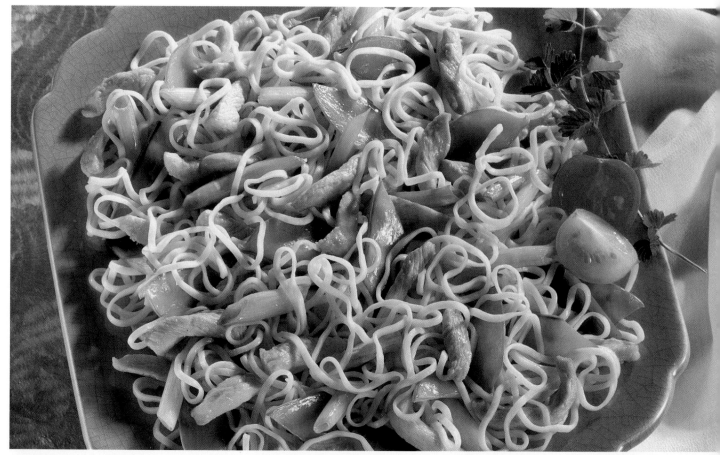

KAHLÚA® STIR–FRY CHICKEN

1½ pounds boneless skinless chicken, cut into ½-inch pieces
2 tablespoons beaten egg
¼ cup plus 2 tablespoons vegetable oil, divided
2 tablespoons plus 1 teaspoon cornstarch, divided
½ cup water chestnuts, sliced

6 asparagus tips, fresh or frozen
1 green bell pepper, cut into ½-inch strips
4 ounces mushrooms, sliced
4 ounces snow peas
3 tablespoons KAHLÚA®
1 cup cashews
3 green onions, chopped

Coat chicken in mixture of egg, 2 tablespoons oil and 2 tablespoons cornstarch. Heat remaining ¼ cup oil in wok or skillet. Add chicken. Cook until golden brown; remove and drain well. Remove all but 2 tablespoons oil from wok; heat. Add all vegetables except green onions. Stir-fry 3 to 5 minutes. Combine Kahlúa® and remaining 1 teaspoon cornstarch; add to vegetables. Bring to a boil, then simmer to slightly thicken. Add chicken and cashews; heat thoroughly. Remove to serving platter. Garnish with green onions.

Makes 4 to 6 servings

PEANUT CHICKEN STIR–FRY

1 package (6.1 ounces) RICE-A-RONI® With ⅓ Less Salt Fried Rice
½ cup reduced-sodium or regular chicken broth
2 tablespoons creamy peanut butter
1 tablespoon reduced-sodium or regular soy sauce
1 tablespoon vegetable oil

¾ pound skinless, boneless chicken breasts, cut into ½-inch pieces
2 cloves garlic, minced
2 cups frozen mixed carrots, broccoli and red bell pepper vegetable medley, thawed, drained
2 tablespoons chopped peanuts (optional)

1. Prepare Rice-A-Roni® Mix as package directs.

2. While Rice-A-Roni® is simmering, combine chicken broth, peanut butter and soy sauce; mix with a fork. Set aside.

3. In second large skillet or wok, heat oil over medium-high heat. Stir-fry chicken and garlic 2 minutes.

4. Add vegetables and broth mixture; stir-fry 5 to 7 minutes or until sauce has thickened. Serve over rice. Sprinkle with peanuts, if desired.

Makes 4 servings

SEAFOOD

HOT AND SOUR SHRIMP

½ package (½ ounce) dried
    shiitake mushrooms*
½ small unpeeled cucumber
1 tablespoon brown sugar
2 teaspoons cornstarch
3 tablespoons rice vinegar
2 tablespoons reduced-sodium
    soy sauce
1 tablespoon vegetable oil

1 pound medium raw shrimp,
    peeled and deveined
2 cloves garlic, minced
¼ teaspoon crushed red pepper
    flakes
1 large red bell pepper, cut into
    short, thin strips
Hot cooked Chinese egg
    noodles (optional)

Place mushrooms in small bowl; cover with warm water. Soak 20 minutes to soften. Drain; squeeze out excess water. Discard stems; slice caps. Cut cucumber in half lengthwise; scrape out seeds. Slice crosswise. Combine brown sugar and cornstarch in small bowl. Blend in vinegar and soy sauce until smooth.

Heat oil in wok or large nonstick skillet over medium heat. Add shrimp, garlic and crushed red pepper; stir-fry 1 minute. Add mushrooms and bell pepper strips; stir-fry 2 minutes or until shrimp are opaque. Stir vinegar mixture; add to wok. Cook and stir 30 seconds or until sauce boils and thickens. Add cucumber; stir-fry until heated through. Serve over noodles, if desired.

Makes 4 servings

*Or substitute ¾ cup sliced fresh mushrooms. Omit procedure for soaking mushrooms.

Hot and Sour Shrimp

THAI–STYLE TUNA FRIED RICE

4 to 5 tablespoons vegetable oil, divided

2 eggs, lightly beaten

⅔ cup raw medium shrimp, peeled, chopped into ¾-inch pieces

3 cloves garlic, minced

1 to 2 tablespoons minced fresh serrano chilies

4 to 6 cups cooked rice, chilled overnight

1 tablespoon sugar

1 tablespoon nam pla (fish sauce) (optional)

1 tablespoon soy sauce

1 can (6 ounces) STARKIST® Solid White or Chunk Light Tuna, drained and chunked

½ cup chopped dry-roasted peanuts

¼ cup chopped fresh basil

2 tablespoons chopped fresh cilantro

Lime wedges for garnish

In wok, heat 1 tablespoon oil over medium-high heat; add eggs and cook, stirring, until partially cooked but still runny. Return eggs to bowl. Wipe out wok with paper towels. Add 2 tablespoons oil to wok; heat.

Add shrimp, garlic and chilies. Stir-fry until shrimp turn pink, about 3 minutes. Remove shrimp mixture; set aside. Add remaining 1 or 2 tablespoons oil to wok; stir-fry rice, sugar, nam pla, if desired, and soy sauce until rice is heated through. Add tuna and peanuts; heat.

Return shrimp mixture and eggs to pan, chopping eggs into pieces with stir-fry spatula. Add basil and cilantro; toss gently to mix. Serve with lime wedges for garnish; squeeze juice on fried rice, if desired.

Makes 4 to 6 servings

Thai-Style Tuna Fried Rice

SCALLOPS WITH VEGETABLES

1 ounce dried mushrooms
2 tablespoons vegetable oil
2 yellow onions, cut into
   wedges and separated
3 stalks celery, diagonally cut
   into ½-inch pieces
8 ounces fresh green beans,
   trimmed and diagonally cut
   into 1-inch pieces
2 teaspoons minced fresh
   ginger
1 clove garlic, minced
1 cup water

2 tablespoons plus
   1½ teaspoons dry sherry
4 teaspoons soy sauce
4 teaspoons cornstarch
2 teaspoons instant chicken
   bouillon granules
1 pound fresh or thawed frozen
   sea scallops, cut into
   quarters
6 green onions, diagonally cut
   into thin slices
1 can (15 ounces) baby corn,
   drained

Place mushrooms in bowl and cover with hot water. Let stand 30 minutes. Drain and squeeze out excess water. Discard stems; thinly slice caps. Heat oil in wok or large skillet over high heat. Add yellow onions, celery, green beans, ginger and garlic; stir-fry 3 minutes. Combine water, sherry, soy sauce, cornstarch and bouillon granules in small bowl. Add to wok; cook and stir until sauce boils. Add scallops, mushrooms, green onions and baby corn. Cook and stir until scallops turn opaque, about 4 minutes.

Makes 4 to 6 servings

SPICY TOFU AND SHRIMP

1 block firm tofu
1 tablespoon vegetable oil
½ pound shrimp, shelled and
   deveined
4 tablespoons LEE KUM KEE®
   Oyster Flavored Sauce,
   divided

1 teaspoon LEE KUM KEE® Chili
   Garlic Sauce
1 tablespoon water
1 green onion, chopped
1 teaspoon LEE KUM KEE®
   Sesame Oil

Drain tofu and cut into ¾-inch cubes. Set aside. Heat skillet or wok until hot; add vegetable oil and stir-fry shrimp with 2 tablespoons Lee Kum Kee® Oyster Flavored Sauce for about 1 minute or until shrimp just begin to turn opaque. Add tofu, remaining 2 tablespoons Lee Kum Kee® Oyster Flavored Sauce, the Lee Kum Kee® Chili Garlic Sauce and water. Gently stir, bringing sauce to a slow simmer. Sprinkle with chopped green onion and Lee Kum Kee® Sesame Oil; serve. *Makes about 4 servings*

Scallops with Vegetables

FRAGRANT BRAISED OYSTERS

- 1 jar (10 or 12 ounces) shucked oysters, drained
- 2 cups plus 1 tablespoon water, divided
- ½ teaspoon salt
- ¼ cup chicken broth
- 1 tablespoon dry sherry
- 1 tablespoon oyster sauce
- 1 teaspoon cornstarch
- ¼ teaspoon sugar
- 2 tablespoons vegetable oil, divided
- 3 slices (about ½-inch each) pared fresh ginger, cut into thin slivers
- ½ small yellow onion, cut into wedges and separated
- 3 green onions, cut into 2-inch pieces

If oysters are large, cut into bite-size pieces. In 2-quart saucepan, bring 2 cups water and salt to a boil. Add oysters. Turn off heat and let stand 30 seconds. Drain, rinse under cold running water and drain again. Combine chicken broth, sherry, oyster sauce, remaining 1 tablespoon water, the cornstarch and sugar in small bowl; mix well. Heat 1 tablespoon oil in wok or large skillet over high heat. Add ginger and yellow onion; stir-fry 1 minute. Add green onions; stir-fry 30 seconds. Remove and set aside. Heat remaining 1 tablespoon oil in wok. Add blanched oysters and stir-fry 2 minutes. Return ginger and onions to wok. Stir cornstarch mixture and add to wok. Cook and stir until sauce boils and thickens.

Makes 2 to 3 servings

Fragrant Braised Oysters

Lemon-Garlic Shrimp

LEMON–GARLIC SHRIMP

1 package (6.2 ounces) RICE-A-RONI® With ¹/₃ Less Salt Broccoli Au Gratin
1 tablespoon margarine or butter
1 pound raw medium shrimp, shelled, deveined or large scallops, halved
1 medium red or green bell pepper, cut into short thin strips

2 cloves garlic, minced
¹/₂ teaspoon Italian seasoning
¹/₂ cup reduced-sodium or regular chicken broth
1 tablespoon lemon juice
1 tablespoon cornstarch
3 medium green onions, cut into ¹/₂-inch pieces
1 teaspoon grated lemon peel, divided

1. Prepare Rice-A-Roni® Mix as package directs.

2. While Rice-A-Roni® is simmering, heat margarine in second large skillet or wok over medium-high heat. Add shrimp, bell pepper, garlic and Italian seasoning. Stir-fry 3 to 4 minutes or until seafood is opaque.

3. Combine chicken broth, lemon juice and cornstarch, mixing until smooth. Add broth mixture and onions to skillet. Stir-fry 2 to 3 minutes or until sauce thickens.

4. Stir ¹/₂ teaspoon lemon peel into rice. Serve rice topped with shrimp mixture; sprinkle with remaining ¹/₂ teaspoon lemon peel.

Makes 4 servings

SEAFOOD COMBINATION

Fried Noodles (recipe
follows)
4 tablespoons vegetable oil,
divided
8 green onions, diagonally cut
into thin slices
3 stalks celery, diagonally cut
into thin slices
1 can (8 ounces) water
chestnuts, drained and cut
into halves
1 can (8 ounces) bamboo
shoots, thinly sliced
8 ounces fresh or thawed
frozen sea scallops, cut into
quarters

8 ounces fresh or thawed
frozen shrimp, shelled and
deveined
8 ounces fresh or thawed
frozen fish fillets, skinned
and cut into 1½-inch-
square pieces
8 ounces cleaned, ready-to-
cook squid (optional)
½ cup water
1 tablespoon soy sauce
2 teaspoons dry sherry
2 teaspoons cornstarch
1 teaspoon instant chicken
bouillon granules

Prepare Fried Noodles; set aside. Heat 2 tablespoons oil in wok or large
skillet over high heat. Add onions, celery, water chestnuts and bamboo
shoots; stir-fry until crisp-tender, about 2 minutes. Remove and set aside.

Heat remaining 2 tablespoons oil in wok over high heat. Add scallops,
shrimp, fish pieces and squid; stir-fry until all seafood turns opaque and is
cooked through, about 3 minutes. Combine water, soy sauce, sherry,
cornstarch and bouillon granules in small bowl. Add to wok. Cook and stir
until liquid boils. Return vegetables to wok; cook and stir 2 minutes more.
Serve with Fried Noodles.

Makes 6 servings

FRIED NOODLES

8 ounces Chinese-style thin egg
noodles

Vegetable oil for frying

Cook noodles according to package directions until tender but still firm,
2 to 3 minutes. Drain; rinse under cold running water and drain again.
Place several layers of paper towels over cookie sheets or jelly-roll pans.
Spread noodles over paper towels and let dry 2 to 3 hours. Heat oil in wok
or large skillet over medium-high heat to 375°F. Using tongs or slotted
spoon, lower a small portion of noodles into hot oil. Cook until golden,
about 30 seconds. Drain on paper towels. Repeat with remaining noodles.

Garlic Shrimp with Wilted Spinach

GARLIC SHRIMP WITH WILTED SPINACH

2 teaspoons olive or vegetable oil

¼ cup diagonally sliced green onions

2 tablespoons sherry or dry white wine (optional)

1 envelope LIPTON® Recipe Secrets® Savory Herb with Garlic Soup Mix*

1 cup water

1 pound uncooked medium shrimp, peeled and deveined

1 large tomato, diced

2 cups fresh trimmed spinach leaves (about 4 ounces)

¼ cup chopped unsalted cashews (optional)

In 12-inch skillet, heat oil over medium heat and cook green onions, stirring occasionally, 2 minutes or until slightly soft. Add sherry and bring to a boil over high heat, stirring frequently. Stir in Savory Herb with Garlic Soup Mix blended with water. Bring to a boil over high heat. Reduce heat to low and simmer 2 minutes or until sauce is thickened. Stir in shrimp, tomato, spinach and cashews. Simmer, stirring occasionally, 2 minutes or until shrimp turn pink. *Makes about 4 servings*

*Also terrific with Lipton® Recipe Secrets® Golden Herb with Lemon or Golden Onion Soup Mix.

Great Tasting Stir-Fries and More   335

HALIBUT WITH CILANTRO AND LIME

1 pound halibut, tuna or
    swordfish steaks
2 tablespoons fresh lime juice
¼ cup reduced-sodium soy
    sauce
1 teaspoon cornstarch
½ teaspoon minced fresh ginger

½ teaspoon vegetable oil
½ cup slivered red or yellow
    onion
2 cloves garlic, minced
¼ cup coarsely chopped
    cilantro
Lime wedges for garnish

Cut halibut into 1-inch pieces; sprinkle with lime juice. Blend soy sauce into cornstarch in cup until smooth. Stir in ginger. Heat oil in wok or large nonstick skillet over medium heat. Add onion and garlic; stir-fry 2 minutes. Add halibut; stir-fry 2 minutes or until halibut is opaque. Stir soy sauce mixture; add to wok. Stir-fry 30 seconds or until sauce boils and thickens. Sprinkle with cilantro. Garnish, if desired.   *Makes 4 servings*

TASTY THAI SHRIMP & SESAME NOODLES

1 pound medium shrimp,
    shelled and deveined
1 (8-ounce) bottle NEWMAN'S
    OWN® Light Italian
    Dressing, divided
2 tablespoons chunky peanut
    butter
1 tablespoon soy sauce
1 tablespoon honey
1 teaspoon grated peeled
    gingerroot

½ teaspoon crushed red pepper
8 ounces capellini or angel hair
    pasta, uncooked
2 tablespoons vegetable oil
1 tablespoon Oriental sesame
    oil
1 medium carrot, peeled and
    shredded
1 cup chopped green onions
¼ cup chopped fresh cilantro
    for garnish

In medium bowl, combine shrimp with ⅓ cup Newman's Own® Light Italian Dressing. Cover and refrigerate 1 hour. In small bowl, with wire whisk or fork, mix peanut butter, soy sauce, honey, ginger, crushed red pepper and remaining dressing; set aside. Prepare capellini as label directs; drain.

Meanwhile, in 4-quart saucepan over high heat, heat vegetable and sesame oils until very hot. Add carrot and cook 1 minute. Drain shrimp; discard dressing. Add shrimp and green onions to carrot and cook, stirring constantly, approximately 3 minutes or until shrimp turn opaque. In large bowl, toss hot capellini with peanut butter and shrimp mixtures. Sprinkle with chopped cilantro, if desired.   *Makes 4 servings*

Halibut with Cilantro and Lime

VEGETABLES & MORE

MOO SHU VEGETABLES

½ package dried shiitake
    mushrooms (6 to
    7 mushrooms)
2 tablespoons peanut or
    vegetable oil
2 cloves garlic, minced
2 cups shredded napa cabbage,
    shredded green cabbage,
    preshredded cabbage or
    coleslaw mix
1 red bell pepper, cut into
    short, thin strips

1 cup fresh or rinsed and
    drained canned bean
    sprouts
2 large green onions, cut into
    short, thin strips
¼ cup hoisin sauce
⅓ cup plum sauce
8 (6- to 7-inch) flour tortillas,
    warmed

Place mushrooms in small bowl; cover with warm water. Soak 20 minutes to soften. Drain, squeezing out excess water. Discard mushroom stems; slice caps. Heat wok or large skillet over medium-high heat. Add oil; heat until hot. Add garlic; stir-fry 30 seconds. Stir in cabbage, mushrooms and bell pepper; stir-fry 3 minutes. Add bean sprouts and onions; stir-fry 2 minutes. Add hoisin sauce; stir-fry 30 seconds or until mixture is hot.

Spread about 2 teaspoons plum sauce down center of each tortilla. Spoon heaping ¼ cup vegetable mixture over sauce. Fold bottom of tortilla up over filling and fold sides over filling to form bundle. *Makes 8 servings*

Moo Shu Vegetables

BROCCOLI & RED PEPPER SAUTÉ

2 tablespoons olive or
   vegetable oil
4 cups small broccoli florets
1 large red bell pepper, cut into
   thin strips
1 medium onion, sliced
1 clove garlic, finely chopped

1 envelope LIPTON® Recipe
   Secrets® Golden Herb with
   Lemon Soup Mix*
1 cup water
¼ cup sliced almonds, toasted
   (optional)

In 12-inch skillet, heat oil over medium heat and cook broccoli, bell pepper, onion and garlic 5 minutes or until onion is tender, stirring occasionally. Combine Golden Herb with Lemon Soup Mix with water; add to vegetable mixture. Simmer covered 5 minutes or until broccoli is tender. Sprinkle with almonds. *Makes about 6 servings*

*Also terrific with Lipton® Recipe Secrets® Savory Herb with Garlic Soup Mix.

BEAN CURD WITH OYSTER SAUCE

2 tablespoons vegetable oil,
   divided
8 ounces tofu, cut into ½-inch
   cubes
½ cup water
2 tablespoons oyster sauce
4 teaspoons dry sherry
4 teaspoons soy sauce
1 tablespoon cornstarch

4 ounces fresh mushrooms,
   sliced
6 green onions, cut into 1-inch
   pieces
3 stalks celery, diagonally cut
   into ½-inch pieces
1 red or green bell pepper, cut
   into ½-inch chunks

Heat 1 tablespoon oil in wok or large skillet over high heat. Add tofu and stir-fry until light brown, about 3 minutes. Remove and set aside. Combine water, oyster sauce, sherry, soy sauce and cornstarch in small bowl. Heat remaining 1 tablespoon oil in wok over high heat. Add remaining ingredients; stir-fry 1 minute. Return tofu to wok; toss lightly to combine. Add oyster sauce mixture to wok. Cook and stir until liquid boils; cook 1 minute more. *Makes 4 servings*

Broccoli & Red Pepper Sauté

CHINESE VEGETABLES

1 pound fresh broccoli
1½ teaspoons vegetable oil
2 medium yellow onions, cut
   into wedges and separated
2 cloves garlic, minced
4½ teaspoons minced fresh
   ginger
8 ounces fresh spinach,
   coarsely chopped
4 stalks celery, diagonally cut
   into ½-inch pieces

8 ounces fresh snow peas *or*
   1 package (6 ounces)
   thawed frozen snow peas,
   trimmed and strings
   removed
4 medium carrots, sliced
8 green onions, diagonally cut
   into thin slices
¾ cup reduced-sodium chicken
   broth
1 tablespoon reduced-sodium
   soy sauce

Cut broccoli tops into florets. Cut stalks into 2×¼-inch strips. Heat oil in wok or large nonstick skillet over high heat. Add broccoli stalks, yellow onions, garlic and ginger; stir-fry 1 minute. Add broccoli florets, spinach, celery, snow peas, carrots and green onions; toss gently. Add broth and soy sauce to vegetables; toss to coat. Bring to a boil; cover and cook 2 to 3 minutes until vegetables are crisp-tender. *Makes 4 servings*

DINER SKILLET POTATOES

1½ pounds all-purpose potatoes,
   peeled and diced
2 large red or green bell
   peppers, chopped

1 envelope LIPTON® Recipe
   Secrets® Onion Soup Mix*
2 tablespoons olive or
   vegetable oil

In large bowl, combine potatoes, bell peppers and Onion Soup Mix until evenly coated.

In 12-inch nonstick skillet, heat oil over medium heat and cook potato mixture, covered, stirring occasionally, 12 minutes. Remove cover and continue cooking, stirring occasionally, 10 minutes or until potatoes are tender. *Makes about 6 servings*

*Also terrific with Lipton® Recipe Secrets® Fiesta Herb with Red Pepper Soup Mix.

Chinese Vegetables

ALMOND BROCCOLI STIR–FRY

1 bunch (about 1 pound)
   broccoli
¾ cup BLUE DIAMOND®
   Chopped Natural Almonds
3 tablespoons vegetable oil
3 cloves garlic, thinly sliced

2 tablespoons soy sauce
1 tablespoon sugar
1 teaspoon grated fresh ginger
   or ¼ teaspoon ground
   ginger
1 teaspoon lemon juice

Cut broccoli into florets. Trim and peel stalks; cut on diagonal into thin slices and reserve. In large skillet or wok cook and stir almonds in oil 1 minute. Add broccoli and stir-fry until barely tender, about 2 minutes. Add garlic and stir-fry until just tender, about 1 minute. Stir in soy sauce, sugar and ginger. Continue stir-frying until sugar dissolves, about 1 minute. Add lemon juice.

Makes 4 servings

STIR–FRY RICE AND VEGETABLES

3 tablespoons vegetable oil
1 bunch green onions, white
   and green parts chopped
   separately
1 medium sweet potato,
   peeled, halved lengthwise
   and thinly sliced
1 small green bell pepper, cut
   into thin strips

2 carrots, thinly sliced
1 zucchini, thinly sliced
2 cups cooked brown rice
1 cup bean sprouts
1 cup fresh mushrooms, sliced
¼ cup honey
¼ cup soy sauce

Heat oil in wok or large, heavy skillet over medium-high heat. Stir-fry white parts of onions, sweet potato, bell pepper, carrots and zucchini until barely tender. Add rice, sprouts, mushrooms and green onion tops. Cook quickly until heated through. If necessary, add more oil. Combine honey and soy sauce in cup. Pour over mixture and stir. Serve immediately.

Makes 6 to 8 servings

Favorite recipe from **National Honey Board**

SPICY ORIENTAL GREEN BEANS

1 pound whole green beans, trimmed

2 tablespoons chopped green onions

2 tablespoons dry sherry or chicken broth

4½ teaspoons reduced-sodium soy sauce

1 teaspoon chili sauce with garlic

1 teaspoon Oriental sesame oil

1 clove garlic, minced
Edible flowers such as pansies, violets or nasturtiums for garnish

Fill Dutch oven with water to depth of ½ inch. Bring water to a boil. Place green beans in steamer basket in Dutch oven. Cover and steam beans about 5 minutes or just until crisp-tender. Drain and set aside.

Combine green onions, sherry, soy sauce, chili sauce, sesame oil and garlic in small bowl. Spray large skillet with nonstick cooking spray; heat over medium heat. Add green beans; pour soy sauce mixture over beans. Toss well to coat. Cook 3 to 5 minutes, stirring constantly until heated through. Garnish, if desired. *Makes 4 servings*

Spicy Oriental Green Beans

BBQ
AND
OUTDOOR
GRILLING

Contents

Burgers, Ribs & Kabobs

BUFFALO TURKEY KABOBS

⅔ cup HELLMANN'S® or
  BEST FOODS® Real or
  Light Mayonnaise or Low
  Fat Mayonnaise
  Dressing, divided
1 teaspoon hot pepper sauce
1½ pounds boneless turkey
  breast, cut into 1-inch
  cubes
2 red bell peppers *or* 1 red
  and 1 yellow bell pepper,
  cut into 1-inch squares

2 medium onions, cut into
  wedges
¼ cup (1 ounce) crumbled
  blue cheese
2 tablespoons milk
1 medium stalk celery,
  minced
1 medium carrot, minced

In medium bowl combine ⅓ cup of the mayonnaise and hot pepper sauce. Stir in turkey. Let stand at room temperature 20 minutes. On 6 skewers, alternately thread turkey, peppers and onions. Grill or broil 5 inches from heat, brushing with remaining mayonnaise mixture and turning frequently, 12 to 15 minutes. Meanwhile, in small bowl blend remaining ⅓ cup mayonnaise with the blue cheese and milk. Stir in celery and carrot. Serve with kabobs. *Makes 6 servings*

Note: For best results, use Real Mayonnaise. If using Light Mayonnaise or Low Fat Mayonnaise Dressing, use sauce the same day.

Buffalo Turkey Kabobs

MEXICALI BURGERS

Guacamole (recipe follows)
1 pound ground chuck
⅓ cup purchased salsa or
   picante sauce
⅓ cup crushed tortilla chips
3 tablespoons finely chopped
   cilantro
2 tablespoons finely chopped
   onion
1 teaspoon ground cumin
4 slices Monterey Jack or
   Cheddar cheese
4 Kaiser rolls or hamburger
   buns, split
Lettuce leaves (optional)
Sliced tomatoes (optional)

1. Prepare barbecue grill with rectangular metal or foil drip pan. Bank briquets on either side of drip pan for indirect cooking.

2. Prepare Guacamole.

3. Combine beef, salsa, tortilla chips, cilantro, onion and cumin in medium bowl. Mix lightly but thoroughly. Shape mixture into 4 (½-inch-thick) burgers, each 4 inches in diameter.

4. Place burgers on grid. Grill burgers, on covered grill, over medium coals 8 to 10 minutes for medium or until desired doneness is reached, turning halfway through grilling time.

5. Place 1 slice cheese on each burger to melt during last 1 to 2 minutes of grilling. If desired, place rolls, cut-side down, on grid to toast lightly during last 1 to 2 minutes of grilling. Place burgers between rolls; top burgers with Guacamole. Serve with lettuce and tomatoes, if desired.

Makes 4 servings

Guacamole

1 ripe avocado
1 tablespoon purchased salsa
   or picante sauce
1 teaspoon fresh lime or lemon
   juice
¼ teaspoon garlic salt

1. Cut avocado lengthwise in half. Remove pit. Scoop avocado flesh out of shells with large spoon; place in medium bowl. Mash roughly with fork or wooden spoon, leaving avocado slightly chunky.

2. Stir in salsa, lime juice and garlic salt. Let stand at room temperature while grilling burgers. Cover and refrigerate if preparing in advance. Bring to room temperature before serving.

Makes about ½ cup

Mexicali Burger

GRILLED PORK AND POTATOES VESUVIO

- 1 **center-cut boneless pork loin roast (1½ pounds), well trimmed**
- 4 **cloves garlic, divided**
- ½ **cup dry white wine**
- 2 **tablespoons olive oil**
- 1½ **to 2 pounds small red potatoes (about 1½ inches in diameter), scrubbed**
- 6 **metal skewers (12 inches long)**
- 6 **lemon wedges
  Salt (optional)
  Pepper (optional)**
- ¼ **cup chopped fresh Italian or curly leaf parsley**
- 1 **teaspoon finely grated lemon peel**

1. Cut pork into 1-inch cubes. Place pork in large resealable plastic food storage bag. Mince 3 cloves garlic; place in small bowl. Add wine and oil; mix well. Pour over pork.

2. Place potatoes in single layer in microwave-safe dish. Pierce each potato with tip of sharp knife. Microwave at HIGH (100% power) 6 to 7 minutes or until almost tender when pierced with fork.

(Or, place potatoes in large saucepan. Cover with cold water. Bring to a boil over high heat. Simmer about 12 minutes or until almost tender when pierced with fork.) Immediately rinse with cold water; drain. Add to pork mixture in bag. Seal bag tightly; turn to coat. Marinate in refrigerator at least 2 hours or up to 8 hours, turning occasionally.

3. Prepare barbecue grill.

4. Meanwhile, drain pork mixture; discard marinade. Alternately thread about 3 pork cubes and 2 potatoes onto each skewer. Place 1 lemon wedge on end of each skewer. Sprinkle salt and pepper over pork and potatoes.

5. Place skewers on grid. Grill skewers, on covered grill, over medium coals 14 to 16 minutes or until pork is juicy and barely pink in center and potatoes are tender, turning halfway through grilling time.

6. Remove skewers from grill. Mince remaining garlic. Place in small bowl. Add parsley and lemon peel; mix well. Sprinkle parsley mixture over pork and potatoes. Squeeze lemon wedges over pork and potatoes.

Makes 6 servings

Grilled Pork and Potatoes Vesuvio

BURGERS CANADIAN

½ cup mayonnaise
⅓ cup A.1.® Steak Sauce
2 tablespoons prepared
   horseradish
1 pound ground beef
2 ounces Cheddar cheese,
   sliced
4 slices Canadian bacon
   (4 ounces)
4 sesame sandwich rolls, split
   and lightly toasted
4 curly lettuce leaves

In small bowl, combine mayonnaise, steak sauce and horseradish. Cover; chill until serving time.

Shape ground beef into 4 patties. Grill burgers over medium heat for 4 minutes on each side or to desired doneness. When almost done, top with cheese; grill until cheese melts. Grill Canadian bacon over medium heat for 1 minute on each side or until heated through. Spread 2 tablespoons sauce on each roll bottom; top with burger, warm Canadian bacon slice, lettuce leaf and roll top. Serve immediately with remaining sauce for dipping.

Makes 4 servings

SEASONED BABY BACK RIBS

1 tablespoon paprika
1½ teaspoons garlic salt
1 teaspoon celery salt
½ teaspoon black pepper
¼ teaspoon ground red pepper
4 pounds pork baby back ribs,
   cut into 3- to 4-rib
   portions, well trimmed
   Barbecue Sauce (page 355)
   Rib rack (optional)

1. Preheat oven to 350°F.

2. For seasoning rub, combine paprika, garlic salt, celery salt, black pepper and ground red pepper in small bowl. Rub over all surfaces of ribs with fingers.

3. Place ribs in foil-lined shallow roasting pan. Bake 30 minutes.

4. Meanwhile, prepare barbecue grill.

5. While coals are heating, prepare Barbecue Sauce.

6. Transfer ribs to rib rack set on grid. Or, place ribs directly on grid. Grill ribs, on covered grill, over medium coals 10 minutes.

7. Remove ribs from rib rack with tongs; brush half the Barbecue Sauce evenly over both sides of ribs. Return ribs to rib rack. Continue to grill, covered, 10 minutes or until ribs are tender and browned. Serve with reserved sauce. Garnish, if desired.

Makes 6 servings

Seasoned Baby Back Ribs

Barbecue Sauce

½ cup ketchup

⅓ cup packed light brown sugar

1 tablespoon cider vinegar

2 teaspoons Worcestershire
    sauce

2 teaspoons soy sauce

Combine ketchup, brown sugar, vinegar, Worcestershire sauce and soy sauce in glass measuring cup or small bowl. Reserve half of sauce for serving.

Makes about ⅔ cup

SWISS BURGERS

1 package (about 1¼ pounds)
   PERDUE® fresh ground
   turkey, ground turkey
   breast meat or ground
   chicken
½ cup thinly sliced scallions
1 teaspoon Worcestershire
   sauce
4 ounces fresh, white
   mushrooms, thinly sliced
2 teaspoons olive oil
½ teaspoon salt
   Ground pepper to taste
4 to 5 pieces Swiss cheese
   Dijon mustard
4 to 5 Kaiser rolls
6 to 8 tablespoons sour cream

Prepare outdoor grill or preheat broiler. In large bowl, combine ground turkey, scallions and Worcestershire sauce. Shape mixture into 4 or 5 patties.

To grill: When coals are medium-hot, place burgers on hottest area of cooking surface of grill; cook 1 to 2 minutes on each side to brown. Move burgers to edge of grill; cook 4 to 6 minutes longer on each side until thoroughly cooked, juices run clear and burgers spring back to the touch.

To broil: Place burgers on rack in broiling pan 4 inches from heat source. Broil 5 to 6 minutes on each side until burgers are thoroughly cooked and spring back to the touch.

Swiss Burger

THE OTHER BURGER

1 pound ground pork
 (80% lean)
1 teaspoon black pepper
¼ teaspoon salt
 Hamburger buns (optional)

Prepare grill. Gently mix together ground pork, pepper and salt; shape into 4 burgers, each about ¾-inch thick. Place burgers on grid. Grill, on covered grill, over medium-hot coals 5 minutes on each side or until barely pink in center. Serve on hamburger buns, if desired.   *Makes 4 servings*

Eastern Burger: Add 2 teaspoons soy sauce, 2 tablespoons dry sherry and 1 tablespoon grated ginger root to pork mixture; grill as directed.

Veggie Burger: Add 3 drops hot pepper sauce, 1 grated carrot and 3 tablespoons chopped parsley to pork mixture; grill as directed.

South-of-the-Border Burger: Add ¼ teaspoon *each* ground cumin, dried oregano leaves, seasoned salt and crushed red pepper to pork mixture; grill as directed.

Prep time: 10 minutes
Cooking time: 10 minutes

Favorite recipe from **National Pork Producers Council**

HONEY DIJON BARBECUE RIBETTES

2½ pounds baby back pork
 spareribs, split
2 cloves garlic, minced
1 tablespoon vegetable oil
⅔ cup chili sauce
⅓ cup GREY POUPON® Dijon
 Mustard
¼ cup honey
6 thin lemon slices
½ teaspoon liquid hot pepper
 seasoning

Place ribs in large heavy pot; fill pot with water to cover ribs. Over high heat, heat to a boil; reduce heat. Cover; simmer for 30 to 40 minutes or until ribs are tender. Drain.

Meanwhile, in medium saucepan, over low heat, cook garlic in oil until tender. Stir in chili sauce, mustard, honey, lemon slices and hot pepper seasoning. Cook over medium heat until heated through, about 2 to 3 minutes. Brush ribs with prepared sauce. Grill over medium heat for 15 to 20 minutes or until done, turning and brushing often with remaining sauce. Slice into individual pieces to serve; garnish as desired. Serve hot.   *Makes 8 servings*

COUNTRY KIELBASA KABOBS

½ cup GREY POUPON®
   COUNTRY DIJON®
   Mustard
½ cup apricot preserves
⅓ cup minced green onions
1 pound kielbasa, cut into
   1-inch pieces
1 large apple, cored and cut
   into wedges
½ cup frozen pearl onions,
   thawed
6 small red skin potatoes,
   parboiled and cut into
   halves
3 cups shredded red and green
   cabbage, steamed

Soak 6 (10-inch) wooden skewers in water for 30 minutes. In small bowl, blend mustard, preserves and green onions; set aside ¼ cup mixture.

Alternately thread kielbasa, apple, pearl onions and potatoes on skewers. Grill or broil kabobs for 12 to 15 minutes or until done, turning and brushing with remaining mustard mixture. Heat reserved mustard mixture and toss with steamed cabbage. Serve hot with kabobs. Garnish as desired.
   Makes 6 servings

BASIC BEEFY BURGERS

1 pound lean ground beef
1 cup CORN CHEX® brand
   cereal, crushed to ⅓ cup
1 egg, slightly beaten
2 tablespoons ketchup
½ teaspoon onion powder
⅛ teaspoon garlic powder

1. Combine beef, cereal, egg, ketchup, onion powder and garlic powder. Shape into 5 patties.

2. Grill 10 to 12 minutes or until no longer pink in center, turning once. Serve on buns with cheese slices, tomato, lettuce, pickles, additional ketchup and mustard, if desired.   *Makes 5 servings*

Cheesy Pizza Burgers: Use 3 tablespoons pizza sauce in place of ketchup. Add ⅔ cup shredded mozzarella cheese and ¼ teaspoon dried oregano leaves to beef mixture. Serve on toasted English muffins topped with additional pizza sauce, if desired.

Tasty Taco Burgers: Use 3 tablespoons taco sauce or salsa in place of ketchup. Add ½ teaspoon chili powder and 2 to 3 dashes ground cumin, if desired, to beef mixture. Serve on buns with sliced Monterey Jack or cheddar cheese, shredded lettuce, chopped tomato and additional taco sauce, if desired.

Country Kielbasa Kabobs

PORK CHOPS WITH GRILLED PINEAPPLE

1 small pineapple, crown,
    stem and rind removed
    (optional)
½ cup WISH-BONE® Italian
    Dressing
¼ cup pineapple juice

½ cup firmly packed brown
    sugar
3 tablespoons soy sauce
6 pork chops, about 1 inch
    thick (about 2 pounds)

Cut pineapple into 6 crosswise slices; set aside.

In large, shallow nonaluminium baking dish or plastic bag, combine Italian dressing, pineapple juice, sugar and soy sauce. Add chops; turn to coat. Cover, or close bag, and marinate in refrigerator, turning occasionally, 3 to 24 hours.

Remove chops, reserving marinade. Bring reserved marinade to a boil. Grill or broil chops, basting frequently with reserved marinade, until chops are done. While chops are cooking, grill or broil pineapple slices, brushing with boiled marinade, until golden and heated through. If desired, bring remaining reserved marinade to a boil and serve over chops.

Makes 6 servings

Nutritional Information Per Serving: Calories 327, Fat 12 g, Sodium 958 mg,
Cholesterol 59 mg

Pork Chop With Grilled Pineapple

PORK ROAST WITH HONEY–MUSTARD GLAZE

Wood chunks or chips for smoking
⅓ **cup honey**
¼ **cup whole-seed or coarse-grind prepared mustard**
Grated peel and juice of 1 medium orange
1 **teaspoon minced fresh ginger** *or* ¼ **teaspoon ground ginger**
½ **teaspoon salt**
⅛ **teaspoon ground red pepper**
Apple juice at room temperature
1 **boneless pork loin roast (3½ to 4 pounds)**

Soak about 4 wood chunks or several handfuls of wood chips in water; drain. Mix honey, mustard, grated orange peel and juice, ginger, salt and red pepper in small bowl.

Arrange medium-low KINGSFORD® Briquets on each side of a rectangular metal or foil drip pan. Pour in apple juice to fill pan half full. Add soaked wood (all the chunks; part of the chips) to the fire.

Oil hot grid to help prevent sticking. Place pork on grid directly above drip pan. Grill pork, on a covered grill, 20 to 30 minutes per pound until meat thermometer inserted in thickest part registers 155°F. (If your grill has a thermometer, maintain a cooking temperature of about 300°F.) Add a few more briquets to both sides of fire every 45 minutes to 1 hour, or as necessary, to maintain a constant temperature. Add more soaked wood chips every 30 minutes. Brush meat with honey-mustard mixture twice during the last 40 minutes of cooking. Let pork stand 10 minutes before slicing to allow the internal temperature to rise to 160°F. Slice and serve with sauce made from pan drippings (directions follow), if desired.

Makes 6 to 8 servings

To make a sauce from pan drippings: Taste the liquid and drippings left in the drip pan. If the drippings have a mild smoky flavor they will make a nice sauce. (If a strong-flavored wood, such as hickory, or too many wood chips were used, the drippings may be overwhelmingly smoky.) Remove excess fat from drip pan with a bulb baster; discard. Measure liquid and drippings; place in a saucepan. For each cup of liquid, use 1 to 2 tablespoons cider vinegar and 2 teaspoons cornstarch mixed with a little cold water until smooth. Stir vinegar-cornstarch mixture into saucepan. Stirring constantly, bring to a boil over medium heat and boil 1 minute. Makes 6 to 8 servings.

ORIENTAL FLANK STEAK

½ cup WISH-BONE® Italian
    Dressing
2 tablespoons firmly packed
    brown sugar
2 tablespoons soy sauce
½ teaspoon ground ginger
    (optional)
1 (1- to 1½-pound) flank or top
    round steak

In large, shallow nonaluminum
baking dish or plastic bag,
combine all ingredients except
steak. Add steak; turn to coat.

Cover, or close bag, and marinate
in refrigerator, turning
occasionally, 3 to 24 hours.

Remove steak, reserving marinade.
Grill or broil steak, turning once,
until steak is done.

Meanwhile, in small saucepan,
bring reserved marinade to a boil
and continue boiling 1 minute.
Pour over steak.

Makes 6 servings

Also terrific with WISH-BONE®
Robusto Italian or Lite Italian
Dressing.

Nutritional Information Per Serving:
Calories 240, Fat 14 g, Sodium 800 mg,
Cholesterol 50 mg

Oriental Flank Steak

RANCH–STYLE FAJITAS

2 **pounds flank or skirt steak**
½ **cup vegetable oil**
⅓ **cup lime juice**
2 **packages (1 ounce each) HIDDEN VALLEY RANCH® Milk Recipe Original Ranch® Salad Dressing Mix**
1 **teaspoon ground cumin**
½ **teaspoon black pepper**
6 **flour tortillas**
   Lettuce
   Guacamole, prepared HIDDEN VALLEY RANCH® Salad Dressing and picante sauce for toppings

Place steak in large baking dish. In small bowl, whisk together oil, lime juice, salad dressing mix, cumin and pepper. Pour mixture over steak. Cover and refrigerate several hours or overnight.

Remove steak; place marinade in small saucepan. Bring to a boil. Grill steak over medium-hot coals 8 to 10 minutes or to desired doneness, turning once and basting with heated marinade during last 5 minutes of grilling. Remove steak and slice diagonally across grain into thin slices. Heat tortillas following package directions. Divide steak strips among tortillas; roll up to enclose. Serve with lettuce and desired toppings.   *Makes 6 servings*

Ranch-Style Fajitas

STEAK AND POTATO SALAD

Roasted Garlic Marinade/Dressing

¾ cup **CRISCO®** Savory
  Seasonings Roasted Garlic
  Flavor
¼ cup red wine vinegar
1 tablespoon dijon-style
  mustard
1 teaspoon salt
½ teaspoon freshly ground
  black pepper
½ teaspoon sugar

Salad

1½ pounds boneless sirloin steak
2 pounds small red potatoes,
  scrubbed
8 ounces fresh green beans
8 ounces white mushrooms
1 medium red bell pepper, cut
  into small strips
1 medium sweet onion, thinly
  sliced
1 cup cherry tomatoes, halved
¼ cup chopped parsley

• For Roasted Garlic Marinade/
Dressing, whisk together all
marinade/dressing ingredients
until well blended.

• Place steak in plastic bag with
resealable top and pour in ⅓ of
the marinade/dressing. Allow to
remain at room temperature for
30 minutes, then chill until ready
to cook.

• Place potatoes in large pot, cover
with cold water and bring to boil.
Cook for about 20 minutes or until
fork-tender. Drain, cool, and cut
into quarters. Toss with half of the
remaining marinade/dressing.

• Steam green beans for
approximately 7 minutes or until
crisp-tender. Refresh in ice water
and drain.

• Rinse, dry and thinly slice
mushrooms. Toss with
2 tablespoons of
marinade/dressing to coat.

• Remove steak from marinade and
discard marinade from plastic bag.
Grill over preheated grill or under
preheated broiler to medium
doneness. Allow to rest 5 minutes.
Cut across grain into thin strips.

• Toss together steak, potatoes,
beans, mushrooms, bell pepper
and onion. Garnish with tomato
halves and parsley.

Makes 6 to 8 servings

BRATS 'N' BEER

1 can or bottle (12 ounces)
    beer (not dark) or
    nonalcoholic beer
4 fresh bratwurst (about
    1 pound)
1 large sweet or Spanish onion,
    (about ½ pound), thinly
    sliced and separated into
    rings
1 tablespoon olive or vegetable
    oil
¼ teaspoon salt
¼ teaspoon pepper
4 hot dog rolls, preferably
    bakery-style or onion, split
    Coarse-grain or sweet-hot
    mustard (optional)
    Drained sauerkraut
    (optional)

1. Prepare barbecue grill for direct cooking.

2. Pour beer into heavy medium saucepan with ovenproof handle. (If not ovenproof, wrap heavy-duty foil around handle.) Set saucepan on one side of grid.

3. Pierce each bratwurst in several places with tip of sharp knife. Carefully add bratwurst to beer; simmer, on uncovered grill, over medium coals 15 minutes, turning once.*

4. Meanwhile, place onion rings on 18×14-inch sheet of heavy-duty foil. Drizzle with oil; sprinkle with salt and pepper. Wrap in foil; place on grid next to saucepan. Grill onions, on uncovered grill, 10 to 15 minutes or until onions are tender.

5. Transfer bratwurst with tongs to grid; remove saucepan using heavy-duty mitt. Discard beer. Grill bratwurst, on covered grill, 9 to 10 minutes or until browned and cooked through, turning halfway through grilling time. If desired, place rolls, cut-side down, on grid to toast lightly during last 1 to 2 minutes of grilling.

6. Place bratwurst in rolls. Open foil packet carefully. Top each bratwurst with onions. Serve with mustard and sauerkraut, if desired.
Makes 4 servings

*If desired, bratwurst may be simmered on rangetop. Pour beer into medium saucepan. Bring to a boil over medium-high heat. Carefully add bratwurst to beer. Reduce heat to low and simmer, uncovered, 15 minutes, turning once.

Brat 'n' Beer

TOURNEDOS WITH MUSHROOM WINE SAUCE DIJON

¼ cup chopped shallots
2 tablespoons
    FLEISCHMANN'S®
    Margarine
1 cup small mushrooms, halved
    (about 4 ounces)
¼ cup GREY POUPON® Dijon
    Mustard, divided
2 tablespoons A.1.® Steak
    Sauce
2 tablespoons Burgundy wine
1 tablespoon chopped parsley
4 slices bacon
4 (4-ounce) beef tenderloin
    steaks (tournedos), about
    1 inch thick
¼ teaspoon coarsely ground
    black pepper

In small saucepan, over medium heat, saute shallots in margarine until tender. Add mushrooms; saute 1 minute. Stir in 2 tablespoons mustard, steak sauce, wine and parsley; heat to a boil. Reduce heat and simmer for 5 minutes; keep warm.

Wrap bacon slice around edge of each steak; secure with toothpicks. Coat steaks with remaining mustard; sprinkle with pepper. Grill steaks over medium heat for 10 to 12 minutes or to desired doneness, turning occasionally. Remove toothpicks; serve steaks topped with warm mushroom sauce.   *Makes 4 servings*

BEEF TENDERLOIN WITH DIJON–CREAM SAUCE

2 tablespoons olive oil
3 tablespoons balsamic vinegar
1 beef tenderloin roast (about
    1½ to 2 pounds)
    Salt
1 tablespoon plus
    1½ teaspoons white
    peppercorns
1 tablespoon plus
    1½ teaspoons black
    peppercorns
3 tablespoons mustard seeds
    Dijon-Cream Sauce (page 369)

Combine oil and vinegar in a cup; rub onto beef. Season generously with salt. Let stand 15 minutes. Meanwhile, coarsely crush peppercorns and mustard seeds in blender or food processor or by hand with mortar and pestle. Roll beef in crushed mixture, pressing into surface to coat.

Oil hot grid to help prevent sticking. Grill beef, on a covered grill, over medium KINGSFORD® Briquets, 16 to 24 minutes (depending on size and thickness of beef) until meat thermometer inserted in center almost registers 150°F for medium-rare, turning halfway through cooking. (Cook until 160°F for medium or 170°F for well-done; add another 5 minutes for every 10°F.) Let stand 5 to 10 minutes before slicing. Slice and serve with a few spoonfuls of Dijon-Cream Sauce.
          Makes 6 servings

Beef Tenderloin with Dijon-Cream Sauce

Dijon-Cream Sauce

1 can (14½ ounces) beef broth
1 cup whipping cream
2 tablespoons butter, softened
1½ to 2 tablespoons Dijon
   mustard
1 to 1½ tablespoons balsamic
   vinegar*
Coarsely crushed black
   peppercorns and mustard
   seeds for garnish

*You may substitute 2 teaspoons
red wine vinegar plus 1 teaspoon
sugar for the balsamic vinegar.*

Bring beef broth and whipping
cream to a boil in a saucepan. Boil
gently until reduced to about
1 cup (sauce will be thick enough
to coat a spoon). Remove from
heat; stir in butter, a little at a
time, until butter is melted. Stir in
mustard and vinegar, adjusting
amounts to taste. Sprinkle with
peppercorns and mustard seeds.

Makes about 1 cup

SUMMER VEGETABLES & FISH BUNDLES

4 fish fillets (about 1 pound)
1 pound thinly sliced
    vegetables*
½ cup water

1 envelope LIPTON® Recipe
    Secrets® Savory Herb
    with Garlic or Golden
    Onion Soup Mix

Use any combination of the following, thinly sliced: mushrooms, zucchini, yellow squash or tomatoes.

On two 18×18-inch pieces heavy-duty aluminum foil, divide fish equally; top with vegetables. Blend water with savory herb with garlic soup mix. Evenly pour over fish. Wrap foil loosely around fillets and vegetables, sealing edges airtight with double fold. Grill or broil pouches, seam sides up, 15 minutes or until fish flakes easily with fork. Serve, if desired, over hot cooked rice.

Makes about 4 servings

Summer Vegetables &
Fish Bundle

TURKEY BURRITOS

1 tablespoon ground cumin
1 tablespoon chili powder
1½ teaspoons salt
1½ to 2 pounds turkey
    tenderloin, cut into
    ½-inch cubes
    Avocado-Corn Salsa (recipe
    follows, optional)
    Lime wedges
    Flour tortillas
    Sour cream (optional)
    Tomato slices for garnish

Combine cumin, chili powder and salt in cup. Place turkey cubes in a shallow glass dish or large heavy plastic bag; pour dry rub over turkey and coat turkey thoroughly. Let turkey stand while preparing Avocado-Corn Salsa. Thread turkey onto metal or bamboo skewers. (Soak bamboo skewers in water at least 20 minutes before using to prevent them from burning.)

Oil hot grid to help prevent sticking. Grill turkey, on a covered grill, over medium KINGSFORD® Briquets, about 6 minutes or until turkey is no longer pink in center, turning once. Remove skewers from grill; squeeze lime wedges over skewers. Warm flour tortillas in microwave oven, or brush each tortilla very lightly with water and grill 10 to 15 seconds per side. Top with Avocado-Corn Salsa and sour cream, if desired. Garnish with tomato slices.

Makes 6 servings

Avocado-Corn Salsa

2 small to medium-size ripe
    avocados, finely chopped
1 cup cooked fresh corn or
    thawed frozen corn
2 medium tomatoes, seeded
    and finely chopped
2 to 3 tablespoons chopped
    fresh cilantro
2 to 3 tablespoons lime juice
½ to 1 teaspoon minced hot
    green chili pepper
½ teaspoon salt

Gently stir together all ingredients in medium bowl; adjust flavors to taste. Cover and refrigerate until ready to serve.

Makes about 1½ cups

Tip: This recipe is great for casual get-togethers. Just prepare the fixings and let the guests make their own burritos.

Turkey Burritos

HEALTHY GRILLED CHICKEN SALAD

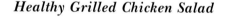

½ cup A.1.® Steak Sauce
½ cup prepared Italian salad
   dressing
1 teaspoon dried basil leaves
1 pound boneless chicken
   breast halves
6 cups mixed salad greens
¼ pound snow peas, blanched
   and halved
1 cup sliced mushrooms
1 medium red bell pepper,
   thinly sliced
   Grated Parmesan cheese
   (optional)

In small bowl, combine steak sauce, dressing and basil. Place chicken in glass dish; coat with ¼ cup steak sauce mixture. Cover; chill 1 hour, turning occasionally.

Arrange salad greens, peas, mushrooms and pepper slices on 6 individual salad plates; set aside.

In small saucepan, over medium heat, heat remaining steak sauce mixture; keep dressing warm.

Remove chicken from marinade; discard marinade. Grill over medium heat for 8 to 10 minutes or until no longer pink in center, turning occasionally. Thinly slice chicken; arrange over salad greens and drizzle warm dressing over prepared salads. Serve immediately; sprinkle with Parmesan cheese if desired. *Makes 6 servings*

Healthy Grilled Chicken Salad

GRILLED PINEAPPLE RICE SALAD WITH TUNA

Rice Salad

  3 cups cooked RICELAND® Extra Long Grain Rice
  2 teaspoons grated orange zest
  ½ cup orange juice
  3 tablespoons fresh lime juice
  1 garlic clove, minced
  1 cup cooked black beans
  1 cup whole kernel corn
  ½ cup diced red bell pepper
  ¼ cup chopped fresh cilantro
     Lettuce leaves

Grilled Tuna/Pineapple

  6 tuna steaks, 1 inch thick*
  ½ large pineapple, peeled, cored and quartered
  2 tablespoons oil
  3 tablespoons fresh lime juice
  2 garlic cloves, minced
  1 teaspoon Italian seasoning
     Fresh ground pepper

Boneless, skinless chicken breasts may be substituted.

In large bowl, combine rice, orange zest, orange juice, lime juice and garlic. Add remaining salad ingredients; toss lightly. Cover and hold at room temperature.

Prepare grill. Rinse tuna; pat dry. Prepare pineapple. Combine remaining ingredients; brush over tuna and pineapple. Grill tuna for approximately 5 minutes per side, basting with marinade. Place pineapple on outer edge of grill, turning and basting until lightly browned.

Chop grilled pineapple and toss into rice salad. Place lettuce leaves on serving plates. Spoon rice mixture on top and place tuna steak on center.

GRILLED SALMON WITH CUCUMBER SAUCE

  ¾ cup HELLMANN'S® or BEST FOODS® Real or Light Mayonnaise or Low Fat Mayonnaise Dressing
  ¼ cup snipped fresh dill *or* 1 tablespoon dried dill weed
  1 tablespoon lemon juice
  6 salmon steaks (4 ounces each), ¾ inch thick
  1 small cucumber, seeded and chopped
  ½ cup chopped radishes
     Lemon wedges

In medium bowl combine mayonnaise, dill and lemon juice; reserve ½ cup for sauce. Brush fish steaks with remaining mayonnaise mixture. Grill 6 inches from heat, turning and brushing frequently with mayonnaise mixture, 6 to 8 minutes or until fish is firm but moist. Stir cucumber and radishes into reserved mayonnaise mixture. Serve fish with cucumber sauce and lemon wedges.

Makes 6 servings

Blackened Sea Bass

BLACKENED SEA BASS

Hardwood charcoal*
2 teaspoons paprika
1 teaspoon garlic salt
1 teaspoon dried thyme leaves, crushed
¼ teaspoon ground white pepper
¼ teaspoon ground red pepper
¼ teaspoon ground black pepper
3 tablespoons butter or margarine
4 skinless sea bass or catfish fillets (4 to 6 ounces each)
Lemon halves
Fresh dill sprigs for garnish

Hardwood charcoal takes somewhat longer than regular charcoal to become hot, but results in a hotter fire than regular charcoal. A hot fire is necessary to seal in the juices and cook fish quickly. If hardwood charcoal is not available, scatter dry hardwood, or mesquite or hickory chunks over hot coals to create a hot fire.

1. Prepare barbecue grill using hardwood charcoal.

2. Meanwhile, combine paprika, garlic salt, thyme, and white, red and black peppers in small bowl; mix well. Set aside.

3. Melt butter in small saucepan over medium heat. Pour melted butter into pie plate or shallow bowl. Cool slightly.

4. Dip sea bass into melted butter, evenly coating both sides.

5. Sprinkle both sides of sea bass evenly with paprika mixture.

6. Place sea bass on grid. (Fire will flare up when sea bass is placed on grid, but will subside when grill is covered.) Grill sea bass, on covered grill, over hot coals 4 to 6 minutes or until sea bass is blackened and flakes easily when tested with fork, turning halfway through grilling time. Serve with lemon halves. Garnish, if desired.

Makes 4 servings

GRILLED SALMON SALAD

1 pound boneless salmon fillet
6 cups torn mixed greens
6 red-skinned new potatoes, cooked, sliced
1 cup fresh green bean pieces, cooked, chilled
1 cup seedless cucumber slices
2 plum tomatoes, sliced
Mustard Vinaigrette (recipe follows)

1. Grill salmon over medium-high coals until fish flakes easily with a fork, about 10 minutes.

2. Meanwhile, place greens on individual serving plates. Arrange potatoes, green beans, cucumber and tomatoes over greens. Break cooked salmon into chunks with fork; arrange on salads.

3. Serve with Mustard Vinaigrette.

Makes 4 servings

Variation: Substitute 1 pound boneless, skinless chicken breast halves for salmon. Grill 5 to 7 minutes on each side or until center is no longer pink; slice. Continue as directed.

Mustard Vinaigrette

½ cup olive oil
⅓ cup lemon juice
3 tablespoons PLOCHMAN'S® Mild Yellow or Dijon Mustard
1 tablespoon water
2 teaspoons minced fresh tarragon leaves *or* ¾ teaspoon dried tarragon leaves
½ teaspoon sugar
¼ teaspoon salt

Mix together all ingredients with a wire whisk.

Variation: Substitute 4 teaspoons minced fresh dill weed or 1 teaspoon dried dill weed for tarragon.

Preparation & Cooking Time: 40 minutes

MARINATED CHICKEN WINGS WITH RED HOT HONEY MUSTARD DIPPING SAUCE

12 chicken wings (about
     2½ pounds), split at joint,
     tips discarded
¼ cup soy sauce
3 tablespoons PLOCHMAN'S®
     Mild Yellow or Dijon
     Mustard
2 tablespoons frozen orange
     juice concentrate, thawed
2 tablespoons honey
1 teaspoon grated orange rind
     Red Hot Honey Mustard
     Dipping Sauce (recipe
     follows)

1. Place chicken wings in glass 12×8-inch baking dish. Combine soy sauce, mustard, orange juice, honey and orange rind. Pour over chicken wings; toss to coat. Marinate in refrigerator 2 hours or overnight, stirring occasionally.

2. Drain marinade from chicken, reserving marinade. Arrange chicken wings on greased grid of grill. Grill over medium coals 15 minutes on each side, basting with reserved marinade halfway through cooking time. Discard any unused marinade. Serve with Hot Honey Mustard Dipping Sauce.
     Makes 8 appetizer servings

Prep & Cook Time: 45 minutes
Marinating Time: 2 hours

RED HOT HONEY MUSTARD DIPPING SAUCE

⅓ cup honey
3 tablespoons PLOCHMAN'S®
     Mild Yellow or Dijon
     Mustard
1 to 2 teaspoons hot pepper
     sauce

Mix together all ingredients.

SHANGHAI FISH PACKETS

4 orange roughy or tilefish
     fillets (4 to 6 ounces each)
¼ cup mirin* or Rhine wine
3 tablespoons soy sauce
1 tablespoon sesame oil
1½ teaspoons grated fresh
     gingerroot
¼ teaspoon crushed red pepper
1 package (10 ounces) fresh
     spinach leaves
1 tablespoon vegetable oil
1 clove garlic, minced

Mirin is a Japanese sweet wine available in Japanese markets and the gourmet section of large supermarkets.

1. Prepare barbecue grill.

2. Place orange roughy in single layer in large shallow dish. Combine mirin, soy sauce, sesame oil, ginger and crushed red pepper in small bowl; pour over orange roughy. Cover; marinate in refrigerator while preparing spinach.

3. Wash spinach leaves in cold water; remove and discard stems. Pat leaves dry with paper towels.

4. Heat vegetable oil in large skillet over medium heat. Add garlic; cook and stir 1 minute. Add spinach; cook and stir until wilted, about 3 minutes.

5. Place spinach mixture in center of each of 4 (12-inch) squares of heavy-duty foil. Remove orange roughy from marinade; reserve marinade. Place 1 orange roughy fillet over each mound of spinach. Drizzle reserved marinade evenly over orange roughy. Wrap in foil.

6. Place packets on grid. Grill packets, on covered grill, over medium coals 15 to 18 minutes or until orange roughy flakes easily when tested with fork.

Makes 4 servings

Shanghai Fish Packet

CALYPSO GRILLED PINEAPPLE

½ cup FRENCH'S®
    Worcestershire Sauce
½ cup honey
½ cup (1 stick) butter or
    margarine

½ cup packed light brown
    sugar
½ cup dark rum
1 pineapple, cut into
    8 wedges and cored*
Vanilla ice cream

To prepare sauce, combine Worcestershire, honey, butter, sugar and rum in 3-quart saucepan. Bring to a full boil over medium-high heat, stirring often. Reduce heat to medium-low. Simmer 12 minutes or until sauce is slightly thickened, stirring often. Remove from heat; cool completely.

Brush pineapple wedges with some of the sauce. Place pineapple on oiled grid. Grill over hot coals 5 minutes or until glazed, turning and basting often with sauce. Serve pineapple with ice cream and remaining sauce. Garnish as desired. Refrigerate any leftover sauce.**   *Makes 8 servings*
(1½ cups sauce)

Prep Time: 15 minutes
Cook Time: 15 minutes

* You may substitute other fruits, such as halved peaches, nectarines or thick slices of mangoes, for the pineapple.

** Leftover sauce may be reheated in microwave. Microwave and stir for 30 seconds at a time.

Calypso Grilled Pineapple

GRILLED GARLIC AND VEGETABLES

8 whole heads fresh garlic*
2 artichokes, trimmed and quartered
4 ears corn, cut in half
2 carrots, cut into 1-inch chunks
2 zucchini, cut into 1-inch chunks
1 cup butter or margarine
4 teaspoons dried rosemary, crushed
½ cup sliced almonds
Salt and black pepper

The whole garlic bulb is called a head.

Prepare grill. Peel outer skin from garlic, keeping cloves intact. Cut 16 (12-inch) squares of heavy-duty foil. On double thickness of foil, place 1 whole head garlic, 1 artichoke quarter, 1 corn half and ⅛ each of carrot and zucchini chunks. Repeat to make 7 more packets. Dot each packet with 2 tablespoons butter; top with ½ teaspoon dried rosemary, and 1 tablespoon almonds. Sprinkle with salt and pepper to taste. Fold up foil, leaving space around edges and crimping all ends to make packets. Place packets on grid. Grill over hot coals 40 to 45 minutes or until vegetables are tender, turning occasionally.
Makes 8 servings

Favorite recipe from **Christopher Ranch Garlic**

BUFFALO CHILI ONIONS

½ cup FRANK'S® REDHOT® Original Cayenne Pepper Sauce
½ cup (1 stick) butter or margarine, melted, or olive oil
¼ cup chili sauce
1 tablespoon chili powder
4 large sweet onions, cut into ½-inch-thick slices

Whisk together RedHot sauce, butter, chili sauce and chili powder in medium bowl until blended; brush on onion slices.

Place onions on grid. Grill over medium-high coals 10 minutes or until tender, turning and basting often with the chili mixture. Serve warm. *Makes 6 servings*

Prep Time: 10 minutes
Cook Time: 10 minutes

Tip: Onions may be prepared ahead and grilled just before serving.

Buffalo Chili Onions

Grilled Tri-Colored Pepper Salad

GRILLED TRI-COLORED PEPPER SALAD

Fresh basil leaves
1 *each* **large red, yellow and green bell pepper, cut into halves or quarters**
⅓ **cup extra-virgin olive oil**
3 **tablespoons balsamic vinegar**
2 **cloves garlic, minced**
¼ **teaspoon salt**
¼ **teaspoon black pepper**
⅓ **cup crumbled goat cheese (about 1½ ounces)**

1. Prepare barbecue grill.

2. Layer basil leaves with largest leaf on bottom, then roll up jelly-roll style. Slice basil roll into very thin slices (enough leaves to measure ¼ cup); separate into strips. Set aside.

3. Place bell peppers, skin-side down, on grid. Grill, on covered grill, over hot coals 10 to 12 minutes or until skin is charred.

4. Place charred bell peppers in paper bag. Close bag; set aside to cool 10 to 15 minutes. Remove skins with paring knife; discard skins.

5. Place bell peppers in shallow glass serving dish. Combine oil, vinegar, garlic, salt and black pepper in small bowl; whisk until well combined. Pour over bell peppers. Let stand 30 minutes at room temperature. (Or, cover and refrigerate up to 24 hours. Bring bell peppers to room temperature before serving.)

6. Sprinkle bell peppers with cheese and basil just before serving.

Makes 4 to 6 servings

STUFFED ZUCCHINI

2 medium zucchini (about
    1 pound), scrubbed
2 tablespoons olive oil
1 large ripe tomato, chopped
1 green or yellow bell pepper,
    finely chopped
1 cup finely cubed boiled
    ham*
½ cup minced fresh basil leaves
1 can (2.8 ounces) FRENCH'S®
    French Fried Onions,
    divided

*You may substitute ¼ pound
spicy sausage for the boiled ham.
Cook with pepper until sausage is
browned.*

Cut each zucchini in half
lengthwise. Using a spoon or
melon baller, scoop out pulp
leaving ¼-inch shell. Set aside
zucchini shells. Finely chop pulp.

Heat oil in large skillet over high
heat. Add zucchini pulp and
tomato; cook until liquid is
evaporated, stirring often. Add
pepper, ham and basil; cook until
pepper is tender. Stir in 1 cup
French Fried Onions. Spoon filling
into shells. Sprinkle remaining
French Fried Onions on top.

Place zucchini on vegetable
grilling rack. Place on grid. Grill
15 minutes over medium coals or
until zucchini are tender.

Makes 4 servings

Prep Time: 15 minutes
Cook Time: 25 minutes

ITALIAN VEGETABLE POCKETS

1 medium eggplant (about
    ¾ pound)
1 small zucchini
1 small yellow squash
4 ripe plum tomatoes
1 can (2.8 ounces) FRENCH'S®
    French Fried Onions
2 tablespoons olive oil
2 tablespoons FRENCH'S®
    Worcestershire Sauce
2 teaspoons Italian seasoning
2 teaspoons seasoned salt
1 teaspoon garlic powder

Cut eggplant, zucchini, squash and
tomatoes into bite-size chunks;
place in large bowl. Add French
Fried Onions. Whisk together oil,
Worcestershire and seasonings in
small bowl. Pour over vegetables.
Toss well to coat evenly. Cut six
12-inch circles of heavy-duty foil.
Spoon about 2 cups vegetables in
center of each piece of foil. Fold
foil in half over vegetables. Seal
edges securely with tight double
folds.

Place packets on grid. Cook over
hot coals 15 minutes or until
vegetables are tender, opening foil
packets carefully. Serve warm.

Makes 6 side-dish servings

Prep Time: 15 minutes
Cook Time: 15 minutes

HERBED MUSHROOM VEGETABLE MEDLEY

4 ounces button or crimini mushrooms, sliced

1 medium red or yellow bell pepper, cut into ¼-inch-wide strips

1 medium zucchini, cut crosswise into ¼-inch-thick slices

1 medium yellow squash, cut crosswise into ¼-inch-thick slices

3 tablespoons butter or margarine, melted

1 tablespoon chopped fresh thyme leaves *or* 1 teaspoon dried thyme leaves, crushed

1 tablespoon chopped fresh basil leaves *or* 1 teaspoon dried basil leaves, crushed

1 tablespoon chopped fresh chives or green onion tops

1 clove garlic, minced

¼ teaspoon salt

¼ teaspoon black pepper

1. Prepare barbecue grill.

2. Combine mushrooms, bell pepper, zucchini and squash in large bowl. Combine butter, thyme, basil, chives, garlic, salt and black pepper in small bowl. Pour over vegetable mixture; toss to coat well.

3. Transfer mixture to 20×14-inch sheet of heavy-duty foil. Wrap in foil. Place foil packet on grid. Grill packet, on covered grill, over medium coals 20 to 25 minutes or until vegetables are fork-tender. Open packet carefully to serve.

Makes 4 to 6 servings

GRILLED POLENTA

2 cups milk

2 cups water

1 cup finely ground yellow cornmeal

2 tablespoons chopped fresh basil

2 tablespoons grated Parmesan cheese

1 teaspoon TABASCO® pepper sauce

1 teaspoon salt

2 tablespoons olive oil

In medium, heavy saucepan, bring milk and water to boil on grill or stovetop. Slowly add cornmeal, stirring constantly. Cook over low heat 30 to 35 minutes, stirring constantly. Add basil, Parmesan cheese, TABASCO and salt; mix well. Pour mixture into lightly greased 10-inch round cake pan and allow to cool.

To serve, slice polenta into wedges, brush with olive oil, and grill on both sides until golden brown.

Makes 6 to 8 servings

Herbed Mushroom Vegetable Medley

GRILLED SWEET POTATO PACKETS WITH PECAN BUTTER

¼ cup chopped pecans
4 sweet potatoes (about 8 ounces each)
1 large sweet or Spanish onion, thinly sliced and separated into rings
3 tablespoons vegetable oil
⅓ cup butter or margarine, softened
2 tablespoons packed light brown sugar
¼ teaspoon salt
¼ teaspoon ground cinnamon

1. Prepare barbecue grill.

2. Meanwhile, to toast pecans, spread in single layer on baking sheet. Bake in preheated 350°F oven 8 to 10 minutes or until golden brown, stirring frequently. Remove pecans from baking sheet; cool to room temperature. Set aside.

3. Peel sweet potatoes; slice crosswise into ¼-inch-thick slices. Alternately place potato slices and onion rings on 4 (14×12-inch) sheets of heavy-duty foil. Brush tops and sides with oil to prevent drying; wrap in foil. Place foil packets on grid.

4. Grill packets, on covered grill, over medium coals 25 to 30 minutes or until potatoes are fork-tender.

5. Meanwhile, to prepare pecan butter, combine butter, brown sugar, salt and cinnamon in small bowl; mix well. Stir in pecans. Open packets carefully; top each with dollop of pecan butter.
Makes 4 servings

GRILLED POTATOES

4 medium baking potatoes, diced
½ cup LIPTON® Onion Butter (recipe follows)
Chopped parsley

On four 18×10-inch pieces heavy-duty aluminum foil, divide potatoes equally; top each with 2 tablespoons Lipton® Onion Butter and sprinkle with parsley. Wrap foil loosely around potatoes, sealing edges airtight with double fold. Grill 30 minutes or until tender. *Makes 4 servings*

LIPTON® ONION BUTTER:
Thoroughly blend 1 envelope LIPTON® Recipe Secrets® Onion Soup Mix with 1 container (8 oz.) whipped butter or soft margarine or ½ pound butter or margarine, softened. Store covered in refrigerator. Makes about 1¼ cups.

Grilled Sweet Potato Packets with Pecan Butter

Contents

Clockwise from top left: Ultimate Chocolate Chip Cookies, page 398; Orange-Glazed Date Nut Bars, page 408; Mocha Chips 'n' Bits, page 403; Frosty's Colorful Cookies, page 406; Cherry Chocolate Chippies, page 406; Pistachio & White Chocolate Cookies, page 399

INTRODUCTION

Cookies have always been well liked, but every year their popularity seems to grow. Since they are quick to make and easy to transport, cookies fit so easily into today's casual lifestyle. They are as welcome in a child's lunch box as they are at a Fourth-of-July picnic.

Chocolate chip, oatmeal, peanut butter, brownie and sugar cookies are everyone's favorites. The Crisco Kitchens have developed five stellar recipes, one for each of these cookies. In addition to being delicious, these five cookies bake up high and stay soft, moist and chewy—just the way you like them. And these basic recipes are as versatile as they are delectable. Take any one of them, make a few changes and you have a new, exciting and sensational cookie. In fact, there is an entire chapter of great cookies that are easy variations of the basic recipe.

The secret to these moist and chewy cookies is Crisco, the country's leading all-vegetable shortening. Since Crisco never needs refrigeration, there is no need to allow it to soften. It is always ready when you are, so cookies made with Crisco can be baked on the spur of the moment. And now that Crisco Sticks are in supermarkets right next to the familiar blue cans of Crisco and the yellow cans of Butter Flavor Crisco, measuring is as easy as can be. Merely cut the pre-measured foil wrapper for the appropriate amount.

Home bakers can feel confident about using Crisco, since it contains half the saturated fat of butter. (Crisco contains 12 grams of total fat per tablespoon, of which 3 grams are saturated fat, while butter contains 7 grams of saturated fat per tablespoon.)

Some of the mouthwatering cookies on the following pages are pictured in specific holiday settings, but they are not exclusive to those times. While Cherry Chocolate Chippies were developed for Christmas, they would be just as enjoyable at Thanksgiving or at a graduation party. So use your imagination and enjoy these cookies all year round. Let the versatility of these five cookie recipes make any get-together a special occasion.

TIPS FOR BAKING GREAT COOKIES EVERY TIME

General Guidelines

• Read the entire recipe before you begin to make sure you have all the ingredients and baking utensils.

• Prepare baking pans and baking sheets according to recipe directions. Grease pans with Crisco only when greasing is called for in directions. Adjust oven racks and preheat the oven.

• Measure all ingredients accurately.

• Follow the recipe directions and baking times exactly. Check for doneness at the minimum baking time using the test given in the recipe.

Measuring

• Use standardized dry measuring cups for all dry ingredients and ingredients such as Crisco, peanut butter, nuts, dried fruit, coconut, fresh fruit, jams and jellies.

• Spoon flour into the correct measuring cup to overflowing and level it off with the straight edge of a metal spatula. Do not dip the measuring cup into the flour or tap the measuring cup on the counter as this will pack the flour.

• Press brown sugar into the correct measuring cup, fill to overflowing and level it off with a straight edge. It should hold the shape of the cup when turned out.

• Press Crisco or Butter Flavor Crisco into the correct measuring cup. Cut through with a knife or spatula and press again to eliminate air pockets. Level it off with a straight edge.

• Use standardized glass or clear plastic liquid measuring cups with a pouring spout to measure all liquid ingredients. Place the cup on a level surface, fill to the desired mark and check the measurement at eye level.

• Use standardized graduated measuring spoons, not eating or serving spoons, for measuring small amounts of ingredients. For dry ingredients, fill the spoon to overflowing and level it off with a straight edge.

Mixing

• Beat Crisco, sugar and other ingredients according to the recipe directions for several minutes to insure proper creaming.

• Sifting of flour is not necessary. Stir together the flour, baking soda, salt and spices before adding to the shortening mixture. Larger amounts of flour should be added gradually to the shortening mixture.

• Do not overmix the dough as this will toughen cookies. If using a hand mixer, it may be necessary to stir in the last portion of flour with a wooden spoon.

• Stir in chips, raisins, nuts and fruit with a wooden spoon.

Baking

• Use sturdy baking sheets with little or no sides. Allow 1 inch of space between the baking sheet and the sides of the oven. This allows heat to circulate in the oven during baking and promotes even browning. Cookies baked on insulated baking sheets may need 1 to 2 minutes longer baking time.

• Bake only one baking sheet at a time in the center of the oven. If cookies brown unevenly, rotate the baking sheet from front to back halfway through the baking time. If you do use more than one baking sheet at a time, rotate the sheets from the top rack to the bottom rack halfway through baking time. Space oven racks 6 inches apart. Allow the baking sheets to cool between batches. Dough will spread if placed on a hot baking sheet.

• Watch cookies carefully during baking to avoid overbaking. Follow the recipe for yield and size since baking time is determined for that size cookie.

• Allow cookies to remain on baking sheets for 2 minutes before removing to sheets of foil, unless otherwise stated. Cool cookies completely before storing.

Problem Solving

• Cookies are dry: This is usually the result of using too much flour or too little liquid. Always measure ingredients accurately.

• Cookies are too brown: If only the bottoms are too brown, the baking sheet may be too close to the bottom of the oven.

Move the rack to a higher position. If both the tops and bottoms of cookies are too brown, either the oven is too hot or there is insufficient air circulation around the baking sheet. Check the oven temperature with an oven thermometer or use a smaller baking sheet. Another cause of overbrowning is overbaking. Check cookies for doneness at the minimum baking time.

• Cookies spread too much or spread into each other: One of the most common causes for cookies spreading too much is using too little flour or too much liquid. Placing cookie dough on hot baking sheets or making cookies too large are other possible causes. Always cool baking sheets to room temperature before reusing and follow recipe directions and yield for proper-sized cookies. If cookies are the correct size but still spread into each other, the portioned dough may have been placed too close together on the baking sheet.

Storage

• Store cooled cookies at room temperature in airtight containers. Store each kind separately to prevent transfer of flavor and changes in texture. Freeze baked cookies in airtight containers or freezer bags for up to six months.

TIPS ON PACKING COOKIES FOR MAILING

• Wrap large, delicate or decorated cookies individually in plastic wrap. Pack cookies in an airtight container. Place heavier cookies at the bottom of the container or pack them in a separate container.

• Place the container in a larger box. Cushion with crumpled newspaper, styrofoam or air–popped popcorn. For a more festive look, wrap the container in gift paper and cushion with crumpled colored tissue paper or metallic tinsel.

• Bar cookies can be baked in disposable aluminum foil pans. When cool, cover pans with foil and pack the pans in a box. Cushion with crumpled newspaper.

• Seal outer box with packing tape.

ULTIMATE CHOCOLATE CHIP COOKIES

Luscious morsels of chocolate and perhaps some crunchy pecans nestled in a soft chewy cookie richly flavored with brown sugar and vanilla—these are the qualities you'll find in Crisco's Ultimate Chocolate Chip Cookies. And, as you will see on the pages that follow, this all-time family favorite recipe can be dressed up for special occasions and the familiar flavors of chocolate and pecans can be traded for a variety of different tastes.

This taste-tempting recipe can be easily varied to create cookies that bear no resemblance to a traditional chocolate chip cookie. Orange-Glazed Date Nut Bars are just right for a bridal shower and Maple Walnut Cookies will become a much loved late-night snack. Captivate the kids with Peanut Butter Treats by simply substituting quartered miniature peanut butter cups for the chocolate chips and pecans.

In this chapter are ideas for festive Christmas cookies, such as Cherry Chocolate Chippies and Frosty's Colorful Cookies. Coffee Chip Drops are perfect for your Valentine's Day sweetheart and Chocolate Chip Ice Cream Sandwiches make a perfect summertime snack. Whatever variations you choose to bake, the results will delight everyone!

Ultimate Chocolate Chip Cookies
(page 398)

Ultimate Chocolate Chip Cookies

1¼ cups firmly packed light
    brown sugar
¾ cup Butter Flavor Crisco
    all-vegetable shortening
    or ¾ Butter Flavor
    Crisco Stick
2 tablespoons milk
1 tablespoon vanilla

1 egg
1¾ cups all-purpose flour
1 teaspoon salt
¾ teaspoon baking soda
1 cup (6 ounces) semisweet
    chocolate chips
1 cup coarsely chopped
    pecans* (optional)

*If pecans are omitted, add an additional ½ cup semisweet chocolate chips.

1. Heat oven to 375°F. Place sheets of foil on countertop for cooling cookies.

2. Place brown sugar, shortening, milk and vanilla in large bowl. Beat at medium speed of electric mixer until well blended. Add egg; beat well.

3. Combine flour, salt and baking soda. Add to shortening mixture; beat at low speed just until blended. Stir in chocolate chips and pecans, if desired.

4. Drop dough by rounded measuring tablespoonfuls 3 inches apart onto ungreased baking sheets.

5. Bake one baking sheet at a time at 375°F for 8 to 10 minutes for chewy cookies, or 11 to 13 minutes for crisp cookies. *Do not overbake.* Cool 2 minutes on baking sheet. Remove cookies to foil to cool completely.

Makes about 3 dozen cookies

Pistachio and White Chocolate Cookies

1 cup shelled pistachio nuts
1¼ cups firmly packed light brown
    sugar
¾ cup Butter Flavor Crisco
    all-vegetable shortening or ¾
    Butter Flavor Crisco Stick
2 tablespoons milk
1 tablespoon vanilla
1 egg
1¾ cups all-purpose flour
1 teaspoon salt
¾ teaspoon baking soda
1 cup white chocolate chips or chunks

1. Heat oven to 350°F. Spread pistachio nuts on baking sheet. Bake at 350°F for 7 to 10 minutes or until toasted, stirring several times. Place nuts in kitchen towel; rub with towel to remove most of skin. Cool nuts. Chop coarsely; reserve.

2. *Increase oven temperature to 375°F.* Place sheets of foil on countertop for cooling cookies.

3. Place brown sugar, shortening, milk and vanilla in large bowl. Beat at medium speed of electric mixer until well blended. Add egg; beat well.

4. Combine flour, salt and baking soda. Add to shortening mixture; beat at low speed just until blended. Stir in white chocolate chips and reserved pistachios.

5. Drop dough by rounded measuring tablespoonfuls 3 inches apart onto ungreased baking sheets.

6. Bake one baking sheet at a time at 375°F for 8 to 10 minutes for chewy cookies, or 11 to 13 minutes for crisp cookies. *Do not overbake.* Cool 2 minutes on baking sheet. Remove cookies to foil to cool completely.
Makes about 3 dozen cookies

For a festive Christmas buffet table, tie the silverware and napkins with brightly colored ribbons, tucking in sprigs of evergreen for an aromatic touch. Or try stuffing silverware into small, inexpensive stockings along with tiny gaily wrapped gifts for each guest.

Maple Walnut Cookies

1¼ cups firmly packed light
    brown sugar
¾ cup Butter Flavor Crisco
    all-vegetable shortening
    or ¾ Butter Flavor
    Crisco Stick
2 tablespoons maple syrup
1 teaspoon vanilla

1 teaspoon maple extract
1 egg
1¾ cups all-purpose flour
1 teaspoon salt
¾ teaspoon baking soda
½ teaspoon cinnamon
1½ cups chopped walnuts
30 to 40 walnut halves

1. Heat oven to 375°F. Place sheets of foil on countertop for cooling cookies.

2. Place brown sugar, shortening, maple syrup, vanilla and maple extract in large bowl. Beat at medium speed of electric mixer until well blended. Add egg; beat well.

3. Combine flour, salt, baking soda and cinnamon. Add to shortening mixture; beat at low speed just until blended. Stir in chopped walnuts.

4. Drop dough by rounded measuring tablespoonfuls 3 inches apart onto ungreased baking sheets. Press walnut half into center of each cookie.

5. Bake one baking sheet at a time at 375°F for 8 to 10 minutes for chewy cookies, or 11 to 13 minutes for crisp cookies. *Do not overbake.* Cool 2 minutes on baking sheet. Remove cookies to foil to cool completely.

Makes about 3 dozen cookies

Top to bottom: Maple Walnut Cookies, Peanut Butter Treats (page 407)

Chocolate Chip Ice Cream Sandwiches

1¼ cups firmly packed light
    brown sugar
¾ cup Butter Flavor Crisco
    all-vegetable shortening
    or ¾ Butter Flavor
    Crisco Stick
2 tablespoons milk
1 tablespoon vanilla

1 egg
1¾ cups all-purpose flour
1 teaspoon salt
¾ teaspoon baking soda
1 cup semisweet chocolate
    chips
1 cup chopped pecans
2 pints ice cream, any flavor

1. Heat oven to 375°F. Place sheets of foil on countertop for cooling cookies.

2. Place brown sugar, shortening, milk and vanilla in large bowl. Beat at medium speed of electric mixer until well blended. Add egg; beat well.

3. Combine flour, salt and baking soda. Add to shortening mixture; beat at low speed just until blended. Stir in chocolate chips and pecans.

4. Measure ¼ cup dough; shape into ball. Repeat with remaining dough. Place balls 4 inches apart on ungreased baking sheets. Flatten balls into 3-inch circles.

5. Bake one baking sheet at a time at 375°F for 10 to 12 minutes or until cookies are lightly browned. *Do not overbake.* Cool 2 minutes on baking sheet. Remove cookies to foil to cool completely.

6. Remove ice cream from freezer to soften slightly. Measure ½ cup ice cream; spread onto bottom of one cookie. Cover with flat side of second cookie. Wrap sandwich in plastic wrap. Place in freezer. Repeat with remaining cookies and ice cream.

Makes about 10 ice cream sandwiches

Note: Chocolate Chip Ice Cream Sandwiches should be eaten within two days. After two days, cookies will absorb moisture and become soggy. If longer storage is needed, make and freeze cookies, but assemble ice cream sandwiches within two days of serving.

Mocha Chips 'n' Bits

Cookies

1¼ cups firmly packed light brown sugar

¾ cup Butter Flavor Crisco all-vegetable shortening or ¾ Butter Flavor Crisco Stick

2 tablespoons milk

1 tablespoon instant coffee powder

1 tablespoon vanilla

1 egg

1¾ cups all-purpose flour

1½ tablespoons unsweetened cocoa powder

1 teaspoon salt

¾ teaspoon baking soda

1 cup (6 ounces) milk chocolate chips

1 cup coarsely chopped pecans

4 ounces bittersweet chocolate, cut into chunks

Icing

1 cup white chocolate chips

1 teaspoon Crisco all-vegetable shortening

1. Heat oven to 375°F. Place sheets of foil on countertop for cooling cookies.

2. Place brown sugar, shortening, milk, instant coffee and vanilla in large bowl. Beat at medium speed of electric mixer until well blended. Add egg; beat well.

3. Combine flour, cocoa, salt and baking soda. Add to shortening mixture; beat at low speed just until blended. Stir in chocolate chips, pecans and chocolate chunks.

4. Drop dough by rounded measuring tablespoonfuls 3 inches apart onto ungreased baking sheets.

5. Bake one baking sheet at a time at 375°F for 8 to 10 minutes for chewy cookies, or 11 to 13 minutes for crisp cookies. *Do not overbake.* Cool 2 minutes on baking sheet. Remove cookies to foil to cool completely.

6. For icing, place white chocolate chips and shortening in heavy, resealable sandwich bag; seal bag. Microwave at 50% (MEDIUM) for 1 minute. Knead bag. If necessary, microwave at 50% for another 30 seconds at a time until mixture is smooth when kneaded. Cut small tip off corner of bag. Pipe shapes on cookies or drizzle randomly.

Makes about 3 dozen cookies

Note: White chocolate chips and shortening can be melted by placing resealable bag in bowl of hot water.

Coffee Chip Drops

Chocolate kiss candies atop these coffee-flavored cookies send a loving message to your sweetheart on Valentine's Day.

1¼ cups firmly packed light brown
    sugar
¾ cup Butter Flavor Crisco
    all-vegetable shortening
    or ¾ Butter Flavor Crisco Stick
2 tablespoons cold coffee
1 teaspoon vanilla
1 egg
1¾ cups all-purpose flour
1 tablespoon finely ground French
    roast or espresso coffee beans
1 teaspoon salt
¾ teaspoon baking soda
½ cup semisweet chocolate chips
½ cup milk chocolate chips
½ cup coarsely chopped walnuts
30 to 40 chocolate kiss candies,
    unwrapped

1. Heat oven to 375°F. Place sheets of foil on countertop for cooling cookies.

2. Place brown sugar, shortening, coffee and vanilla in large bowl. Beat at medium speed of electric mixer until well blended. Add egg; beat well.

3. Combine flour, ground coffee, salt and baking soda. Add to shortening mixture; beat at low speed just until blended. Stir in chocolate chips and walnuts.

4. Drop dough by rounded measuring tablespoonfuls 2 inches apart onto ungreased baking sheets.

5. Bake one baking sheet at a time at 375°F for 8 to 10 minutes or until cookies are lightly browned and just set. *Do not overbake.* Place 1 candy in center of each cookie. Cool 2 minutes on baking sheet. Remove cookies to foil to cool completely.
Makes about 3 dozen cookies

Top to bottom: Coffee Chip Drops,
Chocolate Cheesecake Bars
(page 444)

Frosty's Colorful Cookies

1¼ cups firmly packed light
    brown sugar
¾ cup Butter Flavor Crisco
    all-vegetable shortening
    or ¾ Butter Flavor
    Crisco Stick
2 tablespoons milk

1 tablespoon vanilla
1 egg
1¾ cups all-purpose flour
1 teaspoon salt
¾ teaspoon baking soda
2 cups red and green candy-
    coated chocolate pieces

1. Heat oven to 375°F. Place sheets of foil on countertop for cooling cookies.

2. Place brown sugar, shortening, milk and vanilla in large bowl. Beat at medium speed of electric mixer until well blended. Add egg; beat well.

3. Combine flour, salt and baking soda. Add to shortening mixture; beat at low speed just until blended. Stir in candy-coated chocolate pieces.

4. Drop dough by rounded measuring tablespoonfuls 3 inches apart onto ungreased baking sheets.

5. Bake one baking sheet at a time at 375°F for 8 to 10 minutes for chewy cookies, or 11 to 13 minutes for crisp cookies. *Do not overbake.* Cool 2 minutes on baking sheet. Remove cookies to foil to cool completely.
Makes about 3 dozen cookies

Cherry Chocolate Chippies

1¼ cups firmly packed light
    brown sugar
¾ cup Butter Flavor Crisco
    all-vegetable shortening
    or ¾ Butter Flavor
    Crisco Stick
1 teaspoon vanilla
1 teaspoon almond extract
1 egg

1¾ cups all-purpose flour
1 teaspoon salt
¾ teaspoon baking soda
1 cup (6 ounces) semisweet
    chocolate chips
1 cup well-drained
    maraschino cherries,
    coarsely chopped

1. Heat oven to 375°F. Place sheets of foil on countertop for cooling cookies.

2. Place brown sugar, shortening, vanilla and almond extract in large bowl. Beat at medium speed of electric mixer until well blended. Add egg; beat well.

3. Combine flour, salt and baking soda. Add to shortening mixture; beat at low speed just until blended. Stir in chocolate chips and cherries.

4. Drop dough by rounded measuring tablespoonfuls 2 inches apart onto ungreased baking sheets.

5. Bake one baking sheet at a time at 375°F for 8 to 10 minutes for chewy cookies, or 11 to 13 minutes for crisp cookies. *Do not overbake.* Cool 2 minutes on baking sheet. Remove cookies to foil to cool completely.

Makes about 3 dozen cookies

Peanut Butter Treats

1¼ cups firmly packed light brown sugar	1¾ cups all-purpose flour
¾ cup Butter Flavor Crisco all-vegetable shortening or ¾ Butter Flavor Crisco Stick	1 teaspoon salt
	¾ teaspoon baking soda
2 tablespoons milk	2 cups (about 32) miniature peanut butter cups, unwrapped and quartered or coarsely chopped
1 tablespoon vanilla	
1 egg	

1. Heat oven to 375°F. Place sheets of foil on countertop for cooling cookies.

2. Place brown sugar, shortening, milk and vanilla in large bowl. Beat at medium speed of electric mixer until well blended. Add egg; beat well.

3. Combine flour, salt and baking soda. Add to shortening mixture; beat at low speed just until blended. Stir in peanut butter cup quarters.

4. Drop dough by rounded measuring tablespoonfuls 3 inches apart onto ungreased baking sheets.

5. Bake one baking sheet at a time at 375°F for 8 to 10 minutes or until cookies are lightly browned. *Do not overbake.* Cool 2 minutes on baking sheet. Remove cookies to foil to cool completely.

Makes about 3 dozen cookies

Orange-Glazed Date Nut Bars

Christmas is a great time for entertaining friends and family, but sometimes it's difficult to coordinate everyone's busy schedules. Why not plan an open house that will allow guests to stop in during their busy day? Set a buffet table with make-your-own sandwiches for early afternoon and prepare a large pot of spicy chili or hearty soup for evening. No matter what the menu, an assortment of make-ahead holiday cookies will be welcomed by all your guests.

Cookie Base
1¼ cups firmly packed light brown sugar
¾ cup Butter Flavor Crisco all-vegetable shortening or ¾ Butter Flavor Crisco Stick
2 tablespoons orange juice
1 tablespoon vanilla
1 tablespoon grated orange peel
1 egg
1¾ cups all-purpose flour
1 teaspoon salt
¾ teaspoon baking soda
1 cup chopped dates
1 cup chopped walnuts

Glaze
1½ cups confectioners sugar
2 tablespoons orange juice

1. Heat oven to 350°F. Grease 13 × 9-inch baking pan. Place cooling rack on counter.

2. Place brown sugar, shortening, orange juice, vanilla and orange peel in large bowl. Beat at medium speed of electric mixer until well blended. Add egg; beat well.

3. Combine flour, salt and baking soda. Add to shortening mixture; beat at low speed just until blended. Stir in dates and walnuts.

4. Press dough into prepared pan.

5. Bake at 350°F for 20 to 25 minutes or until lightly browned and firm. *Do not overbake.* Cool completely on cooling rack.

6. For glaze, combine confectioners sugar and orange juice. Stir until smooth. Spread glaze over cookie base. Cut into 2 × 1½-inch bars. Garnish if desired.

Makes 3 dozen bars

Top to bottom: Raspberry Linzer Rounds (page 429), Orange-Glazed Date Nut Bars

CHEWY OATMEAL COOKIES

Dotted with plump raisins and scented with cinnamon, classic oatmeal cookies have been around for most of the 20th century and had changed very little until the Crisco Kitchens developed the Chewy Oatmeal Cookie. What makes these so special is all there in the name—they are chewy and soft, so the nutty flavor and rich texture of the oatmeal does not leave a dry feel in the mouth.

The Crisco Kitchens have also found that Chewy Oatmeal Cookies are extremely versatile. Just by changing a few ingredients in this recipe, you can make a delightful array of new cookies all uniquely different from the basic recipe. Replace the raisins with pineapple and coconut and enjoy Aloha Oatmeal Cookies. Add grated carrots and chopped apple and discover Good 'n' Tasties.

For those who think that a cookie isn't a cookie without a sweet-flavored chip, this chapter includes recipes with bits of white and semisweet chocolate. And like every other recipe in this chapter, they begin with the same easy basic recipe.

Chewy Oatmeal Cookies (page 412)

Chewy Oatmeal Cookies

1¼ cups firmly packed light
    brown sugar
¾ cup Butter Flavor Crisco
    all-vegetable shortening
    or ¾ Butter Flavor
    Crisco Stick
1 egg
⅓ cup milk
1½ teaspoons vanilla

3 cups quick oats, uncooked
1 cup all-purpose flour
½ teaspoon baking soda
½ teaspoon salt
¼ teaspoon cinnamon
1 cup raisins
1 cup coarsely chopped
    walnuts

1. Heat oven to 375°F. Grease baking sheets. Place sheets of foil on countertop for cooling cookies.

2. Place brown sugar, shortening, egg, milk and vanilla in large bowl. Beat at medium speed of electric mixer until well blended.

3. Combine oats, flour, baking soda, salt and cinnamon. Add to shortening mixture; beat at low speed just until blended. Stir in raisins and walnuts.

4. Drop dough by rounded measuring tablespoonfuls 2 inches apart onto prepared baking sheets.

5. Bake one baking sheet at a time at 375°F for 10 to 12 minutes or until cookies are lightly browned. *Do not overbake.* Cool 2 minutes on baking sheet. Remove cookies to foil to cool completely.

Makes about 2½ dozen cookies

Fall Harvest Oatmeal Cookies

1¼ cups firmly packed light
    brown sugar
¾ cup Butter Flavor Crisco
    all-vegetable shortening
    or ¾ Butter Flavor
    Crisco Stick
1 egg
⅓ cup milk
1 tablespoon grated orange
    peel
1½ teaspoons vanilla
3 cups quick oats, uncooked

1 cup all-purpose
    flour
1½ teaspoons cinnamon
½ teaspoon baking soda
½ teaspoon salt
¼ teaspoon nutmeg
¼ teaspoon ground cloves
1 cup coarsely chopped,
    peeled apples
1 cup raisins
1 cup coarsely chopped
    walnuts

1. Heat oven to 375°F. Grease baking sheets. Place sheets of foil on countertop for cooling cookies.

2. Place brown sugar, shortening, egg, milk, orange peel and vanilla in large bowl. Beat at medium speed of electric mixer until well blended.

3. Combine oats, flour, cinnamon, baking soda, salt, nutmeg and cloves. Add to shortening mixture; beat at low speed just until blended. Stir in apples, raisins and walnuts.

4. Drop dough by rounded measuring tablespoonfuls 2 inches apart onto prepared baking sheets.

5. Bake one baking sheet at a time at 375°F for 10 to 12 minutes or until cookies are lightly browned. *Do not overbake.* Cool 2 minutes on baking sheet. Remove cookies to foil to cool completely.

Makes about 2½ dozen cookies

Cranberry Nut Oatmeal Cookies

1¼ cups firmly packed light brown
    sugar
¾ cup Butter Flavor Crisco
    all-vegetable shortening
    or ¾ Butter Flavor Crisco Stick
1 egg
⅓ cup milk
1½ teaspoons vanilla
1 teaspoon grated orange peel
3 cups quick oats, uncooked
1 cup all-purpose flour
½ teaspoon baking soda
½ teaspoon salt
¼ teaspoon cinnamon
1 cup dried cranberries
1 cup coarsely chopped walnuts

1. Heat oven to 375°F. Grease baking sheets. Place sheets of foil on countertop for cooling cookies.

2. Place brown sugar, shortening, egg, milk, vanilla and orange peel in large bowl. Beat at medium speed of electric mixer until well blended.

3. Combine oats, flour, baking soda, salt and cinnamon. Add to shortening mixture; beat at low speed just until blended. Stir in cranberries and walnuts.

4. Drop dough by rounded measuring tablespoonfuls 2 inches apart onto prepared baking sheets.

5. Bake one baking sheet at a time at 375°F for 10 to 12 minutes or until cookies are lightly browned. *Do not overbake.* Cool 2 minutes on baking sheet. Remove cookies to foil to cool completely.
Makes about 2½ dozen cookies

Top to bottom: Fall Harvest Oatmeal Cookies (page 413), *Cranberry Nut Oatmeal Cookies*

While cookies may not be a tradition at your Thanksgiving dinner, they should have a place in the day's festivities. These cranberry and nut-studded cookies will quiet the predinner hungries or top off a late evening snack. Fall Harvest Oatmeal Cookies will make a great dessert for even the most finicky kid on your guest list. No matter which you choose, these make-ahead treats are sure to please.

Aloha Oatmeal Cookies

If friends are embarking on a special trip, send them off in style with a Bon Voyage Party. Serve cookies that are appropriate to their destination. These spicy cookies loaded with pineapple, coconut and macadamia nuts are great whether their destination is Hawaii or some other island paradise. Since cookies are such great travelers, wrap the extras for snacking on the trip.

1¼ cups firmly packed light brown
    sugar
¾ cup Butter Flavor Crisco
    all-vegetable shortening
    or ¾ Butter Flavor Crisco Stick
1 egg
2 tablespoons orange juice
1 tablespoon grated orange peel
1 teaspoon vanilla
½ teaspoon orange or lemon extract
3 cups quick oats, uncooked
1 cup all-purpose flour
½ teaspoon baking soda
½ teaspoon salt
½ teaspoon ground ginger
1 can (8 ounces) crushed pineapple in
    natural juice, well-drained
1 cup flaked coconut
1 cup chopped macadamia nuts

1. Heat oven to 375°F. Grease baking sheets. Place sheets of foil on countertop for cooling cookies.

2. Place brown sugar, shortening, egg, orange juice, orange peel, vanilla and orange extract in large bowl. Beat at medium speed of electric mixer until well blended.

3. Combine oats, flour, baking soda, salt and ginger. Add to shortening mixture; beat at low speed just until blended. Stir in pineapple, coconut and macadamia nuts.

4. Drop dough by rounded measuring tablespoonfuls 2 inches apart onto prepared baking sheets.

5. Bake one baking sheet at a time at 375°F for 10 to 12 minutes or until cookies are lightly browned. *Do not overbake.* Cool 2 minutes. Remove cookies to foil to cool.
Makes about 2½ dozen cookies

Aloha Oatmeal Cookies

Chocolate Cherry Oatmeal Fancies

Everyone loves cookie baking and spending time with loved ones around the holidays. Why not combine the two and invite a group for a cookie-baking session? Ask your guests to bring their favorite recipes. Spend the day baking and everyone goes home with a fantastic assortment of cookies.

½ cup sliced almonds
1¼ cups firmly packed light brown
    sugar
¾ cup Butter Flavor Crisco
    all-vegetable shortening
    or ¾ Butter Flavor Crisco Stick
1 egg
⅓ cup milk
1 teaspoon vanilla
½ teaspoon almond extract
3 cups quick oats, uncooked
1 cup all-purpose flour
½ teaspoon baking soda
½ teaspoon salt
6 ounces white baking chocolate,
    coarsely chopped
6 ounces semisweet chocolate, coarsely
    chopped
½ cup coarsely chopped red candied
    cherries or well-drained, chopped
    maraschino cherries

1. Heat oven to 350°F. Spread almonds on baking sheet. Bake at 350°F for 5 to 7 minutes or until almonds are golden brown. Cool completely; reserve.

2. *Increase oven temperature to 375°F.* Grease baking sheets. Place sheets of foil on countertop for cooling cookies.

3. Place brown sugar, shortening, egg, milk, vanilla and almond extract in large bowl. Beat at medium speed of electric mixer until well blended.

4. Combine oats, flour, baking soda and salt. Add to shortening mixture; beat at low speed just until blended. Stir in white chocolate, semisweet chocolate, cherries and reserved almonds.

5. Drop dough by rounded measuring tablespoonfuls 2 inches apart onto prepared baking sheets.

6. Bake one baking sheet at a time at 375°F for 10 to 12 minutes or until cookies are lightly browned. *Do not overbake.* Cool 2 minutes on baking sheet. Remove cookies to foil to cool completely.

Makes about 4 dozen cookies

Good 'n' Tasties

1¼ cups firmly packed light brown sugar
¾ cup Butter Flavor Crisco all-vegetable shortening or ¾ Butter Flavor Crisco Stick
1 egg
⅓ cup milk
1 tablespoon grated orange peel
1½ teaspoons vanilla
1½ cups quick oats, uncooked
1 cup whole-wheat flour

½ cup all-purpose flour
¼ cup toasted wheat germ
1½ teaspoons cinnamon
1 teaspoon baking soda
½ teaspoon salt
1 cup raisins
1 cup coarsely chopped walnuts or pecans
1 apple, peeled and coarsely chopped
½ cup grated carrots
½ cup flaked coconut

1. Heat oven to 375°F. Grease baking sheets. Place sheets of foil on countertop for cooling cookies.

2. Place brown sugar, shortening, egg, milk, orange peel and vanilla in large bowl. Beat at medium speed of electric mixer until well blended.

3. Combine oats, whole-wheat flour, all-purpose flour, wheat germ, cinnamon, baking soda and salt. Add to shortening mixture; beat at low speed just until blended. Stir in raisins, walnuts, apple, carrots and coconut.

4. Drop dough by rounded measuring tablespoonfuls 2 inches apart onto prepared baking sheets.

5. Bake one baking sheet at a time at 375°F for 10 to 12 minutes or until cookies are lightly browned. *Do not overbake.* Cool 2 minutes on baking sheet. Remove cookies to foil to cool completely.

Makes about 3½ dozen cookies

ULTIMATE SUGAR COOKIES

In the past, sugar cookies were primarily seen as blank canvases begging to be decorated for the holidays. Although pretty, few of us liked the flavor or texture of the cookie. Now meet the Ultimate Sugar Cookie! It was developed by the Crisco Kitchens to be so moist, and above all so delectable, that it will become one of your favorites. And now it is less likely to crumble when iced than a crisper cookie made with butter or margarine. This makes it the ideal cookie for cutting into shapes and decorating.

Browse through this chapter and discover how versatile this recipe can be. With minor variations, you can have a great array of scrumptious cookies in a seemingly endless variety of shapes. You and your family can travel the world right in your kitchen— from the intriguing Scandinavian flavor of Orange-Cardamom Thins to the deliciously different Tropical Lime Cookies. And don't miss the delightful Cappuccino Cookies and Raspberry Linzer Rounds.

So forget your old notions about sugar cookies and discover the whole new world of Ultimate Sugar Cookies—dazzling to the taste buds and exquisite to behold.

Ultimate Sugar Cookies (**page 422**)

Ultimate Sugar Cookies

1¼ cups granulated sugar
1 cup Butter Flavor Crisco
    all-vegetable shortening
    or 1 Butter Flavor
    Crisco Stick
2 eggs
¼ cup light corn syrup or
    regular pancake syrup
1 tablespoon vanilla

3 cups all-purpose flour
    (plus 4 tablespoons),
    divided
¾ teaspoon baking powder
½ teaspoon baking soda
½ teaspoon salt
    Granulated sugar or
    colored sugar crystals

1. Place sugar and shortening in large bowl. Beat at medium speed of electric mixer until well blended. Add eggs, syrup and vanilla; beat until well blended and fluffy.

2. Combine 3 cups flour, baking powder, baking soda and salt. Add gradually to shortening mixture, beating at low speed until well blended.

3. Divide dough into 4 equal pieces; shape each piece into disk. Wrap with plastic wrap. Refrigerate 1 hour or until firm.

4. Heat oven to 375°F. Place sheets of foil on countertop for cooling cookies.

5. Sprinkle about 1 tablespoon flour on large sheet of waxed paper. Place disk of dough on floured paper; flatten slightly with hands. Turn dough over; cover with another large sheet of waxed paper. Roll dough to ¼-inch thickness. Remove top sheet of waxed paper. Cut into desired shapes with floured cookie cutters. Place 2 inches apart on ungreased baking sheet. Repeat with remaining dough.

6. Sprinkle with granulated sugar.

7. Bake one baking sheet at a time at 375°F for 5 to 7 minutes or until edges of cookies are lightly browned. *Do not overbake.* Cool 2 minutes on baking sheet. Remove cookies to foil to cool completely.

Makes about 3½ dozen cookies

Orange-Cardamom Thins

1¼ cups granulated sugar
1 cup Butter Flavor Crisco
    all-vegetable shortening
    or 1 Butter Flavor Crisco Stick
1 egg
¼ cup light corn syrup or regular
    pancake syrup
1 teaspoon vanilla
1 tablespoon grated orange peel
½ teaspoon orange extract
3 cups all-purpose flour
1¼ teaspoons cardamom
¾ teaspoon baking powder
½ teaspoon baking soda
½ teaspoon salt
½ teaspoon cinnamon

1. Place sugar and shortening in large bowl. Beat at medium speed of electric mixer until well blended. Add egg, syrup, vanilla, orange peel and orange extract; beat until well blended and fluffy.

2. Combine flour, cardamom, baking powder, baking soda, salt and cinnamon. Add gradually to shortening mixture, beating at low speed until well blended.

3. Divide dough in half. Roll each half into 12-inch-long log. Wrap with plastic wrap. Refrigerate for 4 hours or until firm.

4. Heat oven to 375°F. Grease baking sheets. Place sheets of foil on counter for cooling cookies.

5. Cut rolls into ¼-inch-thick slices. Place 1 inch apart on prepared baking sheets.

6. Bake one baking sheet at a time at 375°F for 7 to 9 minutes or until bottoms of cookies are lightly browned. *Do not overbake.* Cool 2 minutes on baking sheet. Remove cookies to foil to cool completely.
Makes about 5 dozen cookies

Cardamom, a member of the ginger family, has a pungent aroma and a spicy-sweet flavor. It is used most often in Scandinavian and East Indian cooking.

Toffee Spattered Sugar Stars

1¼ cups granulated sugar
1 cup Butter Flavor Crisco
   all-vegetable shortening
   or 1 Butter Flavor
   Crisco Stick
2 eggs
¼ cup light corn syrup or
   regular pancake syrup
1 tablespoon vanilla

3 cups all-purpose flour
   (plus 4 tablespoons),
   divided
¾ teaspoon baking powder
½ teaspoon baking soda
½ teaspoon salt
1 package (6 ounces) milk
   chocolate English toffee
   chips, divided

1. Place sugar and shortening in large bowl. Beat at medium speed of electric mixer until well blended. Add eggs, syrup and vanilla; beat until well blended and fluffy.

2. Combine 3 cups flour, baking powder, baking soda and salt. Add gradually to shortening mixture, beating at low speed until well blended.

3. Divide dough into 4 equal pieces; shape each into disk. Wrap with plastic wrap. Refrigerate 1 hour or until firm.

4. Heat oven to 375°F. Place sheets of foil on countertop for cooling cookies.

5. Sprinkle about 1 tablespoon flour on large sheet of waxed paper. Place disk of dough on floured paper; flatten slightly with hands. Turn dough over; cover with another large sheet of waxed paper. Roll dough to ¼-inch thickness. Remove top sheet of waxed paper. Sprinkle about ¼ of toffee chips over dough. Roll lightly into dough. Cut out with floured star or round cookie cutter. Place 2 inches apart on ungreased baking sheet. Repeat with remaining dough and toffee chips.

6. Bake one baking sheet at a time at 375°F for 5 to 7 minutes or until cookies are lightly browned around edges. *Do not overbake.* Cool 2 minutes on baking sheet. Remove cookies to foil to cool completely.

Makes about 3½ dozen cookies

Top to bottom: Pecan Cookies (page 426), Toffee Spattered Sugar Stars

Pecan Cookies

1¼ cups confectioners sugar	1 tablespoon vanilla
1 cup Butter Flavor Crisco all-vegetable shortening or 1 Butter Flavor Crisco Stick	2 cups all-purpose flour
	1½ cups finely chopped pecans
2 eggs	¾ teaspoon baking powder
¼ cup light corn syrup or regular pancake syrup	½ teaspoon baking soda
	½ teaspoon salt
	Confectioners sugar

1. Heat oven to 375°F. Place sheets of foil on countertop for cooling cookies.

2. Place 1¼ cups confectioners sugar and shortening in large bowl. Beat at medium speed of electric mixer until well blended. Add eggs, syrup and vanilla; beat until well blended and fluffy.

3. Combine flour, pecans, baking powder, baking soda and salt. Add to shortening mixture; beat at low speed until well blended.

4. Shape dough into 1-inch balls. Place 2 inches apart on ungreased baking sheet.

5. Bake at 375°F for 7 to 9 minutes or until bottoms of cookies are light golden brown. *Do not overbake.* Cool 2 minutes on baking sheet. Roll in confectioners sugar while warm. Remove cookies to foil to cool completely. Reroll in confectioners sugar just before serving.

Makes about 4 dozen cookies

Cappuccino Cookies

1¼ cups firmly packed light brown sugar	1 teaspoon rum extract
1 cup Butter Flavor Crisco all-vegetable shortening or 1 Butter Flavor Crisco Stick	2 tablespoons instant espresso or coffee powder
	3 cups all-purpose flour
2 eggs	¾ teaspoon baking powder
¼ cup light corn syrup or regular pancake syrup	½ teaspoon baking soda
	½ teaspoon salt
1 teaspoon vanilla	½ teaspoon nutmeg
	Chocolate jimmies

1. Place brown sugar and shortening in large bowl. Beat at medium speed of electric mixer until well blended. Add eggs, corn syrup, vanilla, rum extract and coffee; beat until well blended and fluffy.

2. Combine flour, baking powder, baking soda, salt and nutmeg. Add gradually to shortening mixture, beating at low speed until blended. Divide dough in half. Roll each half into two logs approximately 2 inches in diameter. Wrap in waxed paper. Refrigerate several hours.

3. Heat oven to 375°F. Place sheets of foil on countertop for cooling cookies.

4. Cut cookies into ¼-inch-thick slices. Place 2 inches apart on ungreased baking sheet. Sprinkle center of each cookie with jimmies.

5. Bake one baking sheet at a time at 375°F for 7 to 9 minutes or until golden brown. *Do not overbake.* Cool 2 minutes. Remove cookies to foil to cool completely.   *Makes about 4½ dozen cookies*

Tropical Lime Cookies

1¼ cups confectioners sugar
1 cup Butter Flavor Crisco all-vegetable shortening or 1 Butter Flavor Crisco Stick
1 egg
¼ cup light corn syrup or regular pancake syrup
2 tablespoons lime juice

2 tablespoons grated lime peel (about 2 limes)
2½ cups all-purpose flour
¾ teaspoon baking powder
½ teaspoon baking soda
½ teaspoon salt
1 cup flaked coconut
Confectioners sugar

1. Heat oven to 325°F. Place sheets of foil on countertop for cooling cookies.

2. Place confectioners sugar and shortening in large bowl. Beat at medium speed of electric mixer until well blended. Add egg, syrup, lime juice and lime peel; beat until well blended and fluffy.

3. Combine flour, baking powder, baking soda and salt. Add gradually to shortening mixture, beating at low speed until well blended. Stir in coconut.

4. Shape dough into 1-inch balls. Place 2 inches apart on ungreased baking sheet.

5. Bake one baking sheet at a time at 325°F for 15 to 18 minutes or until bottoms of cookies are light golden brown. *Do not overbake.* Cool 2 minutes on baking sheet. Remove cookies to foil. Dust warm cookies with confectioners sugar. Cool completely. Garnish as desired.
Makes about 5 dozen cookies

Maple Pecan Sandwich Cookies

Cookies

- 1¼ cups firmly packed light brown sugar
- 1 cup Butter Flavor Crisco all-vegetable shortening or 1 Butter Flavor Crisco Stick
- 2 eggs
- ¼ cup maple syrup or maple flavored pancake syrup
- 1 teaspoon maple extract
- ½ teaspoon vanilla
- 2½ cups all-purpose flour (plus 4 tablespoons), divided
- 1½ cups finely ground pecans
- ¾ teaspoon baking powder
- ½ teaspoon baking soda
- ½ teaspoon salt
- 20 to 30 pecan halves (optional)

Filling

- 1¼ cups confectioners sugar
- 3 tablespoons Butter Flavor Crisco all-vegetable shortening
- 1 teaspoon maple extract
- Dash salt
- 2½ teaspoons milk

1. For cookies, place brown sugar and shortening in large bowl. Beat at medium speed of electric mixer until well blended. Add eggs, syrup, maple extract and vanilla; beat until well blended and fluffy.

2. Combine 2½ cups flour, ground pecans, baking powder, baking soda and salt. Add gradually to shortening mixture, beating at low speed until well blended. Divide dough into 4 equal pieces; shape each into disk. Wrap with plastic wrap. Refrigerate 1 hour or until firm.

3. Heat oven to 375°F. Place sheets of foil on countertop for cooling cookies.

4. Sprinkle about 1 tablespoon flour on large sheet of waxed paper. Place disk of dough on floured paper; flatten slightly with hands. Turn dough over; cover with another large sheet of waxed paper. Roll dough to ¼-inch thickness. Cut out with floured 3-inch scalloped round cookie cutter. Place 2 inches apart on ungreased baking sheet. Roll out remaining dough. Place pecans in center of half of cookies, if desired.

5. Bake one baking sheet at a time at 375°F for 5 to 7 minutes or until lightly browned around edges. *Do not overbake.* Cool 2 minutes on baking sheet. Remove cookies to foil to cool completely.

6. For filling, place confectioners sugar, shortening, maple extract and salt in medium bowl. Beat at low speed until smooth. Add milk; beat until mixture is smooth. Spread filling on flat side of 1 plain cookie. Cover with flat side of second cookie with pecan. Repeat with remaining cookies and filling. Garnish as desired.

Makes about 2 dozen sandwich cookies

Raspberry Linzer Rounds

1¼ cups granulated sugar
  1 cup Butter Flavor Crisco
      all-vegetable shortening
      or 1 Butter Flavor
      Crisco Stick
  2 eggs
  ¼ cup light corn syrup or
      regular pancake syrup
  1 teaspoon vanilla
  1 teaspoon almond extract
  3 cups all-purpose flour
      (plus 4 tablespoons),
      divided

  1 cup ground almonds
      (about 4 to 5 ounces)
  ¾ teaspoon baking powder
  ½ teaspoon baking soda
  ½ teaspoon salt
  ½ cup seedless raspberry
      preserves, stirred
  Confectioners sugar
      (optional)

1. Place granulated sugar and shortening in large bowl. Beat at medium speed of electric mixer until well blended. Add eggs, syrup, vanilla and almond extract; beat until well blended and fluffy.

2. Combine 3 cups flour, ground almonds, baking powder, baking soda and salt. Add gradually to shortening mixture, beating at low speed until well blended.

3. Divide dough into 4 pieces; shape each piece into disk. Wrap with plastic wrap. Refrigerate several hours or until firm.

4. Heat oven to 375°F. Place sheets of foil on countertop for cooling cookies.

5. Sprinkle about 1 tablespoon flour on large sheet of waxed paper. Place disk of dough on floured paper; flatten slightly with hands. Turn dough over and cover with another large sheet of waxed paper. Roll dough to ¼-inch thickness. Remove top sheet of waxed paper. Cut out with 2- or 2½-inch floured scalloped round cookie cutter. Place 2 inches apart on ungreased baking sheet. Repeat with remaining dough. Cut out centers of half the cookies with ½- or ¾-inch round cutter.

6. Bake one baking sheet at a time at 375°F for 5 to 7 minutes or until edges of cookies are lightly browned.* *Do not overbake.* Cool 2 minutes on baking sheet. Remove cookies to foil to cool completely.

7. Spread a small amount of raspberry jam on bottom of solid cookies; cover with cut-out cookies, bottom sides down, to form sandwiches. Sift confectioners sugar, if desired, over tops of cookies.

Makes about 2 dozen cookies

*Bake larger cookies 1 to 2 minutes longer.

IRRESISTIBLE PEANUT BUTTER COOKIES

Peanut butter cookies are instantly recognized by their familiar crosshatch pattern. But beneath those lines, Crisco's Irresistible Peanut Butter Cookies are brimming with peanut butter flavor. They deliver the maximum in peanut taste as well as the soft moist texture that you prefer.

While the basic Irresistible Peanut Butter Cookie is a favorite with everyone, the Crisco Kitchens have also paired peanut butter with its traditional partners— chocolate, jelly and bananas. Try the dazzling but easy-to-make Inside-Out Peanut Butter Cookie Cups, the kid-pleasing Peanut Butter & Jelly Streusel Bars or the memorable Bananaramas.

Discover the versatility of the basic Irresistible Peanut Butter Cookie recipe. Just turn the page and treat the kid in everyone to dynamic peanut butter creations.

Irresistible Peanut Butter Cookies
(page 432)

Irresistible Peanut Butter Cookies

1¼ cups firmly packed light
    brown sugar
¾ cup creamy peanut butter
½ cup Crisco all-vegetable
    shortening or ½ Crisco
    Stick

3 tablespoons milk
1 tablespoon vanilla
1 egg
1¾ cups all-purpose flour
¾ teaspoon baking soda
¾ teaspoon salt

1. Heat oven to 375°F. Place sheets of foil on countertop for cooling cookies.

2. Place brown sugar, peanut butter, shortening, milk and vanilla in large bowl. Beat at medium speed of electric mixer until well blended. Add egg; beat just until blended.

3. Combine flour, baking soda and salt. Add to shortening mixture; beat at low speed just until blended.

4. Drop dough by rounded measuring tablespoonfuls 2 inches apart onto ungreased baking sheet. Flatten dough slightly in crisscross pattern with tines of fork.

5. Bake one baking sheet at a time at 375°F for 7 to 8 minutes or until cookies are set and just beginning to brown. *Do not overbake.* Cool 2 minutes on baking sheet. Remove cookies to foil to cool completely.

Makes about 3 dozen cookies

Inside-Out Peanut Butter Cookie Cups

Cookies

1¼ cups firmly packed light brown sugar
¾ cup creamy peanut butter
½ cup Crisco all-vegetable shortening or ½ Crisco Stick
3 tablespoons milk
1 tablespoon vanilla
1 egg
1¾ cups all-purpose flour
¾ teaspoon baking soda
¾ teaspoon salt

Filling

1 cup (6 ounces) semi-sweet chocolate chips
1 teaspoon Butter Flavor Crisco all-vegetable shortening*
¼ cup finely chopped peanuts

*Crisco all-vegetable shortening can be substituted for Butter Flavor Crisco.

1. For cookies, place brown sugar, peanut butter, shortening, milk and vanilla in large bowl. Beat at medium speed of electric mixer until well blended. Add egg; beat just until blended.

2. Combine flour, baking soda and salt. Add to shortening mixture; beat at low speed just until blended. Refrigerate about 1 hour or until firm.

3. Heat oven to 375°F. Grease mini-muffin pans. Place sheets of foil on countertop for cooling cookies.

4. Shape dough into 1-inch balls. Place each ball in prepared mini-muffin cup (1¾ inches in diameter). Press dough onto bottom and sides of cup to within ½ inch of top.

5. Bake at 375°F for 7 to 8 minutes or until cookies are set and just beginning to brown. *Do not overbake.* Cool 10 minutes on cooling racks. Remove cookie cups carefully to foil to cool completely.

6. For filling, place chocolate chips and shortening in medium microwave-safe bowl. Microwave at 50% (MEDIUM) for 1 to 2 minutes or until chips are shiny and soft. Stir until smooth. Spoon about ½ teaspoon chocolate mixture into center of each cookie. Sprinkle with chopped peanuts. Cool completely. *Makes about 3½ dozen cookie cups*

Bananaramas

1¼ cups firmly packed light brown sugar
¾ cup creamy peanut butter
½ cup Crisco all-vegetable shortening or ½ Crisco Stick
1 cup mashed banana
3 tablespoons milk
1½ teaspoons vanilla
½ teaspoon almond extract

1 egg
2 cups all-purpose flour
¾ teaspoon baking soda
¾ teaspoon salt
1½ cups milk chocolate chunks or semisweet chocolate chunks*
1 cup peanuts or coarsely chopped pecans (optional)

* A combination of milk chocolate and semisweet chocolate chunks can be used.

1. Heat oven to 350°F. Place sheets of foil on countertop for cooling cookies.

2. Place brown sugar, peanut butter, shortening, banana, milk, vanilla and almond extract in large bowl. Beat at medium speed of electric mixer until well blended. Add egg; beat just until blended.

3. Combine flour, baking soda and salt. Add to shortening mixture; beat at low speed just until blended. Stir in chocolate chunks and nuts, if desired.

4. Drop dough by rounded measuring tablespoonfuls 2 inches apart onto ungreased baking sheets.

5. Bake one baking sheet at a time at 350°F for 11 to 13 minutes or until cookies are light brown around edges. *Do not overbake.* Cool 2 minutes on baking sheet. Remove cookies to foil to cool completely.

Makes about 4 dozen cookies

Top to bottom: Bananaramas, Inside-Out Peanut Butter Cookie Cups (page 433)

Peanut Butter & Jelly Streusel Bars

1¼ cups firmly packed light brown
    sugar
¾ cup creamy peanut butter
½ cup Crisco all-vegetable shortening
    or ½ Crisco Stick
3 tablespoons milk
1 tablespoon vanilla
1 egg
1¾ cups all-purpose flour
¾ teaspoon baking soda
¾ teaspoon salt
1 cup strawberry jam, stirred
½ cup quick oats, uncooked

1. Heat oven to 350°F. Grease 13 × 9-inch baking pan. Place cooling rack on countertop.

2. Place brown sugar, peanut butter, shortening, milk and vanilla in large bowl. Beat at medium speed of electric mixer until well blended. Add egg; beat just until blended.

3. Combine flour, baking soda and salt. Add to shortening mixture; beat at low speed just until blended.

4. Press ⅔ of dough onto bottom of prepared baking pan. Spread jam over dough to within ¼ inch of edges.

5. Add oats to remaining dough. Drop dough by spoonfuls onto jam.

6. Bake at 350°F for 20 to 25 minutes or until edges and streusel topping are lightly browned. *Do not overbake.* Cool completely on cooling rack. Cut into 2 × 1½-inch bars.

Makes about 3 dozen bars

Clockwise from top left: Peanut Butter & Jelly Streusel Bars, Irresistible Peanut Butter Jack O' Lanters (page 439), Peanut Butter Sombreros (page 438)

Plan a fun-filled Halloween party—it's easy to do and popular with any age group. For entertainment choose from a seemingly endless list of games—from silly to ghoulish. Cookies are a perfect fit for your menu because they are quick to prepare and easy to serve. While everyone will love these Peanut Butter & Jelly Streusel Bars, most any cookies will be a hit.

Peanut Butter Sombreros

For even browning, place only one baking sheet at a time in the oven. If the oven does not heat evenly, turn the baking sheet halfway through baking time. Baking sheets can be reused for a second batch of cookies. Just be sure baking sheets have cooled to room temperature before using; otherwise, cookies will spread too much.

1¼ cups firmly packed light brown sugar
¾ cup creamy peanut butter
½ cup Crisco all-vegetable shortening or ½ Crisco Stick
3 tablespoons milk
1 tablespoon vanilla
1 egg
1¾ cups all-purpose flour
¾ teaspoon baking soda
¾ teaspoon salt
Granulated sugar
40 to 50 chocolate kisses, unwrapped

1. Heat oven to 375°F. Place sheets of foil on countertop for cooling cookies.

2. Place brown sugar, peanut butter, shortening, milk and vanilla in large bowl. Beat at medium speed of electric mixer until well blended. Add egg; beat just until blended.

3. Combine flour, baking soda and salt. Add to shortening mixture; beat at low speed just until blended.

4. Shape dough into 1-inch balls. Roll in granulated sugar. Place 2 inches apart on ungreased baking sheets.

5. Bake one baking sheet at a time at 375°F for 6 minutes. Press chocolate kiss into center of each cookie. Bake 3 minutes longer. *Do not overbake.* Cool 2 minutes on baking sheet. Remove cookies to foil to cool completely.   *Makes about 4 dozen cookies*

Irresistible Peanut Butter Jack O' Lanterns

Cookies

1¼ cups firmly packed light brown sugar
¾ cup creamy peanut butter
½ cup Crisco all-vegetable shortening or ½ Crisco Stick
3 tablespoons milk
1 tablespoon vanilla
1 egg
1¾ cups all-purpose flour

¾ teaspoon baking soda
¾ teaspoon salt

Icing

1 cup (6 ounces) semisweet chocolate chips
2 teaspoons Butter Flavor Crisco all-vegetable shortening*

*Crisco all-vegetable shortening can be substituted for Butter Flavor Crisco.

1. Heat oven to 375°F. Place sheets of foil on countertop for cooling cookies.

2. For cookies, place brown sugar, peanut butter, shortening, milk and vanilla in large bowl. Beat at medium speed of electric mixer until well blended. Add egg; beat just until blended.

3. Combine flour, baking soda and salt. Add to shortening mixture; beat at low speed just until blended.

4. Pinch off pieces of dough the size of walnuts. Shape into balls. Place 3 inches apart on ungreased baking sheet. Flatten each ball with bottom of glass to approximately ⅜-inch thickness. Form into pumpkin shape, making indentation on top of round. Pinch off very small piece of dough and roll to form small stem. Attach to top of cookie. Score dough with vertical lines with small, sharp knife to resemble pumpkin.

5. Bake one baking sheet at a time at 375°F for 7 to 8 minutes or until cookies are set and just beginning to brown. *Do not overbake.* Cool on baking sheet 2 minutes. Remove cookies to foil to cool completely.

6. For icing, place chocolate chips and shortening in heavy resealable sandwich bag; seal bag. Microwave at 50% (MEDIUM) for 1 minute. Knead bag. If necessary, microwave at 50% for another 30 seconds at a time until mixture is smooth when bag is kneaded. Cut small tip off corner of bag. Pipe lines and faces on cookies to resemble jack o' lanterns.

Makes about 3 dozen cookies

CHEWY BROWNIE COOKIES

For a true chocolate lover, nothing compares with the rich chocolaty flavor of a brownie. And now that flavor has been captured in the Chewy Brownie Cookie, a luscious drop cookie with a double dose of chocolate. This cookie, developed by the Crisco Kitchens to be moist and chewy, is sure to please any chocoholic on your guest list.

Some of the variations in this chapter are drawn from time-honored, crowd-pleasing chocolate flavor combinations. Chocolate-Mint Brownie Cookies team two old favorites. Friends will love the richness of Toasted Almond Brownie Cookies and German Chocolate Brownie Cookies. Chocolate is a natural with coffee and almonds in Almond Mocha Cookie Bars. Or, press this basic chewy brownie dough into a baking pan and top with a cream cheese layer for heavenly Chocolate Cheesecake Bars.

Chewy Brownie Cookies (page 442)

Chewy Brownie Cookies

1½ cups firmly packed light
    brown sugar
⅔ cup Crisco all-vegetable
    shortening or ⅔ Crisco
    Stick
1 tablespoon water
1 teaspoon vanilla
2 eggs

1½ cups all-purpose flour
⅓ cup unsweetened cocoa
    powder
½ teaspoon salt
¼ teaspoon baking soda
2 cups (12 ounces)
    semisweet chocolate
    chips

1. Heat oven to 375°F. Place sheets of foil on countertop for cooling cookies.

2. Place brown sugar, shortening, water and vanilla in large bowl. Beat at medium speed of electric mixer until well blended. Add eggs; beat well.

3. Combine flour, cocoa, salt and baking soda. Add to shortening mixture; beat at low speed just until blended. Stir in chocolate chips.

4. Drop dough by rounded measuring tablespoonfuls 2 inches apart onto ungreased baking sheet.

5. Bake one baking sheet at a time at 375°F for 7 to 9 minutes or until cookies are set. *Do not overbake.* Cool 2 minutes on baking sheet. Remove cookies to foil to cool completely.

Makes about 3 dozen cookies

Toasted Almond Brownie Cookies

1 cup blanched whole almonds
1½ cups firmly packed light brown sugar
⅔ cup Crisco all-vegetable shortening or ⅔ Crisco Stick
1 tablespoon water
1 teaspoon almond extract
2 eggs
1½ cups all-purpose flour
⅓ cup unsweetened cocoa powder
½ teaspoon salt
¼ teaspoon baking soda
2 cups (12 ounces) semisweet chocolate chips

1. Heat oven to 350°F. Spread almonds on baking sheet; bake at 350°F for 7 to 10 minutes or until golden brown, stirring several times. Cool. Chop coarsely; reserve.

2. *Increase oven temperature to 375°F.* Place sheets of foil on countertop for cooling cookies.

3. Place brown sugar, shortening, water and almond extract in large bowl. Beat at medium speed of electric mixer until well blended. Add eggs; beat well.

4. Combine flour, cocoa, salt and baking soda. Add to shortening mixture; beat at low speed just until blended. Stir in chocolate chips and reserved almonds.

5. Drop dough by rounded measuring tablespoonfuls 2 inches apart onto ungreased baking sheet.

6. Bake one baking sheet at a time at 375°F for 7 to 9 minutes or until cookies are set. *Do not overbake.* Cool 2 minutes on baking sheet. Remove cookies to foil to cool completely.   *Makes about 3 dozen cookies*

Plan ahead! To have freshly baked cookies ready in minutes, place dough in a tightly covered container and refrigerate up to one week or freeze up to six months. Or, form cookies on baking sheet, freeze and transfer to plastic bag for up to six months. Thaw dough before baking.

Chocolate Cheesecake Bars

Brownies

1½ cups firmly packed light brown sugar
⅔ cup Crisco all-vegetable shortening or ⅔ Crisco Stick
1 tablespoon water
1 teaspoon vanilla
2 eggs
1½ cups all-purpose flour
⅓ cup unsweetened cocoa powder
½ teaspoon salt
¼ teaspoon baking soda
2 cups (12 ounces) miniature semisweet chocolate chips

Topping

1 (8-ounce) *plus* 1 (3-ounce) package cream cheese, softened
2 eggs
¾ cup granulated sugar
1 teaspoon vanilla

1. Heat oven to 350°F. Grease 13 × 9-inch baking pan. Place cooling rack on countertop.

2. For brownies, place brown sugar, shortening, water and vanilla in large bowl. Beat at medium speed of electric mixer until well blended. Add eggs; beat well.

3. Combine flour, cocoa, salt and baking soda. Add to shortening mixture; beat at low speed just until blended. Stir in miniature chocolate chips. Spread dough evenly onto bottom of prepared pan.

4. For topping, place cream cheese, eggs, granulated sugar and vanilla in medium bowl. Beat at medium speed until well blended. Spread evenly over top of brownie mixture.

5. Bake at 350°F for 35 to 40 minutes or until set. *Do not overbake.* Place on cooling rack. Run spatula around edge of pan to loosen. Cool completely on cooling rack. Cut into 2 × 1½-inch bars. Garnish as desired.

Makes about 3 dozen brownies

Almond Mocha Cookie Bars

Cookie Base

1 cup slivered almonds
1½ cups firmly packed light brown sugar
⅔ cup Crisco all-vegetable shortening or ⅔ Crisco Stick
2 tablespoons instant or espresso coffee powder
1 tablespoon cold coffee
1 teaspoon vanilla
½ teaspoon almond extract
2 eggs
1½ cups all-purpose flour
⅓ cup unsweetened cocoa powder
½ teaspoon salt
¼ teaspoon baking soda
1 cup (6 ounces) miniature semisweet chocolate chips

Glaze

1 cup confectioners sugar
1 tablespoon cold coffee
1 tablespoon coffee-flavored liqueur or cold coffee (optional)

1. Heat oven to 350°F. Grease 13 × 9-inch baking pan. Place cooling rack on countertop.

2. For cookie base, spread almonds onto baking sheet; bake at 350°F for 7 to 10 minutes or until golden brown, stirring several times. Cool completely. Chop coarsely.

3. Place brown sugar, shortening, coffee powder, coffee, vanilla and almond extract in large bowl. Beat at medium speed of electric mixer until well blended. Add eggs; beat well.

4. Combine flour, cocoa, salt and baking soda. Add to shortening mixture; beat at low speed just until blended. Stir in small chocolate chips and reserved almonds. Spread mixture evenly into prepared pan.

5. Bake at 350°F for 30 to 35 minutes or until set. *Do not overbake.* Cool completely on wire rack. Cut into 2 × 1½-inch bars.

6. For glaze, combine confectioners sugar, coffee and coffee liqueur, if desired, in small bowl. Stir until well blended. Add additional coffee, a little at a time, if icing is too thick, or add additional confectioners sugar, if icing is too thin. Drizzle glaze over bars.

Makes about 3 dozen bars

German Chocolate Brownie Cookies

Cookies
1½ cups firmly packed light
    brown sugar
⅔ cup Crisco all-vegetable
    shortening or ⅔ Crisco
    Stick
1 tablespoon water
1 teaspoon vanilla
2 eggs
1½ cups all-purpose flour
⅓ cup unsweetened cocoa
    powder
½ teaspoon salt
¼ teaspoon baking soda
2 cups (12 ounces)
    semisweet chocolate
    chips

Topping
½ cup evaporated milk
½ cup granulated sugar
¼ cup Butter Flavor Crisco
    all-vegetable shortening
    or ¼ Butter Flavor
    Crisco Stick*
2 egg yolks, lightly beaten
½ teaspoon vanilla
½ cup chopped pecans
½ cup flaked coconut

*Crisco all-vegetable shortening can be substituted for Butter Flavor Crisco or Butter Flavor Crisco Stick.

1. Heat oven to 375°F. Place sheets of foil on countertop for cooling cookies.

2. For cookies, place brown sugar, shortening, water and vanilla in large bowl. Beat at medium speed of electric mixer until well blended. Add eggs; beat well.

3. Combine flour, cocoa, salt and baking soda. Add to shortening mixture; beat at low speed just until blended. Stir in chocolate chips.

4. Drop dough by rounded measuring tablespoonfuls 2 inches apart onto ungreased baking sheet.

5. Bake one baking sheet at a time at 375°F for 7 to 9 minutes or until cookies are set. *Do not overbake.* Cool 2 minutes on baking sheet. Remove cookies to foil to cool completely.

6. For topping, combine evaporated milk, granulated sugar, shortening and egg yolks in medium saucepan. Stir over medium heat until thickened. Remove from heat. Stir in vanilla, pecans and coconut. Cool completely. Frost cookies. *Makes about 3 dozen cookies*

Top to bottom: Maple Pecan Sandwich Cookies (page 428), German Chocolate Brownie Cookies, Good 'n' Tasties (page 419)

Cracked Chocolate Cookies

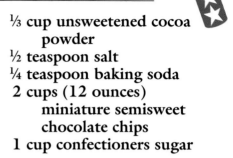

1½ cups firmly packed light brown sugar
⅔ cup Crisco all-vegetable shortening or ⅔ Crisco Stick
1 tablespoon water
1 teaspoon vanilla
2 eggs
1½ cups all-purpose flour

⅓ cup unsweetened cocoa powder
½ teaspoon salt
¼ teaspoon baking soda
2 cups (12 ounces) miniature semisweet chocolate chips
1 cup confectioners sugar

1. Heat oven to 375°F. Place sheets of foil on countertop for cooling cookies.

2. Place brown sugar, shortening, water and vanilla in large bowl. Beat at medium speed of electric mixer until well blended. Add eggs; beat well.

3. Combine flour, cocoa, salt and baking soda. Add to shortening mixture; beat at low speed just until blended. Stir in miniature chocolate chips.

4. Shape dough into 1¼-inch balls. Roll in confectioners sugar. Place 2 inches apart on ungreased baking sheet.

5. Bake one baking sheet at a time at 375°F for 7 to 9 minutes or until cookies are set. *Do not overbake.* Cool 2 minutes on baking sheet. Remove cookies to foil to cool completely.

Makes about 4 dozen cookies

Chocolate Malted Cookies

¾ cup firmly packed light brown sugar
⅔ cup Crisco all-vegetable shortening or ⅔ Crisco Stick
1 teaspoon vanilla
1 egg
1¾ cups all-purpose flour

½ cup malted milk powder
⅓ cup unsweetened cocoa powder
¾ teaspoon baking soda
½ teaspoon salt
2 cups malted milk balls, broken into large pieces*

*Place malted milk balls in heavy resealable plastic bag; break malted milk balls with rolling pin or back of heavy spoon.

1. Heat oven to 375°F. Place sheets of foil on countertop for cooling cookies.

2. Place brown sugar, shortening and vanilla in large bowl. Beat at medium speed of electric mixer until well blended. Add egg; beat well.

3. Combine flour, malted milk powder, cocoa, baking soda and salt. Add to shortening mixture; beat at low speed just until blended. Stir in malted milk pieces.

4. Drop dough by rounded measuring tablespoonfuls 2 inches apart onto ungreased baking sheet.

5. Bake one baking sheet at a time at 375°F for 7 to 9 minutes or until cookies are set. *Do not overbake*. Cool 2 minutes on baking sheet. Remove cookies to foil to cool completely.

Makes about 3 dozen cookies

Chocolate-Mint Brownie Cookies

1½ cups firmly packed light brown sugar
⅔ cup Crisco all-vegetable shortening or ⅔ Crisco Stick
1 tablespoon water
1 teaspoon vanilla
½ teaspoon peppermint extract

2 eggs
1½ cups all-purpose flour
⅓ cup unsweetened cocoa powder
½ teaspoon salt
¼ teaspoon baking soda
2 cups (12 ounces) mint chocolate chips

1. Heat oven to 375°F. Place sheets of foil on countertop for cooling cookies.

2. Place brown sugar, shortening, water, vanilla and peppermint extract in large bowl. Beat at medium speed of electric mixer until well blended. Add eggs; beat well.

3. Combine flour, cocoa, salt and baking soda. Add to shortening mixture; beat at low speed just until blended. Stir in mint chocolate chips.

4. Drop dough by rounded measuring tablespoonfuls 2 inches apart onto ungreased baking sheet.

5. Bake one baking sheet at a time at 375°F for 7 to 9 minutes or until cookies are set. *Do not overbake*. Cool 2 minutes on baking sheet. Remove cookies to foil to cool completely.

Makes about 3 dozen cookies

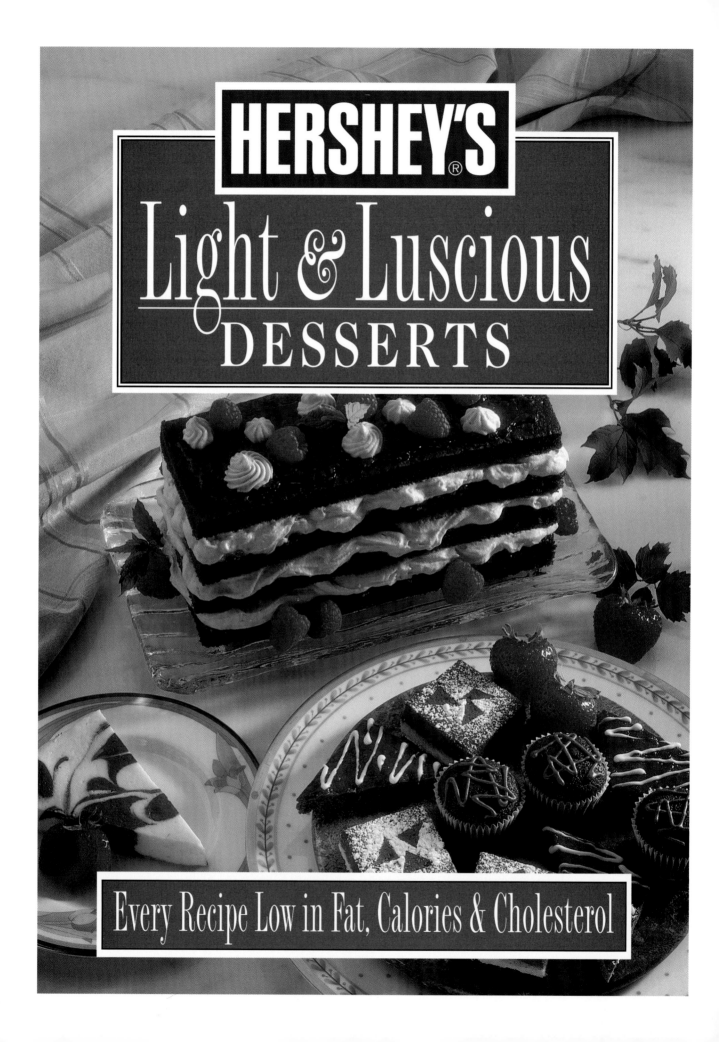

Contents

Clockwise from top: Chocolate and Raspberry Cream Torte, page 460; Choco-Lowfat Strawberry Shortbread Bars, page 466; Mini Brownie Cups, page 468; Chocolate Mousse Squares, page 464; Chocolate Swirled Cheesecake, page 462

ABOUT THE RECIPES

Many Americans today are being advised to reduce the amount of fat in their diets to help keep body weight and blood cholesterol levels in check. Many others are cutting down on fat simply to look and feel better. Does this mean a final good-bye to those delectable chocolate desserts that make life sweeter? Definitely not! By using unsweetened cocoa instead of baking chocolate, chocolate lovers can experience the luscious, rich flavor they love — without all the extra fat and calories.

Hershey's Cocoa is a deep, dark chocolate baking ingredient that contains only .5 grams of fat per tablespoon and is naturally very low in sodium and cholesterol-free. Cocoa is lower in fat than other chocolate baking ingredients because most of the cocoa butter has been removed; it is the only chocolate baking ingredient listed by the American Heart Association (AHA) for use in fat-restricted diets.

The Hershey Kitchens have created a variety of luscious, flavorful desserts designed specifically for chocolate enthusiasts who want the tantalizing taste and texture of a chocolate treat without excess fat, calories and cholesterol. Each recipe has been evaluated by Hershey nutritionists for its nutritional value and has been developed using the following guidelines:

> **Calories** — 180 or less per serving
> **Cholesterol** — 20 mg or less per serving
> **Fat** — 5 g or less per serving

These criteria have been established to help consumers select diets that conform with the AHA's dietary guidelines. The AHA recommends that a person's total dietary fat content be 30 percent or less of total calorie intake. Cholesterol intake should be less than 300 milligrams per day.

The analysis of each recipe includes all the ingredients that are listed in that recipe, *except* ingredients labeled as "optional." If an ingredient is presented with an option ("½ cup strawberries or raspberries") the *first* item listed was used to calculate the nutrition information. If a range is offered for an ingredient (¼ to ⅛ teaspoon, for example) the *first* amount given was used to calculate the nutrition information. Foods shown in photographs on the same serving plate and offered as "serve with" or "garnish with" suggestions at the end of a recipe are not included in the recipe analysis unless otherwise stated.

Every effort has been made to give accurate nutrition data. However, because numerous variables account for a wide range of values for certain foods, all nutrient values that appear in this publication should be considered approximate.

COCOA BASICS

Hershey's Cocoa keeps very well when stored at room temperature in the original container. It retains its freshness and quality almost indefinitely without refrigeration. Cocoa tins now feature an easy-to-use resealable plastic lid.

When storing Hershey's Cocoa, avoid contact with moisture and/or high heat; they could cause clumping and gray discoloration, although neither affect cocoa flavor or quality.

Hershey's Cocoa is a favorite ingredient in recipes developed by the Hershey Kitchens. It is so convenient to use because it is easy to measure, can be used right from the can, blends easily with other ingredients and gives desserts a rich chocolate flavor. To substitute cocoa in your favorite baked recipe, use the appropriate method listed below:

- Three level tablespoons cocoa plus 1 tablespoon shortening (liquid or solid) equals 1 square (1 ounce) unsweetened baking chocolate.

- Six level tablespoons cocoa plus 7 tablespoons sugar plus ¼ cup shortening equals one 6-ounce package (1 cup) semi-sweet chocolate chips or six squares (1 ounce each) semi-sweet chocolate.

- Three level tablespoons cocoa plus 4½ tablespoons sugar plus 2⅔ tablespoons shortening equals 1 bar (4 ounces) sweet baking chocolate.

Hershey's European Style Cocoa is also called "dutch processed" or "alkalized" cocoa. Dutching is a process that neutralizes the natural acidity found in cocoa powder. This results in a darker cocoa with a more mellow chocolate flavor than Hershey's Regular Cocoa. While European Style Cocoa imparts a different color and flavor than regular cocoa, it can easily be substituted in chocolate recipes.

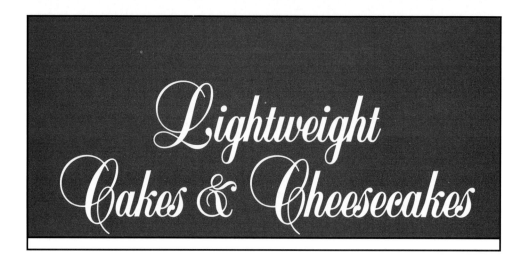

Lightweight Cakes & Cheesecakes

CHOCOLATE CAKE FINGERS

1 cup sugar
1 cup all-purpose flour
⅓ cup HERSHEY'S Cocoa
¾ teaspoon baking powder
¾ teaspoon baking soda
½ cup skim milk
¼ cup liquid egg substitute
¼ cup canola oil or
    vegetable oil

1 teaspoon vanilla extract
½ cup boiling water
    Powdered sugar
1 teaspoon freshly grated
    orange peel
1½ cups frozen light non-dairy
    whipped topping,
    thawed

Heat oven to 350°F. Line bottom of 13X9X2-inch baking pan with wax paper. In large mixer bowl, stir together sugar, flour, cocoa, baking powder and baking soda. Add milk, egg substitute, oil and vanilla; beat on medium speed of electric mixer 2 minutes. Stir in boiling water (batter will be thin). Pour into prepared pan.

Bake 16 to 18 minutes or until wooden pick inserted in center comes out clean. With knife or metal spatula, loosen cake from edges of pan. Place clean, lint-free dishtowel on wire rack; sprinkle lightly with powdered sugar. Invert cake on towel; peel off wax paper. Cool completely. Invert cake, right side up, on cutting board. Cut cake into small rectangles (about 2X1¼ inches). Stir orange peel into whipped topping; spoon dollop on each piece of cake. Garnish as desired. Store ungarnished cake, covered, at room temperature.

42 pieces

Nutritional Information Per Serving	
(2 pieces)	
100 Calories	0 mg Cholesterol
1 gm Protein	70 mg Sodium
16 gm Carbohydrate	15 mg Calcium
3.5 gm Fat	

Chocolate Cake Fingers

SECRET STRAWBERRY FILLED ANGEL CAKE

1 package (about
    15 ounces) angel food
    cake mix
1½ teaspoons unflavored
    gelatin
¼ cup cold water

1 container (8 ounces)
    vanilla lowfat yogurt
⅓ cup HERSHEY'S Strawberry
    Syrup
    Chocolate Syrup Whipped
    Topping (recipe follows)

Place oven rack in lowest position, Mix, bake and cool cake as directed on package. In small microwave-safe bowl, sprinkle gelatin over water; let stand 2 minutes to soften. Microwave at HIGH (100%) 40 seconds; stir thoroughly. Let stand 2 minutes or until gelatin is completely dissolved; cool slightly. In medium bowl, stir together yogurt, strawberry syrup and gelatin mixture until smooth; refrigerate until mixture mounds slightly when dropped from spoon, about 15 to 20 minutes.

Place cake, rounded side down, on cutting board. Using serrated knife, cut 1-inch layer from top of cake; lift off in one piece. Set aside. Using serrated knife, cut around cake 1 inch from center hole and 1 inch from outer edge, leaving cake walls and cake base 1¼ inches thick. Using fork, carefully remove cake in cavity without breaking through sides or bottom. Place hollowed-out cake on serving plate. Spoon strawberry syrup mixture into cavity. Cover with reserved cake top. Cover; refrigerate while preparing Chocolate Syrup Whipped Topping. Spread Chocolate Syrup Whipped Topping evenly over top and outside of cake. Refrigerate 4 hours or until strawberry syrup mixture is set before serving. Garnish as desired. Cover; refrigerate leftover cake.

18 servings

Chocolate Syrup Whipped Topping: In medium bowl, stir together 2 cups frozen light non-dairy whipped topping, thawed and ¼ cup HERSHEY'S Syrup.

Nutritional Information Per Serving

140 Calories	0 mg Cholesterol
3 gm Protein	190 mg Sodium
30 gm Carbohydrate	25 mg Calcium
1 gm Fat	

Secret Strawberry Filled Angel Cake

LUSCIOUS CHOCOLATE CHEESECAKE

2 cups (16 ounces) nonfat cottage cheese
¾ cup liquid egg substitute
⅔ cup sugar
4 ounces (½ of 8-ounce package) Neufchatel cheese (light cream cheese), softened
⅓ cup HERSHEY'S Cocoa or HERSHEY'S European Style Cocoa

½ teaspoon vanilla extract
Yogurt Topping (recipe follows)
Sliced strawberries or mandarin orange segments (optional)

Heat oven to 300°F. Spray 9-inch springform pan with vegetable cooking spray. In food processor, place cottage cheese, egg substitute, sugar, Neufchatel cheese, cocoa and vanilla; process until smooth. Pour into prepared pan.

Bake 35 minutes or until edge is set. Meanwhile, prepare Yogurt Topping. Carefully spread topping over top of warm cheesecake. Return cheesecake to oven; bake 5 minutes. With knife, loosen cheesecake from side of pan. Cool completely in pan on wire rack. Cover; refrigerate until chilled. Just before serving, remove side of pan. Serve with strawberries or oranges, if desired. Garnish as desired. Cover; refrigerate leftover cheesecake.   *Makes 9 servings*

Yogurt Topping: In small bowl, stir together ⅔ cup plain nonfat yogurt and 2 tablespoons sugar until well blended.

Nutritional Information Per Serving

170 Calories	10 mg Cholesterol
12 gm Protein	290 mg Sodium
22 gm Carbohydrate	70 mg Calcium
4 gm Fat	

Luscious Chocolate Cheesecake

CHOCOLATE AND RASPBERRY CREAM TORTE

6 tablespoons (40% oil)
   lower-fat margarine
1 cup sugar
1 cup skim milk
1 tablespoon white vinegar
½ teaspoon vanilla extract
1¼ cups all-purpose flour

⅓ cup HERSHEY'S Cocoa or
   HERSHEY'S European
   Style Cocoa
1 teaspoon baking soda
¼ cup red raspberry jam
Raspberry Cream (recipe
   follows)

Heat oven to 350°F. Spray 15½X10½X1-inch jelly-roll pan with vegetable cooking spray. In medium saucepan over low heat, melt margarine; stir in sugar. Remove from heat; stir in milk, vinegar and vanilla. In small bowl, stir together flour, cocoa and baking soda; add gradually to sugar mixture, stirring with whisk until well blended. Pour into prepared pan.

Bake 16 to 18 minutes or until wooden pick inserted in center comes out clean. Cool 10 minutes; remove from pan to wire rack. Cool completely. To assemble, cut cake crosswise into four pieces. Place one piece on serving plate; spread 1 tablespoon jam over top. Carefully spread a scant ¾ cup Raspberry Cream over jam. Repeat procedure with remaining cake layers, jam and Raspberry Cream, ending with plain layer on top. Spread remaining 1 tablespoon jam over top. Spoon or pipe remaining Raspberry Cream over jam. Refrigerate torte until ready to serve. Garnish as desired. Cover; refrigerate leftover torte.

15 servings

Raspberry Cream: Thaw and thoroughly drain 1 package (10 ounces) frozen red raspberries. In blender container, place raspberries. Cover; blend until smooth. Strain in sieve; discard seeds. In small mixer bowl, prepare 1 envelope (1.3 ounces) dry whipped topping mix as directed on package, using ½ cup cold skim milk, omitting vanilla and adding 2 to 3 drops red food color, if desired. Fold in pureed raspberries.

Nutritional Information Per Serving

170 Calories	0 mg Cholesterol
3 gm Protein	120 mg Sodium
33 gm Carbohydrate	40 mg Calcium
3.5 gm Fat	

---

*Chocolate and Raspberry
Cream Torte*

CHOCOLATE SWIRLED CHEESECAKE

Yogurt Cheese (recipe follows)
2 tablespoons graham cracker crumbs
1 package (8 ounces) Neufchatel cheese (light cream cheese), softened
1½ teaspoons vanilla extract
¾ cup sugar
1 tablespoon cornstarch
1 carton (8 ounces) liquid egg substitute
¼ cup HERSHEY'S Cocoa
¼ teaspoon almond extract

Prepare Yogurt Cheese. Heat oven to 325°F. Spray bottom of 8- or 9-inch springform pan with vegetable cooking spray. Sprinkle graham cracker crumbs on bottom of pan. In large mixer bowl, beat Yogurt Cheese, Neufchatel cheese and vanilla on medium speed of electric mixer until smooth. Add sugar and cornstarch; beat just until well blended. Gradually add egg substitute, beating on low speed until blended. Transfer 1½ cups batter to medium bowl; add cocoa. Beat until well blended. Stir almond extract into vanilla batter. Alternately spoon vanilla and chocolate batters into prepared pan. With knife or metal spatula, cut through batters for marble effect.

Bake 35 minutes for 8-inch pan; 40 minutes for 9-inch pan or until edge is set. With knife, loosen cheesecake from side of pan. Cool completely in pan on wire rack. Cover; refrigerate at least 6 hours before serving. Just before serving, remove side of pan. Garnish as desired. Cover; refrigerate leftover cheesecake.   *16 servings*

Yogurt Cheese: Use one 16-ounce container plain lowfat yogurt, no gelatin added. Line non-rusting colander or sieve with large piece of double thickness cheesecloth or large coffee filter; place colander over deep bowl. Spoon yogurt into prepared colander; cover with plastic wrap. Refrigerate until liquid no longer drains from yogurt, about 24 hours. Remove yogurt from cheesecloth and place in separate bowl; discard liquid.

Nutritional Information Per Serving	
110 Calories	15 mg Cholesterol
4 gm Protein	100 mg Sodium
14 gm Carbohydrate	45 mg Calcium
4 gm Fat	

Chocolate Swirled Cheesecake

Guilt-Free Cookies & Bars

CHOCOLATE MOUSSE SQUARES

¾ cup plus 2 tablespoons all-purpose flour, divided
⅔ cup plus 3 tablespoons granulated sugar, divided
¼ cup (½ stick) cold margarine
¼ cup HERSHEY'S Cocoa

½ teaspoon powdered instant coffee
¼ teaspoon baking powder
½ cup liquid egg substitute
½ teaspoon vanilla extract
½ cup plain lowfat yogurt
½ teaspoon powdered sugar

Heat oven to 350°F. In medium bowl, stir together ¾ cup flour and 3 tablespoons granulated sugar. With pastry blender or 2 knives, cut in margarine until fine crumbs form. Press mixture onto bottom of ungreased 8-inch square baking pan. Bake 15 minutes or until golden. Reduce oven temperature to 300°F.

Meanwhile, in small mixer bowl, stir together remaining ⅔ cup granulated sugar, cocoa, remaining 2 tablespoons flour, instant coffee and baking powder. Add egg substitute and vanilla; beat on medium speed of electric mixer until well blended. Add yogurt; beat just until blended. Pour over prepared crust.

Bake 30 minutes or until center is set. Cool completely in pan on wire rack. Cut into squares. If desired, place small paper cutouts over top. Sift powdered sugar over cutouts. Carefully remove cutouts. Store, covered, in refrigerator. *16 squares*

Nutritional Information Per Serving (1 square)	
100 Calories	0 mg Cholesterol
2 gm Protein	55 mg Sodium
17 gm Carbohydrate	20 mg Calcium
3 gm Fat	

Chocolate Mousse Squares

CHOCO-LOWFAT STRAWBERRY SHORTBREAD BARS

¼ cup (½ stick) (56-60%) vegetable oil spread
½ cup sugar
1 egg white
1¼ cups all-purpose flour
¼ cup HERSHEY'S Cocoa or HERSHEY'S European Style Cocoa

¾ teaspoon cream of tartar
½ teaspoon baking soda
Dash salt
½ cup strawberry all-fruit spread
White Chip Drizzle (recipe follows)

Heat oven to 375°F. Lightly spray 13X9X2-inch baking pan with vegetable cooking spray. In mixer bowl, combine vegetable oil spread and sugar; beat on medium speed of electric mixer until well blended. Add egg white; beat until well blended. In small bowl, stir together flour, cocoa, cream of tartar, baking soda and salt; beat gradually into sugar mixture. Gently press mixture onto bottom of prepared pan.

Bake 10 to 12 minutes or just until set. Cool completely in pan on wire rack. Spread fruit spread evenly over crust. Cut into bars or other desired shapes with small cookie cutters. Drizzle White Chip Drizzle over tops of bars. Let stand until set. Store, covered, at room temperature.   *3 dozen bars*

White Chip Drizzle: In small microwave-safe bowl, place ⅓ cup HERSHEY'S Premier White Milk Chips and ½ teaspoon shortening (do not use butter, margarine or oil). Microwave at HIGH (100%) 30 seconds; stir vigorously. If necessary, microwave at HIGH an additional 15 seconds until chips are melted and mixture is smooth when stirred. Use immediately.

Nutritional Information Per Serving
(1 bar with drizzle)

60 Calories	0 mg Cholesterol
1 gm Protein	30 mg Sodium
11 gm Carbohydrate	5 mg Calcium
1.5 gm Fat	

Choco-Lowfat Strawberry Shortbread Bars

MINI BROWNIE CUPS

¼ cup (½ stick) (56-60% oil)
 vegetable oil spread
2 egg whites
1 egg
¾ cup sugar
⅔ cup all-purpose flour

⅓ cup HERSHEY'S Cocoa
½ teaspoon baking powder
¼ teaspoon salt
 Mocha Glaze (recipe
 follows)

Heat oven to 350°F. Line 24 small muffin cups (1¾ inches in diameter) with paper bake cups or spray with vegetable cooking spray. In small saucepan over low heat, melt vegetable oil spread; cool slightly. In small mixer bowl, beat egg whites and egg on medium speed of electric mixer until foamy; gradually add sugar, beating until slightly thickened and light in color. In small bowl, stir together flour, cocoa, baking powder and salt; add gradually to egg mixture, beating until blended. Gradually add vegetable oil spread; beat just until blended. Fill muffin cups ⅔ full with batter.

Bake 15 to 18 minutes or until wooden pick inserted in centers comes out clean. Remove from pans to wire racks. Cool completely. Drizzle Mocha Glaze over tops of brownie cups. Let stand until set. Store, covered, at room temperature.   *2 dozen brownie cups*

MOCHA GLAZE

¼ cup powdered sugar
¾ teaspoon HERSHEY'S
 Cocoa
¼ teaspoon powdered
 instant coffee

2 teaspoons hot water
¼ teaspoon vanilla extract

In small bowl, stir together powdered sugar and cocoa. Dissolve coffee in water; add to sugar mixture, stirring until well blended. Stir in vanilla.

Nutritional Information Per Serving
(2 brownie cups with glaze)

120 Calories	20 mg Cholesterol
2 gm Protein	105 mg Sodium
22 gm Carbohydrate	5 mg Calcium
3.5 gm Fat	

FRUIT-FILLED CHOCOLATE DREAMS

1 envelope (1.3 ounces) dry whipped topping mix
1 tablespoon HERSHEY'S Cocoa
½ cup cold skim milk

½ teaspoon vanilla extract
Assorted fresh fruit, cut up
Chocolate Sauce (recipe follows)

Place foil on cookie sheet. In small mixer bowl, stir together topping mix and cocoa. Add ½ cup milk and ½ teaspoon vanilla. Beat on high speed of electric mixer until stiff peaks form. Spoon topping into 5 mounds onto prepared cookie sheet. With spoon, shape into 4-inch shells. Freeze until firm, about 1 hour. To serve, fill center of each frozen shell with about ⅓ cup assorted fresh fruit; drizzle with 1 tablespoon Chocolate Sauce. Garnish as desired. Serve immediately.

5 servings

CHOCOLATE SAUCE

¾ cup sugar
⅓ cup HERSHEY'S Cocoa
1 tablespoon cornstarch

¾ cup water
1 tablespoon margarine
1 teaspoon vanilla extract

In small saucepan, combine sugar, cocoa and cornstarch; gradually stir in water. Cook over medium heat, stirring constantly, until mixture comes to a boil; boil 1 minute. Remove from heat; add margarine and vanilla, stirring until smooth. Cover; refrigerate until cold.

Nutritional Information Per Serving

110 Calories
2 gm Protein
16 gm Carbohydrate
4 gm Fat

0 mg Cholesterol
30 mg Sodium
45 mg Calcium

Fruit-Filled Chocolate Dreams

LUSCIOUS COLD CHOCOLATE SOUFFLES

1 envelope unflavored
   gelatin
¼ cup cold water
2 tablespoons reduced-
   calorie tub margarine
1½ cups cold skim milk,
   divided
½ cup sugar

⅓ cup HERSHEY'S Cocoa or
   HERSHEY'S European
   Style Cocoa
2½ teaspoons vanilla extract,
   divided
1 envelope (1.3 ounces) dry
   whipped topping mix

Measure lengths of foil to fit around 6 small souffle dishes (about 4 ounces each); fold in thirds lengthwise. Tape securely to outside of dishes to form collar, allowing collar to extend 1 inch above rims of dishes. Lightly oil inside of foil.

In small microwave-safe bowl, sprinkle gelatin over water; let stand 2 minutes to soften. Microwave at HIGH (100%) 40 seconds; stir thoroughly. Stir in margarine until melted; let stand 2 minutes or until gelatin is completely dissolved. In small mixer bowl, stir together 1 cup milk, sugar, cocoa and 2 teaspoons vanilla. Beat on low speed of electric mixer while gradually pouring in gelatin mixture. Beat until well blended. Prepare topping mix as directed on package, using remaining ½ cup milk and remaining ½ teaspoon vanilla; carefully fold into chocolate mixture until well blended.

Spoon into prepared souffle dishes, filling ½-inch from top of collars. Cover; refrigerate until firm, about 3 hours. Carefully remove foil. Garnish as desired.

6 servings

Note: Six (6-ounce) custard cups may be used in place of souffle dishes; omit foil collar.

Nutritional Information Per Serving	
170 Calories	0 mg Cholesterol
5 gm Protein	60 mg Sodium
25 gm Carbohydrate	80 mg Calcium
5 gm Fat	

Luscious Cold Chocolate Souffles

TIDAL WAVE COCOA ALMOND MOUSSE

⅔ cup sugar
⅓ cup HERSHEY'S Cocoa
1 envelope unflavored
   gelatin
1½ cups (12-ounce can)
   evaporated skim milk

½ teaspoon almond extract
1 envelope (1.3 ounces) dry
   whipped topping mix
½ cup cold skim milk
½ teaspoon vanilla extract

In medium saucepan, stir together sugar, cocoa and gelatin; stir in evaporated milk until blended. Let stand 1 minute to soften gelatin. Cook over low heat, stirring constantly, until gelatin is completely dissolved, about 5 minutes. Remove from heat; pour mixture into large bowl. Stir in almond extract. Refrigerate, stirring occasionally, until mixture mounds slightly when dropped from spoon.

Prepare topping mix as directed on package, using ½ cup milk and ½ teaspoon vanilla. Reserve ½ cup topping for garnish (cover and refrigerate until ready to use); fold remaining topping into chocolate mixture. Let stand a few minutes; spoon into 7 individual dessert dishes. Cover; refrigerate until firm. Garnish with reserved topping.

7 servings

Nutritional Information Per Serving

170	Calories	<5 mg Cholesterol
7	gm Protein	80 mg Sodium
31	gm Carbohydrate	170 mg Calcium
2.5	gm Fat	

CHOCOLATE-BANANA YOGURT FREEZE

¾ cup sugar
¼ cup HERSHEY'S Cocoa
1½ cups (12-ounce can)
   evaporated skim milk

1 container (8 ounces) plain
   nonfat yogurt
⅓ cup ripe mashed banana
1 teaspoon vanilla extract

In medium microwave-safe bowl or 4-cup measure, stir together sugar and cocoa. Stir in evaporated milk. Microwave at HIGH (100%) 2 to 3 minutes or until mixture comes to a boil; stir with whisk until smooth. Refrigerate 30 minutes. Stir in yogurt, banana and vanilla. Cover; refrigerate until cold, about 6 hours.

Pour mixture into 1-quart ice cream freezer container. Freeze according to manufacturer's directions. (If harder texture is desired, spoon into freezerproof container; cover and place in freezer until of desired consistency.)

8 servings

Nutritional Information Per Serving

140 Calories	<5 mg Cholesterol
6 gm Protein	80 mg Sodium
30 gm Carbohydrate	200 mg Calcium
0 gm Fat	

CHOCOLATE-ORANGE ICE

2 cups water
⅔ cup sugar
2 tablespoons HERSHEY'S Cocoa

Strips of peel from 1 orange
½ cup fresh orange juice

In medium saucepan, stir together water, sugar, cocoa and orange peel. Cook over medium heat, stirring constantly, until mixture comes to a boil. Reduce heat; simmer 5 minutes, without stirring. Strain to remove orange peel; discard. Cover; refrigerate mixture several hours until cold.

Stir orange juice into chocolate mixture. Pour into 1-quart ice cream freezer container. Freeze according to manufacturer's directions.

6 servings

Nutritional Information Per Serving

100 Calories	0 mg Cholesterol
<1 gm Protein	0 mg Sodium
25 gm Carbohydrate	10 mg Calcium
0 gm Fat	

FRUIT IN A CHOCOLATE CLOUD

Yogurt Cheese (recipe follows)
2 cups (1 pint) fresh strawberries, rinsed and drained
¼ cup sugar
¼ cup HERSHEY'S Cocoa or HERSHEY'S European Style Cocoa
2 tablespoons hot water

2 teaspoons vanilla extract, divided
½ to 1 teaspoon freshly grated orange peel (optional)
2 envelopes (1.3 ounces each) dry whipped topping mix
1 cup cold skim milk
2 large bananas, sliced

Prepare Yogurt Cheese. Remove hulls of strawberries; cut strawberries in half vertically. In medium bowl, stir together sugar, cocoa and water until smooth and well blended. Stir in 1 teaspoon vanilla. Gradually stir in Yogurt Cheese and orange peel, if desired; blend thoroughly. In large mixer bowl, prepare topping mixes as directed on packages, using 1 cup milk and remaining 1 teaspoon vanilla; fold into chocolate mixture.

Into 1½-quart glass serving bowl, carefully spoon half of chocolate mixture; place one-half of strawberry halves, cut sides out, around inside of entire bowl. Layer banana slices over chocolate mixture. Cut remaining strawberry halves into smaller pieces; layer over banana slices. Carefully spread remaining chocolate mixture over fruit. Cover; refrigerate several hours before serving. Garnish as desired.

12 servings

Yogurt Cheese: Use two 8-ounce containers vanilla lowfat yogurt, no gelatin added. Line non-rusting colander or sieve with large piece of double thickness cheesecloth or large coffee filter; place colander over deep bowl. Spoon yogurt into prepared colander; cover with plastic wrap. Refrigerate until liquid no longer drains from yogurt, about 24 hours. Remove yogurt from cheesecloth and place in separate bowl; discard liquid.

Nutritional Information Per Serving	
130 Calories	<5 mg Cholesterol
4 gm Protein	45 mg Sodium
21 gm Carbohydrate	75 mg Calcium
3.5 gm Fat	

Fruit in a Chocolate Cloud

TROPICAL CHOCOLATE ORANGE ICE MILK

²/₃ cup nonfat dry milk
    powder
²/₃ cup sugar
¼ cup HERSHEY'S Cocoa
2 tablespoons cornstarch
4 cups (1 quart) skim milk,
    divided

¼ teaspoon freshly grated
    orange peel
⅛ teaspoon orange extract
    Orange Cups (optional,
    directions follow)
    Additional freshly grated
    orange peel (optional)

In medium saucepan, stir together milk powder, sugar, cocoa and cornstarch. Gradually stir in 2 cups skim milk. Cook over medium heat, stirring constantly, until mixture is smooth and slightly thickened, about 5 minutes. Remove from heat. Stir in remaining 2 cups milk, ¼ teaspoon orange peel and orange extract. Cover; refrigerate several hours until cold.

Pour mixture into 2-quart ice cream freezer container. Freeze according to manufacturer's directions. Before serving, let stand at room temperature until slightly softened. Scoop ½ cup ice milk into each Orange Cup or 8 individual dessert dishes. Garnish with additional orange peel, if desired. *8 servings*

Orange Cups: Cut about 1-inch slice from tops of 8 oranges; discard. Using sharp knife, cut out and remove small triangle shaped notches around tops of oranges to make zig-zag pattern. Scoop out pulp; reserve for other uses.

Nutritional Information Per Serving

150 Calories	<5 mg Cholesterol
7 gm Protein	95 mg Sodium
29 gm Carbohydrate	225 mg Calcium
1 gm Fat	

Tropical Chocolate Orange Ice Milk

CHOCOLATE-FILLED MERINGUE SHELLS WITH STRAWBERRY SAUCE

2 egg whites
¼ teaspoon cream of tartar
  Dash salt
¾ cup sugar
¼ teaspoon vanilla extract

Chocolate Filling (recipe follows)
1 package (10 ounces) frozen strawberries in syrup, thawed

Heat oven to 275°F. Line 10 muffin cups (2½ inches in diameter) with paper bake cups. In small mixer bowl, beat egg whites with cream of tartar and salt at high speed of electric mixer until soft peaks form. Beat in sugar, 1 tablespoon at a time, beating well after each addition until stiff peaks hold their shape, sugar is dissolved and mixture is glossy. Fold in vanilla. Spoon about 3 tablespoons mixture in each muffin cup. Using back of spoon or small spatula, push mixture up sides of muffin cups forming well in center.

Bake 1 hour or until meringues turn delicate cream color and feel dry to the touch. Cool in pan on wire rack. Before serving, carefully remove paper from shells. For each serving, spoon 1 heaping tablespoonful Chocolate Filling into meringue shell. In blender container, place strawberries with syrup. Cover; blend until smooth. Spoon over filled shells. Garnish as desired. To store leftover unfilled shells, peel paper bake cups from remaining shells; store shells loosely covered at room temperature. *10 servings*

Chocolate Filling: In small mixer bowl, beat 4 ounces (½ of 8-ounce package) softened Neufchatel cheese (light cream cheese) and ¼ cup HERSHEY'S Cocoa on medium speed of electric mixer until blended. Gradually add ¾ cup powdered sugar, beating until well blended. Fold in 1 cup frozen light non-dairy whipped topping, thawed.

Nutritional Information Per Serving

180 Calories	10 mg Cholesterol
3 gm Protein	60 mg Sodium
33 gm Carbohydrate	10 mg Calcium
3.5 gm Fat	

Chocolate-Filled Meringue Shells with Strawberry Sauce

CHOCOLATE-BANANA SHERBET

2 ripe medium bananas
1 cup apricot nectar or
   peach or pineapple
   juice, divided

½ cup HERSHEY'S Semi-Sweet
   Chocolate Chips
2 tablespoons sugar
1 cup lowfat 2% milk

Into blender container or food processor, slice bananas. Add ¾ cup fruit juice. Cover; blend until smooth. In small microwave-safe bowl, place chocolate chips, remaining ¼ cup fruit juice and sugar. Microwave at HIGH (100%) 30 seconds; stir. If necessary, microwave at HIGH an additional 15 seconds at a time, stirring after each heating, just until chips are melted and mixture is smooth when stirred. Add to mixture in blender. Cover; blend until thoroughly combined. Add milk. Cover; blend until smooth. Pour into 8- or 9-inch square pan. Cover; freeze until hard around edges, about 2 hours.

In large mixer bowl or food processor, spoon partially frozen mixture; beat until smooth but not melted. Return mixture to pan. Cover; freeze until firm, stirring several times before mixture freezes. Before serving, let stand at room temperature 10 to 15 minutes until slightly softened. Scoop into 8 individual dessert dishes.   *8 servings*

Nutritional Information Per Serving	
130 Calories	<5 mg Cholesterol
2 gm Protein	15 mg Sodium
22 gm Carbohydrate	45 mg Calcium
4 gm Fat	

Chocolate-Banana Sherbet

Chocolate Potpourri

ORANGE CHOCOLATE CHIP BREAD

½ cup skim milk
½ cup plain nonfat yogurt
⅓ cup sugar
¼ cup orange juice
1 egg, slightly beaten
1 tablespoon freshly grated
   orange peel

3 cups all-purpose biscuit
   baking mix
½ cup HERSHEY'S MINI CHIPS
   Semi-Sweet Chocolate

Heat oven to 350°F. Grease 9X5X3-inch loaf pan or spray with vegetable cooking spray. In large bowl, stir together milk, yogurt, sugar, orange juice, egg and orange peel; add baking mix. With spoon, beat until well blended, about 1 minute. Stir in small chocolate chips. Pour into prepared pan.

Bake 45 to 50 minutes or until wooden pick inserted in center comes out clean. Cool 10 minutes; remove from pan to wire rack. Cool completely before slicing. Garnish as desired. Wrap leftover bread in foil or plastic wrap. Store at room temperature or freeze for longer storage.

1 loaf (16 slices)

Nutritional Information Per Serving	
(1 slice)	
150 Calories	15 mg Cholesterol
4 gm Protein	280 mg Sodium
24 gm Carbohydrate	30 mg Calcium
4.5 gm Fat	

Orange Chocolate Chip Bread

CHOCOLATE CREAM PIE WITH SKIM MILK

⅓ cup sugar
¼ cup cornstarch
3 tablespoons HERSHEY'S
  Cocoa or HERSHEY'S
  European Style Cocoa
2 cups skim milk
1 teaspoon vanilla extract
1 packaged graham
  cracker crumb crust
  (6 ounces)

Frozen light non-dairy
  whipped topping,
  thawed (optional)
Assorted fresh fruit
  (optional)

To Microwave: In large microwave-safe bowl, stir together sugar, cornstarch and cocoa; gradually stir in milk. Microwave at HIGH (100%) 2 minutes; stir well. Microwave at HIGH 2 to 5 minutes or until mixture just begins to boil; stir well. Microwave at HIGH 30 seconds to 1 minute or until mixture is very hot and thickened. Stir in vanilla. Pour into crust. Press plastic wrap directly onto surface; refrigerate several hours or until set. Garnish with whipped topping and fruit, if desired. Store, covered, in refrigerator.

10 servings

Nutritional Information Per Serving

120 Calories	0 mg Cholesterol
3 gm Protein	120 mg Sodium
24 gm Carbohydrate	65 mg Calcium
4.5 gm Fat	

COCOA FRUIT BALLS

2½ cups (about 12 ounces)
  mixed dried fruits, such
  as apples, apricots,
  pears and prunes
1¼ cups (8 ounces) dried
  Mission figs

1 cup MOUNDS Sweetened
  Coconut Flakes
½ cup HERSHEY'S Cocoa
2 tablespoons orange juice
2 tablespoons honey
¼ cup powdered sugar

Remove pits from prunes and stems from figs, if necessary. Using metal blade of food processor, process dried fruits, figs and coconut until ground and almost paste-like (or put through fine blade of food grinder). In large bowl, combine cocoa, orange juice and honey with fruit mixture; mix well. Cover; refrigerate until chilled. Shape mixture into 1¼-inch balls. Store in airtight container at room temperature for 3 to 4 days. Store in airtight container in refrigerator or freezer for longer storage. Roll in powdered sugar just before serving. *3 dozen balls*

Nutritional Information Per Serving
(1 ball rolled in powdered sugar)

70 Calories	0 mg Cholesterol
<1 gm Protein	10 mg Sodium
14 gm Carbohydrate	15 mg Calcium
1 gm Fat	

PEANUT BUTTER 'N' CHOCOLATE CHIPS SNACK MIX

6 cups bite-size crisp corn, rice or wheat squares cereal
3 cups miniature pretzels
2 cups toasted oat cereal rings

1 cup raisins or dried fruit bits
1 cup HERSHEY'S Semi-Sweet Chocolate Chips
1 cup REESE'S Peanut Butter Chips

In large bowl, stir together all ingredients. Store in airtight container at room temperature. *14 cups snack mix*

Nutritional Information Per Serving
(½ cup)

130 Calories	0 mg Cholesterol
3 gm Protein	160 mg Sodium
21 gm Carbohydrate	15 mg Calcium
4 gm Fat	

SINFULLY RICH NONFAT FUDGE SAUCE

½ cup sugar
¼ cup HERSHEY'S Cocoa or HERSHEY'S European Style Cocoa
1 tablespoon plus 1 teaspoon cornstarch
½ cup evaporated skim milk

2 teaspoons vanilla extract
Assorted fresh fruit, cut up (optional)
Cake (optional)
Nonfat frozen yogurt (optional)

In small saucepan, stir together sugar, cocoa and cornstarch; gradually stir in evaporated milk. Cook over low heat, stirring constantly with whisk, until mixture boils; continue cooking and stirring until thickened and smooth. Remove from heat; stir in vanilla. Serve warm or cold with assorted fresh fruit, cake or nonfat frozen yogurt, if desired. Cover; refrigerate leftover sauce. *9 servings*

Nutritional Information Per Serving
(2 tablespoons sauce)

70 Calories	0 mg Cholesterol
2 gm Protein	15 mg Sodium
15 gm Carbohydrate	55 mg Calcium
0 gm Fat	

PEACHY CHOCOLATE YOGURT SHAKE

⅔ cup peeled fresh peach slices or 1 package (10 ounces) frozen peach slices, thawed and drained

¼ teaspoon almond extract
2 cups (1 pint) vanilla nonfat frozen yogurt
¼ cup HERSHEY'S Syrup
¼ cup skim milk

In blender container, place peaches and almond extract. Cover; blend until smooth. Add frozen yogurt, syrup and milk. Cover; blend until smooth. Serve immediately. *Four 6-ounce servings*

Nutritional Information Per Serving

160 Calories	0 mg Cholesterol
6 gm Protein	80 mg Sodium
34 gm Carbohydrate	20 mg Calcium
0 gm Fat	

Sinfully Rich Nonfat Fudge Sauce

HOT COCOA WITH CINNAMON

3 tablespoons sugar
3 tablespoons HERSHEY'S
   Cocoa
½ cup hot water

1 (3-inch) piece stick
   cinnamon
3 cups skim milk
½ teaspoon vanilla extract

In medium saucepan, stir together sugar and cocoa; gradually stir in water. Add cinnamon. Cook over medium heat, stirring constantly, until mixture boils; boil and stir 1 minute. Immediately stir in milk; continue cooking and stirring until mixture is hot. Do not boil. Remove from heat; discard cinnamon stick. Stir in vanilla. Beat with rotary beater or whisk until foamy. Serve immediately.

Four 7-ounce servings

Nutritional Information Per Serving	
110 Calories	<5 mg Cholesterol
7 gm Protein	95 mg Sodium
20 gm Carbohydrate	240 mg Calcium
1 gm Fat	

CREAMY CHOCOLATE CUPCAKE FROSTING

¼ cup (½ stick) (40% oil)
   lower-fat margarine,
   softened
2¾ cups powdered sugar

½ cup HERSHEY'S Cocoa
⅓ cup plain nonfat yogurt
½ teaspoon vanilla extract

In small mixer bowl, beat margarine on medium speed of electric mixer until creamy. Add powdered sugar and cocoa alternately with yogurt; beat to spreading consistency. Blend in vanilla. Use frosting immediately. Cover; refrigerate leftover frosting and frosted cupcakes.

1¾ cups frosting; frosts 24 cupcakes

Nutritional Information Per Serving (1 tablespoon frosting only)	
60 Calories	0 mg Cholesterol
1 gm Protein	10 mg Sodium
13 gm Carbohydrate	10 mg Calcium
1 gm Fat	

Hot Cocoa with Cinnamon

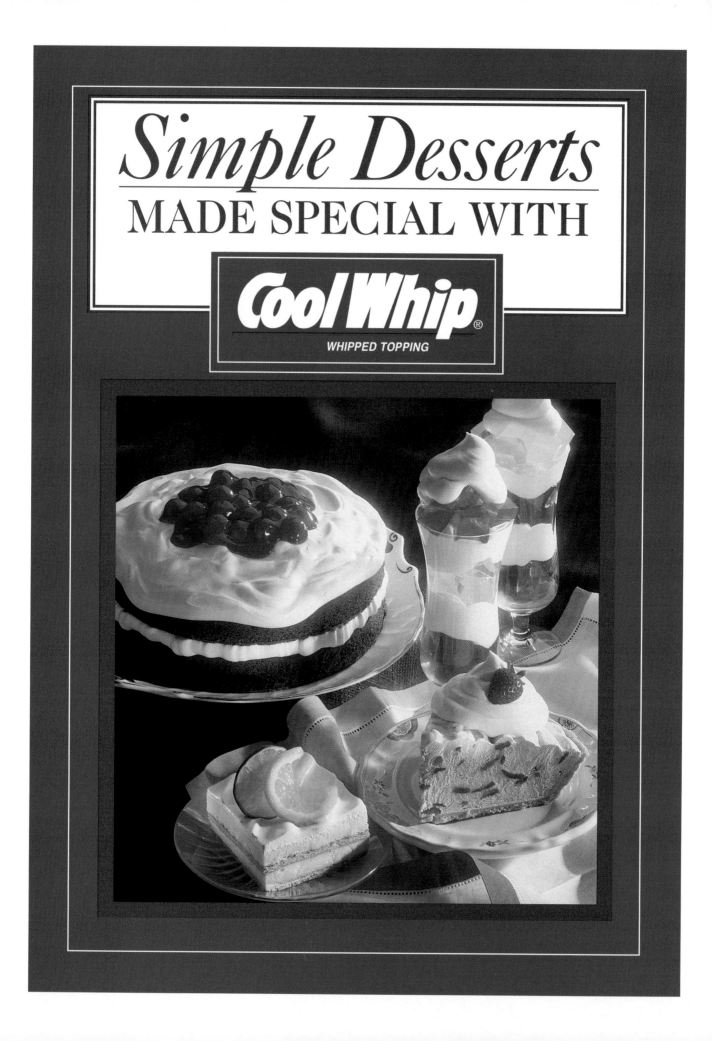

Contents

Clockwise from top left: Black Forest Torte, page 509;
Wild Side Sundaes, page 554; Frozen Strawberry Yogurt
Pie, page 534; Lemon Cheese Square, page 535

Introduction

Special desserts that are fun and easy to make add a festive touch to any celebration. COOL WHIP Whipped Topping is that special ingredient that helps make every occasion an extraordinary one. Whatever the event or day, these fabulous recipes will help make each one a memorable occasion for family and friends.

Included is a whole calendar of recipes that will help you entertain with style and ease throughout the year. For quick and easy reference, this book is divided by seasons. Recipes for the winter holidays and events can be found in the chapter " 'Tis the Season." If you're looking for a special dessert to make for Christmas, Super Bowl Sunday or even President's Day, this is where to look.

"Spring Sensations" will provide you with dessert ideas for Easter, Mother's Day, Sunday brunch and baby showers. Another chapter includes favorite summer celebrations such as graduations, picnics and family reunions. "Autumn Delights" features desserts that make fall festivities special. Last but not least, an entire chapter is devoted to kids' favorites—perfect activities for year-round fun.

Simple Desserts Made Special with COOL WHIP is more than a collection of wonderful recipes—it's also a guide to creative entertaining. The easy-to-follow instructions are the key to the delicious desserts presented on the following pages. You'll find everything you need to know in order to duplicate the recipes in your own kitchen. Every recipe takes less than 30 minutes to prepare (excluding refrigerating and freezing time) so there's more time for you to spend with your family and guests.

COOL WHIP Basics

How To Thaw COOL WHIP

- Place tub of COOL WHIP Whipped Topping, unopened, in the refrigerator. For complete thawing, allow these times:

  - 1 hour for 4-ounce tub

  - 4 hours for 8-ounce tub

  - 5 hours for 12-ounce tub

  - 6 hours for 16-ounce tub

- Thawing COOL WHIP in the microwave is not recommended. The timing is too critical. A second or so too long in the microwave will liquify COOL WHIP.

How To Store COOL WHIP

- For long-term storage, keep COOL WHIP Whipped Topping in the freezer. Once thawed, keep refrigerated no more than 2 weeks. For longer storage, refreeze. Don't let the container stand in a hot kitchen—the topping will soften and may begin to liquify.

■ ■ ■

COOL WHIP Whipped Topping comes in four different sizes. To estimate your recipe needs, the content amounts are listed in the chart below.

COOL WHIP Whipped Toppings			
Tub Size	**COOL WHIP Non-Dairy** Amount	**COOL WHIP Extra Creamy** Amount	**COOL WHIP LITE** Amount
4 ounces	1¾ cups		
8 ounces	3½ cups	3 cups	3¼ cups
12 ounces	5¼ cups	4½ cups	5 cups
16 ounces	7 cups		

Serving Tips for COOL WHIP

- COOL WHIP Whipped Topping is best thawed before use, but it can also be used as a topping before it has thawed entirely. Take it right from freezer or refrigerator and spoon onto dessert about 5 minutes before serving.

- Thaw COOL WHIP Whipped Topping completely before measuring or stirring into ingredients.

- When serving thawed frozen fruit with COOL WHIP Whipped Topping, drain the fruit first. The juice may make the topping appear curdled.

- Stir a few drops of food coloring into thawed COOL WHIP Whipped Topping to make tinted frostings and toppings.

- For fluted borders and rosettes, spoon thawed COOL WHIP Whipped Topping into a pastry bag or decorating tube and press through desired tip.

- When using COOL WHIP Whipped Topping as a frosting or as an ingredient in a frosting, store cake in refrigerator.

How To Use COOL WHIP in Recipes

- COOL WHIP Non-Dairy, Extra Creamy and COOL WHIP LITE Whipped Toppings can usually be used interchangeably in recipes. If COOL WHIP LITE is used with gelatin or higher acid fruits, the recipe may not set as firmly. Make sure to use the cup measurement specified in the recipe.

- Substitute equal amounts of COOL WHIP Whipped Topping for sweetened whipped cream. When a recipe calls for liquid cream that is to be whipped, double the measure and substitute COOL WHIP.

- All recipes prepared with COOL WHIP Whipped Topping should be stored either in the refrigerator or the freezer.

Easy Garnishes with COOL WHIP

Whipped Topping Dollops

1. Swirl spoon, held upright, through thawed COOL WHIP, creating rippled surface on the whipped topping.

2. Dip spoon into rippled whipped topping to scoop up heaping spoonful of whipped topping, maintaining rippled surface.

3. Gently touch spoon onto surface of dessert and release whipped topping gradually onto surface, pulling spoon up into a crowning tip.

Whipped Topping Piping

Insert decorating tip into pastry bag; fill with thawed COOL WHIP Whipped Topping. Fold down pastry bag. Holding bag firmly with one hand and squeezing topping down into tip, guide tip around surface to be decorated. If desired, double back whipped topping at intervals for decorative wave effect.

Crust Basics

The simplest approach is to purchase a 9-inch ready-to-use crumb crust. These are available in 6-ounce packages and in a variety of flavors. However, you can make your own. Here's how:

Use packaged graham cracker crumbs or follow one of the following methods for crushing crackers or cookies:

Plastic Bag Method: Place crackers or cookies in large zipper-style plastic bag. Press out excess air; seal. Using a rolling pin, roll the crackers until they are crushed into fine crumbs.

Food Processor Method: Break crackers or cookies. Place in food processor container; cover. Process until fine crumbs form.

To Prepare Crust: Mix 1 1/2 cups graham cracker or cookie crumbs, 3 tablespoons sugar and 1/3 cup margarine, melted. Press onto bottom and up sides of 9-inch pie plate. Refrigerate until ready to use.

To Toast Nuts

Heat oven to 400°F. Spread nuts in an even layer in a shallow baking pan. Toast 8 to 10 minutes or until golden brown, stirring frequently.

Tips for Success

Some Tips for Success When Using JELL-O Brand Gelatin

- To make a mixture that is clear and uniformly set, be sure the gelatin is *completely* dissolved in boiling water or other boiling liquid before adding the cold liquid.

- To store prepared gelatin overnight or longer, cover to prevent drying.

- Always store gelatin cakes, desserts or pies in the refrigerator.

Some Tips for Success When Using JELL-O Instant Pudding and Pie Filling

- Always use *cold* milk. Beat pudding mix slowly, not vigorously.

- For best results, use whole or 2% lowfat milk. Skim milk, reconstituted nonfat dry milk, light cream or half-and-half can also be used.

- Always store prepared pudding desserts, snacks and pies in the refrigerator.

Coconut Know-How

- *To Store Coconut:* Unopened packages of BAKER'S ANGEL FLAKE Coconut can be kept on your kitchen shelf. After opening the package, store the coconut in a tightly closed package or in an airtight container. Refrigerate or freeze coconut for up to 6 months.

- *To Toast Coconut:* Heat oven to 350°F. Spread 1⅓ cups BAKER'S ANGEL FLAKE Coconut in an even layer in a shallow baking pan. Toast 7 to 12 minutes or until lightly browned, stirring the coconut frequently so that it will brown evenly. Or, toast in microwave in a microwavable bowl on HIGH 5 minutes, stirring several times.

- *To Tint Coconut:* Place 1 cup BAKER'S ANGEL FLAKE Coconut in a plastic bag. Dilute a few drops of food coloring with ½ teaspoon of water and add to the coconut. Close the bag and shake until the coconut is evenly tinted. Repeat with more food coloring and water for a darker shade, if desired.

Baking Chocolate Know-How

- Store chocolate in a cool, dry place, below 75°F, if possible, but not in the refrigerator.

- We strongly recommend that you use the microwave method for melting chocolate. Chocolate scorches easily on the top of the stove so use very low heat and a heavy saucepan when using this method.

- Use the type of chocolate called for in a recipe. As a rule, semi-sweet chocolate and unsweetened chocolate are not interchangeable in recipes.

How to Melt Chocolate

- *Microwave Method:* Heat 1 unwrapped square of BAKER'S Semi-Sweet or Unsweetened Chocolate or 1 unwrapped 4-ounce bar of BAKER'S GERMAN'S Sweet Chocolate, broken in half, in microwavable bowl on HIGH 1 to 2 minutes or until almost melted, stirring halfway through heating time. Semi-Sweet and GERMAN'S Sweet Chocolates will retain some of their original shapes. Remove from oven. **Stir until chocolate is completely melted.** Add 10 seconds for each additional square of Semi-Sweet or Unsweetened Chocolate.

- *Top of Stove Method:* Place unwrapped chocolate in heavy saucepan on very low heat; stir constantly until just melted.

Easy Chocolate Garnishes

Chocolate Curls

1. Melt 4 squares BAKER'S Semi-Sweet Chocolate. Spread with spatula into very thin layer on cookie sheet. Refrigerate about 10 minutes or until firm, but still pliable.

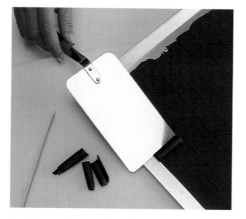

2. To make curls, slip tip of straight-side metal spatula under chocolate. Push spatula firmly along cookie sheet, under chocolate, so chocolate curls as it is pushed. (If chocolate is too firm to curl, let stand a few minutes at room temperature; refrigerate again if it becomes too soft.)

3. Carefully pick up each chocolate curl by inserting toothpick in center. Lift onto wax paper-lined cookie sheet.

4. Refrigerate about 15 minutes or until firm. Arrange on desserts. (Lift with toothpick to prevent breakage or melting.) Refrigerate until ready to serve.

Dipping Fruit and Nuts

Melt BAKER'S Semi-Sweet Chocolate or BAKER'S GERMAN'S Sweet Chocolate. Dip fruit or nuts into chocolate, covering at least half; let excess chocolate drip off. Let stand or refrigerate on wax paper-lined tray about 30 minutes or until chocolate is firm.

Chocolate Cutouts

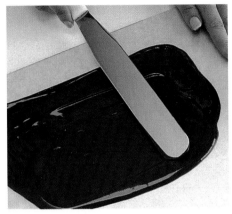

1. Melt 4 squares BAKER'S Semi-Sweet Chocolate. Pour onto wax paper-lined cookie sheet; spread to ⅛-inch thickness with spatula. Refrigerate about 15 minutes or until firm.

2. Cut out shapes with cookie cutters.

3. Immediately lift shapes carefully from wax paper with spatula or knife. Refrigerate until ready to use.

Chocolate Drizzle

1. Place 1 square BAKER'S Semi-Sweet Chocolate in zipper-style plastic sandwich bag. Close bag tightly. Microwave on HIGH about 1 minute or until chocolate is melted. Fold down top of bag tightly; snip tiny piece off corner (about ⅛ inch).

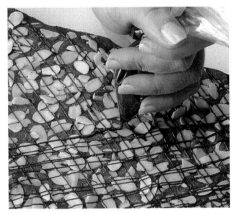

2. Holding top of bag tightly, drizzle chocolate through opening over brownies, cookies, cakes or desserts.

Easy Fruit Garnishes

Citrus Twists

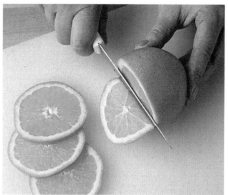

1. With sharp knife, cut orange, lemon or lime into thin slices.

2. Cut slit through slices to centers.

3. Twist slices from slits in opposite directions to form twists.

Fruit Fans

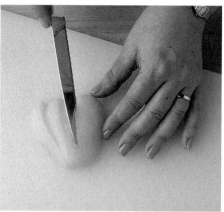

1. With sharp knife, cut drained canned pear halves into thin slices (about 5 or 6), cutting up to, but not through, stem ends. (Use same technique for strawberries.)

2. Hold stem end in place and gently fan out slices from stem before placing on plate for fruit desserts or using as garnish.

Gumdrop Garnishes

Gumdrop Shapes

1. Flatten gumdrops with rolling pin on a smooth flat surface or sheet of wax paper sprinkled with sugar. Roll until very thin (about 1/16-inch thick), turning frequently to coat with sugar. Cut into desired shapes.

2. For **Gumdrop Flowers**, hold flattened gumdrop at center; overlap edges slightly to give petal effect, pressing piece together at base to resemble flower. For open blossom, bend gumdrop petals outward from center. Insert small piece of gumdrop in centers with toothpick, if desired. Use toothpick to attach flowers to cake if necessary.

Gumdrop Ribbon

1. Line up gumdrops in a row on a smooth flat surface or a sheet of wax paper sprinkled with sugar. Flatten into long strips with a rolling pin, turning frequently to coat with sugar.

2. Cut flattened gumdrops into a strip as needed.

Note: If you can't find large gumdrops, simply press several small gumdrops together before flattening with the rolling pin. Chewy fruit snack rolls can also be used for cutting out shapes.

'Tis the Season

This most wonderful time of the year provides a variety of holidays and other events to celebrate with family and friends.

Create your own delicious Yuletide traditions with a mouthwatering selection of holiday recipes, such as **Chocolate Peppermint Pie, Candy Cane Cake** and **Merry Berry Desserts**.

And on President's Day, inaugurate a new tradition with **Cherries Jubilee** or **Black Forest Torte**.

Fan or not, Super Bowl Sunday has become a popular reason to have a party. Try **Football Cut-Up Cake** or **Dessert Nachos** at halftime.

Clockwise from top left: Candy Cane Cake (page 506), Chocolate Peppermint Pie (page 506), Merry Berry Dessert (page 507)

Chocolate Peppermint Pie
Photo on page 505

1 cup crushed chocolate-covered mint-flavored cookies
3 tablespoons hot water
1 prepared graham cracker crumb crust (6 ounces)
4 ounces PHILADELPHIA BRAND Cream Cheese, softened
⅓ cup sugar
2 tablespoons milk
¼ teaspoon peppermint extract
1 tub (8 ounces) COOL WHIP Whipped Topping, thawed
6 to 10 drops green food coloring
    Additional thawed COOL WHIP Whipped Topping
    Green gumdrop spearmint leaves (optional)
    Red cinnamon candies (optional)

MIX cookies and hot water in small bowl. Spread evenly in bottom of crust.

BEAT cream cheese in large bowl with electric mixer on medium speed until smooth. Gradually beat in sugar, milk and peppermint extract until well blended. Gently stir in whipped topping. Divide mixture in half; stir food coloring into ½ of the whipped topping mixture until evenly colored. Spoon green and white whipped topping mixtures alternately into crust. Smooth top with spatula.

REFRIGERATE 3 hours or until set. Garnish with additional whipped topping before serving. Decorate with spearmint leaves and cinnamon candies to make holly leaves and berries. Store leftover pie in refrigerator.

Makes 8 servings

Candy Cane Cake
Photo on page 505

1 package (9 ounces) chocolate wafer cookies
3 tablespoons (about) milk
1 tub (8 ounces) COOL WHIP Whipped Topping, thawed
    BAKER'S ANGEL FLAKE Coconut (optional)
    Red and green food colorings (optional)
    Red string licorice (optional)

BRUSH cookies with milk; spread with whipped topping, using about 2 cups. (Refrigerate remaining whipped topping.) Stack cookies in groups of 4 or 5. Place stacks on plastic wrap to form a roll, pressing together lightly. Bend top of roll to form a "cane." Wrap in plastic wrap.

REFRIGERATE at least 6 hours or freeze 4 hours until firm. Just before serving, unwrap and place on serving plate.

FROST with remaining whipped topping. Garnish with coconut tinted with red and green food colorings (see page 499 for directions) and pieces of licorice. To serve, cut cake diagonally into slices. Store leftover cake in refrigerator.

Makes 8 servings

Merry Berry Desserts

Photo on page 505

½ cup sliced strawberries
    and/or banana
1 package (4-serving size)
    JELL-O Brand Strawberry
    Flavor Gelatin
1 cup boiling water
1 cup cold water
1 ripe banana, cut up
1 tub (8 ounces) COOL WHIP
    Whipped Topping,
    thawed

ARRANGE strawberry and/or banana slices in bottoms of 6 muffin cups. Dissolve gelatin completely in boiling water in medium bowl. Stir in cold water. Spoon 3 tablespoons of the gelatin into each muffin cup. Refrigerate until set but not firm.

PLACE remaining gelatin and banana in blender container; cover. Blend on high speed 1 minute. Add 1½ cups of the whipped topping; cover. Blend until well mixed. Spoon over clear gelatin.

REFRIGERATE 4 hours or until firm. To unmold, run small metal spatula around edge of each muffin cup. Dip pan into warm water, just to rim, for about 10 seconds. Place moistened tray on top of pan. Invert; holding pan and tray together, shake slightly to loosen. Gently remove pan. Place desserts on individual serving plates. Garnish with remaining whipped topping.

Makes 6 servings

German Sweet Chocolate Pie

1 package (4 ounces)
    BAKER'S GERMAN'S Sweet
    Chocolate
⅓ cup milk
4 ounces PHILADELPHIA
    BRAND Cream Cheese,
    softened
2 tablespoons sugar
1 tub (8 ounces) COOL WHIP
    Whipped Topping, thawed
1 prepared graham cracker
    crumb crust (6 ounces)
    Chocolate Curls (see page
    500 for directions)
    (optional)

MICROWAVE chocolate and 2 tablespoons of the milk in large microwavable bowl on HIGH 1½ to 2 minutes or until chocolate is almost melted, stirring halfway through heating time. Stir until chocolate is completely melted.

BEAT in cream cheese, sugar and remaining milk until well blended. Refrigerate about 10 minutes to cool. Gently stir in whipped topping until smooth. Spoon into crust.

FREEZE 4 hours or until firm. Garnish with chocolate curls, if desired. Let stand at room temperature 15 minutes or until pie can be cut easily. Store leftover pie in freezer.   *Makes 8 servings*

Black Forest Torte

Even after a long day of shopping, there's still time to make dessert!

2 baked 9-inch round devil's food or chocolate cake layers, cooled
1/4 cup almond- or cherry-flavored liqueur or orange juice
1 tub (8 ounces) COOL WHIP Whipped Topping, thawed
1 can (21 ounces) cherry pie filling

SPRINKLE cake layers with liqueur or orange juice.

SPOON or pipe 1/2 cup whipped topping into 3-inch circle in center of 1 cake layer on serving plate. Spoon or pipe 1 cup of the whipped topping around top edge of cake layer. Spoon 1/2 of the pie filling between circle and border.

PLACE second cake layer on top. Spoon or pipe remaining whipped topping around top edge of cake layer. Spoon remaining pie filling in center.

REFRIGERATE 1 hour or until ready to serve.

Makes 12 servings

Note: Torte is best made and served the same day. Store leftover torte in refrigerator.

Cherries Jubilee

1 1/4 cups cold milk
1/4 teaspoon almond extract (optional)
1 package (4-serving size) JELL-O Vanilla Flavor Instant Pudding and Pie Filling
1 tub (8 ounces) COOL WHIP Whipped Topping, thawed
3/4 cup cherry pie filling

POUR milk and almond extract into large bowl. Add pudding mix. Beat with wire whisk 1 to 2 minutes.

STIR in 2 cups of the whipped topping. Spoon whipped topping mixture and pie filling alternately into 6 parfait glasses.

REFRIGERATE until ready to serve. Garnish with remaining whipped topping.

Makes 6 servings

Top to bottom: Cherries Jubilee, Black Forest Torte

Simple Desserts Made Special with Cool Whip®

Dessert Nachos

12 whole graham crackers
1 tub (8 ounces) COOL WHIP
    Whipped Topping,
    thawed
1 cup chopped strawberries
1 cup chopped peeled kiwi
1 cup sliced bananas
    Strawberry dessert
    topping

BREAK graham crackers in half. Score each half diagonally with knife; break apart to form triangles.

ARRANGE ½ of the triangles in single layer on serving plates. Spread evenly with ½ of the whipped topping; top with ½ of the fruit. Drizzle with dessert topping. Repeat layers.

REFRIGERATE until ready to serve.   *Makes 6 servings*

Football Cut-Up Cake

1 package (2-layer size) cake
    mix, any flavor except
    angel food
1 tub (8 ounces) COOL WHIP
    Whipped Topping,
    thawed
5 packages (1.4 ounces each)
    chocolate-covered
    English toffee bars,
    chopped
8 KRAFT Caramels, cut in
    half
    Chocolate bar, broken into
    rectangles

PREPARE and bake cake mix as directed on package for 13×9-inch baking pan. Cool 15 minutes; remove from pan. Cool completely on wire rack.

CUT cake as shown in illustration 1. Using small amount of whipped topping to hold pieces together, arrange cake on serving tray as shown in illustration 2.

FROST cake with remaining whipped topping. Decorate sides with chopped candy bars. Arrange caramel halves to resemble bands and chocolate bar rectangles to resemble laces. Store cake in refrigerator.

Makes 12 to 16 servings

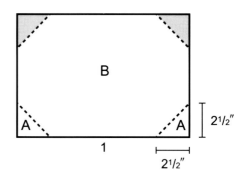

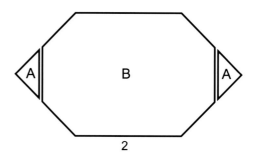

*Top to bottom: Football Cut-Up
Cake, Dessert Nachos*

Spring Sensations

Fresh air, blossoming flowers and the first warm day signal the arrival of spring and a calendar full of special occasions.

Mark the arrival of spring with friends and an informal Sunday brunch including **Boston Cream Croissants, Dessert Waffles** and **Heavenly Ambrosia in a Cloud**.

Colored eggs and jelly beans mean a visit from the Easter Bunny. Why not make a **Hippity Hop Bunny Cake** to celebrate his arrival?

Surprise your mother with a stunning **Lemon Berry Charlotte** on her Sunday in May.

While the berries of the season are at their luscious peak, you'll want to try our easy-to-prepare **Strawberry Dip** for a fast and easy treat.

Clockwise from top left: Heavenly Ambrosia in a Cloud (page 519), Dessert Waffle (page 517), Boston Cream Croissants (page 520)

Come for
Brunch

Raspberry Vanilla Pudding Supreme
Photo on page 516

This luscious pudding is perfect for large family parties.

5 1/2 cups cold milk
4 packages (4-serving size) JELL-O French Vanilla or Vanilla Flavor Instant Pudding and Pie Filling
24 shortbread or vanilla wafer cookies, crumbled (about 1 1/2 cups)
1 package (10 ounces) BIRDS EYE Raspberries in a Lite Syrup, thawed
1/4 teaspoon red food coloring
1 tub (8 ounces) COOL WHIP Whipped Topping, thawed
Fresh raspberries (optional)
Fresh mint leaves (optional)

POUR 4 cups of the milk into large bowl. Add 2 packages of the pudding mix. Beat with wire whisk 1 to 2 minutes. Spoon into 3-quart serving bowl. Refrigerate 15 minutes. Sprinkle with crumbled cookies.

POUR remaining 1 1/2 cups milk, raspberries in syrup and food coloring into large bowl. Add remaining 2 packages pudding mix. Beat with wire whisk 1 to 2 minutes. Let stand 5 minutes or until slightly thickened. Gently stir in 2 1/2 cups of the whipped topping. Spoon over cookies in bowl.

REFRIGERATE 4 hours or until set. Garnish with remaining whipped topping, fresh raspberries and mint leaves.

Makes 16 servings

Chocolate Truffle Loaf
Photo on page 516

2 packages (8 squares each) BAKER'S Semi-Sweet Chocolate
1/2 cup (1 stick) margarine or butter
1/4 cup milk
2 eggs, slightly beaten
1 teaspoon vanilla
1 tub (8 ounces) COOL WHIP Whipped Topping, thawed

HEAT 15 squares of the chocolate, margarine and milk in large heavy saucepan on very low heat until chocolate is melted and mixture is smooth, stirring constantly. Stir in eggs with wire whisk; cook 1 minute, stirring constantly. Remove from heat. Stir in vanilla.

REFRIGERATE about 20 minutes or until just cool, stirring occasionally. Gently stir in 2 3/4 cups of the whipped topping. Pour into 8×4-inch loaf pan which has been lined with plastic wrap.

REFRIGERATE 6 hours or overnight or freeze 3 hours until firm. Invert pan onto serving plate; remove plastic wrap. Melt remaining 1 square chocolate; drizzle over dessert (see page 501 for directions). Garnish with remaining whipped topping. Store leftover dessert in refrigerator.

Makes 16 servings

Creamy Lemon Bars

1 1/2 cups graham cracker
    crumbs
1/2 cup sugar
1/3 cup margarine or butter,
    melted
1 package (8 ounces)
    PHILADELPHIA BRAND
    Cream Cheese, softened
2 tablespoons milk
1 tub (8 ounces) COOL WHIP
    Whipped Topping,
    thawed
3 1/2 cups cold milk
2 packages (4-serving size)
    JELL-O Lemon Flavor
    Instant Pudding and Pie
    Filling

MIX graham cracker crumbs,
1/4 cup of the sugar and margarine
in 13×9-inch pan. Press firmly
into bottom of pan. Refrigerate
15 minutes.

BEAT cream cheese, remaining 1/4
cup sugar and 2 tablespoons milk
until smooth. Gently stir in 1/2 of
the whipped topping. Spread over
crust.

POUR 3 1/2 cups cold milk into
large bowl. Add pudding mixes.
Beat with wire whisk 1 to
2 minutes. Pour over cream cheese
layer.

REFRIGERATE 4 hours or
overnight. Spread remaining
whipped topping over pudding
just before serving.
Makes 15 servings

Berries Delight: Prepare as
directed above, using French
vanilla or vanilla flavor pudding
mix. Arrange 2 pints strawberries,
halved, over cream cheese mixture
before topping with pudding.

Strawberry Cool 'n Easy Pie

1 package (4-serving size)
    JELL-O Brand Strawberry
    Flavor Gelatin
2/3 cup boiling water
1/2 cup cold water
    Ice cubes
1 tub (8 ounces) COOL WHIP
    Whipped Topping,
    thawed
1 cup chopped strawberries
1 prepared graham cracker
    crumb crust (6 ounces)

DISSOLVE gelatin completely in
boiling water in large bowl. Mix
cold water and ice to make
1 1/4 cups. Add to gelatin, stirring
until slightly thickened. Remove
any remaining ice.

STIR in whipped topping with
wire whisk until smooth. Mix in
strawberries. Refrigerate 20 to
30 minutes or until mixture is
very thick and will mound. Spoon
into crust.

REFRIGERATE 4 hours or until
firm. Garnish with additional
whipped topping and strawberries.
Store leftover pie in refrigerator.
Makes 8 servings

Lemon Chiffon Pie: Prepare as
directed above, using lemon flavor
gelatin. Add 2 teaspoons grated
lemon peel and 2 tablespoons
lemon juice to dissolved gelatin
with cold water and ice. Garnish
with additional whipped topping
and grated lemon peel or Citrus
Twists (see page 502 for
directions).

Dessert Waffles
Photo on page 513

12 small frozen Belgian waffles
1 package (10 ounces) BIRDS EYE Red Raspberries in a Lite Syrup, thawed
3 cups assorted fresh fruit
1 tub (8 ounces) COOL WHIP Whipped Topping, thawed

HEAT waffles as directed on package.

PLACE raspberries in blender container; cover. Blend until smooth. Strain to remove seeds, if desired.

SERVE waffles with raspberry sauce, fruit and whipped topping.
Makes 12 servings

Baby Booties

4 cups BAKER'S ANGEL FLAKE Coconut
Assorted food colorings
24 baked cupcakes, cooled
4 cups thawed COOL WHIP Whipped Topping
Decorating gel
Miniature star candies

DIVIDE coconut into 4 (1-cup) portions. Tint each cup of coconut a different color using assorted food colorings (see page 499 for directions).

LEAVE 16 cupcakes whole; cut remaining cupcakes as shown in illustration. Using small amount of the whipped topping to hold pieces together, assemble booties on serving tray as shown in photograph.

FROST booties with remaining whipped topping. Press a different color of coconut into whipped topping on each of 4 booties. Pipe decorating gel on the booties to form shoelaces. Decorate with candies. Store cakes in refrigerator.
Makes 16 servings

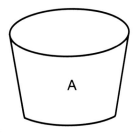

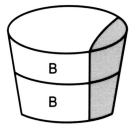

Clockwise from top: Baby Booties, Raspberry Vanilla Pudding Supreme (page 514), Chocolate Truffle Loaf (page 514)

Lemon Berry Charlotte

Any mother would love this stunning dessert.

   1 package (8-serving size) or
     2 packages (4-serving
     size) JELL-O Brand
     Lemon Flavor Gelatin
1 1/2 cups boiling water
  3/4 cup cold water
     Ice cubes
   1 tub (12 ounces)
     COOL WHIP Whipped
     Topping, thawed
   1 cup chopped strawberries
   1 package (3 ounces)
     ladyfingers, split
     Cloth ribbon (optional)
     Strawberry halves
     (optional)
     Fresh mint leaves
     (optional)

DISSOLVE gelatin completely in boiling water in large bowl. Mix cold water and ice to make 1 3/4 cups. Add to gelatin, stirring until ice is melted. Refrigerate 10 minutes or until slightly thickened, if necessary.

STIR in 3 1/2 cups of the whipped topping and strawberries. Spoon into 2-quart saucepan (about 3 1/2 inches deep) which has been lined with plastic wrap.

REFRIGERATE 4 hours or until firm. Invert saucepan onto serving plate; remove plastic wrap. Spread top and sides of dessert with 1 cup of the whipped topping.

PRESS cut sides of ladyfingers into sides of dessert. Tie ribbon around dessert. Garnish with remaining whipped topping, strawberry halves and mint leaves. Store leftover dessert in refrigerator.   *Makes 12 servings*

Heavenly Ambrosia in a Cloud
Photo on page 513

   1 tub (8 ounces) COOL WHIP
     Whipped Topping,
     thawed
   2 cans (11 ounces each)
     mandarin orange
     sections, drained
   1 can (20 ounces) crushed
     pineapple, drained
   3 cups KRAFT Miniature
     Marshmallows
   2 cups BAKER'S ANGEL
     FLAKE Coconut
     Toasted sliced almonds
     (see page 498 for
     directions) (optional)

SPREAD whipped topping onto bottom and up sides of 2 1/2-quart serving bowl. Refrigerate.

MIX oranges, pineapple, marshmallows and coconut in large bowl. Spoon into whipped topping-lined bowl.

REFRIGERATE at least 1 hour or until ready to serve. Garnish with almonds.   *Makes 16 servings*

Classic Ambrosia: Gently stir whipped topping into fruit mixture. Refrigerate at least 1 hour or until ready to serve. Stir before serving.

Lemon Berry Charlotte

Strawberry Dip

1 tub (8 ounces) COOL WHIP
    LITE Whipped Topping,
    thawed
1 container (8 ounces)
    strawberry flavored
    lowfat yogurt
1/2 cup crushed strawberries
1 tablespoon grated orange
    peel
    Assorted fresh fruit, such
    as strawberries, grapes,
    kiwi, sliced oranges or
    pineapple

MIX whipped topping, yogurt,
strawberries and orange peel until
well blended. Spoon into serving
bowl. Refrigerate until ready to
serve.

SERVE as a dip with fresh fruit.
Makes about 5 cups

Boston Cream Croissants

Photo on page 513

1 1/4 cups cold milk
1 package (4-serving size)
    JELL-O French Vanilla or
    Vanilla Flavor Instant
    Pudding and Pie Filling
1 cup thawed COOL WHIP
    Whipped Topping
12 miniature croissants
1 square BAKER'S
    Unsweetened Chocolate
1 tablespoon margarine or
    butter
3/4 cup powdered sugar
2 tablespoons water

POUR milk into large bowl. Add
pudding mix. Beat with wire
whisk 1 to 2 minutes. Gently stir
in whipped topping.

SPLIT croissants horizontally; fill
with whipped topping mixture.
Refrigerate.

MELT chocolate and margarine in
small heavy saucepan on very low
heat, stirring constantly. Remove
from heat. Stir in sugar and water
until smooth. Drizzle over tops of
croissants.

REFRIGERATE until ready to
serve.   *Makes 12 servings*

Caramel Apple Salad

3 Granny Smith or other
    green apples, diced
3 red apples, diced
6 packages (2.07 ounces
    each) chocolate-covered
    caramel peanut nougat
    bars, chopped
1 tub (8 ounces) COOL WHIP
    Whipped Topping,
    thawed
    Apple slices (optional)

MIX apples and chopped candy
bars until well blended. Gently stir
in whipped topping.

REFRIGERATE 1 hour or until
ready to serve. Garnish with apple
slices.   *Makes 20 servings*

Note: Salad is best made and
served the same day.

*Top to bottom: Caramel Apple
Salad, Strawberry Dip*

Easter Bonnet Cake

1 package (2-layer size)
  yellow cake mix
1½ cups cold milk
1 package (4-serving size)
  JELL-O Lemon Flavor
  Instant Pudding and Pie
  Filling
1 tub (8 ounces) COOL WHIP
  Whipped Topping,
  thawed
2⅔ cups (7 ounces) BAKER'S
  ANGEL FLAKE Coconut
  Cloth ribbon (optional)
  Gumdrop Flowers (see
  page 503 for directions)
  (optional)

HEAT oven to 350°F.

PREPARE cake mix as directed on package. Pour 3½ cups of the batter into greased and floured 1½-quart metal or ovenproof glass bowl. Pour remaining batter into greased and floured 12×¾-inch pizza pan. Bake 15 minutes for the pan and 50 minutes for the bowl or until toothpick inserted in centers comes out clean. Cool 10 minutes; remove from pan and bowl. Cool completely on wire racks. If bottom of bowl-shaped cake is very rounded, thinly slice to make flat. Cut bowl-shaped cake horizontally into 3 layers.

POUR milk into small bowl. Add pudding mix. Beat with wire whisk 1 to 2 minutes.

PLACE 12-inch cake layer on serving tray. Spread with 1½ cups of the whipped topping. Center bottom layer of bowl-shaped cake on frosted layer; spread with ⅔ of the pudding. Add second layer; spread with remaining pudding. Add top layer, forming the crown.

SPREAD remaining whipped topping over the crown. Sprinkle coconut over cake. Tie ribbon around the crown to form hat band. Garnish with Gumdrop Flowers. Store cake in refrigerator.

Makes 16 servings

Cannoli Parfaits

1 cup ricotta cheese
⅓ cup powdered sugar
1 to 2 teaspoons grated
  orange peel
2 tablespoons orange juice
1½ teaspoons vanilla
1 tub (8 ounces) COOL WHIP
  Whipped Topping,
  thawed
¼ cup chopped dried
  apricots
¼ cup BAKER'S Semi-Sweet
  Real Chocolate Chips
¼ cup raisins
10 thin crisp butter cookies,
  coarsely chopped (about
  ¾ cup)

MIX cheese, sugar, orange peel, juice and vanilla in medium bowl. Gently stir in 2 cups of the whipped topping.

STIR in apricots, chips and raisins. Layer cookies and whipped topping mixture alternately in 6 parfait glasses.

REFRIGERATE at least 1 hour or until ready to serve. Garnish with remaining whipped topping.

Makes 6 servings

Top to bottom: Easter Bonnet Cake, Cannoli Parfaits

Hippity Hop Bunny Cake

Surprise the kids after the Easter egg hunt with this cake.

2 ¼ cups BAKER'S ANGEL FLAKE Coconut
Red food coloring
2 baked 9-inch round cake layers, cooled
1 tub (8 ounces) COOL WHIP Whipped Topping, thawed
Assorted candies

TINT ¼ cup of the coconut pink using red food coloring (see page 499 for directions).

LEAVE 1 cake layer whole; cut remaining cake layer as shown in illustration. Using small amount of whipped topping to hold pieces together, arrange cake on serving tray as shown in photograph.

FROST cake with remaining whipped topping. Sprinkle center of bunny's ears with pink coconut. Sprinkle remaining 2 cups white coconut over bunny's head and outer edges of ears. Decorate with candies. Store cake in refrigerator.

Makes 12 to 16 servings

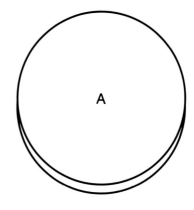

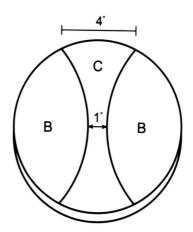

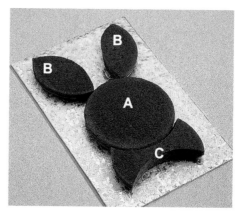

Summertime Celebrations

Most of us wish summer celebrations would last all year. Memorial Day signals the unofficial beginning of summer and the first picnic of the season. You'll want to make **Watermelon Slices,** a real crowd-pleaser.

There's nothing more patriotic than the **Stars and Stripes Dessert** for a glorious Fourth of July barbecue or other event celebrating the red, white and blue holiday.

Simply elegant desserts like **Romanoff Tarts** and **Lemon Berry Terrine** are perfect standouts for a garden wedding reception.

An annual event of grand proportions, such as a family reunion, calls for a dessert of grand proportions! **Dessert Pizza** or **Creamy Orange Cake** will feed a large crowd after a day full of activities.

Watermelon Slices (page 539)

Father's Day Cheesecake Pie

Dad will welcome a slice of this delicious cheesecake after a day of fishing or golf.

1 package (8 ounces) PHILADELPHIA BRAND Cream Cheese, softened
⅓ cup sugar
1 teaspoon vanilla
1 tub (8 ounces) COOL WHIP Whipped Topping, thawed
1 prepared graham cracker crumb crust (6 ounces)
Additional thawed COOL WHIP Whipped Topping (about ½ cup)
KRAFT Miniature Marshmallows
Strawberry dessert topping or jam

BEAT cream cheese, sugar and vanilla with wire whisk in large bowl until smooth. Gently stir in whipped topping. Spoon into crust.

REFRIGERATE at least 4 hours or until set.

DECORATE top of pie with additional whipped topping and marshmallows to resemble a tie. Fill in tie and outline edge of pie with dessert topping. Store leftover pie in refrigerator.

Makes 8 servings

Dessert Grillers

4 cups assorted fruit, such as strawberries, sliced kiwi, oranges or pineapple
12 thin wooden skewers
½ cup (1 stick) margarine or butter
1 package (12 ounces) pound cake, cut into 12 slices
2 tablespoons sugar
1 teaspoon ground cinnamon
1 tub (8 ounces) COOL WHIP Whipped Topping, thawed

ARRANGE fruit on skewers; set aside. Heat grill or broiler.

SPREAD margarine evenly on cake slices. Mix sugar and cinnamon in small bowl; sprinkle over cake slices.

PLACE cake slices on grill over hot coals or on rack of broiler pan. Grill or broil on both sides until lightly toasted. Cool. Serve with whipped topping and fruit kabobs.
Makes 12 servings

Top to bottom: Father's Day Cheesecake Pie, Dessert Griller, Pistachio Pineapple Delight (page 534)

This card is good for ONE CAR WASH!

World Class Dad

Lemon Berry Terrine

An easy but elegant dessert for a gala affair.

    1 package (12 ounces)
        pound cake
    1 package (8 ounces)
        PHILADELPHIA BRAND
        Cream Cheese,
        softened
 1½ cups cold milk
    1 package (4-serving size)
        JELL-O Lemon Flavor
        Instant Pudding and Pie
        Filling
    1 teaspoon grated lemon
        peel
    1 tub (8 ounces) COOL WHIP
        Whipped Topping,
        thawed
    1 pint strawberries, hulled

LINE bottom and sides of
8×4-inch loaf pan with wax paper.

CUT rounded top off cake; reserve
for another use. Trim edges of
cake. Cut cake horizontally into
5 slices. Line bottom and long
sides of pan with 3 cake slices.
Cut another cake slice in half;
place on short sides of pan.

BEAT cream cheese and ½ cup
of the milk in large bowl with
electric mixer on low speed until
smooth. Add remaining milk,
pudding mix and lemon peel; beat
1 to 2 minutes. Gently stir in
1 cup of the whipped topping.

SPOON ½ of the filling into
cake-lined pan. Arrange ½ of the
strawberries, stem-side up, in
filling, pressing down slightly. Top
with remaining filling. Place
remaining cake slice on top of
filling.

REFRIGERATE 3 hours or until
firm. Invert pan onto serving
plate; remove wax paper. Garnish
with remaining whipped topping
and strawberries. Store leftover
dessert in refrigerator.
        Makes 16 servings

Romanoff Tarts

    1 cup cold milk
    2 tablespoons orange-
        flavored liqueur or
        orange juice
    1 package (4-serving size)
        JELL-O French Vanilla or
        Vanilla Flavor Instant
        Pudding and Pie Filling
    1 cup thawed COOL WHIP
        Whipped Topping
    1 cup chopped strawberries
    6 prepared graham cracker
        tart shells
        Assorted fruit (optional)

POUR milk and liqueur into large
bowl. Add pudding mix. Beat with
wire whisk 1 to 2 minutes.

STIR in whipped topping and
strawberries. Spoon into tart
shells.

REFRIGERATE 1 hour or until
ready to serve. Garnish with
additional whipped topping and
fruit.   *Makes 6 servings*

*Clockwise from top: Romanoff
Tarts, Lemon Berry Terrine,
Strawberry Heart Pillows
(page 533)*

Dessert Pizza

This pizza is lots of fun. Try your favorite combination of fruit and dessert toppings.

> 1 package (20 ounces)
>   refrigerated chocolate
>   chip cookie dough
> 2 cups thawed COOL WHIP
>   Whipped Topping
> 2 cups assorted fruit, such
>   as blueberries, halved
>   green grapes and sliced
>   strawberries
>   Strawberry dessert
>   topping

HEAT oven to 350°F.

LINE 12-inch pizza pan with foil; grease foil. Press dough into prepared pan. Bake 20 minutes or until golden brown. Cool in pan on wire rack. Remove foil. Place cookie crust on serving plate.

SPREAD whipped topping on cookie crust. Garnish with fruit. Drizzle with dessert topping. Serve immediately or refrigerate until ready to serve.

Makes 12 servings

Strawberry Banana Split Pie

> 1 banana, sliced
> 1 prepared chocolate flavor
>   crumb crust (6 ounces)
> ³⁄₄ cup cold milk or
>   half-and-half
> ³⁄₄ cup pureed strawberries
>   Red food coloring
> 1 package (4-serving size)
>   JELL-O Vanilla Flavor
>   Instant Pudding and Pie
>   Filling
> 1 tub (8 ounces) COOL WHIP
>   Whipped Topping,
>   thawed
>   Sliced bananas and
>   strawberries
>   Chocolate dessert topping
>   Additional thawed
>   COOL WHIP Whipped
>   Topping
> 1 maraschino cherry

ARRANGE banana slices in bottom of crust.

POUR milk, strawberry puree and food coloring into large bowl. Add pudding mix. Beat with wire whisk 1 to 2 minutes. Let stand 5 minutes. Gently stir in whipped topping. Spoon into crust.

FREEZE 6 hours or overnight until firm. Let stand at room temperature 15 minutes or until pie can be cut easily.

GARNISH with sliced bananas and strawberries. Drizzle with dessert topping. Top with dollop of additional whipped topping and cherry. Store leftover pie in freezer. *Makes 8 servings*

Chocolate Peanut Butter Truffles

1 package (8 squares)
  BAKER'S Semi-Sweet
  Chocolate
½ cup peanut butter
1 tub (8 ounces) COOL WHIP
  Whipped Topping,
  thawed
  Powdered sugar, finely
  chopped nuts, BAKER'S
  ANGEL FLAKE Coconut,
  unsweetened cocoa or
  multi-colored sprinkles

MICROWAVE chocolate in large microwavable bowl on HIGH 2 minutes or until chocolate is almost melted, stirring halfway through heating time. Stir until chocolate is completely melted.

STIR in peanut butter until smooth. Cool to room temperature. Stir in whipped topping.

REFRIGERATE 1 hour. Shape into 1-inch balls. Roll in powdered sugar, nuts, coconut, cocoa or sprinkles. Store in refrigerator.
Makes about 3 dozen

Cool Christmas Fudge: Prepare as directed above, substituting 4 ounces PHILADELPHIA BRAND Cream Cheese for peanut butter. Stir in ½ cup chopped nuts with whipped topping. Spread in foil-lined 8-inch square pan. Refrigerate 4 hours or until firm. Remove from pan. Cut into squares. Store in refrigerator. Makes about 4 dozen.

Strawberry Heart Pillows

Photo on page 531

1 frozen ready-to-bake puff
  pastry sheet
1 cup strawberry jam or
  preserves
1 tub (8 ounces) COOL WHIP
  Whipped Topping,
  thawed
  Sliced strawberries

THAW pastry as directed on package. Heat oven to 350°F. Unfold pastry. Using 2-inch heart-shaped cookie cutter, cut into 16 hearts. Or, using sharp knife, cut into 30 (1½-inch) squares. Place on ungreased cookie sheets.

BAKE 20 minutes or until golden. Remove from cookie sheets. Cool completely on wire racks. Split each pastry horizontally in half.

SPREAD 1 teaspoon jam on bottom half of each heart. Top with dollop of whipped topping. Cover with top half of heart. Garnish with whipped topping and strawberries.

REFRIGERATE until ready to serve.
Makes 16 hearts or 30 squares

Pistachio Pineapple Delight

Photo on page 529

1 package (4-serving size) JELL-O Pistachio Flavor Instant Pudding and Pie Filling
1 can (20 ounces) crushed pineapple in syrup
1 cup KRAFT Miniature Marshmallows
1/2 cup chopped nuts
1 3/4 cups thawed COOL WHIP Whipped Topping
    Sliced strawberries (optional)

STIR pudding mix, pineapple, marshmallows and nuts in large bowl until well blended. Gently stir in whipped topping.

REFRIGERATE 1 hour or until ready to serve. Garnish with additional whipped topping and sliced strawberries.

Makes 8 servings

Frozen Strawberry-Yogurt Pie

Photo on page 536

2 containers (8 ounces each) vanilla or strawberry flavored yogurt
1 tub (8 ounces) COOL WHIP Whipped Topping, thawed
2 cups sweetened chopped strawberries
1 prepared graham cracker crumb crust (6 ounces)

STIR yogurt gently into whipped topping until well blended. Stir in strawberries. Spoon into crust.

FREEZE 4 hours or overnight until firm. Let stand in refrigerator 15 minutes or until pie can be cut easily.

GARNISH with additional whipped topping and whole strawberries. Store leftover pie in freezer. *Makes 8 servings*

Cookies and Cream Pie

1 1/2 cups cold milk or half-and-half
1 package (4-serving size) JELL-O Vanilla Flavor Instant Pudding and Pie Filling
1 tub (8 ounces) COOL WHIP Whipped Topping, thawed
1 cup chopped chocolate sandwich cookies
1 prepared chocolate flavor crumb crust (6 ounces)

POUR milk into large bowl. Add pudding mix. Beat with wire whisk 1 to 2 minutes. Let stand 5 minutes. Gently stir in whipped topping and chopped cookies. Spoon into crust.

FREEZE 6 hours or overnight until firm. Let stand at room temperature 15 minutes or until pie can be cut easily.

GARNISH with additional chocolate sandwich cookies, if desired. Store leftover pie in freezer. *Makes 8 servings*

Creamy Orange Cake

1 can (6 ounces) frozen
    orange juice concentrate,
    thawed
1 package (2-layer size)
    yellow cake mix
1 package (3 ounces)
    PHILADELPHIA BRAND
    Cream Cheese, softened
1/4 cup sugar
1 tub (12 ounces)
    COOL WHIP Whipped
    Topping, thawed
    Mandarin orange sections
    (optional)
    Fresh mint leaves
    (optional)

POUR concentrate into 2-cup measuring cup, reserving 2 tablespoons for cake filling. Add enough water to remaining concentrate to make the amount of liquid needed for cake mix. Prepare cake mix as directed on package, using measured liquid. Pour into 2 greased and floured 9-inch round cake pans. Bake and cool as directed on package.

BEAT cream cheese and sugar in large bowl with electric mixer on low speed until smooth. Beat in reserved concentrate. Gently stir in 1/2 cup of the whipped topping.

PLACE 1 cake layer on serving plate. Spread with cream cheese mixture. Top with second cake layer. Frost cake with remaining whipped topping. Pipe additional whipped topping around bottom of cake (see page 497 for directions), if desired. Garnish with orange sections and mint leaves. Store cake in refrigerator.

Makes 12 to 16 servings

Lemon Cheese Squares

15 whole graham crackers,
    broken in half
2 packages (8 ounces each)
    PHILADELPHIA BRAND
    Cream Cheese, softened
3 cups cold milk
2 packages (6-serving size)
    JELL-O Lemon Flavor
    Instant Pudding and Pie
    Filling
1 tub (8 ounces) COOL WHIP
    Whipped Topping,
    thawed
1 can (21 ounces) blueberry
    pie filling or Citrus
    Twists (see page 502)

ARRANGE 1/2 of the crackers in bottom of 13×9-inch pan, cutting crackers to fit, if necessary.

BEAT cream cheese in large bowl with electric mixer on low speed until smooth. Gradually beat in 1 cup of the milk. Add remaining milk and pudding mixes. Beat 1 to 2 minutes. Gently stir in 2 cups of the whipped topping.

SPREAD 1/2 of the pudding mixture over crackers. Add second layer of crackers; top with remaining pudding mixture and whipped topping.

FREEZE 2 hours or until firm. Let stand at room temperature 15 minutes or until squares can be cut easily. Garnish with pie filling. Store leftover dessert in freezer.

Makes 18 servings

Lemonade Stand Pie

1 can (6 ounces) frozen
   lemonade or pink
   lemonade concentrate,
   partially thawed
1 pint vanilla ice cream
   (2 cups), softened
1 tub (8 ounces) COOL WHIP
   Whipped Topping,
   thawed
1 prepared graham cracker
   crumb crust (6 ounces)
   Citrus Twists (see page 502
   for directions) (optional)
   Fresh mint leaves
   (optional)

BEAT concentrate in large bowl
with electric mixer on low speed
about 30 seconds. Gradually
spoon in ice cream; beat until well
blended. Gently stir in whipped
topping until smooth. Freeze until
mixture will mound, if necessary.
Spoon into crust.

FREEZE 4 hours or overnight
until firm. Let stand at room
temperature 15 minutes or until
pie can be cut easily.

GARNISH with Citrus Twists and
mint leaves. Store leftover pie in
freezer. *Makes 8 servings*

Summer Lime Pie

1 package (4-serving size)
   JELL-O Brand Lime
   Flavor Gelatin
²/₃ cup boiling water
¹/₂ teaspoon grated lime peel
3 tablespoons lime juice
¹/₂ cup cold water
   Ice cubes
1 tub (8 ounces) COOL WHIP
   Whipped Topping,
   thawed
1 prepared graham cracker
   crumb crust (6 ounces)
   Lime slices, cut into
   quarters (optional)

DISSOLVE gelatin completely in
boiling water in large bowl. Stir in
lime peel and juice. Mix cold
water and ice to make 1¹/₄ cups.
Add to gelatin, stirring until ice is
melted.

STIR in whipped topping with
wire whisk until smooth.
Refrigerate 10 to 15 minutes or
until mixture is very thick and
will mound. Spoon into crust.

REFRIGERATE 2 hours or until
firm. Garnish with additional
whipped topping and lime slices.
Store leftover pie in refrigerator.
Makes 8 servings

Clockwise from top: Lemonade
Stand Pie, Frozen Strawberry-
Yogurt Pie (page 534), Summer
Lime Pie

Stars and Stripes Dessert

2 pints strawberries
1 package (12 ounces) pound cake, cut into 8 slices
1 1/3 cups blueberries
1 tub (8 ounces) COOL WHIP Whipped Topping, thawed

SLICE 1 cup of the strawberries; set aside. Halve remaining strawberries; set aside.

LINE bottom of 12×8-inch baking dish with cake slices. Top with 1 cup sliced strawberries, 1 cup of the blueberries and whipped topping.

PLACE strawberry halves and remaining 1/3 cup blueberries on whipped topping to create a flag design.

REFRIGERATE until ready to serve. *Makes 15 servings*

Watermelon Slices
Photo on page 527

Slices of ice cold "watermelon" are a refreshing summer treat.

1 tub (8 ounces) COOL WHIP Whipped Topping, thawed
3 to 4 drops green food coloring
1 pint raspberry or strawberry sherbet or sorbet (2 cups), softened
1 square BAKER'S Semi-Sweet Chocolate, chopped

LINE 1 1/2-quart bowl with plastic wrap. Mix 1/2 of the whipped topping with food coloring in another large bowl until well blended. Spread on bottom and up sides of prepared bowl. Freeze 30 minutes or until firm.

SPREAD remaining whipped topping over green layer. Freeze 1 hour or until firm.

MIX sherbet and chopped chocolate in medium bowl. Spoon into center of whipped topping.

FREEZE at least 4 hours or overnight until firm. Invert bowl onto serving plate; remove plastic wrap. Let stand at room temperature 5 minutes or until dessert can be cut easily. Cut into slices. Serve immediately. Store leftover dessert in freezer.
Makes 10 to 12 servings

Stars and Stripes Dessert

Star Spangled Snack

1 package (4-serving size) JELL-O Brand Berry Blue Flavor Gelatin
1 package (4-serving size) JELL-O Brand Gelatin, any red flavor
2 cups boiling water
1 cup cold water
1 tub (8 ounces) COOL WHIP Whipped Topping, thawed

DISSOLVE each package of gelatin completely in 1 cup boiling water in separate bowls. Stir 1/2 cup cold water into each bowl of gelatin. Pour each mixture into separate 8-inch square pans. Refrigerate at least 3 hours or until firm. Cut gelatin in each pan into 1/2-inch cubes.

SPOON blue cubes evenly into 8 dessert dishes. Cover with whipped topping. Top with red cubes. Garnish with remaining whipped topping.

REFRIGERATE until ready to serve.   *Makes 8 servings*

4th of July Dessert

1 package (8-serving size) or 2 packages (4-serving size) JELL-O Brand Gelatin, any red flavor
2 cups boiling water
2 cups cold water
1 tub (8 ounces) COOL WHIP Whipped Topping, thawed
1 cup sliced strawberries
1/4 cup blueberries

DISSOLVE gelatin completely in boiling water in large bowl. Stir in cold water. Pour into 2-quart serving bowl. Refrigerate at least 3 hours or until firm.

SPREAD whipped topping over gelatin. Decorate with strawberries to create a star design. Sprinkle with blueberries.

REFRIGERATE until ready to serve.   *Makes 8 servings*

Firecrackers

5 cups BAKER'S ANGEL FLAKE Coconut
Blue food coloring
24 baked cupcakes, cooled
1 tub (12 ounces) COOL WHIP Whipped Topping, thawed
Red decorating gel
Red string licorice

TINT coconut using blue food coloring (see page 499).

TRIM any "lips" off top edges of cupcakes. Using small amount of whipped topping, attach bottoms of 2 cupcakes together. Repeat with remaining cupcakes. Stand attached cupcakes on 1 end on serving plate or tray.

FROST with remaining whipped topping. Press coconut onto sides.

DRAW a star on top of each firecracker with decorating gel. Insert pieces of licorice for fuses. Store cakes in refrigerator.
                              Makes 12

Clockwise from top: 4th of July Dessert, Firecrackers, Star Spangled Snack

Autumn Delights

The cool, crisp air and wonderful, warm colors of autumn are so inviting you'll look for any reason to plan an event to bring family and friends together.

When the kids go back to school, surprise them with a variety of after-school treats such as **Rainbow Sandwiches, Creamy Cookie Parfaits** or **Chocolate Peanut Butter Desserts**. And, you'll want to make sure that **Boo the Ghost** makes a special appearance for Halloween.

Try one of our fruit desserts for your next fall get-together. **Caramel Apple Squares** or **Peaches and Cream Dessert** is sure to please both adults and kids.

When it's time for America's oldest celebration, **Double Layer Pumpkin Pie** or **Cranberry Raspberry Mousse** makes a grand finale to your traditional Thanksgiving menu.

Top to bottom: Caramel Apple Squares (page 545), Apple Crunch (page 545)

Creamy Cookie Parfaits

24 to 32 miniature cookies
2⅔ cups thawed COOL WHIP Whipped Topping

LAYER cookies and whipped topping alternately in 4 parfait glasses. Top with additional cookies. Serve immediately or refrigerate until ready to serve.

Makes 4 servings

Crazy Colored Halloween Desserts

Photo on page 551

1 package (8 ounces) PHILADELPHIA BRAND Cream Cheese, softened
4 scoops KOOL-AID Sugar-Sweetened Soft Drink Mix, any green or orange flavor
½ cup milk
1 tub (8 ounces) COOL WHIP Whipped Topping, thawed
12 sponge cake dessert shells Assorted candies and cookies

BEAT cream cheese and soft drink mix in large bowl until well blended. Gradually beat in milk until smooth. Gently stir in whipped topping.

SPOON about ⅓ cup whipped topping mixture into each dessert shell. Decorate with candies and cookies to resemble pumpkins, spiders and witches. Refrigerate until ready to serve.

Makes 12 servings

Rainbow Sandwiches

1 package (4-serving size) JELL-O Brand Gelatin, any flavor
1 cup boiling water
¾ cup cold water
1 package (12 ounces) pound cake, cut into ¼-inch slices
Thawed COOL WHIP Whipped Topping

DISSOLVE gelatin completely in boiling water in small bowl. Stir in cold water. Pour into 9-inch square pan. Refrigerate at least 3 hours or until firm. Cut gelatin and cake slices into circles, squares and/or rectangles.

SPREAD whipped topping on cake slices. Place gelatin shapes on ½ of the cake slices. Top with remaining cake slices, whipped topping side down.

REFRIGERATE until ready to serve. *Makes 8 to 12 servings*

Caramel Apple Squares

Photo on page 543

Creamy COOL WHIP complements the best of the season's apple harvest.

11 graham cracker squares
22 KRAFT Caramels
3 tablespoons milk
⅔ cup chopped walnuts
1 cup cold milk
1 package (4-serving size) JELL-O Vanilla Flavor Instant Pudding and Pie Filling
2 cups thawed COOL WHIP Whipped Topping
2 cups diced red and/or green apples
¼ cup KRAFT Miniature Marshmallows

ARRANGE crackers on bottom of 12×8-inch baking dish, cutting crackers to fit, if necessary.

MICROWAVE 15 of the caramels and 2 tablespoons of the milk in small microwavable bowl on HIGH 1 to 1½ minutes or until caramels are melted and mixture is smooth, stirring after 1 minute. Spread over crackers; sprinkle with ⅓ cup of the walnuts. Refrigerate.

POUR 1 cup milk into large bowl. Add pudding mix. Beat with wire whisk 1 to 2 minutes. Gently stir in 1 cup of the whipped topping. Spread over caramel layer.

REFRIGERATE at least 3 hours or until ready to serve. Garnish with remaining whipped topping, ⅓ cup walnuts, apples and marshmallows. Microwave remaining 7 caramels and 1 tablespoon milk in small microwavable bowl on HIGH 1 minute or until caramels are melted and mixture is smooth, stirring after 30 seconds. Drizzle over top of dessert. Store leftover dessert in refrigerator.

Makes 10 servings

Apple Crunch: Mix equal amounts of **COOL WHIP LITE Whipped Topping** and plain or vanilla flavored lowfat yogurt. Spoon over diced red and green apples and granola cereal. Sprinkle with ground cinnamon.

Frosted Spice Cake

Photo on page 547

1 cup cold milk
1 package (4-serving size) JELL-O Vanilla Flavor Instant Pudding and Pie Filling
1 tablespoon grated orange peel
½ teaspoon ground cinnamon
¼ teaspoon ground nutmeg
1 tub (8 ounces) COOL WHIP Whipped Topping, thawed
2 baked 9-inch round spice or yellow cake layers, cooled
Chopped nuts (optional)

POUR milk into large bowl. Add pudding mix, orange peel and spices. Beat with wire whisk 1 to 2 minutes. Gently stir in whipped topping.

FILL and frost cake layers with whipped topping mixture. Pipe additional whipped topping mixture around bottom of cake (see page 497 for directions), if desired. Garnish with chopped nuts. Store cake in refrigerator.

Makes 12 servings

Double Layer Pumpkin Pie

4 ounces PHILADELPHIA
  BRAND Cream Cheese,
  softened
1 tablespoon milk or
  half-and-half
1 tablespoon sugar
1½ cups thawed COOL WHIP
  Whipped Topping
1 prepared graham cracker
  crumb crust (6 ounces)
1 cup cold milk or
  half-and-half
2 packages (4-serving size)
  JELL-O Vanilla Flavor
  Instant Pudding and Pie
  Filling
1 can (16 ounces) pumpkin
1 teaspoon ground
  cinnamon
½ teaspoon ground ginger
¼ teaspoon ground cloves
  Additional thawed
    COOL WHIP Whipped
    Topping

BEAT cream cheese, 1 tablespoon milk and sugar in large bowl with wire whisk until smooth. Gently stir in whipped topping. Spread on bottom of crust.

POUR 1 cup milk into another large bowl. Add pudding mixes. Beat with wire whisk 1 to 2 minutes. (Mixture will be thick.) Stir in pumpkin and spices with wire whisk until well mixed. Spread over cream cheese layer.

REFRIGERATE 4 hours or until set. Garnish with additional whipped topping. Store leftover pie in refrigerator.
Makes 8 servings

Helpful Tip: Soften cream cheese in microwave on HIGH 15 to 20 seconds.

Cranberry Raspberry Mousse

1 cup cranberry juice
  cocktail
1 package (4-serving size)
  JELL-O Brand Raspberry
  Flavor Gelatin
1 container (12 ounces)
  cranberry raspberry
  crushed fruit
1 tub (12 ounces)
  COOL WHIP Whipped
  Topping, thawed

BRING cranberry juice to boil in small saucepan. Dissolve gelatin completely in boiling liquid in large bowl. Stir in fruit. Refrigerate until slightly thickened.

STIR in 2 cups of the whipped topping until well blended. Layer cranberry mixture and 2 cups of the remaining whipped topping alternately in 8 dessert glasses.

REFRIGERATE 3 hours or until firm. Garnish each dessert with dollop of remaining whipped topping.   *Makes 8 servings*

Clockwise from top right: Frosted Spice Cake (page 545), Double Layer Pumpkin Pie, Cranberry Raspberry Mousse

Snacks are often a dieter's worst enemy. With the help of **COOL WHIP LITE Whipped Topping**, you'll be ready for your next snack attack.

Peaches and Cream Dessert

>   3 cups frozen sliced
>   peaches, thawed
>   4 tablespoons sugar
>   1 cup light sour cream
>   1/4 teaspoon ground
>   cinnamon
>   1 1/2 cups thawed COOL WHIP
>   LITE Whipped Topping
>   1 cup granola cereal
>   Cinnamon sticks (optional)

DICE peaches, reserving several slices for garnish, if desired. Mix peaches and 2 tablespoons of the sugar in large serving bowl.

MIX sour cream, remaining 2 tablespoons sugar and cinnamon in another large bowl. Gently stir in whipped topping. Sprinkle 3/4 cup of the granola over peaches. Top with whipped topping mixture.

REFRIGERATE until ready to serve. Sprinkle with remaining 1/4 cup granola. Garnish with additional whipped topping, reserved peach slices and cinnamon sticks.

Makes 6 to 8 servings

Note: Recipe can be doubled.

Mini Ladyfinger Napoleons

SPLIT ladyfingers; spread bottom halves with **COOL WHIP LITE Whipped Topping**. Top with sliced strawberries. Cover with top halves of ladyfingers to make "sandwiches."

Chocolate Peanut Butter Desserts

>   2 tablespoons skim milk
>   2 tablespoons peanut butter
>   1 cup thawed COOL WHIP
>   LITE Whipped Topping
>   2 cups cold skim milk
>   1 package (4-serving size)
>   JELL-O Chocolate Flavor
>   Sugar Free Instant
>   Pudding and Pie Filling

MIX 2 tablespoons milk into peanut butter in small bowl. Stir in whipped topping.

POUR 2 cups milk into large bowl. Add pudding mix. Beat with wire whisk 1 to 2 minutes. Spoon pudding and whipped topping mixture alternately into 6 parfait glasses.

REFRIGERATE 1 hour or until ready to serve. Garnish with additional whipped topping.

Makes 6 servings

Clockwise from top: Peaches and Cream Dessert, Chocolate Peanut Butter Desserts, Chocolate Mousse (page 550), Mini Ladyfinger Napoleons

Boo the Ghost

1 baked 13×9-inch cake,
   cooled
1 tub (8 ounces) COOL WHIP
   Whipped Topping,
   thawed
2 chocolate wafer cookies
2 green candy wafers
   Candy corn
1 black jelly bean
   Black or red string licorice

CUT cake as shown in illustration. Using small amount of whipped topping to hold pieces together, arrange cake on serving tray as shown in photograph.

FROST cake with remaining whipped topping. Decorate with cookies and candy wafers for eyes and candy corn for mouth. Make a spider using the jelly bean for its body and pieces of licorice for its legs. Store cake in refrigerator.

Makes 12 to 16 servings

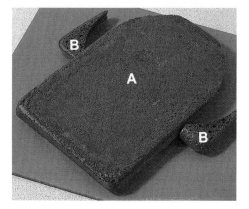

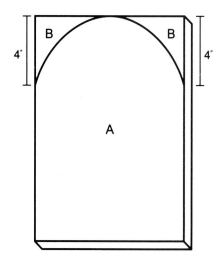

Chocolate Mousse
Photo on page 549

Chocolate mousse on a diet? You bet, when it's made with this recipe.

1½ cups cold skim milk
  1 package (4-serving size)
     JELL-O Chocolate Sugar
     Free Instant Pudding and
     Pie Filling
1½ cups thawed COOL WHIP
     LITE Whipped Topping
  ¼ cup fresh raspberries
     (optional)

POUR milk into large bowl. Add pudding mix. Beat with wire whisk 1 to 2 minutes.

STIR in 1 cup of the whipped topping. Spoon into serving bowl or individual dessert dishes.

REFRIGERATE until ready to serve. Garnish with remaining whipped topping and raspberries.
Makes 5 servings

Top to bottom: Crazy Colored Halloween Desserts (page 544), Boo the Ghost

Year-Round Fun for Kids

Looking for fun activities you can do with your child? This chapter features easy-to-follow recipes that are fun to make and delicious to eat. Many are so simple that the kids can even help.

Create magic with **Butterfly Cupcakes, Wild Side Sundaes** or **Electrifying Slide Dessert** at your child's next party. Or let the kids help make **Honey Bees** and **Wormy Apples**.

Recipes like **Flowerpot Pie** and **Clown Cones** will help moms and dads make every day a "funday."

Wild Side Sundaes (page 554)

Wild Side Sundaes
Photo on page 553

    4 packages (4-serving size)
       JELL-O Brand Gelatin,
       4 different flavors
    4 cups boiling water
    2 cups cold water
    1 tub (8 ounces) COOL WHIP
       Whipped Topping,
       thawed
       Additional thawed
       COOL WHIP Whipped
       Topping

DISSOLVE each package of gelatin completely in 1 cup boiling water in separate bowls. Stir ½ cup cold water into each bowl of gelatin. Pour each mixture into separate 8-inch square pans. Refrigerate at least 3 hours or until firm. Cut gelatin in each pan into ½-inch cubes.

LAYER gelatin cubes alternately with whipped topping in sundae glasses. Garnish with dollop of additional whipped topping.

REFRIGERATE until ready to serve.   *Makes 16 servings*

Electrifying Slide Dessert

    2 packages (4-serving size)
       JELL-O Brand Gelatin,
       any flavor
    2 cups boiling water
    1 cup cold water
       Ice cubes
    2 cups thawed COOL WHIP
       Whipped Topping

LINE bottom and sides of 2 loaf pans with wet paper towels. Tilt 3 (8-ounce) glasses in each loaf pan.

DISSOLVE 1 package of the gelatin completely in 1 cup boiling water in large bowl. Mix ½ cup cold water and ice to make 1 cup. Add to gelatin, stirring until ice is melted. Refrigerate 10 minutes or until slightly thickened. Gently stir in 1 cup of the whipped topping. Spoon into tilted glasses. Refrigerate 1 hour or until set but not firm.

DISSOLVE remaining package gelatin completely in 1 cup boiling water in medium bowl. Mix ½ cup cold water and ice to make 1 cup. Add to gelatin, stirring until ice is melted. Refrigerate about 10 minutes or until slightly thickened. Spoon into glasses over set gelatin mixture. Set glasses upright.

REFRIGERATE at least 1 hour or until firm. Garnish with dollop of remaining whipped topping.
          Makes 6 servings

Wormy Apples
Photo on page 556

    2 small apples
    ½ cup thawed COOL WHIP
       Whipped Topping
    2 gummy worms

CORE apples, if desired. Cut each apple horizontally into 3 slices.

SPREAD slices with whipped topping. Reassemble apples. Cut small holes in apples; insert gummy worms into holes. Serve immediately.   *Makes 2 servings*

Clown Cones

2 cups cold milk
1 package (4-serving size)
  JELL-O Vanilla or
  Chocolate Flavor Instant
  Pudding and Pie Filling
1 tub (8 ounces) COOL WHIP
  Whipped Topping,
  thawed
  Paper baking cups
12 sugar ice cream cones
  Assorted candies and
  sprinkles
  Decorating gel

POUR milk into large bowl. Add
pudding mix. Beat with wire
whisk 1 or 2 minutes. Let stand 5
minutes. Gently stir in whipped
topping. Pour into 2-quart freezer
container; cover.

FREEZE 6 hours or overnight
until firm. Let stand to soften
slightly. Scoop onto flattened
baking cups.

TOP with ice cream cones for
hats. Make clown faces with
candies and decorating gel.
Decorate cones as desired. Serve
immediately.   *Makes 12*

Butterfly Cupcakes

1 cup cold milk
1 package (4-serving size)
  JELL-O Instant Pudding
  and Pie Filling, any flavor
1 tub (8 ounces) COOL WHIP
  Whipped Topping,
  thawed
24 baked cupcakes, cooled
  Multi-colored sprinkles
  Miniature flower candies
  Black or red string licorice

POUR milk into large bowl. Add
pudding mix. Beat with wire
whisk 1 to 2 minutes. Gently stir
in whipped topping. Reserve 1
teaspoon pudding mixture; set
aside.

CUT top off each cupcake. Cut
each top in half; set aside. Spoon
2 heaping tablespoons pudding
mixture on top of each cupcake.
Sprinkle with mutli-colored
sprinkles.

PLACE 2 cupcake top halves, cut
sides together, into pudding
mixture, raising outside ends
slightly to resemble butterfly
wings. Lightly dip candies into
reserved pudding mixture; arrange
on cupcake wings. Insert pieces of
licorice into pudding mixture to
resemble antennae. Store
cupcakes in refrigerator.
          Makes 24

Flowerpot Pie

1 cup cold milk
1 package (4-serving size) JELL-O Chocolate Flavor Instant Pudding and Pie Filling
1 tub (8 ounces) COOL WHIP Whipped Topping, thawed
20 chocolate sandwich cookies, finely crushed
1½ cups "rocks"*
1 prepared chocolate flavor or graham cracker crumb crust (6 ounces)
Gumdrop Flowers (see directions on this page) (optional)
*Use any combination of the following:
BAKER'S Semi-Sweet Real Chocolate Chips
Chopped peanuts
Granola

POUR milk into large bowl. Add pudding mix. Beat with wire whisk 1 to 2 minutes. Gently stir in whipped topping.

STIR 1 cup of the crushed cookies and "rocks" into pudding mixture. Spoon into crust. Sprinkle with remaining crushed cookies.

FREEZE 4 hours or until firm. Let stand at room temperature 15 minutes or until pie can be cut easily. Garnish with Gumdrop Flowers. Store leftover pie in freezer. *Makes 8 servings*

Gumdrop Flowers: Flatten small gumdrops. Cut with small cookie cutters. Attach to pretzel sticks to form flowers and leaves as shown in photograph.

Honey Bees

A hint of honey adds zip to this cute snack.

1 cup cold milk
3 tablespoons honey
Yellow food coloring (optional)
1 package (4-serving size) JELL-O Vanilla Flavor Instant Pudding and Pie Filling
2 cups thawed COOL WHIP Whipped Topping
¾ cup finely crushed chocolate wafer cookies
12 chocolate wafer cookie halves
6 large black gumdrops
Black or red string licorice

POUR milk, honey and food coloring into large bowl. Add pudding mix. Beat with wire whisk 1 to 2 minutes.

STIR in whipped topping. Layer alternately with crushed cookies in 6 dessert dishes.

REFRIGERATE 1 hour or until ready to serve. Place cookie halves in whipped topping mixture to form wings. Decorate with gumdrops. Insert small pieces of licorice to form antennae and stinger. Sprinkle with additional crushed cookies, if desired.
Makes 6 servings

Clockwise from top: Honey Bees, Wormy Apples (page 554), Flowerpot Pie

Acknowledgments

The publisher would like to thank the companies and organizations listed below for the use of their recipes and photographs in this publication.

American Spice Trade Association

Best Foods, a Division of CPC International Inc.

Birds Eye

Blue Diamond Growers

Bob Evans Farms®

California Tomato Commission

Christopher Ranch Garlic

Del Monte Corporation

Dole Food Company, Inc.

Farmhouse Foods Company

Florida Department of Agriculture and Consumer Services, Bureau of Seafood and Aquaculture

Golden Grain/Mission Pasta

Hershey Foods Corporation

Holland House, a division of Cadbury Beverages, Inc.

The HVR Company

Kahlúa® Liqueur

Kikkoman International Inc.

The Kingsford Products Company

Kraft Foods, Inc.

Lawry's® Foods, Inc.

Lee Kum Kee (USA) Inc.

Thomas J. Lipton Co.

McIlhenny Company

Minnesota Cultivated Wild Rice Council

Nabisco, Inc.

National Broiler Council

National Cattlemen's Beef Association

National Honey Board

National Onion Association

National Pork Producers Council

National Turkey Federation

Nestlé Food Company

Newman's Own, Inc.®

Perdue® Farms

Plochman, Inc.

The Procter & Gamble Company

Ralston Foods, Inc.

Reckitt & Colman Inc.

Riceland Foods, Inc.

Riviana Foods Inc.

Sargento Foods Inc.®

StarKist® Seafood Company

Surimi Seafood Education Center

USA Rice Council

Washington Apple Commission

Wesson/Peter Pan Foods Company

Index

METRIC CONVERSION CHART

VOLUME MEASUREMENTS (dry)

1/8 teaspoon = 0.5 mL
1/4 teaspoon = 1 mL
1/2 teaspoon = 2 mL
3/4 teaspoon = 4 mL
1 teaspoon = 5 mL
1 tablespoon = 15 mL
2 tablespoons = 30 mL
1/4 cup = 60 mL
1/3 cup = 75 mL
1/2 cup = 125 mL
2/3 cup = 150 mL
3/4 cup = 175 mL
1 cup = 250 mL
2 cups = 1 pint = 500 mL
3 cups = 750 mL
4 cups = 1 quart = 1 L

VOLUME MEASUREMENTS (fluid)

1 fluid ounce (2 tablespoons) = 30 mL
4 fluid ounces (1/2 cup) = 125 mL
8 fluid ounces (1 cup) = 250 mL
12 fluid ounces (1 1/2 cups) = 375 mL
16 fluid ounces (2 cups) = 500 mL

WEIGHTS (mass)

1/2 ounce = 15 g
1 ounce = 30 g
3 ounces = 90 g
4 ounces = 120 g
8 ounces = 225 g
10 ounces = 285 g
12 ounces = 360 g
16 ounces = 1 pound = 450 g

DIMENSIONS

1/16 inch = 2 mm
1/8 inch = 3 mm
1/4 inch = 6 mm
1/2 inch = 1.5 cm
3/4 inch = 2 cm
1 inch = 2.5 cm

OVEN TEMPERATURES

250°F = 120°C
275°F = 140°C
300°F = 150°C
325°F = 160°C
350°F = 180°C
375°F = 190°C
400°F = 200°C
425°F = 220°C
450°F = 230°C

BAKING PAN SIZES

Utensil	Size in Inches/Quarts	Metric Volume	Size in Centimeters
Baking or Cake Pan (square or rectangular)	8 × 8 × 2	2 L	20 × 20 × 5
	9 × 9 × 2	2.5 L	22 × 22 × 5
	12 × 8 × 2	3 L	30 × 20 × 5
	13 × 9 × 2	3.5 L	33 × 23 × 5
Loaf Pan	8 × 4 × 3	1.5 L	20 × 10 × 7
	9 × 5 × 3	2 L	23 × 13 × 7
Round Layer Cake Pan	8 × 1½	1.2 L	20 × 4
	9 × 1½	1.5 L	23 × 4
Pie Plate	8 × 1¼	750 mL	20 × 3
	9 × 1¼	1 L	23 × 3
Baking Dish or Casserole	1 quart	1 L	—
	1½ quart	1.5 L	—
	2 quart	2 L	—